Elements of Indian Art

Including Temple Architecture, Iconography & Iconometry

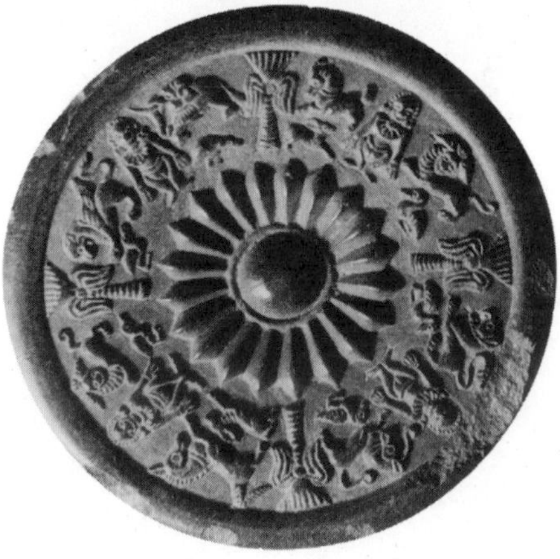

Perspectives in Indian Art & Archaeology Series

(ISSN 0971-4723)

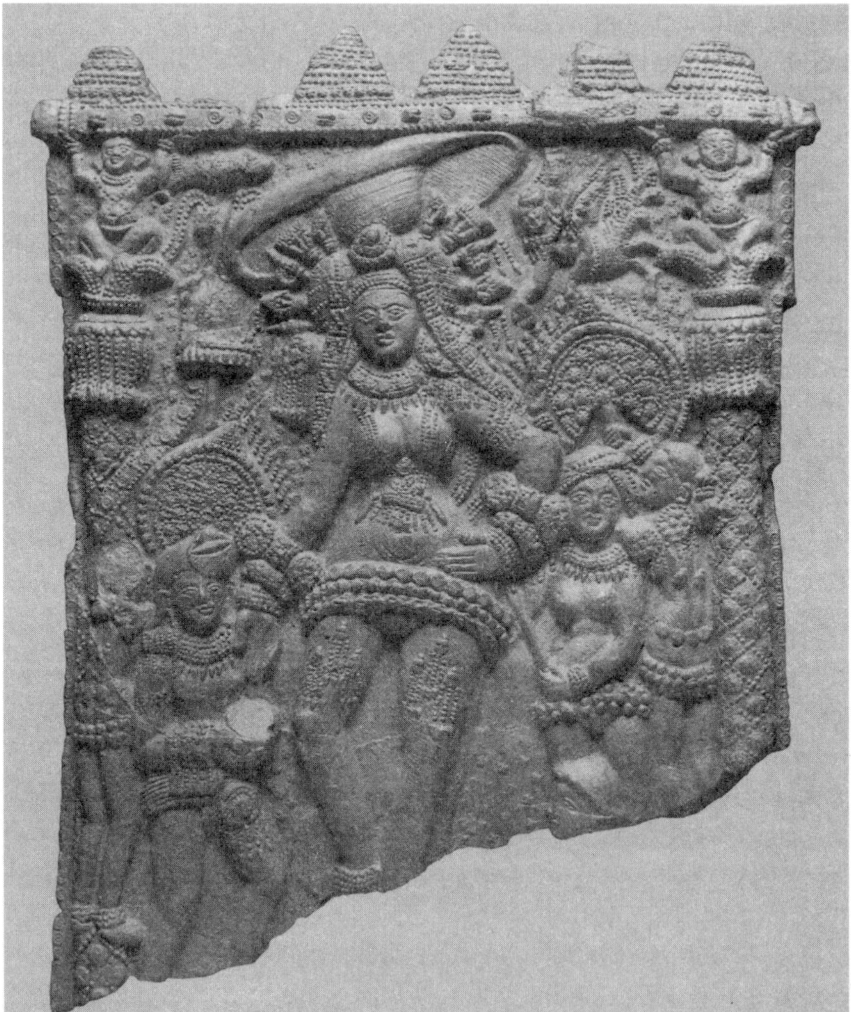

Devī with attendants, terracotta, Candraketugarh, West Bengal, 2nd century BCE
(courtesy: The Metropolitan Museum of Art, New York)

Perspectives in Indian Art & Archaeology, no. 4

Elements of Indian Art

Including Temple Architecture, Iconography & Iconometry

Second revised and enlarged edition comprising new chapters on

- Rock Art in India
- The Haṛappan Art
- Indian Art Beyond the Indian Frontiers (South and South-East Asia)

S.P. Gupta
Shashi Prabha Asthana

Indraprastha Museum of Art and Archaeology
New Delhi - 110 016

DK PRINTWORLD
Publishers of Indian Traditions

Cataloging in Publication Data — DK

Courtesy: D.K. Agencies (P) Ltd. <docinfo@dkagencies.com>

Gupta, S. P. (Swarajya Prakash), 1931-2007, **author.**
Elements of Indian art : including temple architecture, iconography & iconometry / S.P. Gupta, Shashi Prabha Asthana.
pages cm. – (Perspectives in Indian art & archaeology, ISSN 0971-4723 ; no. 4)
Includes passages in Sanskrit (Sanskrit in roman).
Fourth reprint of: Second revised and enlarged edition published in 2007. Comprising new chapters on rock art in India, the Haṛappan art, Indian art beyond the Indian frontiers (South and South-East Asia).
Includes bibliographical references and index.
ISBN 9788124602133 (HB)
ISBN 9788124602140 (PB)

1. Art, Indic. 2. Architecture – India. 3. Idols and images – India. 4. Idols and images – India – Measurement. I. Asthana, Shashi, author. II. Indraprastha Museum of Art and Archaeology, publisher. III. Title. IV. Series: Perspectives in Indian art & archaeology ; no. 4.

LCC N7302.G87 2025 | DDC 709.54 23

ISBN 978-81-246-0213-3 (HB)
ISBN 978-81-246-0214-0 (PB)
First published in India in 2002
Second revised and enlarged edition published in 2007
Reprints: First 2009; Second 2015; Third 2020; Fourth 2025

Authors: S.P. Gupta (1931-2007); Shashi Prabha Asthana (1947-1997)

Published by:
Indraprastha Museum of Art and Archaeology
B-17, Qutub Institutional Area
New Delhi - 110016

and

D.K. Printworld (P) Ltd.
Regd. Office: "Vedaśrī", F-395, Sudarshan Park
ESI Hospital Metro Station, New Delhi - 110015
Phones: (011) 4172 2626, 98713 94815
e-mail: indology@dkprintworld.com
Website: www.dkprintworld.com

Printed by: D.K. Printworld (P) Ltd., New Delhi - 110015

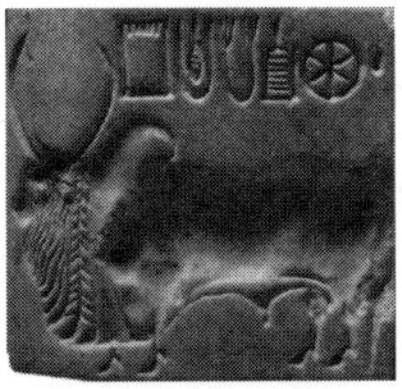

Preface to the Second Edition

It is a matter of certain amount of satisfaction that the first edition of this book, published in late 2002, was almost completely sold out by mid-2006. Although, of late, I am not keeping good health, on the insistence of the students and the members of the Faculty of the National Museum Institute, New Delhi, particularly Prof. (Dr.) Anupa Pande, Head of the History of Art Department, who kept on goading me to do it so very affectionately that I could not refuse. I decided to bring out a revised second edition. My friends Shri K.N. Dikshit and Sri Madneshwar Trivedi are to some extent also responsible for it. Having once decided to enlarge the text, I decided to add three new chapters in this edition of the publication — one, dealing with the Rock Art, also called "Pre-historic Art" or "Stone Age Art," second dealing with the "Proto-historic Art" or "The Bronze Age Art," same as "The Haṛappan Art," also called "The Indus" or "The Indus–Sarasvatī Art," and the third dealing with the "Indian Art Beyond the Indian Frontiers" encompassing the ancient art of some of the neighbouring countries located on the south and the east of India — Sri Lanka, Myanmar, Thailand, Cambodia and Indonesia — since these countries have shared India's culture for centuries together and produced a lot similar works of art and architecture within their own local matrix.

I will be failing in my duty if I do not record the most valuable assistance I received from my young colleagues in the Indian Archaeological Society, New Delhi, Sarvashri Suresh Bomble and S. Vijayakumar. On the Secretarial and Internet front, Sarvashri Mohit Srivastava, Lakhan Trivedi and Bharat Singh were of great help, for which I am thankful to them. Ms. Raj Rani, Librarian, helped me by providing most the books I needed.

Lastly, a word of appreciation for Shri Susheel Mittal, the young and energetic owner of D.K. Printworld, who lovingly placed a very tall order to me — "Kindly complete it within two weeks since I am under pressure from the students of the Art Appreciation Course of the National Museum Institute who have expressed great desire to own the book very soon." Was it not cruelty? But then I thoroughly enjoyed doing it.

New Delhi **Swarajya Prakash Gupta**
5, September 2006

The illustrations for the three new chapters have been taken from the following publications for which I acknowledge the courtesy of their authors and publishers.

For the Rock Art

Chakravarty, K.K. and R.G. Bednarik, 2004, *Indian Rock Art and its Global Context.*

Purakala, Annual Journal of the Rock Art Society of India, Nos. 14-15, 2005.

Wakankar, V.S., 2005, *Painted Rock-Shelters of India,* Bhopal: Directorate of Archaeology and Museums, Madhya Pradesh Government.

Wakankar, V.S. and R.R.R. Brooks, 1976, *Stone Age Painting in India.*

For the Haṛappan Art

Gupta, S.P., 1996, *The Indus-Saraswati Civilization.*

Gupta, S.P. (ed.), 2003, *Masterpieces of the National Museum Collection.*

Jarrige, C., J.F. Jarrige, R.H. Meadow, and G. Quivron, 1995, *Mehrgarh: Field Reports 1974-1985.*

Lal, B.B., 2002, *The Saraswati Flows On.*

For South and South-East Asian Art

Beek, S.V. and L.I. Tettoni, 1999, *The Arts of Thailand.*

Briggs, L.P., 1999, *The Ancient Khmer Empire.*

Lokesh Chandra, S.P. Gupta (eds.), *India's Contribution to World Thought and Culture.*

Coomaraswamy, A.K., 1965, *History of Indian and Indonesian Art.*

Kvorn, N.J., 1927, *Barabudur*, Archaeological Description.

Miksic, John, 1990, *Borobudur — Golden Tales of the Buddhas.*

Snellgrove, David, 2004, *Angkor — Before and After: A Cultural History of Khmers.*

Turner, Jane (ed.), 1996, *The Dictionary of Art*, vol. 29.

Preface to the First Edition

Having served the National Museum, New Delhi and the Allahabad Museum for more than thirty years, I felt that the visitors to museums rarely get to know the context and meaning of the works of art that they see there. Often the available books are either too large to consult or too small to learn even the basic facts. This is true of the foreign as well as national visitors. We, therefore, thought of producing a book of medium size, almost like a handbook, which a visitor can easily take with him or her in galleries devoted to ancient Indian art and learn about it through this book. For this purpose we have embellished the book with a large number of illustrations.

For a number of years I have been taking classes and delivering lectures in the National Museum Institute. There also I felt the same lack of basic knowledge about the art and architecture of ancient India amongst the students of M.A. courses, and the Tour Guides who join the courses of Art History. The book will serve them also because they are supposed to tell the tourists visiting museums and monuments all about our ancient art and architecture.

The National Museum Institute also runs courses in Art Appreciation for the common people who are eager to know the fundamentals of Indian art. I have been taking some lectures for them also. I am sure they will certainly benefit from this book.

Finally, what about scholars? Yes, there will be enough food for their thought also, since at times I have given views which are a lot different from those propounded by others.

It is common knowledge that in ancient India works of art were not produced for their own sake. Instead, these were required to be the parts of temples, either as deities to be worshipped or as parts of the structures. It was, therefore, felt necessary to include here the subject of iconography as well as temple architecture; the subject of iconometry included here is only an extension of iconography. We have here not included the Prehistoric and Protohistoric Art since they form different cycles of Indian Art and are rarely connected with the Art Tradition which started in the Mauryan period.

There is a small story behind this book. In the year 1982 the second author of this book, the late Dr. Shashi Asthana, had to appear for the post of Keeper (Archaeology) in the National Museum. For this purpose she prepared a manuscript on the subject of Iconography. Unfortunately, it remained unpublished in her lifetime; she died in 1997 at the age of less than 50 years because of kidney failure. Last year, I found it in a bundle of papers she had left behind. When I called the publishers to publish it, they asked me not only to enlarge it but also add a few chapters to make it more meaningful and useful. As a mark of my love and respect for her, who was one time my student, who did her Ph.D. under my guidance, and later my colleague in the National Museum — she was Asstt. Director there when she passed away — I decided to do it.

This book is dedicated to the memory of late S. Ganesh Rao, my friend from 1957 when we were together working at Nāgārjunakoṇḍa excavations. He was then a surveyor. Later on we both moved to New Delhi; he was working in the Archaeological Survey of India and I was in the National Museum. In the 1970s and 1980s whatever I wrote I generally showed it to him for critical evaluation. Dr. Asthana also did the same. He used to be very ruthless. We liked it and changed many parts of our writings since he felt that much more data were required to buttress our claims. Today he is not with us, but I do cherish my memories with him. I am sure, had Dr. Asthana been alive she would also have decided to dedicate this book to the memory of our friend Shri Ganesh Rao.

In the preparation of this book I was greatly helped in many ways by Ms. Anuja Geetali and Ms. Mahua Bhattacharyya. Shri M.S. Mani has been very kind to me in preparing all the drawings appearing in this book. Shri Jassu Ram made the maps. Shri Tejas Garge and Shri Laxmi Narain helped me in selecting the photographs for which I am beholden to them. I am equally beholden to Sarvashri Rakesh Dutta and Manoj Harbola for typing the manuscript; Shri Himanshu Joshi, in addition, generated maps and charts on computer. Dr. B.S. Harishankar and Shri B.S. Rajput helped me in getting books from the library for which I am indeed thankful to them.

To Sarvashri K.S. Ramachandran and K.N. Dikshit, the authors will ever remain thankful for their most friendly advice and support.

I acknowledge my indebtedness to the writers whose books we have consulted and from which we have drawn not only material but also illustrations. The first and foremost is the book entitled *Indian Art* authored by Dr. V.S. Agarwala. The second major book is the *Iconography of the Hindus, Buddhists and Jains* by Dr. R.S. Gupte. The third major book is *Pratimā Kośa* by Shri S.R. Ramachandran. The fourth major work is the *Encyclopaedia of Temple Architecture* in several volumes published by the American Institute of Indian Studies, Gurgaon, New Delhi. The fifth major work is the *Development of Hindu Iconography* by J.N. Banerjea. There are several other books also which have helped me in various ways, e.g. *Mathurā Kalā* by Dr. Shashi Prabha Asthana, *Kuṣāṇa Prastara Mūrtiyoṅ meṅ Samāja Evaṁ Dharma* by Dr. Rani Srivastava and *Bhubaneswar*, a guide book beautifully written and illustrated by Dr. (Ms.) Debala Mitra and published by the Archaeological Survey of India, New Delhi. I have also drawn a lot from my own book *The Roots of Indian Art.*

I am also thankful to the National Museum, New Delhi and Archaeological Survey of India, New Delhi for a number of photographs, which they supplied to us.

Shri Susheel Mittal of D.K. Printworld deserves my appreciation for the personal care which he took in seeing the book through the press.

New Delhi
30-08-2002 **S.P. Gupta**

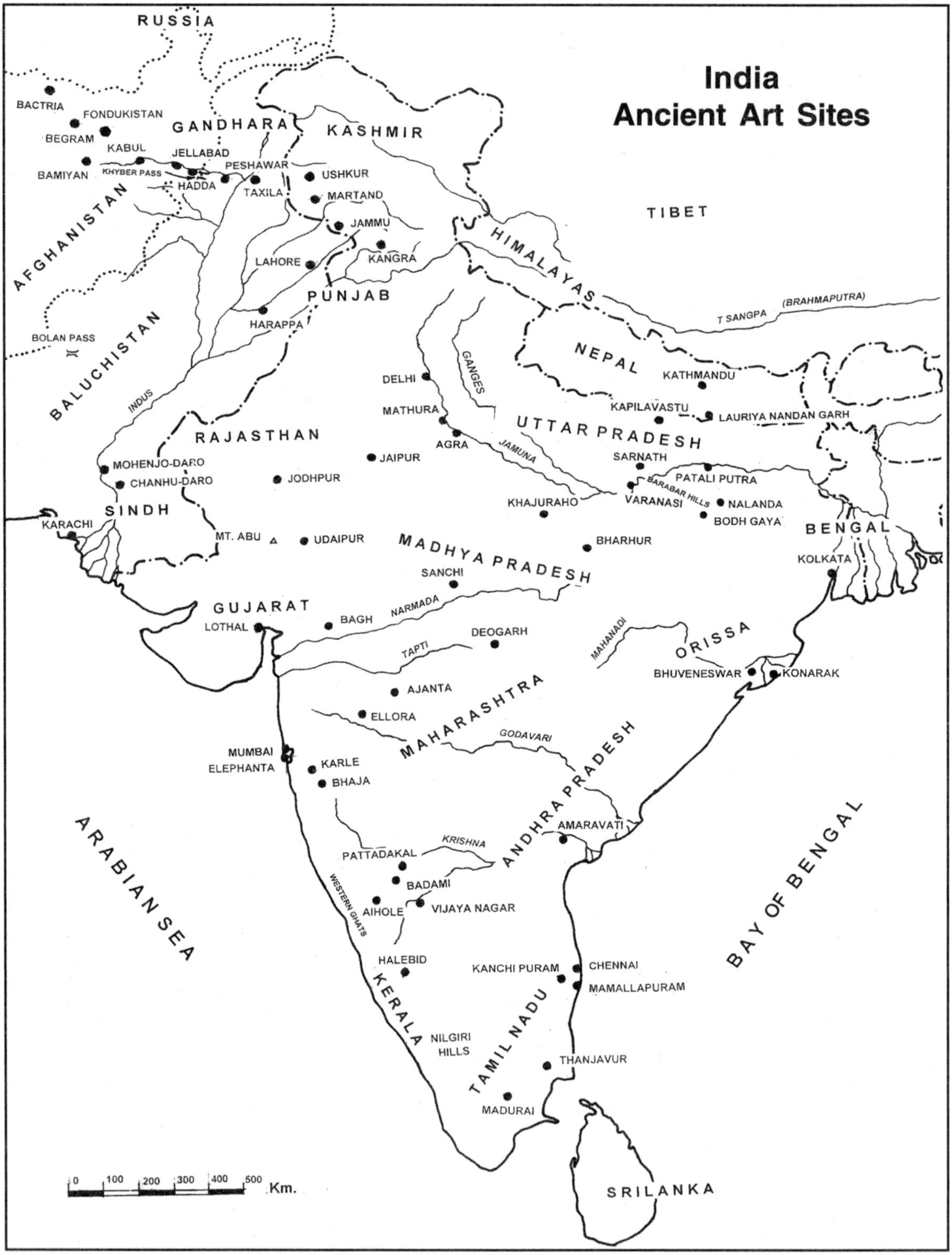

Map of Ancient India showing important Art Sites

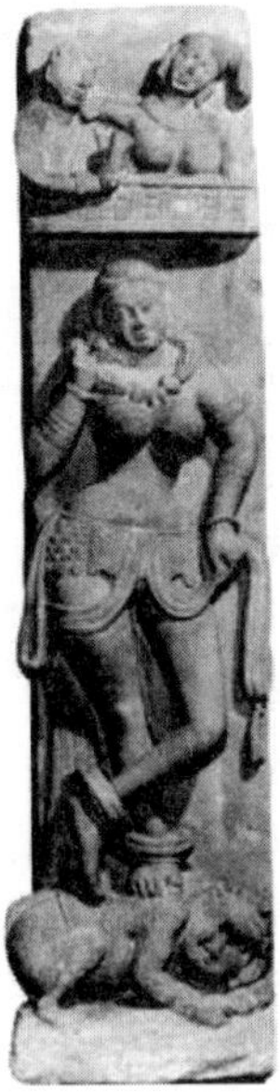

Contents

Preface to the Second Edition v

Preface to the First Edition vii

Map of Ancient India showing important Art Sites x

Transliteration Chart xv

Map of India showing Sites of Principal Temples xvi

1. Rock Art in India **1**
- Various Kinds of Rock Art 2
- Distribution and Chronology 2
- Bhīmbeṭkā 3
- The Purpose of Rock Art 5
- Dating the Rock Art 5
- Other Forms of Stone Age Art & Architecture 7

2. The Haṛappan Art **9**
- Materials Used 11
- Subject Matter & Common Motifs 12
- Stone & Bronze Sculptures 12
- Terracottas 13
- Steatite Seals 14
- Pottery Paintings, Metal Art, Glazing, etc. 15
- Haṛappan Architecture 17
- The Continuity of Haṛappan Traditions 20

3. Fundamentals of Indian Art **21**
- Religion and Art 22
- Hinduism has no Hierarchy Amongst Gods 23
- Hinduism *vis-à-vis* Christianity and Islam 24
- The *Avatāras* of Viṣṇu 24

Buddha: The Life and Teaching 25
Mahāvīra: The Life and Teaching 26
Art and Architecture 27
Sacred Structures 27
Hindu Temple 31
Temples of North India 34
Temples of South India 40
Temples of Orissa 44
The Icons 48
Symbols 49
Hindu Iconography 53
Śiva 53
Viṣṇu 54
Brahmā 55
The Śākta 56
The Tantra 63
Īhāmṛga 66
Mythology: What it is in Hinduism? 67
Buddha 68
Bodhisattva 68
Jina 69
Basic Nature of Indian Art 70
Paintings 73
Nine *Rasas* 75
Tempera and Fresco Techniques 75
Differing Attitudes towards Indian Art 77
The Role of European Travellers Coming with Christian Bias 78

4. Indian Art in Historical Perspective 81
The Terminology 81
Vedic Heritage 82
Mauryan Art (fourth–third centuries BCE) 83
Śuṅga-Sātavāhana Art (second–first centuries BCE) 89
Kuṣāṇa Art (first–third centuries) 94
Bactrian, Mathurā and Gāndhāra Schools of Kuṣāṇa Art 101
Gupta Art (fourth–sixth centuries) 103

Post-Gupta Art — Phase I (sixth–eighth centuries) 109
Maitrakas Art (sixth–seventh centuries) 109
Early Cāḷukyan Art (sixth–seventh centuries) 110
Rāṣṭrakūṭa Art (eighth–ninth centuries) 110
Pallava Art (sixth–eighth centuries) 111
Post-Gupta Art — Phase II (ninth–twelfth centuries) 112
Gurjara–Pratihāra Art (eighth–tenth centuries) 112
Coḷa Art (ninth–twelfth centuries) 112
Pāla Art (eighth–eleventh centuries) 115
Hoyasaḷa Art (eleventh–thirteenth centuries) 116
Orissa School (eighth–thirteenth centuries) 117
Candela Art (tenth–eleventh centuries) 118
Other Mediaeval Monuments and Art Traditions 119
North India 119
South India 119

5. Iconography: The Making of Cult Images 121
Iconometric Sources 122
Texts governing the Northern Schools 122
Texts governing the Southern Schools 122
Non-iconometric or *Śāstrīya* (शास्त्रीय) Sources 122
Tantras 123
Other Works 124
Some Classifications of Images 125
Cala (चल) or Portable Images 126
Acala (अचल) or Stationary Images 126
Pūrṇa (पूर्ण) or Complete Images 126
Apūrṇa (अपूर्ण) or Incomplete Images 126
Śānta (शांत) Images or Images with Pleasing Countenance 127
Aśānta (अशांत) Images or Images with Agitated Countenance 127
*Mudrā*s 127
*Hasta-mudrā*s (हस्त-मुद्राएं) or Hand Poses 128
*Pāda-mudrā*s (पाद-मुद्राएं) or Foot Poses 133
*Śarīra-mudrā*s (शरीर-मुद्राएं) or Body Poses 134
Attributes or objects held in hands 135
Weapons of War and Chase 135
Household and Agricultural Objects and Implements 137

Fruits	138
Flowers	138
Animal World	139
Musical Instruments	139
Others	140
Āsanas (आसन) or Sitting Postures	141
Āsanas or *Pīṭhas* ('आसन' अथवा 'पीठ') (Pedestals)	142
Vāhanas (वाहन) or Mounts	143
Mukuṭas and Headgears (मुकुट एवं केश-विन्यास)	144
Ābhūṣaṇa (आभूषण) or Ornaments	145
Karṇābhūṣaṇa (कर्णाभूषण) or Ear ornaments	145
Kaṇṭhābhūṣaṇa (कण्ठाभूषण) or Neck ornaments	146
Vakṣābhūṣaṇa (वक्षाभूषण) or Chest ornaments	146
Kaṭi-ābhūṣaṇa (कटि-आभूषण) or Hip ornaments	147
Pāda-ābhūṣaṇa (पाद-आभूषण) or Feet ornaments	148
Bāhu (बाहु) and *Bhujā-ābhūṣaṇa* (भुजा-आभूषण) or Armlets and Wristlets	148
Nāsa-ābhūṣaṇa (नास-आभूषण) or Nose ornaments	148
Paridhāna (परिधान) or Dress	148
Bandha (बन्ध) or Belt	148
Vastra (वस्त्र) or Cloth	148
Special dress of the Buddha (बुद्ध के वस्त्र)	149
6. Principles of Iconometry	**151**
Tāla (ताल) as Main Unit of Measurement	152
Aṅgula (अंगुल) as the First Unit of Measurement	152
Height and Girth Measurements	152
Measurements of Different Parts of the Body	153
Uttama (उत्तम) *Madhyama* (मध्यम) and *Adhama* (अधम) Measurements	154
Some Textual Differences	155
7. Indian Art Beyond the Indian Frontiers	**157**
Sri Lanka, 159; Myanmar, 162; Thailand, 166; Cambodia, 170; Indonesia, 177	
Select Bibliography	183
Index	187

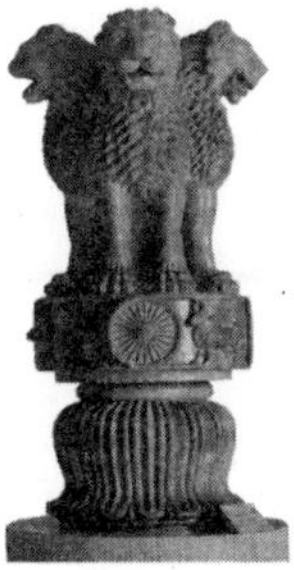

Transliteration Chart

VOWELS

अ *a*	आ *ā*	इ *i*	ई *ī*	उ *u*	ऊ *ū*	ऋ *ṛ*	ॠ *ṝ*[1]
(Roman)	(palm)	(it)	(police)	(put)	(rule)	(rig)	
ऌ *ḷ*	ॡ *ḹ*[1]	ए *e*	ऐ *ai*	ओ *o*	औ *au*		
(able)		(there)	(aisle)	(no)	(loud)		

CONSONANTS

Guttural	क *ka*	ख *kha*[2]	ग *ga*	घ *gha*[2]	ङ *ṅa*
	(skate)	(blockhead)	(gate)	(ghost)	(sing)
Palatal	च *ca*	छ *cha*[2]	ज *ja*	झ *jha*[2]	ञ *ña*
	(chunk)	(catch him)	(john)	(hedgehog)	(bunch)
Cerebral	ट *ṭa*	ठ *ṭha*[2]	ड *ḍa*	ढ *ḍha*[2]	ण *ṇa*
	(start)	(anthill)	(dart)	(godhead)	(under)
Dental	त *ta*	थ *tha*[2]	द *da*	ध *dha*[2]	न *na*
	(path)	(thunder)	(that)	(this)	(numb)
Labial	प *pa*	फ *pha*[2]	ब *ba*	भ *bha*[2]	म *ma*
	(spin)	(philosophy)	(bin)	(abhor)	(much)
Semi-vowels	य *ya*	र *ra*	ल *la*[3]	व *va*[4]	
	(young)	(drama)	(luck)	(vile)	
Sibilants	श *śa*[5]	ष *ṣa*[5]	स *sa*	ह *ha*	
	(shove)	(bushel)	(so)	(hum)	
Others	क्ष *kṣa*	त्र *tra*	ज्ञ *jña*		
	(*kṣatriya*)	(*triśūla*)	(*jñānī*)		

अं (ं) *ṁ anusvāra* is a nasal off-glide that immediately follows the pronunciation of a vowel as in *saṁskṛti*.

अः *visarga* = *ḥ* consists in abrupt release of breath after a vowel as in *prātaḥ*.

ऽ *Avagraha* shows non-pronunciation, that is, deletion of "a" after "e" or "o" as in *ime 'vasthitāḥ*. In Vedic Sanskrit, it can also show word division.

HINDI LETTERS (extras)

ँ = *m̐*	ं = ṅ	ड़ = *ṛa*	ढ़ = *ṛha*
(*candrabindu*)	(*anusvāra*)		

---

1 Longer form of the preceding vowel.

2 Aspirated forms of the preceding consonants. The compound words given as examples should be pronounced without a syllabic break at the underlined places. "tha" and "pha" should not be pronounced as fricatives.

3 retroflexed and written as "L *la*" in certain phonetic contexts.

4 Pronounced like "w," without aspiration.

5 "śa" is palatal; "ṣa" cerebral or retroflex.

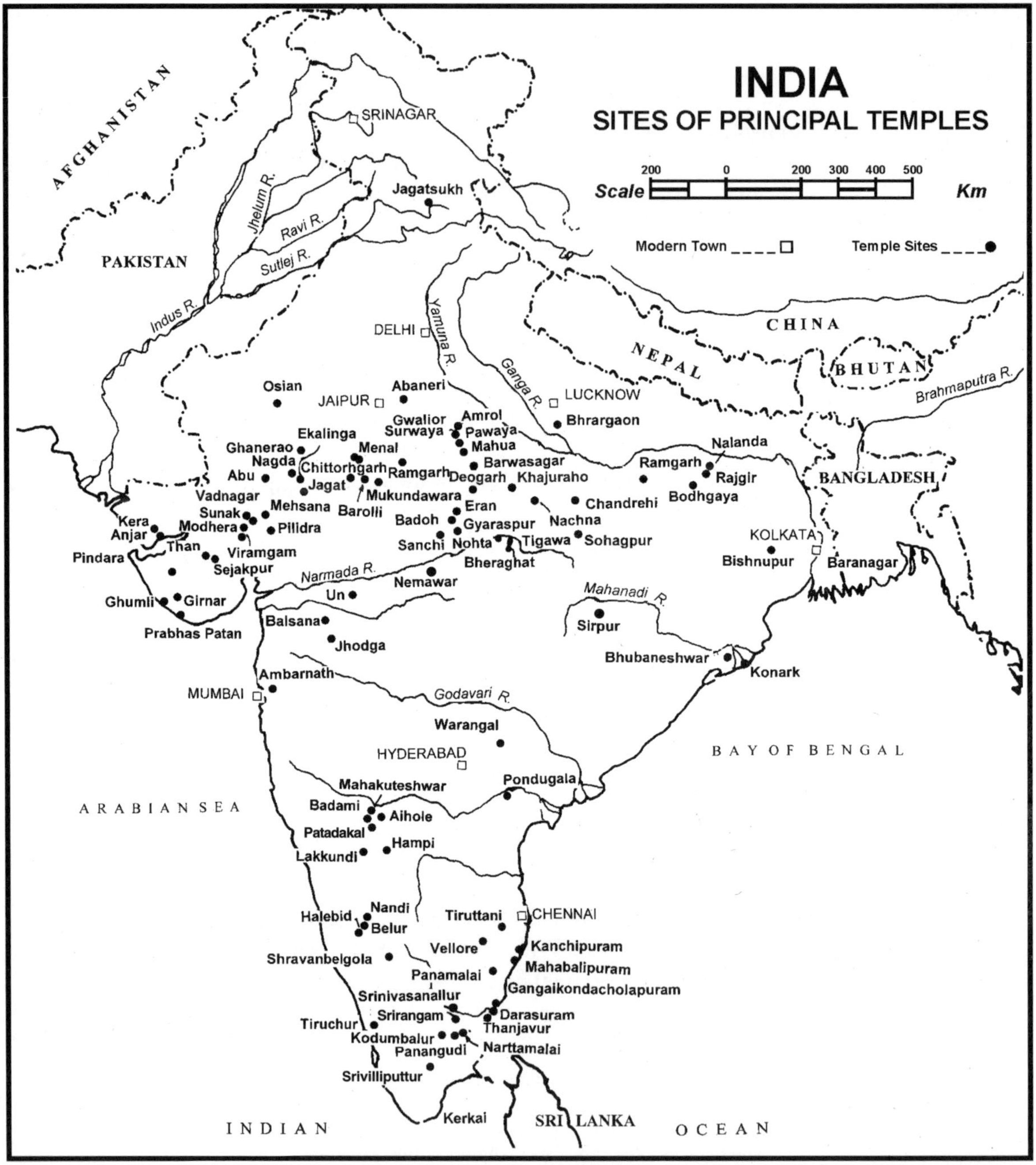

Map of India showing sites of Principal Temples

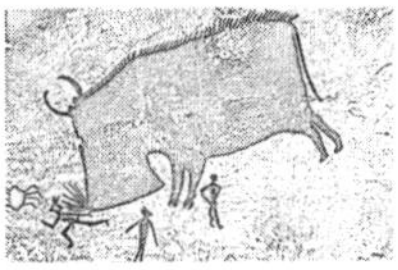

1

Rock Art in India

THE term "Rock Art" is generally used for the prehistoric art, belonging mainly to the Stone Age, although in many regions it continued in the historical periods as well. Since, in the Stone Age, human beings depended for their supply of food primarily on hunting animals and other creatures as well as gathering fruits, vegetables, edible roots, honey, etc. the arts mainly depict themes centring around these items. This art generally includes representations of wild animals, individually or in groups, stationary or fleeing, usually shown being hunted by human beings. However, there are also

Cavalry, Likhniyādarī, Mirẓāpur, U.P.

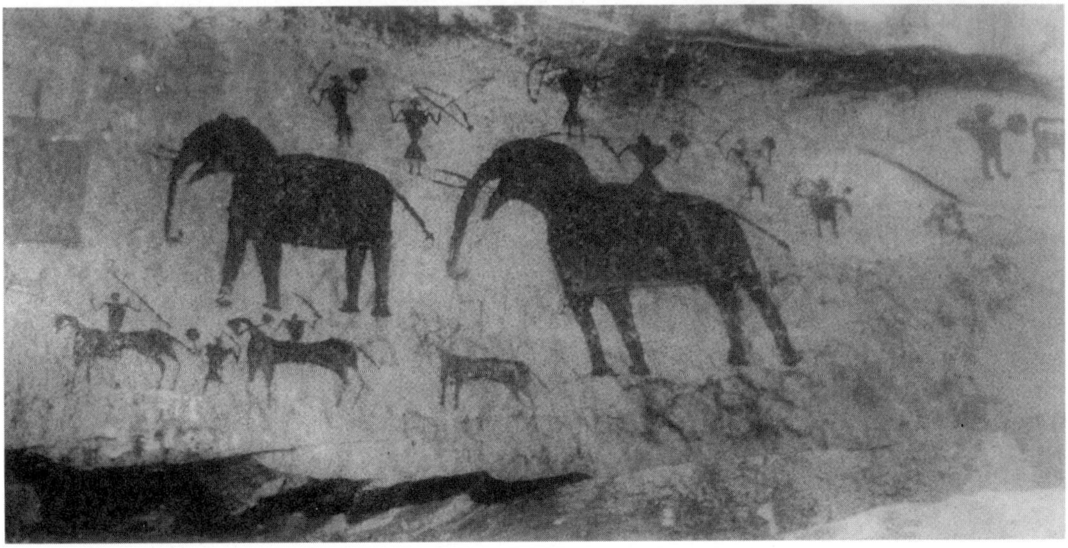

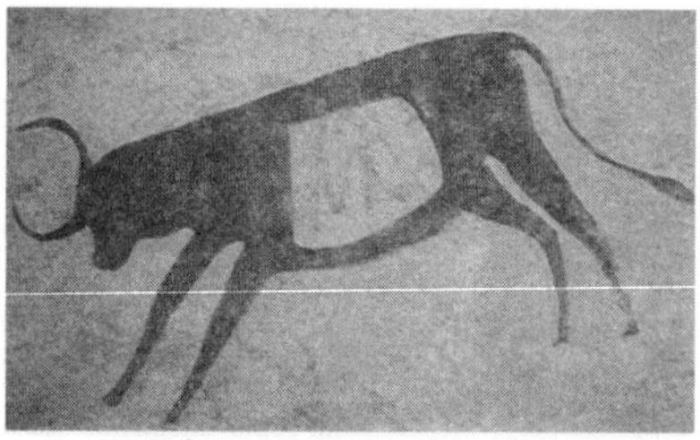

Ādamgaṛh: Bison, Mesolithic

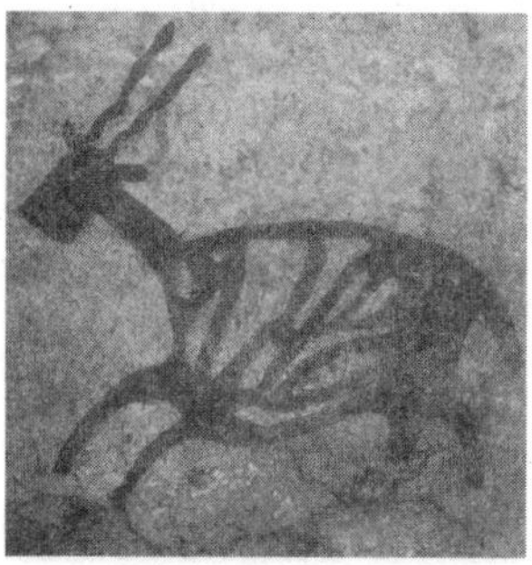

Bhopal: Black buck, Late Mesolithic

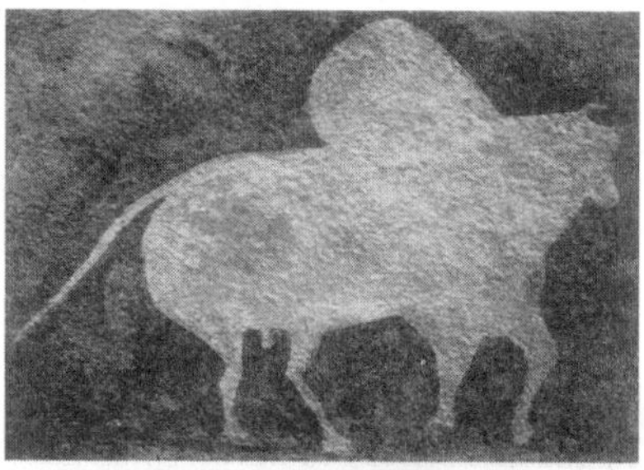

Kharvai: Zebu bull, Neolithic/Chalcolithic

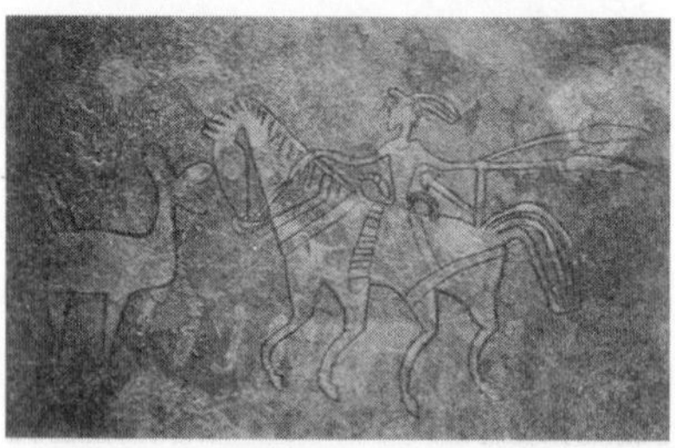

Bhīmbeṭkā: Mounted warrior and jungle cock, Early Historic

the representations of the floral world as well as geometric forms.

Various Kinds of Rock Art

The Rock Art includes (i) paintings done in caves and rock-shelters as well as on open-air boulders, (ii) engravings etched in linear forms on rock surfaces, irrespective of their formations and location, (iii) peckings carried out on rock surfaces in clusters of dots making different forms, human, animal and geometric, (iv) cup-marks or cupule created on rock surfaces in the form of deep or shallow roundels, and (v) carvings, leading to works of art in relief, or else in the round, done on pieces of bone, stone and ivory as well as large rock surfaces. Although all these categories, and a few more, are important, the largest number of them account for paintings which are found in many parts of the world — India, Africa, Europe, America, Australia, Russia and Asia. Many of these works of art were discovered during the last two decades of the nineteenth century and the first half of the twentieth century; but these are still being discovered all over the world. In India these were first discovered by John Cockburn and A. Carlleyle in the Vindhyan ranges of Bāndā and Mirẓāpur districts. Much work was done in the late twentieth century by S.K. Pandey, Jagdish Gupta, Giriraj Kumar, besides V.S. Wakankar, Manoranjan Ghosh, D.H. Gordon, and several others of the past generations.

Distribution and Chronology

Of the most famous prehistoric rock paintings located outside India are those of Altamira caves located in Spain, and Lascaux caves located in France. In India, the ones in the Vindhyan rock-shelters of Bhīmbeṭkā are outstanding due to which the entire site has been included in the "World Heritage Site" by the UNESCO. However, similar paintings are found at Ādamgaṛh near Hośaṅgābād on the Narmadā in Madhya Pradesh and at Lekhaniā in Mirẓāpur, Uttar Pradesh, Pañcamaṛhī in Madhya Pradesh, etc. There are, of course, many more rock-shelters in the Kaimūr ranges in central India also — so also in Tamil Nadu, Karnataka, Andhra Pradesh, Kerala, Orissa and Gujarat.

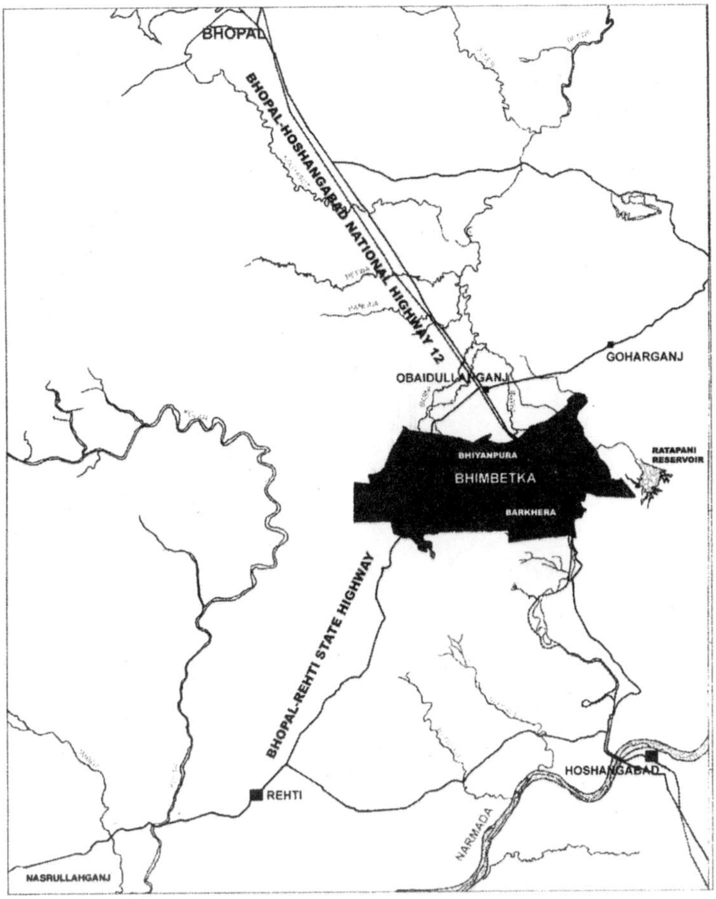

The location of Bhīmbeṭkā (Courtesy: ASI)

While the earliest pre-historic paintings of Europe are generally dated to the Upper Palaeolithic period, starting from the times of the Aurignacian Culture, going back to the period from 33,000 BCE, this tradition continued up to the end of the Pleistocene Period or the Glacial Age almost 10,000 BCE. The Indian ones, however, start only around 8000-5000 BCE time-bracket, belonging to the Mesolithic period — but they continue till almost the end of the eighteenth century CE. Whether or not some paintings belong to the Upper Palaeolithic times is difficult to say at this stage.

Bhīmbeṭakā

Discovered in 1957 by V.S. Wakankar, the rock-shelters of Bhīmbeṭkā, located in Distt. Raisen of Madhya Pradesh, are only 50 km from Bhopal. Like

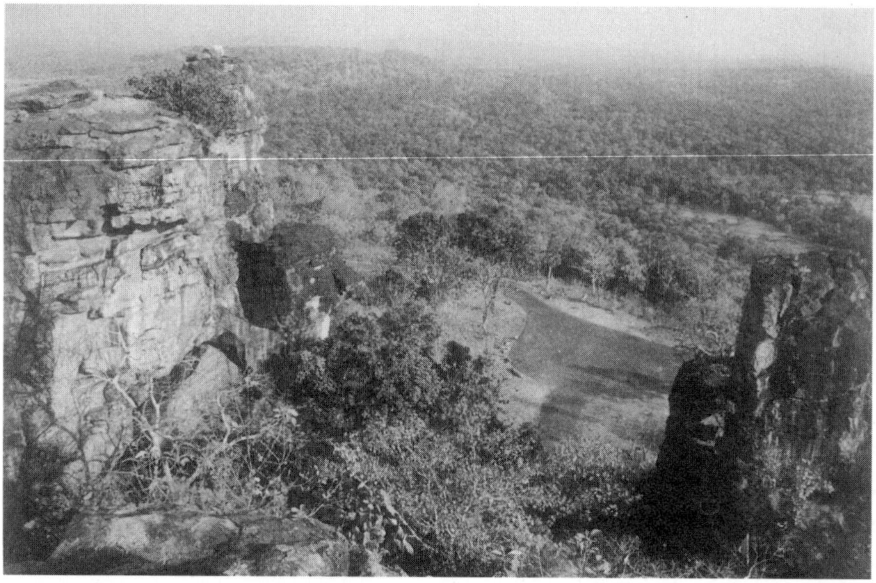

View from Bhīmbeṭkā Rock-shelters

many other rock-shelter paintings, most of the paintings at Bhīmbeṭkā are found done in different shades of red — from deep brown to yellowish red. However, black, yellow and white are also used extensively; only sometimes colours like green and blue are found used. The paints used are invariably non-organic, i.e. mineral or products of minerals or earth-produced ochres. The most popularly used mineral is brown-coloured haematite, which is iron-based and found in nature in various forms of nodules, some in the form of pencils. Copper-bearing pyrites were also used to produce green, but only occasionally. Calcium-based nodules, such as *kaṅkara*s, produced various shades of white and dull yellow. Carbon was used to produce black. The colours were generally mixed with water, natural glues, blood and animal fats.

Dārā kī Chattan: Cup marks

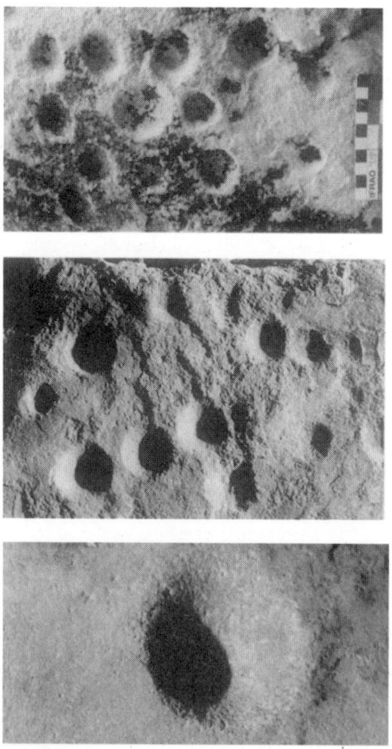

The paintings were executed directly on the exposed surfaces of the rocks; there was no preparation of the ground with any kind of paste of clay or lime to make the surface plain and smooth to make paintings on, as was done at Ajantā in the historical times. The colours, therefore, entered into the pores of the coarse surface of the rocks. The rocks are either a variety of sandstone formations, or their metamorphosed forms like quartzite; the other formations, i.e. those of the igneous rocks, for example, granite, basalt or gabbros, mainly in south India and the Deccan, are found only rarely used for executing paintings, although engravings and peckings are found executed on them very often, particularly during the Neolithic period and later in the historical times.

The paintings are done either in lines or outlines, some filled in with hatched lines, the others filled in fully or partially in solid colours.

The pictures, sometimes covering large spaces, are usually filled with multiple figures of humans and animals. However, small and large individual figures of men, women and animals are also found depicted in the rock-shelters of not only India but also Africa, Australia and other countries.

Rock-shelters paintings of various styles from various sites

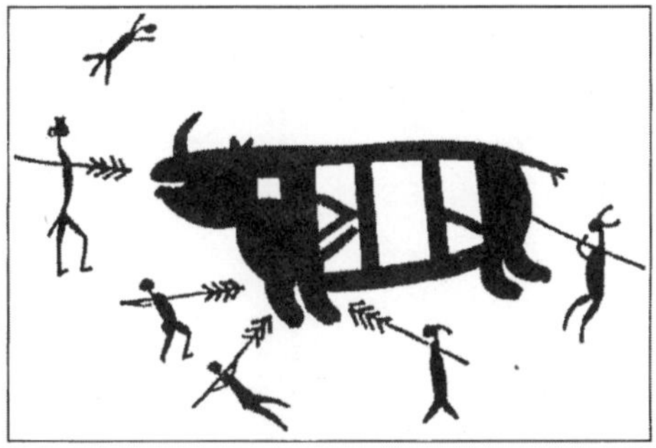

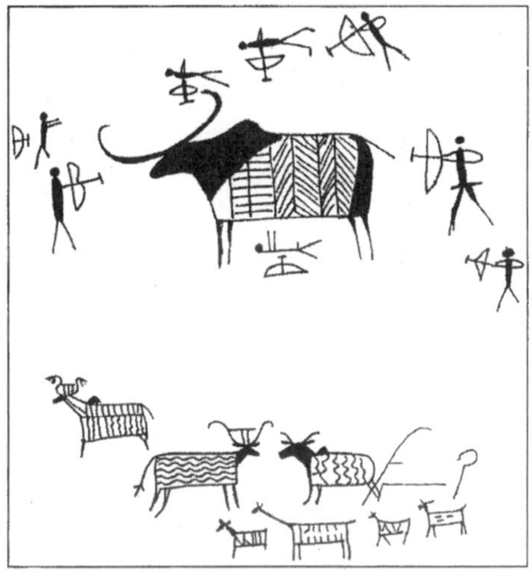

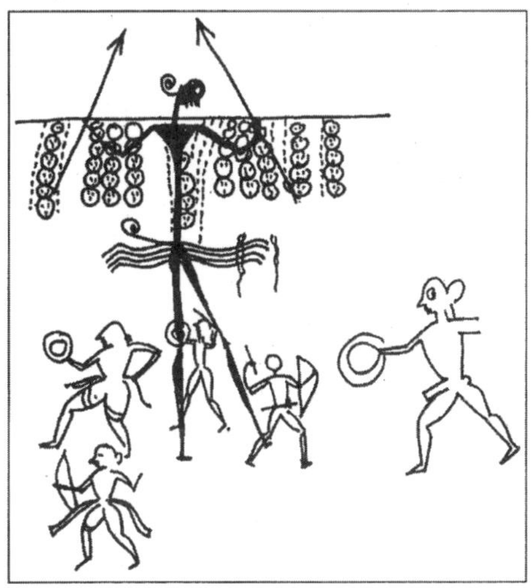

The Purpose of Rock Art

No one knows exactly the purpose for which the people executed these paintings; only some guesses have been made. Thus, according to one view these were magico-religious in nature. For example, some polychrome paintings of wild animals found in the caves of Lascaux have arrows depicted in their bodies which may mean that by doing that the hunter-painter ensured that he will kill the animal when he goes to hunt that species of the animal. Others, however, take them only as the products of natural behaviour of human beings, to depict the world around them when in leisure. Some even associate them with belief-systems comparable to those found amongst the tribals in the contemporary period. But then how far can we impose the present on the past?

Dating the Rock Art

These paintings are often found superimposed by paintings done in later periods, without any regard

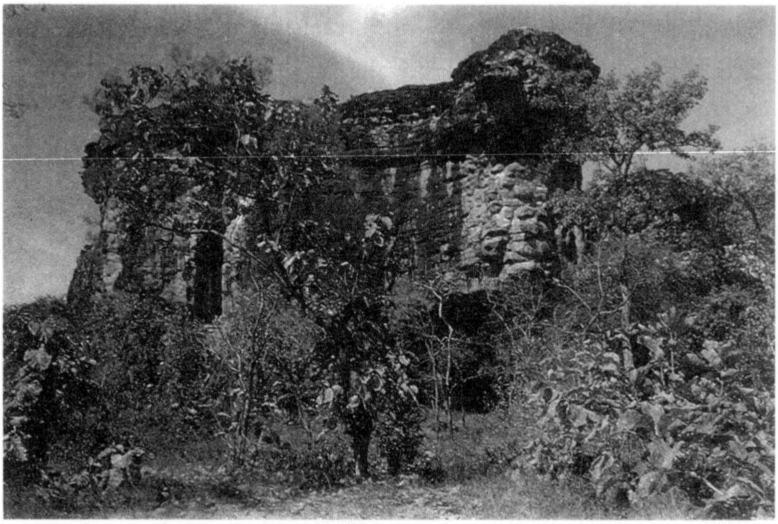

Auditorium Rock, Bhīmbeṭkā Mountain, formed by differential erosion of the top-layer of the mountain

to the pre-existing paintings. It is thus not very easy to separate them periodwise although some sequences have been made out by applying the method of "later ones override the earlier ones." However, in India, since some paintings depict the scenes found on the potteries of the Chalcolithic period of the second millennium BCE, these are dated to that period. Similarly, some paintings carry inscriptions of the Mauryan-Śuṅga Brāhmī, thus these are dated to the period bracketed between 300 BCE and CE 50. There are then pictures of marriages in which costumes as well as the weapons depicted belong stylistically to the eighteenth century. In this way attempts have been made by some scholars to date them to various time-frames. However, physical and chemical methods of dating, such as the radiocarbon and AMS methods, have also been used but only rarely, generally in some foreign countries, such as Australia, where white paint has been dated, but their results are more or less tentative. In recent years, it has been claimed, generally on the basis of stratigraphy, that the cup-marks in India as well as elsewhere belong to the Lower and Middle Palaeolithic periods, datable to 200,000 to 50,000 years BCE or more but opinions are divided on the issue to include or not to include them in the category of Rock Art although their locations make them almost certain that these are not functional in everyday life, these are often located on the vertical sides of the rocks and are generally executed in groups. What magico-religious purpose they may have served is hardly possible to know at this stage of research.

Lastly, how were these prehistoric painting traditions tied up with the classical traditions of Indian paintings, generally bracketed between 200 BCE and CE 1100, and later? Perhaps, not. There is no positive evidence for doing that. For example, the earliest, the Śuṅga–Sātavāhana paintings of Ajantā of the second and first century BCE time-bracket, was in no way inspired by the rock-shelter paintings. All the classical traditions were inspired by the organized religions — Buddhism, Jainism, Vaiṣṇavism, Śaivism, Śāktism, etc. — and not by the Rock Art, although in some rock-shelters we do find them, as at some places in Gujarat, *stūpa* is depicted but then it is more than clear that the former influenced the latter, and not the other way round.

Deers, humped bulls and humans, Sātakuṇḍā Raisen, Madhya Pradesh, (Courtesy: K.K. Chakravarty)

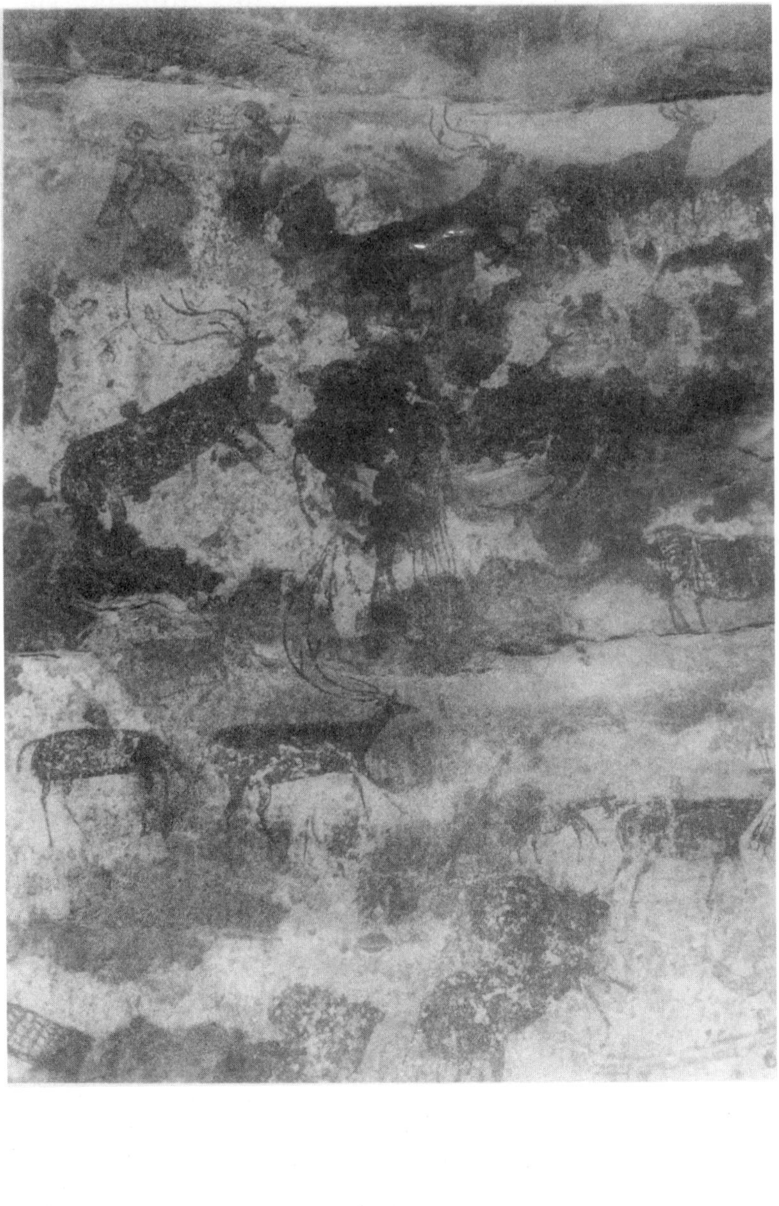

Other Forms of Stone Age Art & Architecture

The other forms of Rock Art done by engravings, peckings, etc. are very few in India. At Paṭne, located near Ajantā, the excavations yielded engravings done on ostrich egg shells found embedded in the Upper Palaeolithic deposits. The rock engravings of the Neolithic period found in Andhra Pradesh, Goa and Karnataka generally include cattle and some wild animals.

Caves and rock-shelters are the natural abodes of men and gods although at times the Stone Age people erected some walls by piling up stones of one kind or the other found in their vicinity. These walls served as protection devices against wind, rains and wild animals. The excavations conducted at Bhīmbeṭkā rock-shelters have yielded the evidence of a few such structures.

Some kind of open-air shrines have been suspected in the Son Valley, in the Vindhyas, Mesolithic sites since heaps of stones, bearing naturally occurring parallel triangles, one within the other, due to water action, in the region of sandstone formations, were marked by the explorers. Since similar stones are still worshipped by the villagers living nearby, the explorers, J.D. Clarke and G.R. Sharma, felt that it could be the continuation of an old tradition — the triangles represent females in their mother goddess aspect.

Thus, in terms of Stone Age Art there is a lot of data-base but in terms of Stone Age Architecture in India, we have very limited evidence to work upon. In fact, bone and stone sculptures and engravings found in the Upper Palaeolithic deposits in Europe, have only rarely been found in Indian rock-shelter deposits. Only in deposits of the Billasurgam caves in Karnataka bone art works in engravings have been reported.

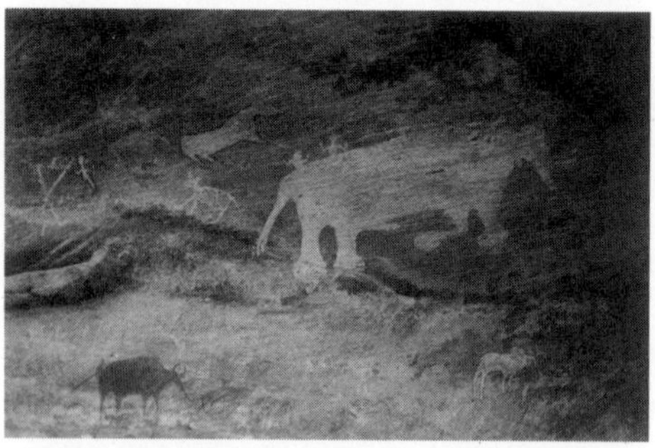

Bhīmbeṭkā Rock-shelters: Paintings in white and red colours

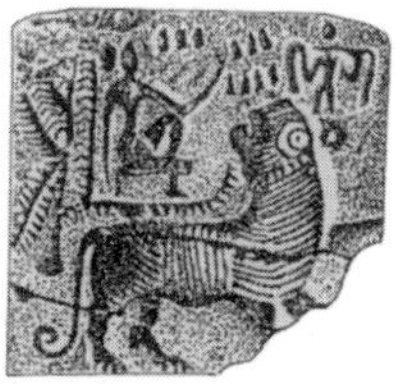

2

The Harappan Art

THE epithet "Haṛappan" is used for a literate urban civilization which is also known as the "Indus Valley" or "Indus" or "Indus–Sarasvatī" civilization. It belongs to the Bronze Age India, mainly of the third millennium BCE (3000–2000 BCE). During this period, India witnessed the birth of several large cities, spreading from Maharashtra in the south to Jammu in the north and from Makran coast in the west to upper Gaṅgā–Yamunā Doab in the east, covering broadly 1600 × 1600 km area, which is four times more than any known civilization of its times, for example the Egyptian and the Mesopotamian. However, unlike these two, the Haṛappan civilization still remains somewhat enigmatic since its writing has yet not been deciphered. This has been so even though India had close commercial contacts with Mesopotamia and, therefore, there should have been several bilingual inscriptions. However not one has been found anywhere which could help us in reading the inscriptions found engraved on seals and sealings, copper and bronze objects and pottery.

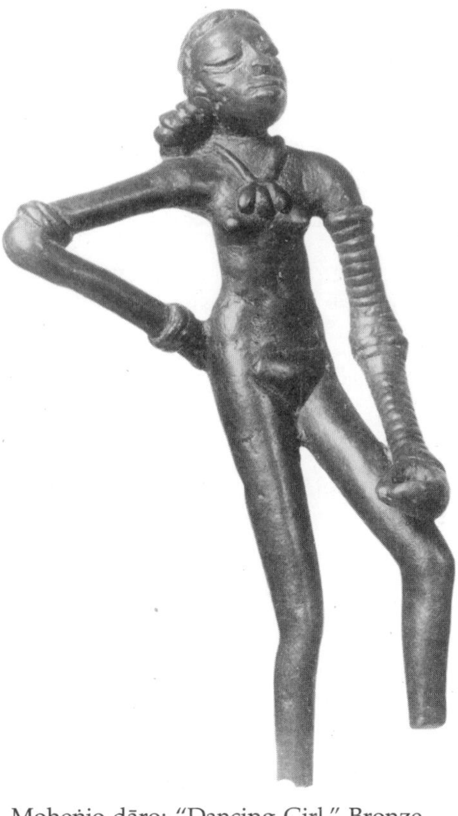

Moheṅjo-dāṛo: "Dancing Girl," Bronze

The term "Haṛappan" is derived from the name of an ancient site located on the River Rāvī in the Sahiwal district of present-day Pakistan. Although this site was explored in the nineteenth century itself by one Charles Masson and then by Alexander

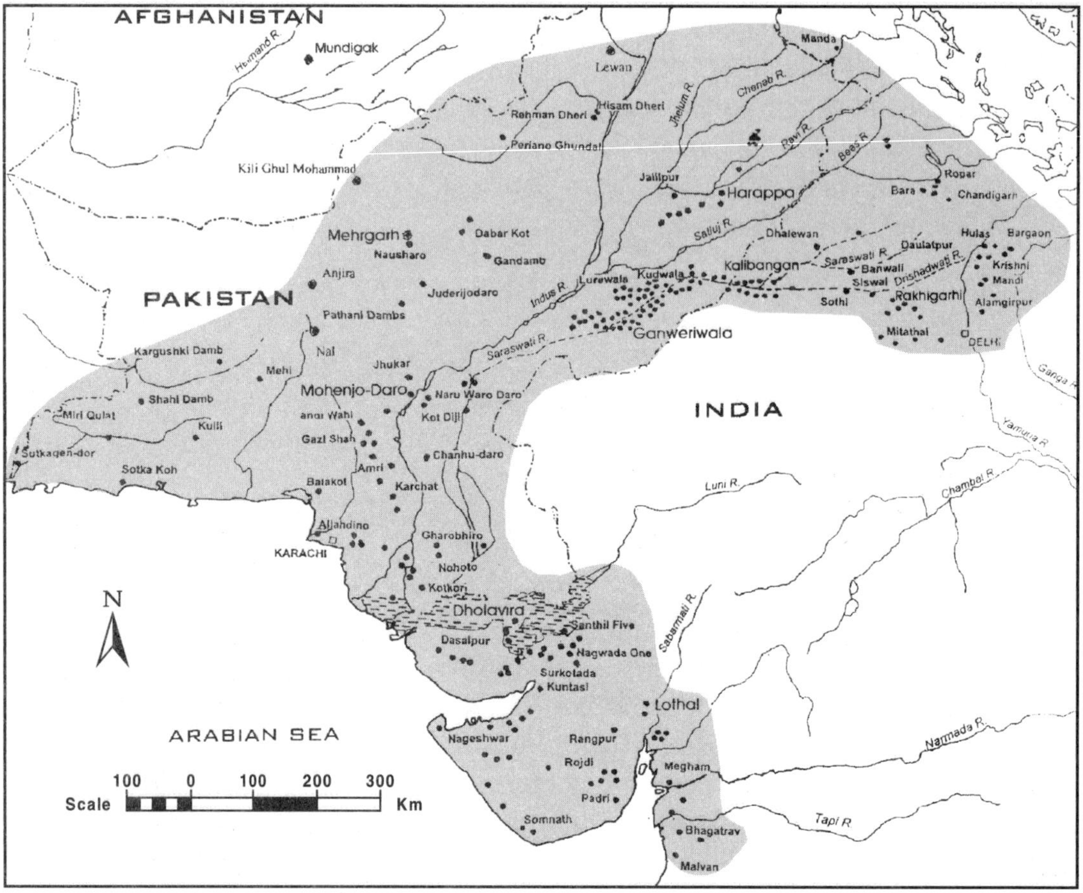

Map of Haṛappan Civilization

Cunningham, it was excavated only in the winter of 1921-22, when yet another site of the same civilization, Moheṅjo-dāṛo, located on the River Indus in Sindh, Pakistan, was also excavated. The archaeological excavations were conducted at these sites under the general direction of John Marshall for more than two to three decades. Later on, more work was done at many other Haṛappan sites, including pre-Haṛappan and Late Haṛappan sites, both in India and Pakistan. In Pakistan, a major pre-Haṛappan site was excavated by the French archaeologist J.F. Jarrige. It is Mehrgaṛh, located on the Bolan River, in Baluchistan. In India, the major Haṛappan sites excavated are Lothal, located in southern Gujarat; Sūrkoṭaḍā, Dholāvīrā and Jūnī

Kurāṇ in Kachchh; Kālībaṅgā, Tarkhānewālā Ḍerā, and Baroṛ located in northern Rajasthan; and Baṇāwalī, Rākhīgaṛhī and Bhirrānā in northern Haryana, by scholars like B.B. Lal, S.R. Rao, J.P. Joshi, R.S. Bisht and several others. While the major Haṛappan sites in Pakistan are located in the valleys of the Indus and her tributaries, such sites in India are found located on the banks of the present-day dried up river known as Sarasvatī and also her tributaries like Dṛṣadvatī. In fact, there are around four times more number of Early and Mature Haṛappan period sites on the Sarasvatī system of rivers than the Indus system of rivers. Put together, these are around 2000. The Haṛappan civilization was, therefore, undoubtedly the gift of not only the Indus but also the Sarasvatī. Therein, therefore, lies the justification of the new term, the Indus–Sarasvatī civilization for the Haṛappan culture-complex.

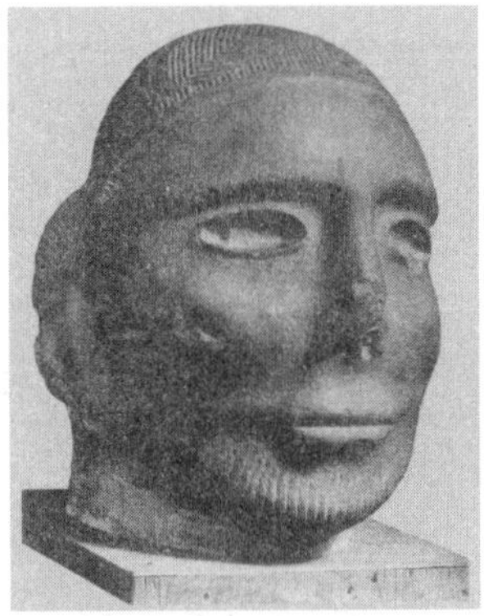

Moheṅjo-dāṛo: Steatite head of an elite male

Materials Used

The works of art produced at Haṛappan sites are generally small in size, less than 30 cm in height. These were carved with the help of bronze tools on a variety of stones and clays. Others were cast in metals, usually bronze. The stones generally used include sandstone, steatite, alabaster, jasper, agate, carnelian and many other semi-precious stones as well. The clays used are generally the ordinary clay, burnt to terracotta, and kaolin, very fine whitish clay. The metals used are bronze, an alloy of copper (approx. 90 per cent) and tin (approx. 10 per cent) with a small content of arsenic (less than 1 per cent). Gold and silver, and their alloy electrum, sometimes even lead, were also used to produce works of art and crafts, including jewellery items. Some of the smaller works of art and crafts were glazed in colours like white, turquoise, grey and black.

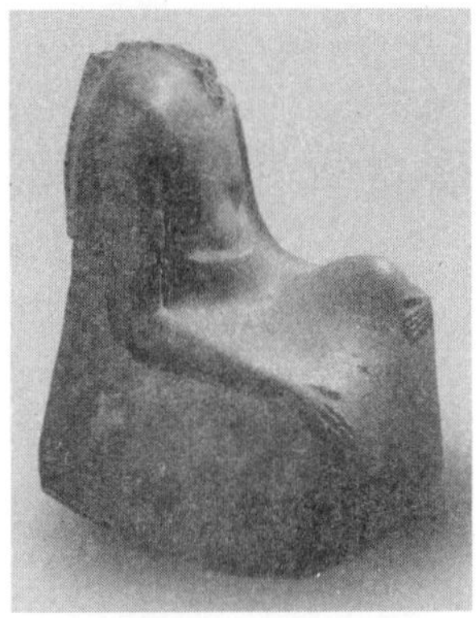

Moheṅjo-dāṛo: Priest in sitting posture

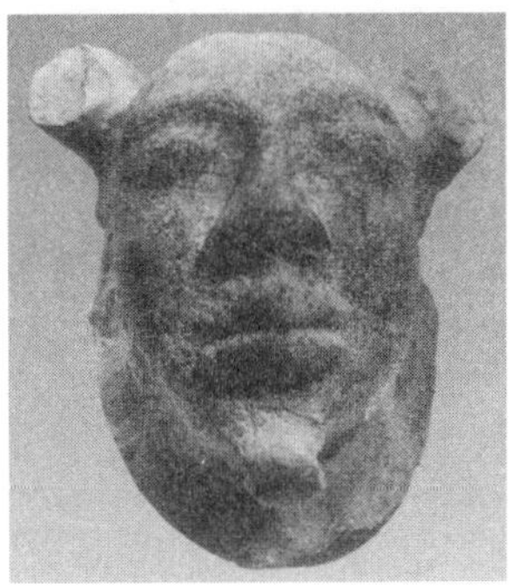

Moheṅjo-dāṛo: Terracotta mask of a bearded mythical male

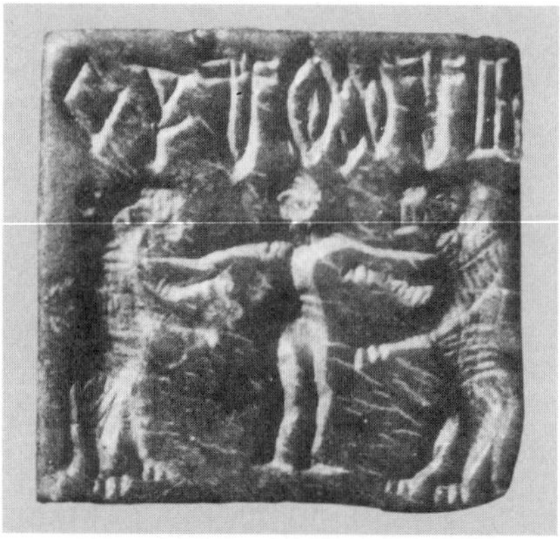

Moheṅjo-dāṛo: "Gilgemesh" seal

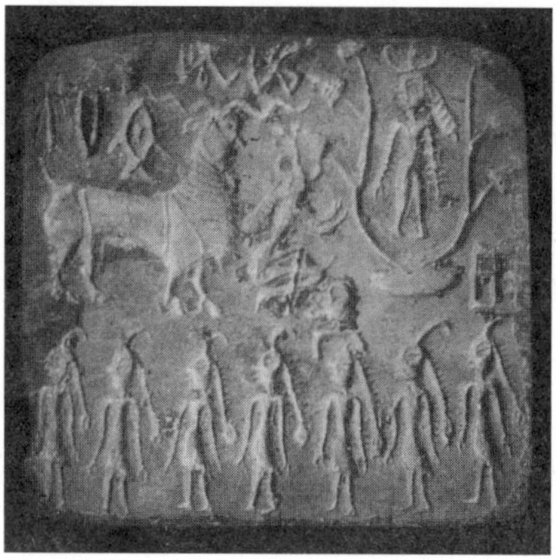

Moheṅjo-dāṛo: Seal with sacrificial scene

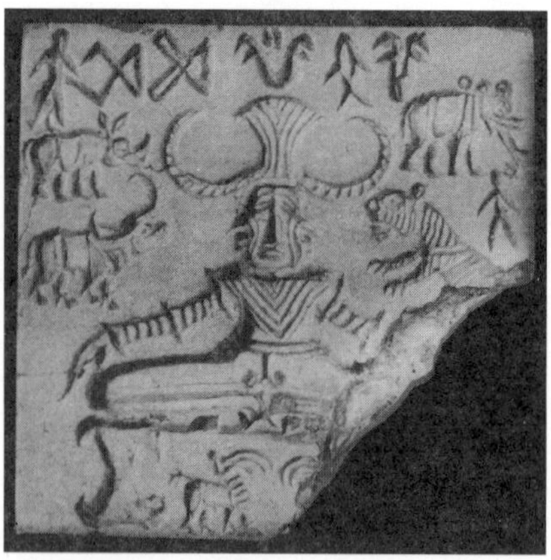

Moheṅjo-dāṛo: "Paśupati" seal

Subject Matter & Common Motifs

The subject matter of the works of Haṛappan art include faunal as well as floral representations, besides geometric motifs. The faunal elements of art include human beings and animals, as well as birds, reptiles, aquatic beings and many other creatures. The category of human beings includes both males and females while animals include bulls, buffaloes, tigers, elephants, goats, rams, unicorns, stags, camels, dogs, etc. There are also the representations of snakes, scorpions, tortoise, peacock, crow, parrot, and others. The floral elements of art include *pīpala* leaf, multi-petalled flowers and trees and grasses. The geometric elements include triangles, rectangles, squares, roundels, fish-scales and the like. But there is also yet one more category, which includes mythological characters and hybrid personages such as the human image with three faces, single body but many heads, of one and the same animal or of different animals.

Stone & Bronze Sculptures

The most famous stone sculptures, made in the round, include the bust of the so-called "priest-king"; but he may have been just a member of the elite since India had no system of the Mesopotamian polity in which the two positions, that of the priest and the king, were combined in one person. It is shown with half-closed slit-open eyes, combed hair tied with a broad band or fillet with a prominent ring in the centre, combed and trimmed beard, clean moustache and shawl decorated with trefoil design, covering the body and one shoulder. This bust and the head of a high ranking person, with well-combed hair and half-closed eyes with hollows in which white shell or steatite may have been inserted — both were recovered from Moheṅjo-dāṛo. The other well-known stone sculptures include a sitting personage clad in plain shawl and also a goat (?), both from Moheñjo-dāṛo. There are a few others, of human beings and animals from Moheñjo-dāṛo and other sites. From Haṛappā, on the other hand, there is a small nude male headless torso carved in red jaspery stone and a nude headless male dancer in black jaspery stone. The famous bronzes, on the other hand, include the so-called nude "Dancing Girl" with thick lips, slit eyes, elaborate hair-do and hands covered fully with bangles, and a "buffalo" from Moheñjo-dāṛo. There is a bronze buffalo from Kālībaṅgā also. Both are robust and well modelled, with naturalistic treatment of body elements. The tiny little figurines of dogs, stags and squirrels, and of several other creatures as well as of human beings come from Moheñjo-dāṛo, Haṛappā, Canhū-dāṛo and other sites. These are equally cute and beautiful, used perhaps as toys.

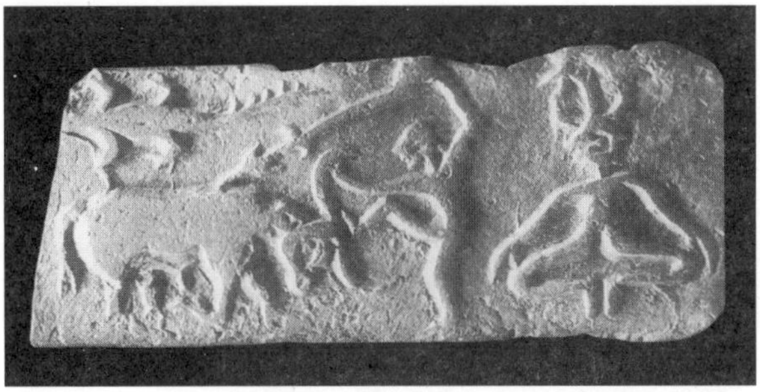

Haṛappā: Terracotta sealing, depicting the Śiva-like seated figure and a person attempting to kill a buffalo, perhaps as a sacrifice

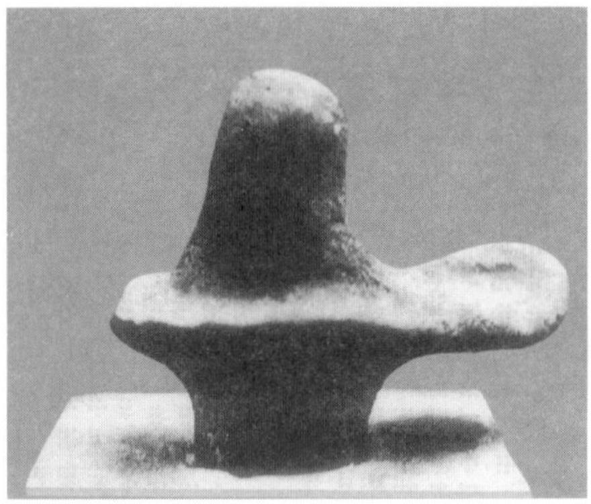

Kālībaṅgā: Terracotta Śivaliṅga

Terracottas

The bulk of art objects, however, include terracottas. These objects usually depict what is called "mother goddess," although all of them do not seem to be cult objects. These are hand modelled female figurines with open breasts but loins or the mid-lower part covered with a plain piece of cloth. The headdress is very often formal, sometimes placed in between two small but deep cups. In some examples, the hairdo is pleated. In some others these are shown pregnant. A few of them have babies.

Haṛappā: Engravings on copper tablets

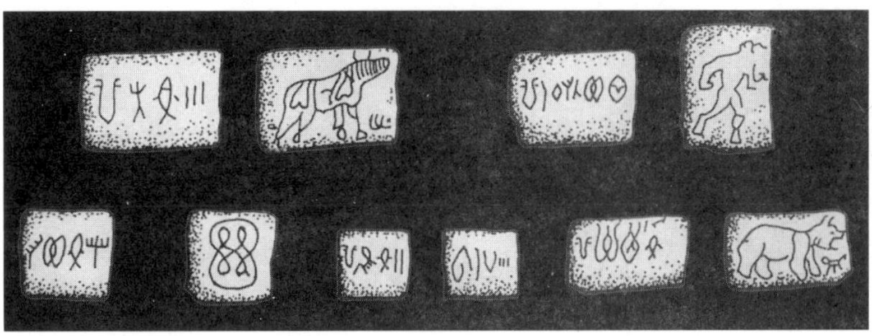

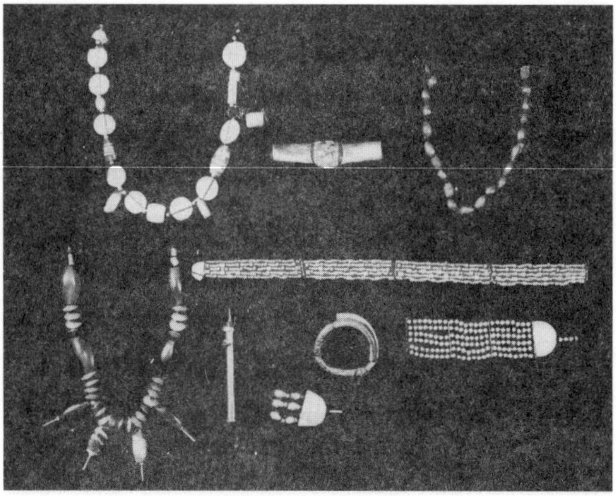

Moheṅ jo-dāṛo: Jewellery of gold and semi-precious stones

These are generally shown wearing a large variety of ornaments. There are some mythical figures as well as caricatures. The terracottas are hand-modelled with pinched nose and appliqué breasts. However, a few of the terracottas are produced by moulds, such as the masks. These have been found largely at Haṛappā, Moheṅjo-dāṛo and Canhū-dāṛo. At other sites bull figurines, often crudely made, are found in large numbers. The female figurines are shown standing, sitting and squatting with hands folded in *namaskāra-mudrā* or else in yogic postures, or else engaged in some household works.

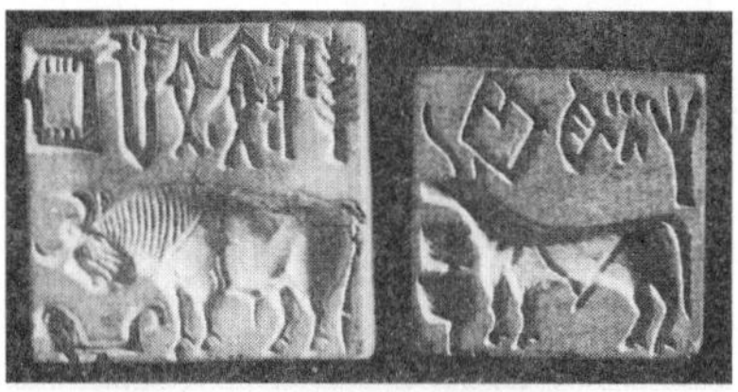

Bull and Unicorn seals

The tradition of making terracotta female figurines with a variety of hairdo had its predecessor in the Baluchi sites of the fourth and fifth millennia BCE in the Zhob and Bolan valleys at sites like Periāno Ghuṇḍaī, Kauḍaṇī, Sūr-Jaṅgal, Ḍābar Koṭ, Dāmb Sadāt and Mehrgaṛh. These were not necessarily cult objects. In this context it may also be mentioned that there are very few male figurines, some of them, however, shown nude.

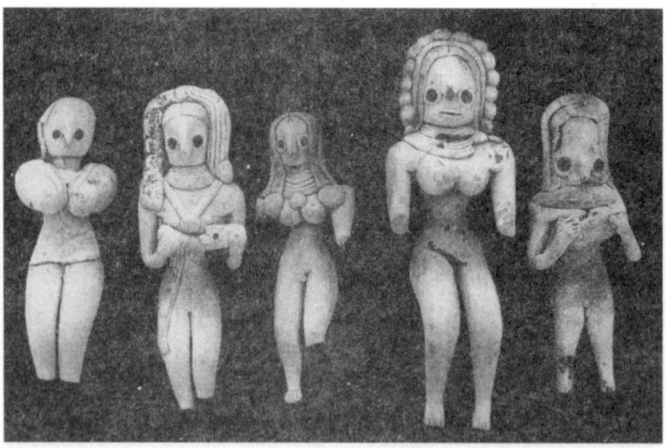

Mehrgaṛh: Pre-Haṛappan terracotta figurine — males, females and females with child

Steatite Seals

The works of art with perfect modelling of naturalistic kind made with great sensitivity and care are not only in stone and bronze but also in the carvings in the negative, i.e. intaglio, mostly carved on a soft variety of fine stone known as soap stone or steatite. When stamped on wet clay they leave behind in high relief the pictures engraved with precision. The images on them include animals like bulls, elephants and unicorns in largest numbers. Tigers come next. The other animals, real and mythical, are fewer in number. The human beings include the most famous image of the so-called "Paśupati" — a male sporting a horned headgear, and sitting cross-legged on a couch below which were depicted stags. The image is supposed to have three faces as well as ithyphallic. It is surrounded by small figures of animals like bull and tiger as well as a human being, in all five of them — hence Paśupati or "Lord of Animals" form of Śiva, according to one view. There are a few other seals depicting sitting male figures carrying the horned headdress. There are some examples of pictures depicting some events of a mythological narrative, for example one standing male fighting simultaneously two tigers, one on either side. It is sometimes called "Gilgamesh" on the analogy of a war-hero in Mesopotamia. In another example a male is sitting on a tree while a tiger is looking at him from the surface. In yet another example there is a scene of human or goat sacrifice with seven human beings clad in peaked tunic and standing in a row below the scene depicting sacrifice. Engravings on stone and terracotta as well as bronze and copper pieces, account only for just a few.

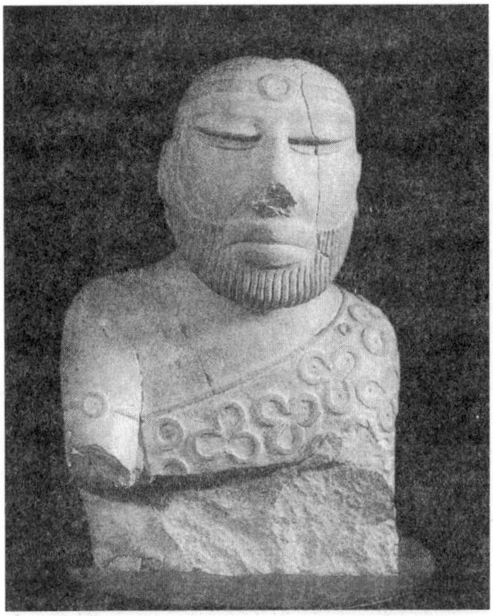

Mohenjo-dāṛo: "Priest King"

Mohenjo-dāṛo: Terracotta "Mother Goddess"

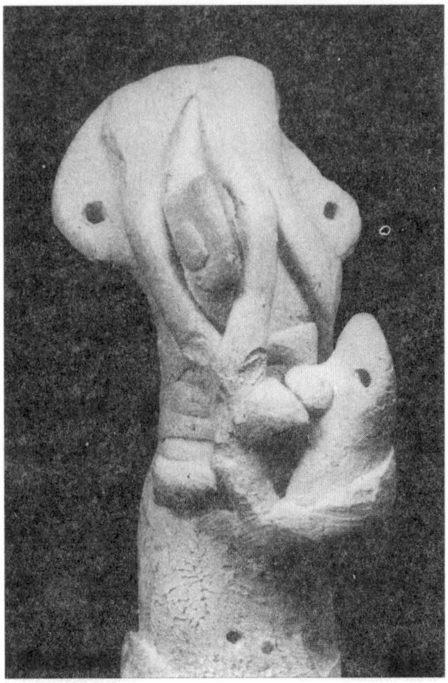

Pottery Paintings, Metal Art, Glazing, etc.

The paintings are found executed in black on pottery, mostly red in colour. However, white and chocolate colours were also used. In some instances yellow and green were also included, as at Nal. The motifs included *pīpala* leaf, peacocks, humans, fish, birds, animals, plants, trees and a large number of geometric designs.

A word about the bronze figurines. These are produced by what is called in French *cire-perdue* and in English "lost-wax" process. In this technique the image is carved first in wax (in those days bees-wax),

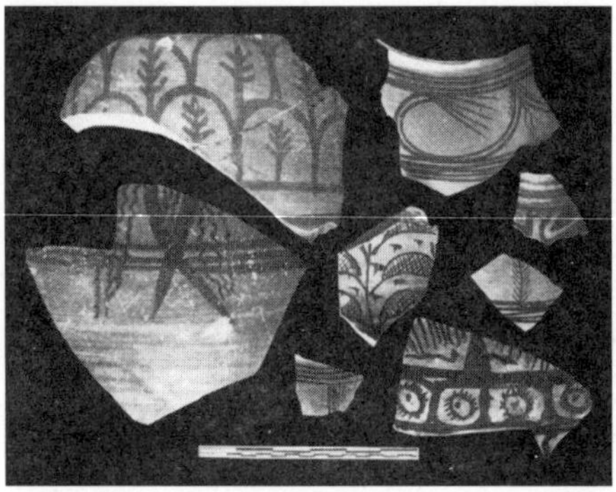

Lothal: Painted designs on pots

it was then fully covered with the finest sticky clay and then pressed, so that the image made in wax, as the original, makes its impression in all details on the surface of the clay. In the bottom of the covering clay a hole is made. It is then left in the shadow to dry slowly and gradually. This is then fired in an oven. On this, the wax melts out through the hole, leaving behind the burnt clay or terracotta mould, hollow from inside. Some time after this, the hole is plugged and the molten metal, the bronze, is poured into the mould which is constantly stirred so that no bubble is formed. When cooled, the terracotta mould is broken to get the image fully cast. Some retouches and filing and rubbing make the image fully finished like the original one made in wax.

Mohenjo-dāṛo: Painted earthen pot

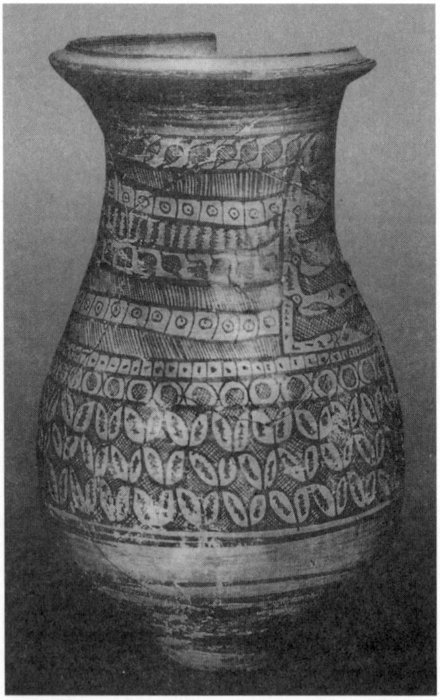

Glazing, often turquoise in colour, found on some works of art and crafts, is called "faience." It was produced with the mixture of powdered silica, lime, and oxides of iron and copper, under high temperature. Faience was mainly used for making small animal figures, beads and bangles. The gold and silver, as well as electrum (an alloy of gold and silver) and lead, as well as steatite, and paste, made of steatite powder, and shell and semi-precious stones were used in a variety of ways to produce crafts of jewellery, ornaments, utensils and tiny figurines, as well as beads. One kind of the latter, called "etched carnelian beads" were carved out of red or yellow carnelian bearing geometric motifs first by etching and then filling the negative with white paste and fired.

The Haṛappan works of art are not as large in dimension as the Egyptian and Mesopotamian ones, mainly because of their differences in polity, religion and ideological frameworks and conceptual perceptions. For example, we have yet to discover a palace for the king and monumental temple at the

Haṛappan sites, unlike Egypt and Mesopotamia where they are numerous. However, the variety in subject matter and the naturalistic treatment of humans and animals, as well as of the items of the floral world, make the Haṛappan art stand quite apart from the rest of its contemporaries.

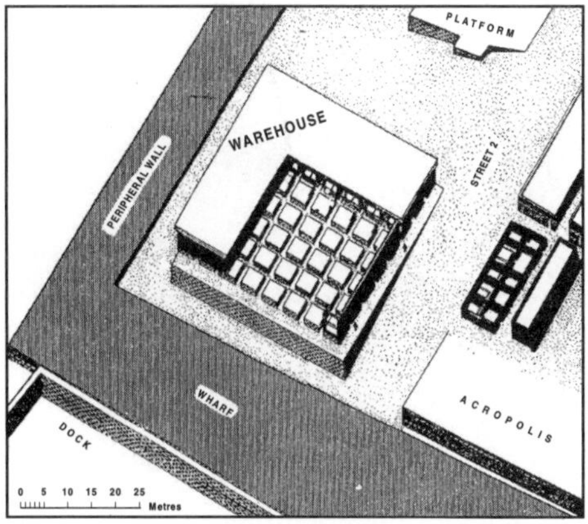

Lothal: Warehouse

Haṛappan Architecture

The Haṛappan architecture, on the other hand, is really monumental — large and spacious, constructed with the help of burnt and unburnt bricks, generally in the standard size of 11" × 5.5" × 2.5" in the ratio of 4 : 2 : 1, as at Haṛappā, Moheṅjo-dāṛo, Lothal and Kālībaṅgā. The popular method of joining them was the alternate courses of headers and stretchers, nowadays called the "English Bond" style. It gives perfect strength to the brick walls since no two joints fall one below the other. However, in the rocky regions, small and large pieces of stones were also used in constructions, usually fortifications, as at Dholāvīra and Sūrkoṭaḍā in Kachchh. There are some monuments which are partly structured and partly rock-cut as are the large water reservoirs at Dholāvīrā.

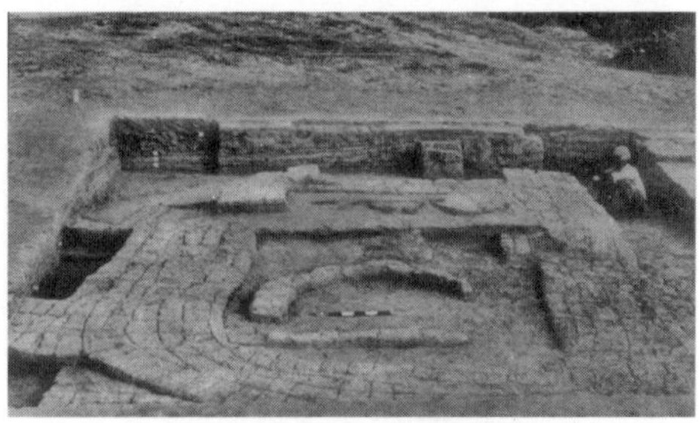

Baṇāwalī: Apsidal fire temple

Some of the architectural marvels of the Haṛappan or the Indus–Sarasvatī times are as follows:

1. *The Great Bath of Moheṅjo-dāṛo*: It is a large burnt-brick structure with a tank measuring in length: 11.7 m, width: 6.9 m and depth: 2.4 m, located in the centre of a complex of related structures, approached by flights of steps, and a series of rooms, wells and drains at the ground and below the ground levels. The basal bricks were made water tight with the use of bitumen and gypsum.

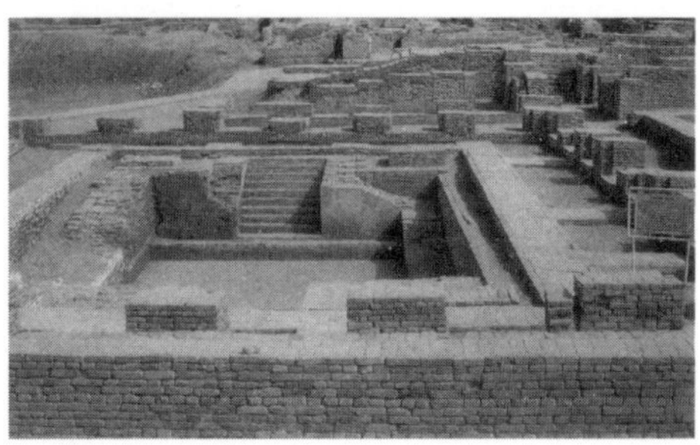

Moheṅjo-dāṛo: The "Great Bath"

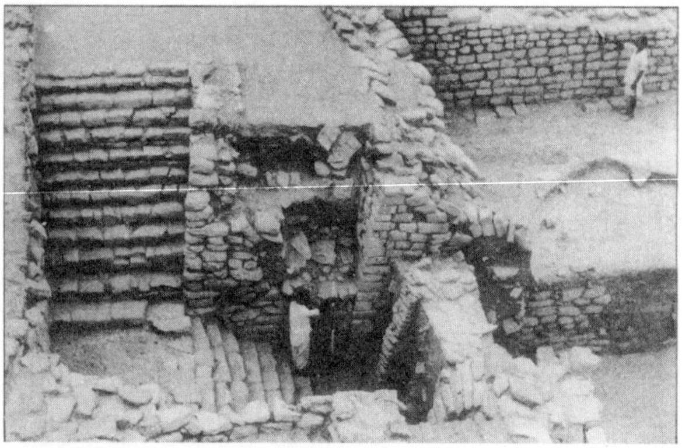

Dholāvīrā: Staircase in the northern gateway of the Citadel

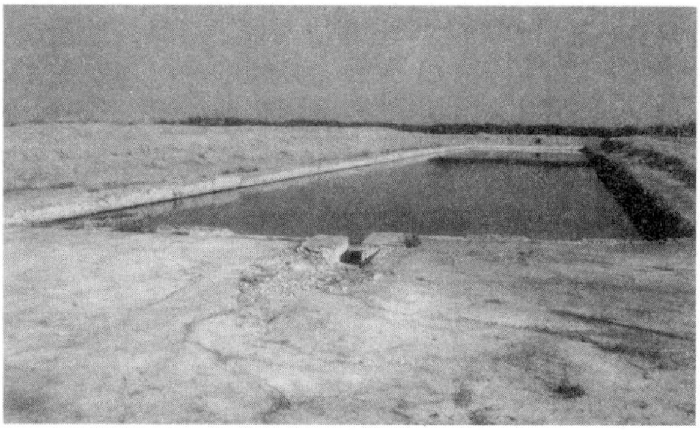

Lothal: The Dockyard

Kālībaṅgā: The Fire Altars

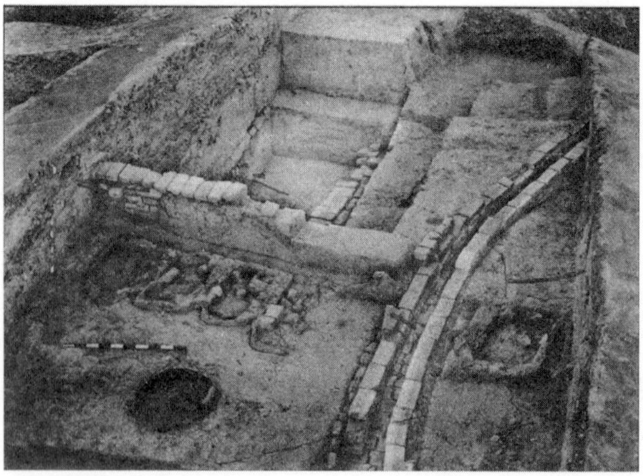

2. *The Granary of Haṛappā*: It is a huge structure, covering 850 m^2 of space, built of burnt bricks with loading and unloading platforms and a warehouse of several parallel platforms, which probably carried wooden rooms with air-ducts in between the platforms to save grain, etc. from fungus and other diseases. Lothal has a similar structure called "Warehouse."

3. *The Dockyard of Lothal*: It is a large, roughly rectangular burnt-brick structure, measuring 215 m × 37 m, with inlets and outlets, to bring water from a sea-ending river, the Bhogao, and to regulate the volume of the water in the reservoir for safe berthing of boats carrying bales of goods, respectively.

4. *The Water Reservoirs of Dholāvīrā*: There are several large tanks with landing steps, partly carved into the bed-rock and partly (the upper portion) built of stone pieces. The later day "stepped wells" or *wao* or *bāolī* in Gujarat and other places, possibly emerged out of this experiment.

5. *The Fire Altars of Kālībaṅgā*: A series of seven fire altars in the form of ash-filled oblong ovens with a vertically placed brick-like clay object in the centre, was found on a mud-brick platform. These are the earliest examples of fire worship in India. Many other Haṛappan sites have also yielded this kind of evidence.

6. *The Apsidal Fire temple of Baṇāwalī*: An apsidal mud-brick structure found with a series of Kālībaṅgā type fire altars in the central part and series of alcoves, measuring from 1 × 1 m to 1 × 2 m, set within the thickness of the wall along one side, appears to be the evidence of the earliest structural temple in India, the plan of which was followed in the historical times by Buddhists and others.

7. *The Fortifications of Dholāvīra and Sūrkoṭaḍā*: The main cities of Dholāvīrā and Sūrkoṭaḍā were protected by a huge fortification of stones. However, those in the plains, such as at Haṛappā, Kālībaṅgā, Baṇāwalī, Rākhīgaṛhī and many others had fortifications of mud-bricks.

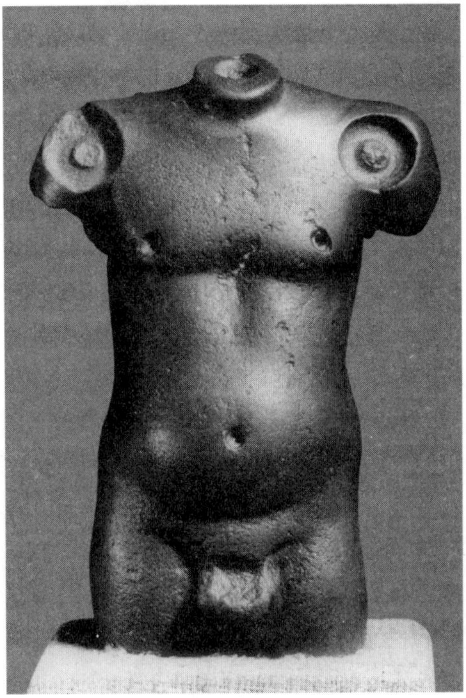

Haṛappā: Red stone male torso

There are, certainly, many more monumental structures at the Haṛappan sites, including single- and double-storied houses built along streets and lanes with covered and open drains with corbelled arches; shops built along the main roads; wells dug in the corners of cross-roads and individual houses; and halls with brick and stone pillars, both monolithic and structural. There is, in fact, an endless variety of structures at every Haṛappan or Indus–Sarasvatī site but that is a matter of details. What is important to note is that most of the Haṛappan cities were planned and meant for not only the elite but also the common men, the features which were hardly present at that point of time at any Egyptian and Mesopotamian settlement, which cared only for the abodes of gods, kings and courtiers as also the burial monuments like the pyramids; the common men lived only in huts. The

Mohenjo-dāṛo: Bronze buffalo

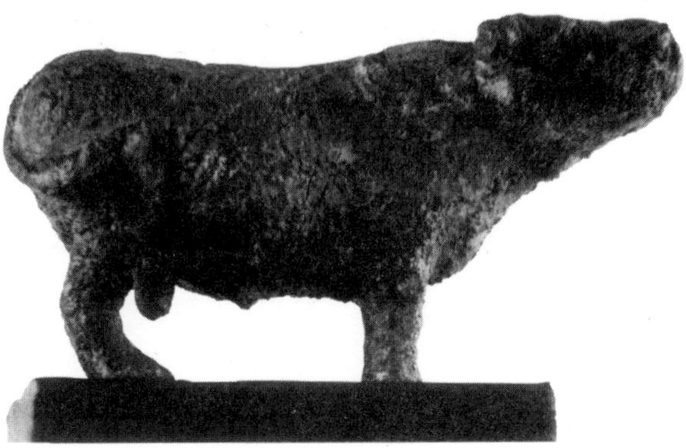

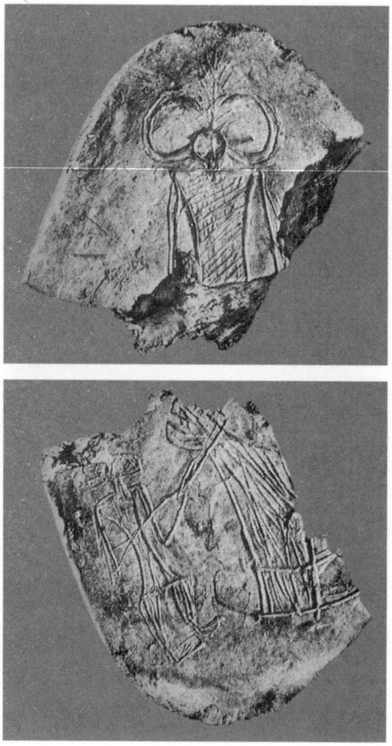

Kālībaṅgā: Engraved images on two terracotta pieces

Haṛappan was, therefore, unique as well as much ahead of its times — democratic, peace-loving and caring for all its citizens.

The Continuity of Haṛappan Traditions

The overall view of the Haṛappan Art and Architecture when assessed in terms of Haṛappan Civilization and its contributions to the later-day Hindu Civilization, as noted by John Marshall and B.B. Lal, shows the following:

- the Haṛappan belief-systems in water-worship, tree-worship, serpent worship, fire-worship, *pīpala* worship, *svastika* worship, Śiva-liṅga worship, Paśupati Śiva worship, bull worship, mother-goddess worship, etc;
- the system of wearing bangles right up to the forearm;
- the tradition of putting red-coloured vermillion by women in the centre of the parted hair;
- the system of saluting each other in *namaskāra-mudrā;*
- the yogic posture of showing eyes covered more than three-fourth by the upper lid so as to concentrate the vision on the tip of the nose;
- wearing shawl in a fashion to cover the entire lower body except one shoulder; and
- basic apsidal plan of temple architecture, etc.

Truly, the Haṛappan art was the product of its unique culture. Also, many of its art, crafts and belief-systems have continued to be in practice in one form or the other till this day.

3

Fundamentals of Indian Art

FOR an average Indian it is very easy to understand and appreciate Indian art since everything is both old and contemporary; everyday he lives with it. For foreigners also it is not difficult to appreciate it provided he or she devotes just a little time to know the background of the Indian traditions. The Indian traditions are manifested in Vedic literary texts such as the Vedas, the Upaniṣads, the Epics, the Purāṇas, the Āgamas and Śilpa-śāstras as well as in folk and local practices, oral literature and the classics. There are also several Śaiva, Vaiṣṇava, Buddhist and Jaina literary works. There are some treatises on various aspects of art and architecture, including iconography and iconometry.

Art is not for Art Sake, it is for "Dharma"

To begin with, what goes in the name of Indian Art of pre-modern period has been part and parcel of Hindu concept of *dharma* (धर्म) and all religions born in India but following various belief-systems and modes of worship. Many of the basic ideas underlying these religions seem to have originated in the Vedic times. These ideas, however, developed through various literary works of the succeeding periods. It is through them that we come to know about the socio-cultural life of the people and its foundations. Thus, in India, we find that during the olden days "art was not for art sake" as it is now.

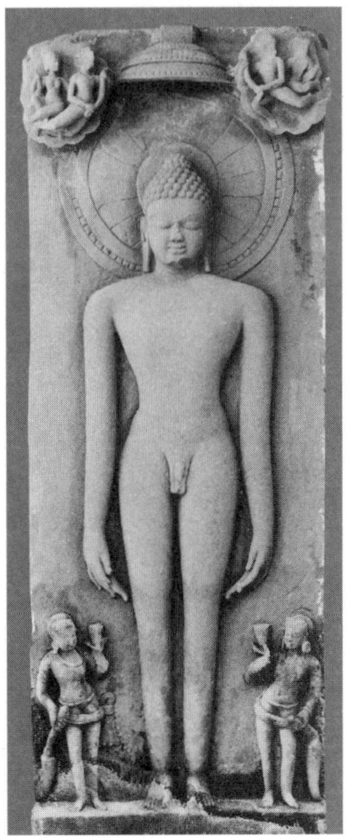

Jina, Deogaṛh, U.P.
10th century CE

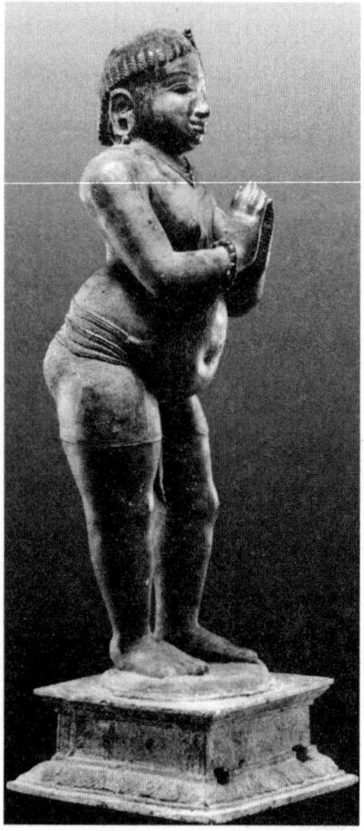

A *bhakta* (devotee), Tiruvenkaḍu, Tamil Nadu, 11th century CE

The so-called "works of art" were parts of some belief-system, written or unwritten, and some monument, religious or secular with religious beliefs attached to it. It was also spiritual, the ultimate goal of all Indian religions. That is why "art" was always manifested in temples and shrines of one kind or the other in the form of images, icons, idols, votive objects, symbols, etc. Its purpose was to heighten one's spiritual experience. Hence, in order to appreciate Indian art one has to have some knowledge of Indian religious literature and village-based traditions. Of social ideals and social behaviour. Of moral precepts. Of the way a human life is to be lived to fulfil its mission and goal in an atmosphere of conflictlessness. This is much beyond the concept of "religion." It is called *dharma* which can hardly be translated in English language because this concept is exclusively Hindu, its roots lie in the Ṛgvedic concept of *ṛta* (ऋत). And it is also universal in its application as Vivekananda used to say. The roots of Indian art lie in this holistic concept. Not that there were no pictures or sculptures of non-religious themes, these were there but in ancient period these were generally incidental; only in the medieval period we find the secular art as an independent stream of art flowing mainly in paintings, made in the courts of the kings or else for the kings and the nobility.

Religion and Art

The religious establishments and edifices in India belong to countless sects and sub-sects of religions, but all of them can be grouped in five categories, Śaiva, Vaiṣṇava, Śākta, Bauddha and Jaina. However, the first three are sometimes collectively called "Hindu," although great art historians like Ludwick Bachhofer used "Hindu" for all religions which originated in India, including Bauddha and Jaina, since these were basically only the streams of a single system, i.e. Indian view of life as a whole, including its spiritual moorings, starting from the Vedic times. Thus, religious cults led to the growth of cult-icons, iconography and icon-making techniques.

Hinduism has no Hierarchy Amongst Gods

It may, however, be noted that there is no concept of "hierarchy" amongst gods in Hinduism in which one is the highest and the others are level-wise lower than the previous one. As a matter of fact, by turn Śiva, Viṣṇu, Brahmā and Śakti becomes the Supreme Deity, the others are shown paying homage to Him or Her, depending on the occasion arising in the narrative of the mythology. The notion of One Supreme Reality is, however, very much there since in the ultimate analysis that alone is sought to be realized by the devotee. The gods are many; one, if so wishes, can select any one of them as per his or her own choice for the purpose of concentrating his or her mind on the Ultimate. But it is not idolatry since the idols themselves are not worshipped, what is in reality worshipped is the Supreme Being, called by various names, including Brahmā, Īśvara, Paramātmā, etc. One attains Godhood through the realization of the True Nature of the Self which too is God. In other words, there is no duality, man and God are the same, only the ignorance of man makes him feel that he is different from God. This concept is "I am Brahma," अहं ब्रम्हास्मि. This is called "advaita" (अद्वैत). But this also is only one view, although the dominant view. The others are slightly modified views, e.g. "viśiṣṭādvaita" (विशिष्टाद्वैत) in which "I" and "He" are one and the same yet both exist independently in a particular sense.

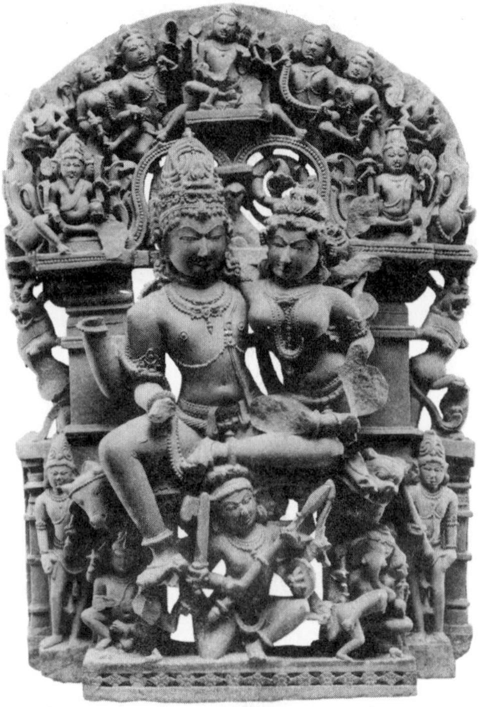

Rāvaṇa shaking Kailāsa where Śiva and Pārvatī are sitting, Hiṅglājgaṛh, M.P. 11th century CE

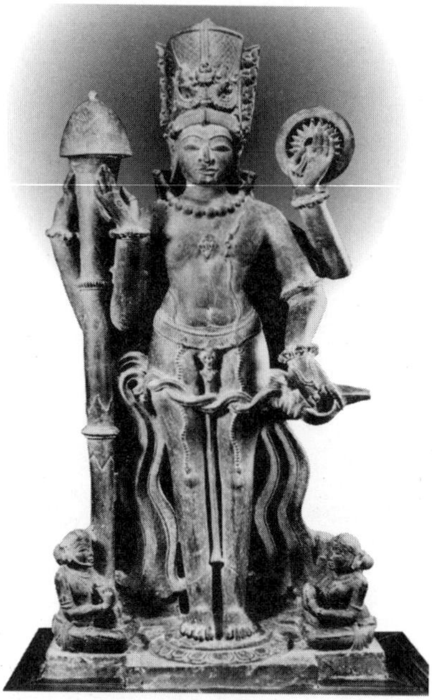

Viṣṇu, Madhya Pradesh, 11th century

Hinduism vis-à-vis Christianity and Islam

In this respect Hinduism is entirely different from Christianity and Islam where there is the concept of only one God and one *paigambar* (पैगम्बर) or prophet, the Son, or the "Chosen One" by God, Jesus Christ and Prophet Muhammad, respectively. This is their fundamental concept. For example, the words of Koran Sharif are the words of God communicated to the world through the last Prophet, Mohammad Saheb. These therefore cannot be changed. In Hinduism the words of the Vedas (वेद) are not the words of God; these were of the *ṛṣis* (ऋषि) or saints who composed the hymns, one could accept or reject their authority. That has been happening all the time. Buddha and Mahāvīra openly rejected them. So did many others. Ṛṣi Cārvāka, for example, was absolutely a materialist philosopher. That is why Hinduism has no fundamental concepts. It is only a way of life and each one has countless alternative paths to choose from for attaining salvation.

THE AVATĀRAS OF VIṢṆU

THE CONCEPT OF AVATĀRA OR INCARNATION OF GOD

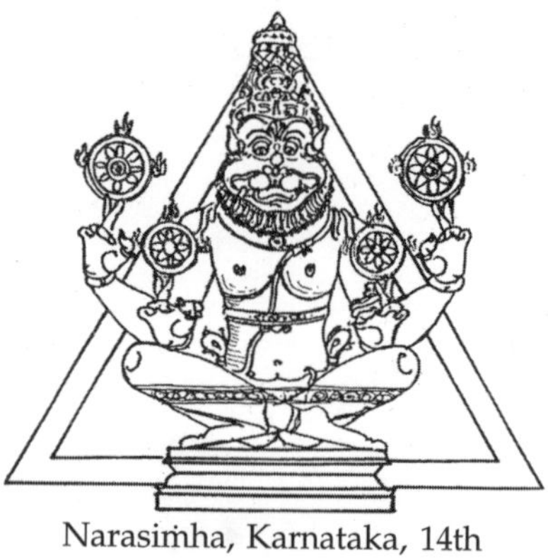

Narasiṁha, Karnataka, 14th century

Of all the Hindu gods, Viṣṇu has one aspect which is different from the rest — it is the concept of *avatāra* (अवतार), i.e. incarnation or God taking human or animal or partially human and partially animal form. These are ten in number, *daśāvatāra* (दशावतार). In each incarnation God Viṣṇu took one form to fulfil one specific mission in order to save the world from evil. For example, Viṣṇu incarnated himself as Rāma in order to kill the wicked king Rāvaṇa; as Kṛṣṇa to defeat the Kauravas by their righteous brothers, the Pāṇḍvas and establish the rule of *dharma* or Righteousness; as Narasiṁha to kill the demon

Hiraṇyakaśyipu; as Varāha to save the mother Earth or *Pṛthvī* (पृथ्वी) from the demon who took her to the depths of ocean, etc. There are also *Vāmanāvatāra*, *Kūrmāvatāra*, and *Matsyāvatāra*. Balarāma, Paraśurāma and Kalki are the other *avatāras*. From the seventh century even Buddha was included in the list of *avatāras* as is proved from an inscription discovered on the plinth of the Shore Temple at Mahābalipuram.

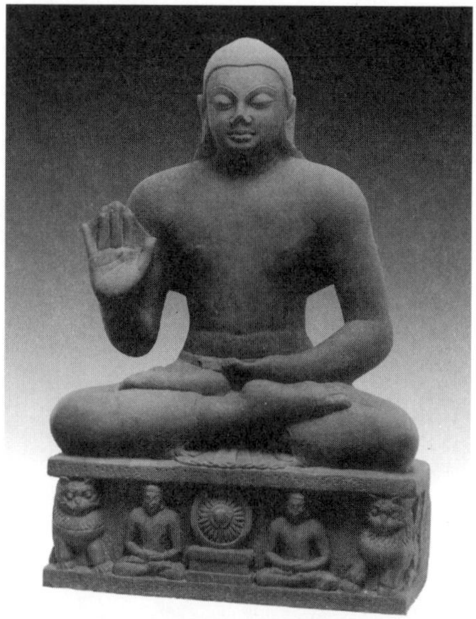

Buddha, Maṅkuwar, U.P., Gupta, 5th century CE

BUDDHA: THE LIFE AND TEACHING

The case of Buddhism is slightly different. Buddha, the originator of Buddhism, has been considered as a historical being with definite date of birth and death backed by a genealogy. He was born as Siddhārtha, the son of the Śākya king Śuddhodhana and queen Māyā, more than 2500 years ago, in the year 563 BCE. He was born in a garden at Lumbinī, located in south-east Nepal, while his mother was on way to her mother's house. He, however, grew up at Kapilavastu, the capital city of his father, located at Siddhārth Nagar in eastern Uttar Pradesh. One day he left home, leaving behind his wife Yaśodharā and son Rāhul, in search of the Truth. The "Truth" dawned upon him at Bodh-Gayā located in north-eastern Bihar while meditating under a *pīpala* tree. On getting Enlightenment, or *nirvāṇa* (निर्वाण), a Buddhist term, he came to Sārnāth near Varaṇasi and delivered his First Sermon. This act is called *dharmacakra-pravartana* (धर्मचक्र-प्रवर्तन) or "Rolling the Wheel of *dharma*," often written as *dhamma* (धम्म), the Pāli form of Sanskrit *dharma*.

He preached what he called "The Middle Path," *madhyama mārga* (मध्यम मार्ग), not too much of austerity and not too much of indulgence, no killing of the animals and no rituals connected with Vedic Fire Sacrifice, instead accumulate merit by doing

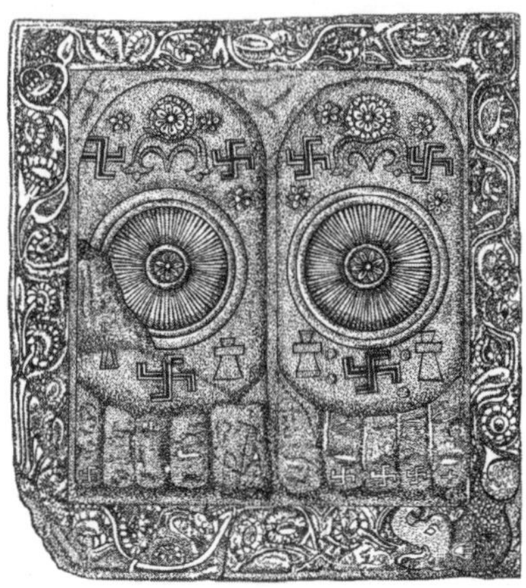

Footprints of Buddha with auspicious marks, Amarāvatī, A.P. 2nd century BCE

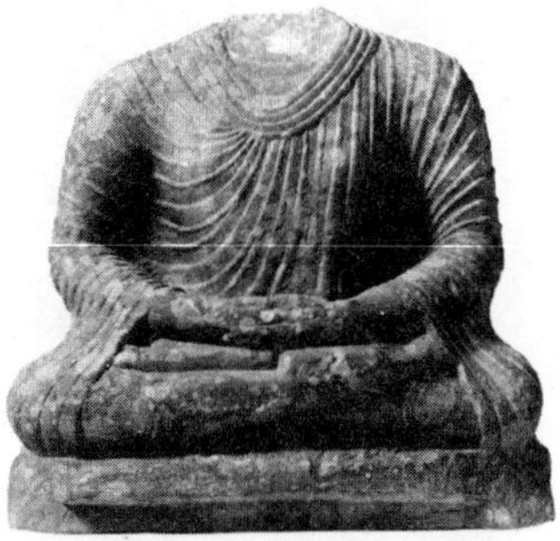

Buddha, Mathurā, U.P., Kuṣāṇa, 1st century CE

good to fellow beings since *karma* alone will determine the nature of the next birth. However, one should aim at annihilating the "cycle of birth and death" and thus achieve what he called *nirvāṇa* (निर्वाण). He died at Kuśīnagara, in eastern Uttar Pradesh, at the age of 80. He was the originator of the Bauddha Dharma in which celibacy and monastic life for the aspirants of *nirvāṇa* were recommended.

MAHĀVĪRA: THE LIFE AND TEACHING

Jainism was also founded in the middle of sixth century BCE in northern Bihar. Vaiśālī was its main centre of activities. Its greatest teacher was Mahāvīra, etymologically "great hero," but his original name was Vardhamāna. He was born in 599 BCE at Kauṇḍinyapur near Vaiśālī, in a princely family. He was the son of Siddhārtha and queen Tristā, a daughter of the Licchavi king of Vaiśālī. At the age of 30 he, like Buddha, left his wife and daughter at home and became an ascetic. He believed in great austerity and thus was called *jina*, (जिन्) meaning "conqueror," the conqueror of all passions, greed and hatred which, according to Jainas even Hindu gods could not conquer. By rightful thought and conduct one could easily achieve salvation, according to him. Although he never met Buddha he too stood for ascetic life and monastic order which had been ordained centuries ago by twenty-three previous *jina*s, called *tīrthaṁkara*s (तीर्थंकर), the first of them called "Ādinātha" as well as Ṛṣabhanātha. He stood for extreme austerity and adopted the principle of *syādvāda* (स्याद्वाद) which stands for the fact that the Truth cannot be absolute and only one, there may be at least seven alternatives such as the elephant according to seven blind men could be like a fan (one who touches the ears alone)

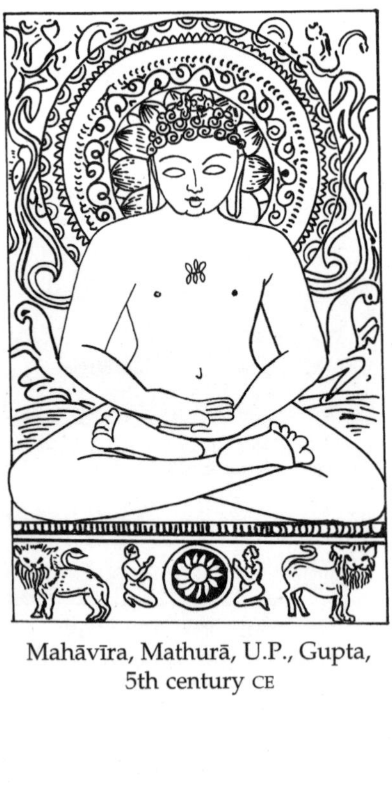

Mahāvīra, Mathurā, U.P., Gupta, 5th century CE

or like a trunk of a tree (one who touches only the legs), etc.

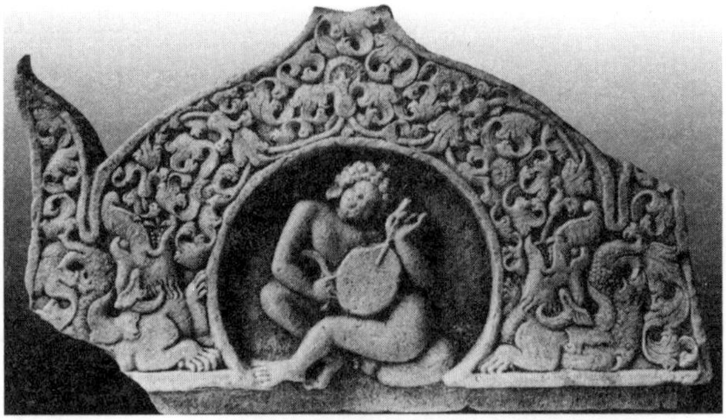

Architectural piece with drum-player decoration, Gupta, Mukandara, Rajasthan, 5th century CE

Art and Architecture

Art in India includes architecture. It is so because most of the works of art are the architectural members of some temple or shrine, only a portion of which is carved, the remaining part is used to build the inside of the architecture. The independent images are many but not as many as the sculptured architectural pieces. It applies to rock-cut temples and shrines as well, which were, strictly speaking, not architecture but sculpture carved with great care and devotion besides great technical skill and huge labour in giving it the form of a built structure.

Sacred Structures

KUṬĪ AND PRĀSĀDA

The earliest form of sacred structures or temple emerged from the huts (कुटी) in which human beings themselves lived, round huts with domical roofs, called *kūṭa* (कूट), and rectangular huts with gable roofs, called *śālā* (शाला), both made of bamboos. With the growth of civilization the system of kingship emerged and along with this institution the concept of palace (home for the king) architecture developed. It became not only larger in dimension but also multistoreyed. Obviously, bamboo was replaced by hard wood to give it a proper shape and also bear the weight of upper floors with pavilions and residential quarters. The palace is called *prāsāda* (प्रासाद), hence very often the temples are also called *prāsāda*, or Palace of God.

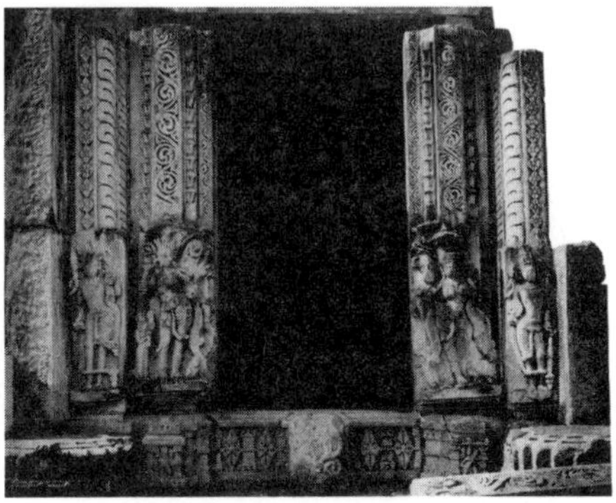

Temple-door, Garhwa, U.P. 10th century CE

The temple architecture emerged out of these two traditions in a mixed manner. It replaced the open-air platform system of shrines at many places, particularly where organized religious sects had the backing of money and men.

Thus, the *kūṭa* and *śālā* put together gave the elephant-back ended or apsidal *śālā* architecture. Later on, the rounded form was largely replaced by square and rectangular forms. Most of the temples from Gupta period onwards adopted these geometric forms because now stone started replacing the wood and brick as construction materials, which if square or rectangle in shape made things easy and strong.

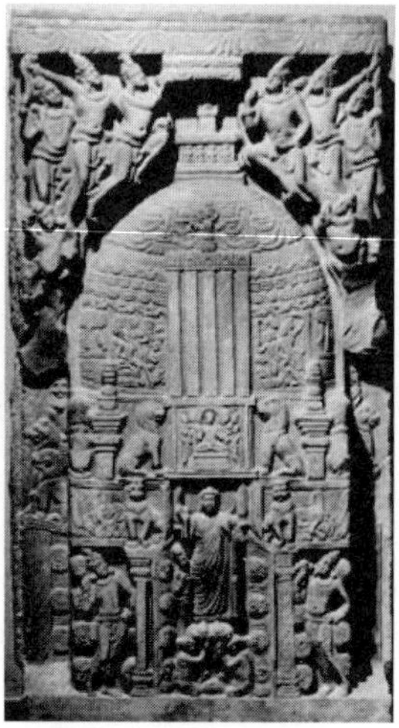

Slab covering the *aṇḍa* of a *stūpa*, Nāgārjunakoṇḍa, Ikṣvāku, A.P., 3rd century CE

STŪPA

Stūpa (स्तूप) as an object of veneration in its own right, as a replacement of Buddha himself, became very popular with Buddhists although Jainas also erected *stūpas*. *Stūpa* is, in fact, a sepul-chral monument, in which the ashes of the cremated bodies of the saints were buried. It is a domical structure, called *aṇḍa* (अण्ड), erected on the ground or on a platform. At a later date, a railing *vedikā* (वेदिका) was erected round it on the ground level, leaving in between sufficient space *patha* (पथ) for the devotees to go round it in the ritual called *pradakṣiṇā* (प्रदक्षिणा). If the *stūpa* is very large, such as at Sāñcī, such a path was also created on a higher level, approached by a series of steps called *sopāna* (सोपान). Generally a *stūpa* has on the top of the *aṇḍa*

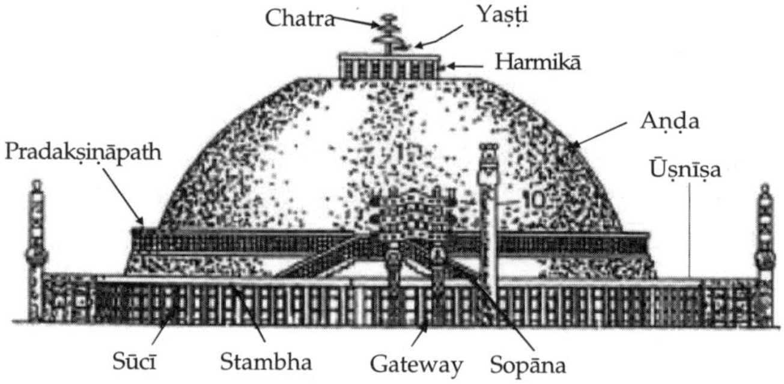

Sāñcī Stūpa, 2nd century BCE

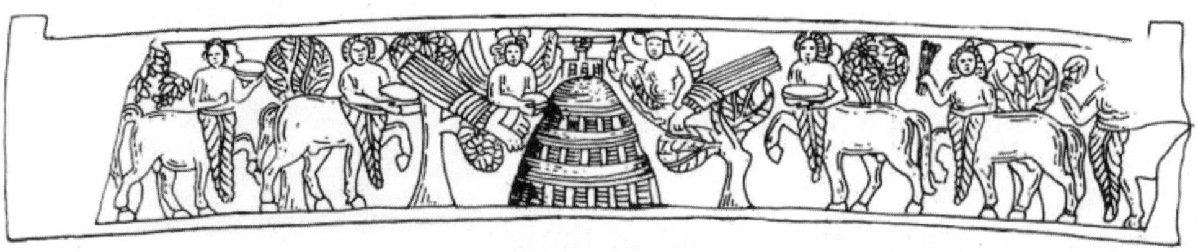

Stūpa being worshipped by semi-divine beings, the *gandharvas* and *kinnaras*, tympanum, Kaṅkālī Ṭīlā, Mathurā, Śuṅga, 2nd century BCE

a small square railing, called *harmikā* (हर्मिका), in the centre of which one can see a stick *yaṣṭi* (यष्टि) with three discs called *chatra* (छत्र) in diminishing sizes, placed one above the other. As time passed, the hemispherical or bubble like *aṇḍa* started becoming elongated, so much so that it became a tower with several storeys or floors, as in China and Japan. *Stūpa* of earth, brick or stone, is also called *caitya* (चैत्य) because it was, to begin with, raised at the very place where the dead body was cremated on *citā* (चिता), the pile of wood. The term *caitya* was also used for the *pīpala* tree under which Buddha got Enlightenment. As a matter of fact, this term was used for all sacred items which the Buddhist worshipped, including the image of Buddha and the *bodhisattvas*.

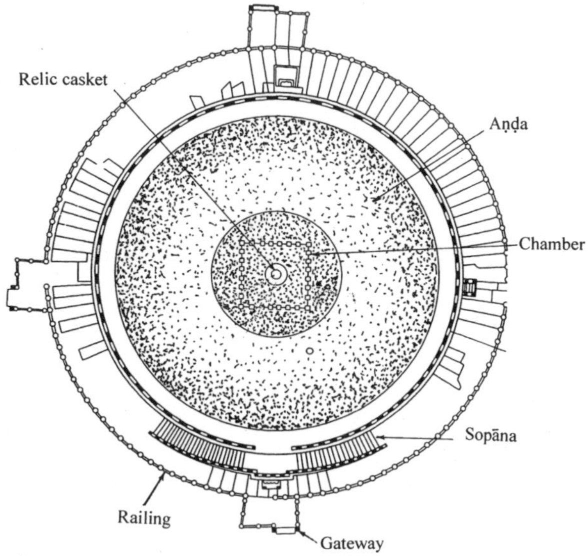

Plan of Sāñcī Mahāstūpa

There are some regional variations also. For example, in Andhra Pradesh, the *stūpas* had on four sides small platforms and five independent pillars standing in a row. These are called *āyaka* (आयक) platform and *āyaka* pillars. On the platform offerings were placed. Amarāvatī and Nāgārjunakoṇḍa have such *stūpas*.

CAITYAGṚHA

The covered structure or temple in which such sacred objects are kept for worship is called *caitya-gṛha* (चैत्यगृह), sometimes the term *bodhi-ghara* (बोधि-घर) is used for the temple housing *pīpala* tree.

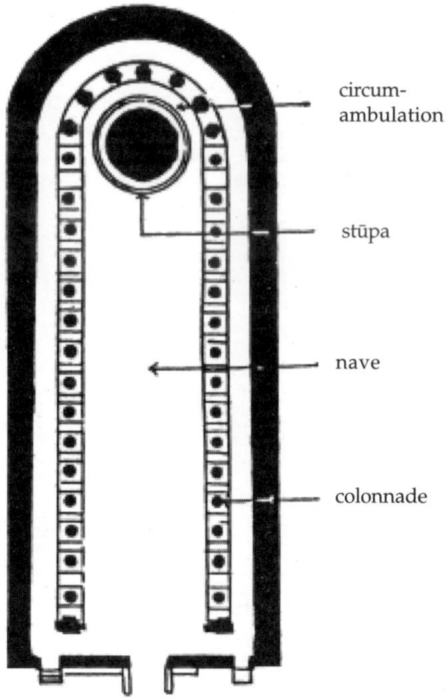

Plan of *caityagṛha*, Kanherī, Maharashtra, 2nd century CE

The *caityagṛha* is an elongated building, structural or rock-cut, with apsidal end. Near the apsidal end, a *stūpa* with Buddha image, or Buddha image in sitting or standing posture, etc. is erected with a path for circumambulation (*pradakṣiṇā*).

In a developed *caityagṛha* we see a colonnade or series of columns, starting from near the entrance and passing behind the *stūpa* and returning right up to the entrance. It, therefore, leaves a lot of space in front of the *stūpa* for the devotees. This is also the plan of a Christian church where this hall is called "nave." Since the entire ceiling is ribbed, the architecture is certainly a copy of the wooden architecture; as a matter of fact in the rock-cut *caityagṛha* the wooden ribs are still intact.

THE VEDIKĀ

A large *stūpa* in the open, as noted above, is seen surrounded by a *vedikā* (वेदिका) or railing. This is also a copy in stone of an original wooden fencing with uprights, *stambhas* (स्तम्भ) and cross-beams *sūcīs* (सूची) topped by coping *uṣṇīṣa* (उष्णीष).

The railing had one to four gateways erected on two uprights and three cross-beams, the entire surface of which is embellished with various kinds of decorative elements, sacred as well as non-sacred, such as the scenes of everyday life.

There are also independent pillars (स्तम्भ), standing with a capital (शीर्ष) fixed on top of it. The shaft could be round and smooth or faceted. The capital may bear the images of sacred animals or else the images of gods, besides several other decorative elements carved on the abacus.

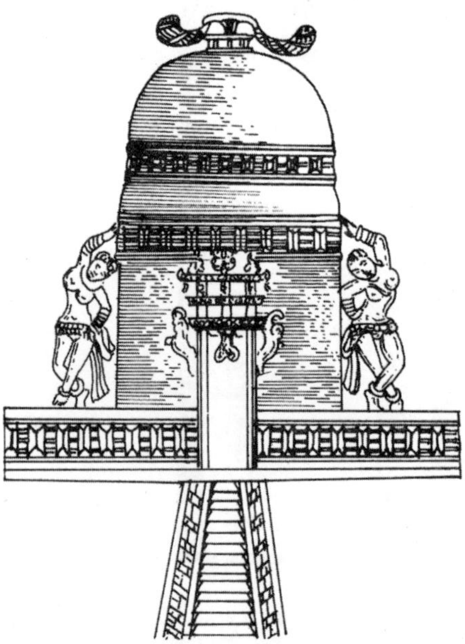

Jaina *stūpa*, Kaṅkālī Ṭīlā, Mathurā, Kuṣāṇa, 1st century CE

THE ENTRANCE

One of the most fascinating elements of the *caitya-gṛhas* is the entrance which is very richly carved, particularly in rock-cut caves. These are marked by huge windows, called *gavākṣas* (गवाक्ष) in the form of ogee or pointed arches with flat ended base resting on the two inward tilted pillars of the entrance. On the sides of the window-arch are depicted series (or *jāla* (जाल), i.e. *pañjara* (पञ्जर) of small *caitya* windows and other decorations filling up vacant spaces.

THE VOTIVE STŪPA

There is a class of *stūpa*s called *votive stūpas*, usually small in size, either built or carved in the round. These *stūpa*s had no funerary remains. These solid structures were meant for receiving offerings. When built they served as the subsidiary shrines to which offering were offered.

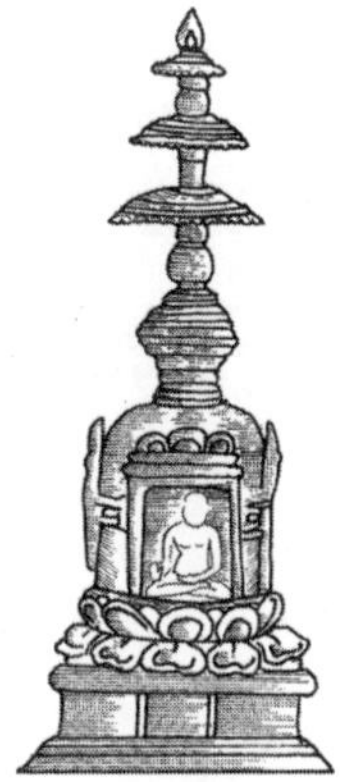

Votive *stūpa*, Gāndhāra, 2nd century CE

HINDU TEMPLE

THE CONCEPTS

Generally speaking, a temple is a "Place of Worship." It is also called the "House of God." However, for a Hindu, it is both and yet still more. It is the whole cosmos in the miniature form. Stella Kramrisch defined temple as "monument of manifestation" in her *The Hindu Temple.* Hence its morphology is not arbitrary. From top to bottom the Hindu temple seeks to represent everything of which the cosmic world *brahmāṇḍa* (ब्रह्माण्ड), the entire universe, is composed of: the earthly world, the heavenly world, the astral world, and the world below the waters — *pṛthvī* (पृथ्वी), *ākāśa* (आकाश) with *svarga* (स्वर्ग), and *pātāla* (पाताल), respectively. That is why on the walls of a Hindu temple one can see the representations of men, women, children, animals, birds, pests, insects, reptiles, trees, rivers, flowers, seas, mountains, houses, forts, palaces, villages, huts, etc., which constitute the earthly world. It includes even copulation amongst men and among animals since it is through this mode of life that creation takes place.

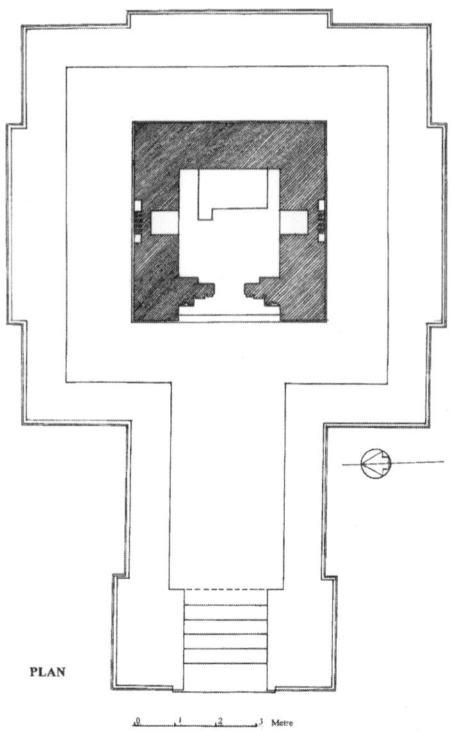

Plan of north Indian Temple, Pārvatī Temple, Nachnā, M.P., Gupta, 5th century CE

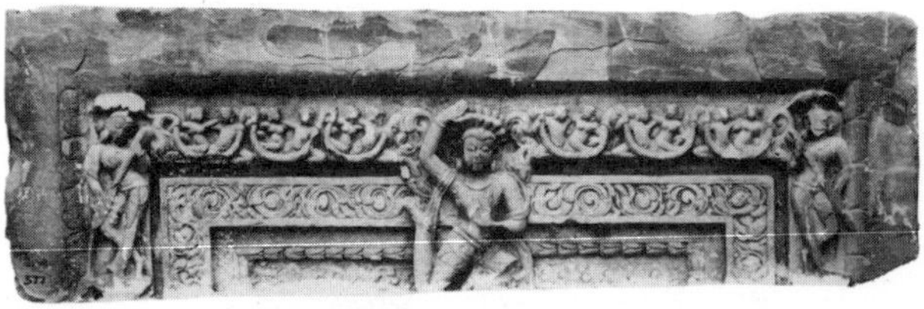

Lintel of a temple, Dudhai, U.P., 8th century CE

The Hindu temple architecture, i.e. its morphology, follows the requirements of man's vision of the cosmos which he wants to recreate on the earth; it is not the fancy of the architect. Visions differ, therefore forms differ but forms are not experiments of architects.

The temple also contains the images of gods and goddesses as well as semi-divine and mythical beings, including half-human and half-animal or half-bird and half-reptile forms, as described in Hindu mythologies contained in epics, Purāṇas, and *kāvyas*. The world of waters with fish, tortoise, crocodile, coral, plants, rocks, etc. which constitute the life below the seas is also represented.

Underlying all these so simple yet so complex ideas is the water cosmology (science of universe) as well as water cosmogony (origin of the universe) which means that water is the basis of all creation and sustainer. It is for this very reason that from the Gupta time itself the temple pillars are shown emerging from *kalaśa* (कलश) or water-pot, and the finial or top is embellished with a *kalaśa*.

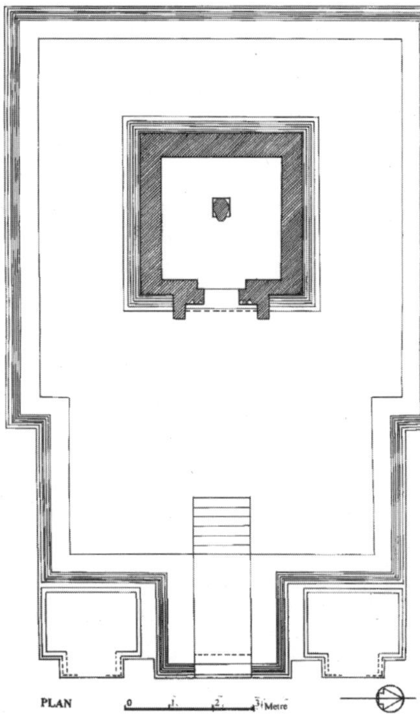

Plan of north Indian Temple, Śiva Temple, Bhūmarā, M.P., Gupta, 5th century CE

HINDU AND NON-HINDU VIEWS ON SACRED STRUCTURE

Thus, a Hindu views his temple slightly differently than a Christian views his church or a Muslim views his mosque. For a Christian, the church is just a "place of worship," it is neither the House of God nor Mini Cosmos; for a Muslim, the mosque is just a "place for offering prayer to God."

A Hindu may worship many gods at one and the same time since he believes that in whatever form or forms one may worship, all will eventually reach God, the only one, the ultimate Reality "as wherever the rain water from heaven may fall it goes to the ocean," similarly "prayers offered to one and all gods go to God alone."

THE PLACEMENTS OF IMAGES

The sculptures representing gods and goddesses can be placed anywhere and worshipped even under a tree, or over a platform, or in a cave, or under a rock-shelter, or on the bank of river, or a tank, or ocean; in fact, anywhere and everywhere. However, from purely temporal point of view, a temple is a cover to protect the image from the vagaries of nature as well as animals. A temple may be either in the form of a huge sculptured rock, called rock-cut temple, or else it is a built-structure using bricks, or wood, or stone pieces; sometimes even terracotta is used.

FORMS OF TEMPLES

However, it is not the material used which is important, what is really important is the "form" of the temple. The form is not one but many, depending upon regional traditions. The temples of northern India generally belong to the category called "Nāgara" (नागर), those of south India are called "Drāviḍa" (द्राविड). Those belonging to the middle region (Karnataka) and of mixed types (Nāgara and Drāviḍa) are called '"Vesara" (वेसर) or "Besara" (बेसर). However, this classification is very old and based upon some south Indian texts, but at the scholarly level there are many more of them. Here we will deal only with three most basic forms of temples, the northern, the southern and the Orissan because of elevational differences and forms of the

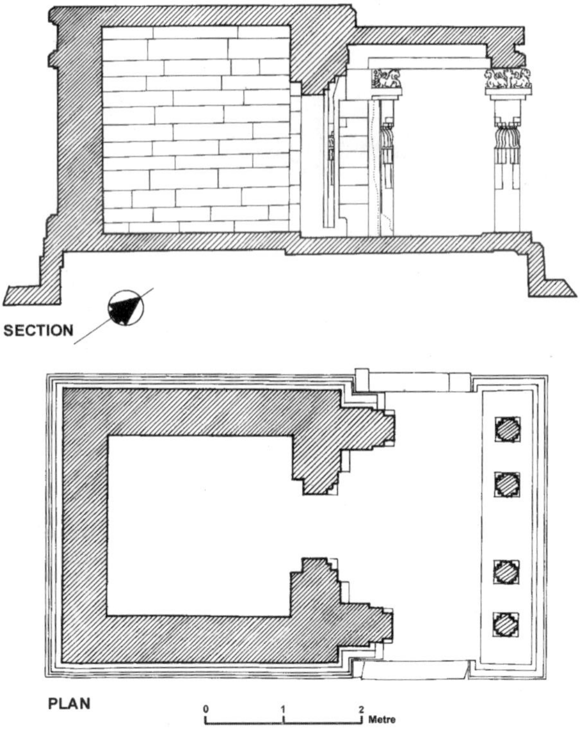

Temple, Sāñcī, Gupta, late 4th century CE
(Temple No. 17, probably Bauddha temple)

*śikhara*s. However, the three traditional types mentioned in the southern texts can been explained in the following terms on the basis of the morphology of temples.

A Nāgara type is four-sided. The *garbha-gṛha* (गर्भ-गृह) is perfect square, but the whole temple plan could be oblong. Its elevation is marked by four-sided neck or *grīvā* (ग्रीवा) and a tall tapering *śikhara.* A Drāviḍa type temple, marked with terraces, is, on the other hand, hexagonal or octagonal from the plinth to the finial. Or else, it is marked by hexagonal or octagonal *grīvā* or *śikhara.* A Vesara type temple is, however, circular, or else ellipsoidal, or else apsidal from base to the top. Or else it is marked by this plan (circular, ellipsoidal or apsidal) in its *grīvā* and *śikhara*.

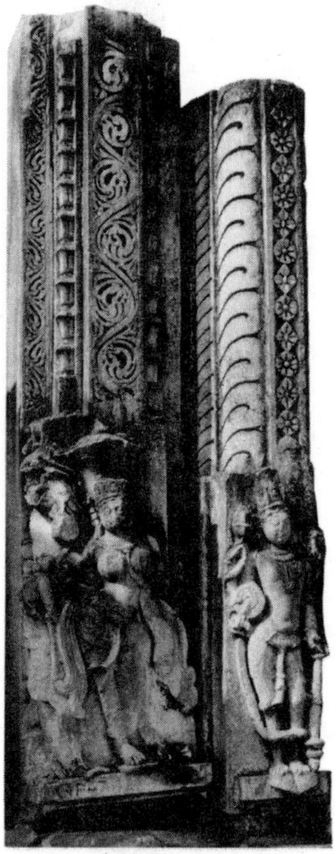

Dvāra of a temple, Garhwā, U.P., 10th century CE

It may be noted that while the Nāgara and Drāviḍa are considered the pure types, the Vesara type is considered *mixed*, in which the elements of both the pure types are found mixed in a variety of ways. Thus, one can see a Vesara temple having a square body at different *tala*s (तल) but the *grīvā* (ग्रीवा) and *śikhara* circular, octagonal or apsidal in form. In the same way the body may be oblong but the *grīvā* and *śikhara* may be elliptical.

It may, therefore, be clearly noted that what is really important is not so much the shape or form of the basal parts of the temple, or even of the body, it is the plan of the *grīvā* and *śikhara* components which is critical in this classification.

TEMPLES OF NORTH INDIA

A north Indian temple of Prāsāda (प्रासाद) or Nāgara (नागर) style has two basic components:

(i) *Garbha-gṛha* (गर्भ-गृह) or *sanctum sanctorum* or central cella, with only one door, in which the image of the main deity is placed, and

(ii) *Maṇḍapa* (मण्डप) or porch in front of the *garbha-gṛha,* usually open from three sides for the worshippers to stand under shade to have *darśana* (दर्शन) (a concept in which the deity is revealing himself or herself and the devotee is perceiving it within the depths of his or her inner-most consciousness) or view the deity and offer prayers while looking at the image and experiencing his or her spiritual presence.

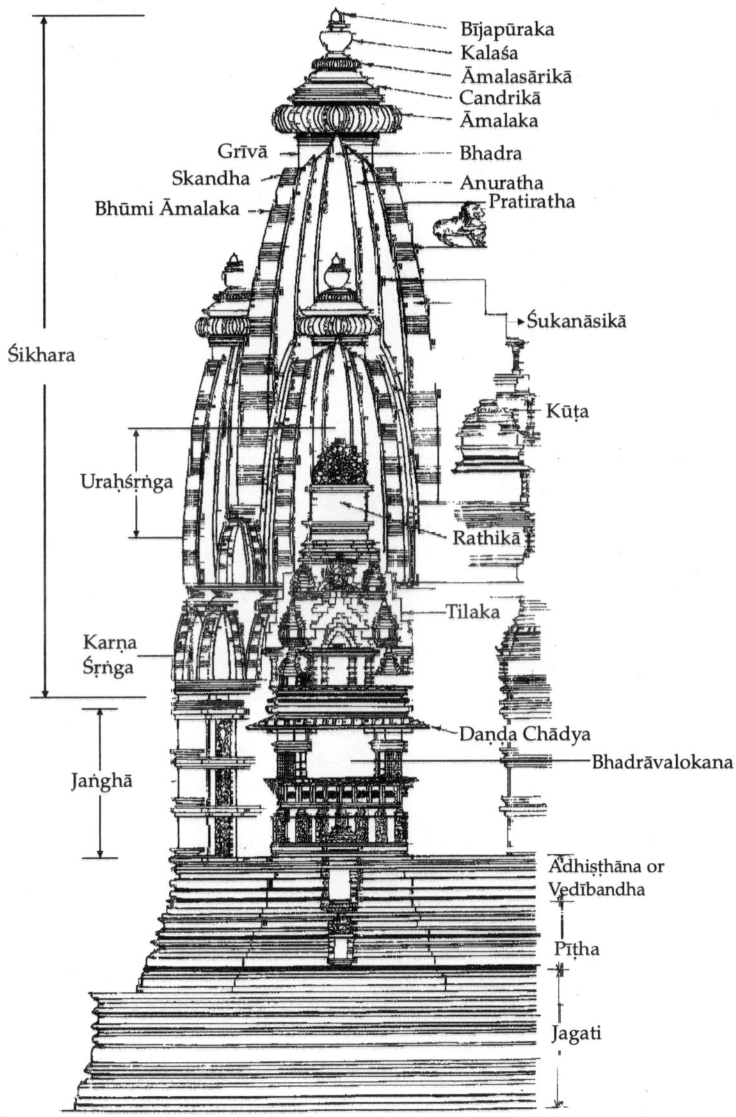

Elements of a north Indian Temple

We have such a simple temple (Temple No. 17) with flat roof at Sāñcī, in Madhya Pradesh, belonging to the Gupta period (fifth century CE); it was possibly a Buddhist temple. During the same period but towards the end of the century, perhaps, at Deogaṛh, near Jhānsī, Uttar Pradesh, a slightly more elaborate temple for Viṣṇu was built; in this the roof over the *garbha-gṛha* became pyramidal, i.e. tall and

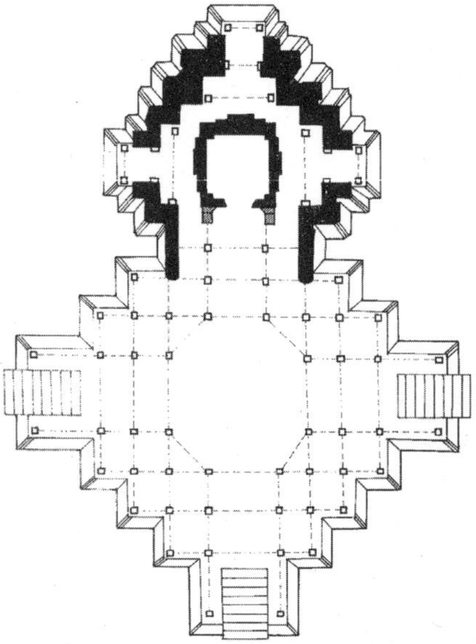

Plan of a north Indian Temple with *pradikṣiṇā patha* around *garbha-gṛha*

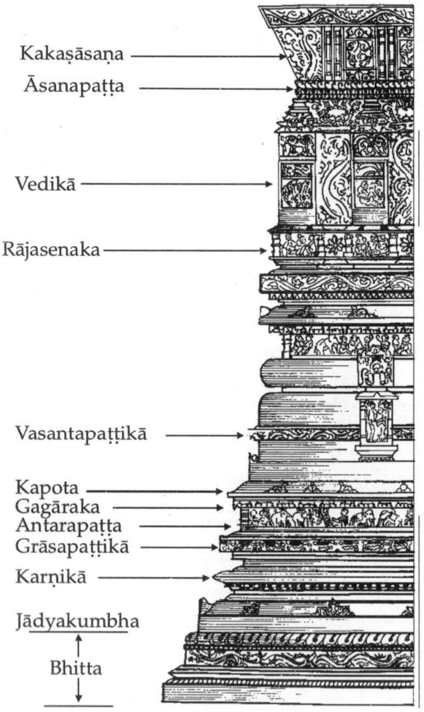

Elements of the base of a north Indian Temple

pointed, resembling a mountain. It is called *śikhara* (शिखर) which is, in fact, the spire, a tall structure that tapers to a point above. The *śikhara,* the walls and the pillars, as well as the roofs over the *garbha-gṛha* and the *maṇḍapa,* are often decorated with floral and geometric patterns as well as with the images of gods and goddesses and scenes from mythologies.

In the third stage a couple of more *maṇḍapa*s (मण्डप) are found added, the narrow covered area or the *maṇḍapa* in front of the *garbha-gṛha* is called *antarāla* (अन्तराल) or vestibule. The large hall in front of the *antarāla* is called *mahāmaṇḍapa* (महामण्डप) or *gūḍha-maṇḍapa* (गूढ़मण्डप). A smaller *maṇḍapa* in front of the *mahāmaṇḍapa* is called *ardha-maṇḍapa* (अर्धमण्डप), or half porch, which is reached by a *dvāra* (द्वार), i.e. doorway, with flights of steps. In this stage of development, the *garbha-gṛha* is surrounded by a corridor or *pradakṣiṇāpatha* (प्रदक्षिणापथ) or circum-ambulatory path, through which the devotees moved round the *garbha-gṛha.* At times windows, called *gavākṣa* (गवाक्ष), were added at different points to allow light and air pass through the entire inner space.

The Concept of Vāstupuruṣa: Parts of Temples

A Hindu temple is also called *vāstupuruṣa* (वास्तुपुरुष), i.e. an architectural piece resembling the body of a human being. "Human being" here stands for God or "Supreme Being" since he is conceived in the form of man. Later this concept developed into the *maṇḍala* concept called *Vāstupuruṣa-maṇḍala* (वास्तु-पुरुष मण्डल). Generally, a Nāgara style temple stands on a large and high platform, called *jagati,* made of stone or bricks, with several mouldings. It represents the feet of man. Over this stands a smaller platform of stones, called *pīṭha* (पीठ). Over the *pīṭha* rises a still smaller platform, called *adhiṣṭhāna* (अधिष्ठान) or *vedī-bandha* (वेदी-बन्ध), the immediate base of the superstructure of the temple. It is on this platform that the pillars and walls of the temple are raised; the top of this *adhiṣṭhāna* or platform is the floor of the temple. Three parts of the temple represent the ankle, lower feet and upper feet of the human body.

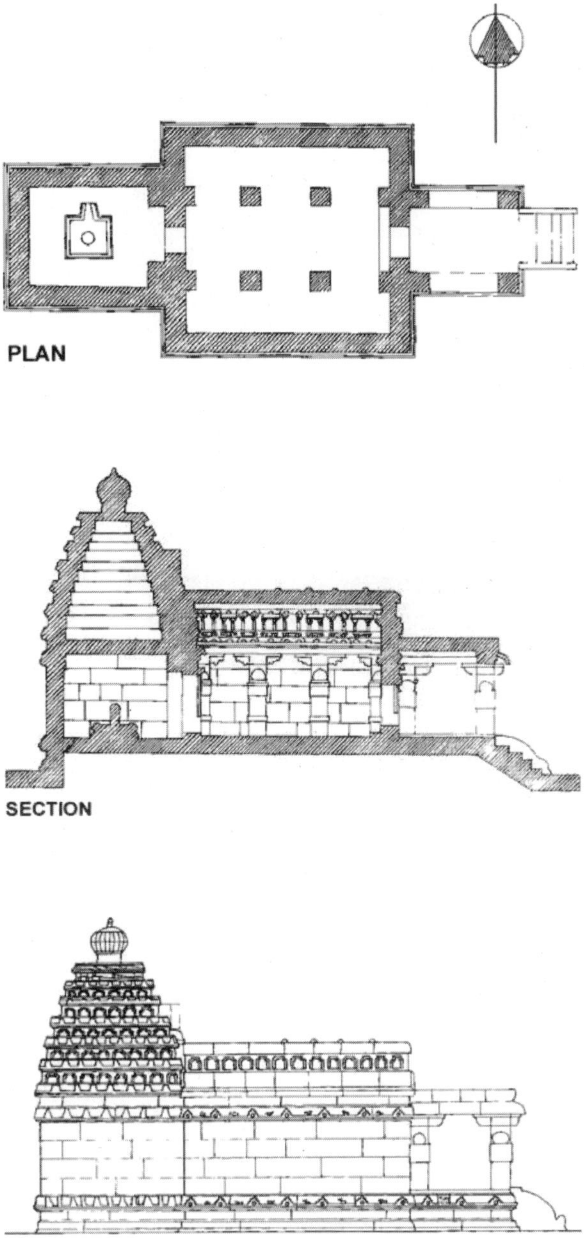

Plan, Section and Side Elevation of a north Indian Temple style in Karnataka, Mallikārjuna Temple, Aihoḷe, early 8th century CE

THE ŚIKHARA

The pillared area of the temple forms the *jaṅghā* (जंघा) or the thighs. On the gateway, at the top level of the *jaṅghā* is *chādya* (छाद्य) or sun-shade, while on the top level of the pillars are the mouldings called *varāṇḍikā* (वराण्डिका). It is from this level that the *śikhara* or spire emerges. Since there is a series of small *śikhara*s, in the form of pilasters, i.e. half *śikhara*, placed one above the other along the corners of the *śikhara*s, till the top of the entire *śikhara* is reached, these are called *śṛṅga śikhara*s (शृंग शिखर); the first or the lowest one is named *karṇa* (कर्ण) or corner *śṛṅga* and the above ones as *uru-śṛṅga*s (उरु-शृंग). The areas beyond the *karṇa* and *uru-śṛṅga*s have a series of *āmalaka*s, shaped like cogged wheels, or *āmalā* fruit, called *bhūmi- āmalaka*s (भूमि-आमलक), each one of which represents one floor or one storey of the building. In fact, all Hindu temples, both in the north and south are found following the principle of *prāsāda* or terraced palace, or multi-storeyed structure. In north Indian *śikhara* the terraces are compressed but clearly marked by *bhūmi-āmalaka*s. This is true of Orissa temples also.

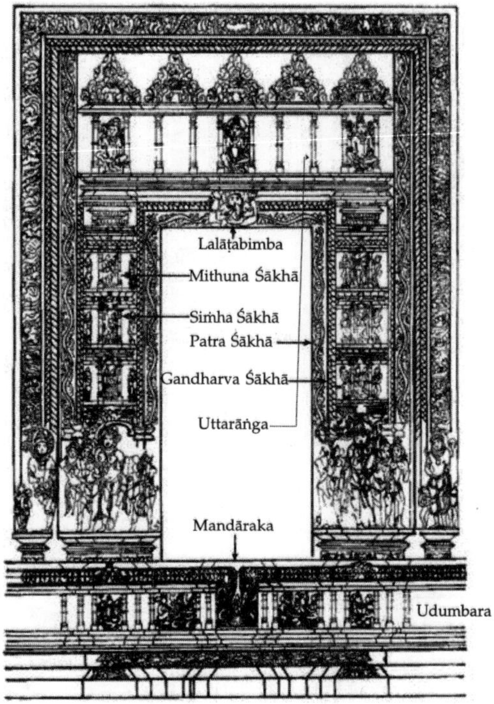

Gateway of a north Indian Temple

THE BHADRA

The front pleat or tall and tapering facet, called *bhadra* (भद्र), with parallel narrower facets called *prati-bhadras* (प्रतिभद्र), above the gate, usually decorated with floral and geometric designs, called *latā* (लता), are cut in stencil style.

THE ŚĪRṢA: ĀMALAKA (आमलक) AND BĪJAPŪRAKA (बीजपूरक)

On the top of this body of the temple, i.e. *śīrṣa* (शीर्ष), is a constricted moulding, called *skandha* (स्कंध), i.e. *kandhā* or shoulder, followed by *grīvā* or neck. It is topped by a large *āmalaka.* On the *āmalaka* are a series of discs, called *candrikā* (चन्द्रिका), over which lies a small *āmalaka,* called *āmalā-sārikā* (सारिका) and on the top of all these is the *kalaśa* (कलश) with a coconut fruit called *bījapūraka,* inserted in its mouth. The whole thing represents the head of man and represents the finial.

THE CHĀDYA (छाद्यय) AND RATHIKA (रथिक)

On the gateway and above the *chādya* one or two, one above the other, are small gateways with *śikharas*, called *rathika,* representing storeys.

THE SUKANĀSIKĀ (सुकनासिका) AND BHŪMI-ĀMALAKA (भूमि-आमलक)

On the top of an upper *bhūmi-āmalakas* sometimes a fabulous lion, carved in the round, is fixed which is called *sukanāsikā,* representing the nose.

Somewhere in the *grīvā,* or near about, a ring-stone is fixed, meant for hoisting a flag.

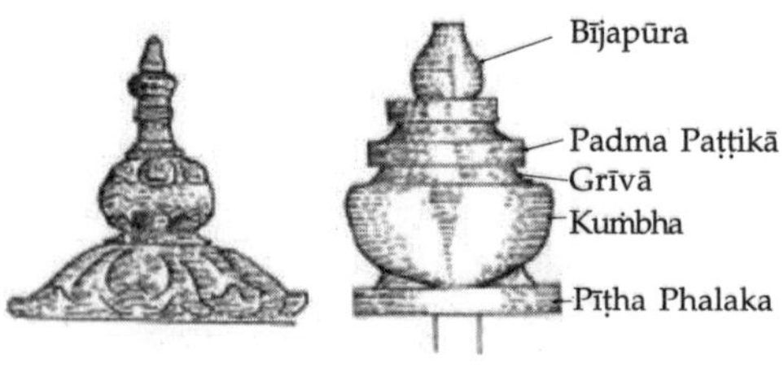

Top of a north Indian Temple

THE DOOR-FRAME AND ITS DECORATIONS: LALĀṬA-BIMBA (लंलाट-बिम्ब) AND DVĀRA-ŚĀKHĀS (द्वार-शाखा)

A Nāgara style temple has a highly decorated entrance door-frame, including the threshold, with vertical and horizontal friezes, panels and runners. In the centre of the lintel is placed the image of some god or goddess, called *lalāṭa-bimba.* The doorjambs may have one, three, five or seven parallel vertical *śākhās* or offsets, called *dvāra-śākhās* each one decorated with friezes and panels depicting gods and goddesses, floral and geometrical designs. At the bottom there may be panels depicting either the *dvārapālas* (द्वारपाल), i.e. security guards, or Gaṅgā and Yamunā, the two sacred rivers.

THE PILLARS AND THEIR DECORATIONS

The pillars are also decorated in a number of ways with *pūrṇa-ghaṭas* (पूर्णघट), *devakanyās* (देवकन्या), *apsaras* (अप्सरस्), *yakṣas* (यक्ष), *yakṣīs* (यक्षी), *padma* (पद्म), *āmalakas* (आमलक), floral garlands (माला), capitals (शीर्ष), chains with bells (जंजीर एवं घंटिका), etc.

THE OTHER PARTS AND THEIR DECORATIONS

The *jagati* (जगति), *pīṭha* (पीठ) and *adhiṣṭhāna* (अधिष्ठान) are also beautifully decorated with a variety of offsets and mouldings with definitive nomenclature, like *grāsapaṭṭī* (ग्रासपट्टी), *khura* (खुर), *kapota* (कपोत), *antarpātra* (अन्तर्पात्र), *vedikā* (वेदिका), etc., friezes and panels, including those depicting elephants (*gaja-thara* गज-थर), horses (*aśva-thara* अश्व-थर), human beings (*nara-thara* नर-थर), etc.

In short, a north Indian temple is generally marked by a *garbha-gṛha* (गर्भगृह) or room in which the image of the main deity is placed and can be seen only from one door placed in the front, generally

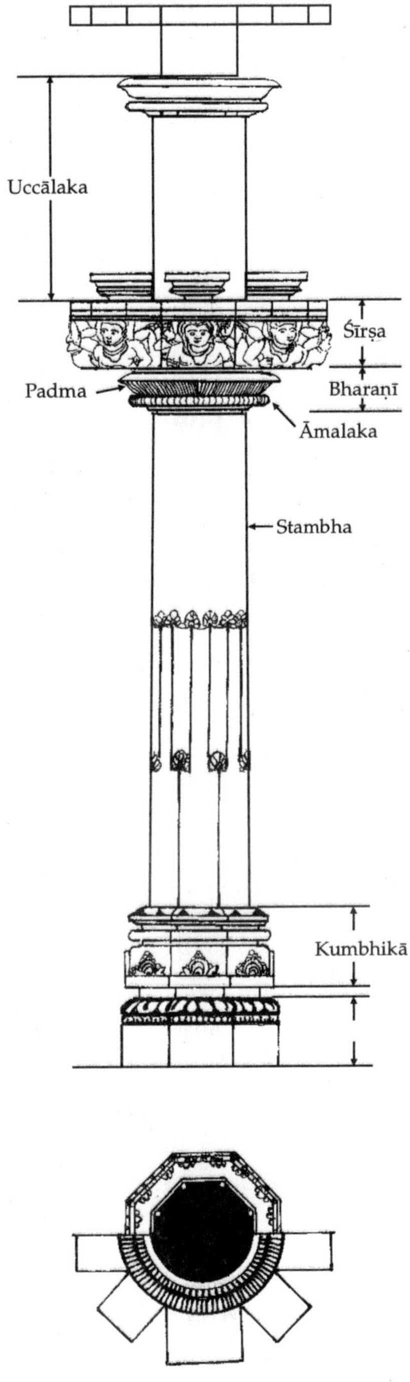

Architectural Components of a Temple Pillar, north India

facing east. In front of this room are one or more side-opened or covered spaces, called *maṇḍapa*s (मण्डप). There is also a circumambulatory path or *pradakṣiṇāpatha* (प्रदक्षिणापथ) for the devotees to go round the *garbha-gṛha.* This structure is placed over a high platform called *jagati.* There is also a tall spire raised over the *garbha-gṛha* which is called *śikhara.*

TEMPLES OF SOUTH INDIA

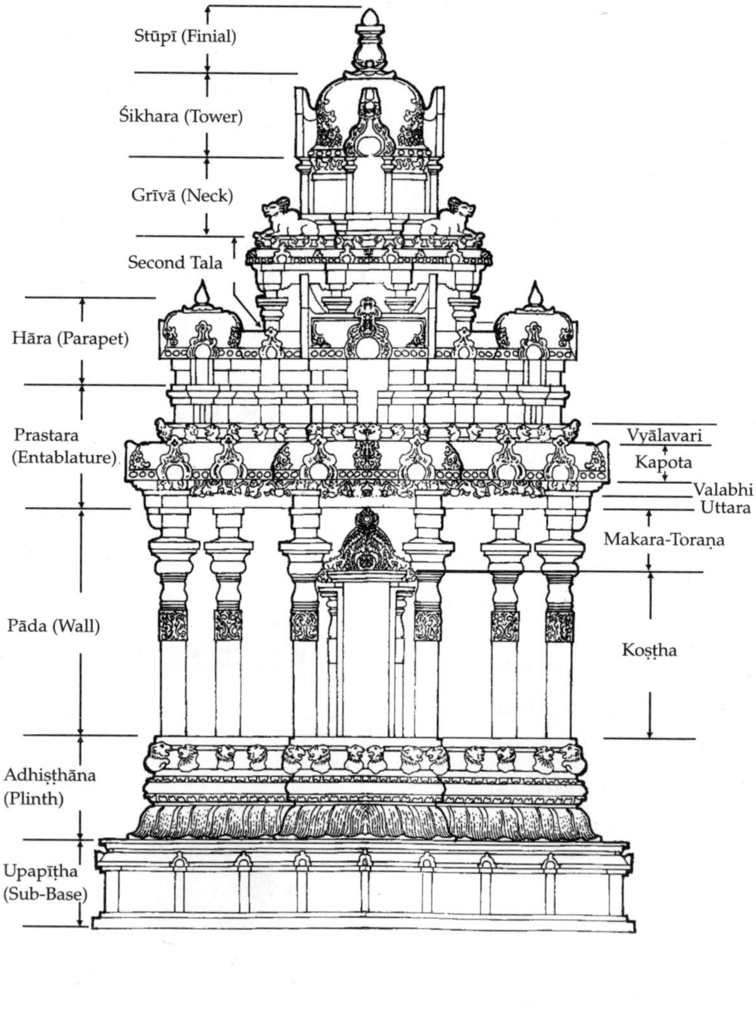

Elements of a *vimāna* of south Indian Temple (elevation)

A general south Indian or Drāviḍa type temple, commonly called "*Vimāna* type," *vimāna* (विमान) means ship or boat, is based upon Āgamas (आगम), and, Śilpa (शिल्प) and Vāstuśāstras (वास्तुशास्त्र). It is marked by six major body parts or *aṅga*s (अंग):

(i) the *adhiṣṭhāna* (अधिष्ठान): the base or pedestal or platform on which the whole superstructure rests;

(ii) the *pāda* (पाद): walls (*bhitti* भित्ति) with pillars (*stambha*s स्तम्भ) in between them which make and enclose the cella or room, the *garbha-gṛha*, in which the main or presiding deity is placed;

(iii) the *prastara* (प्रस्तर): the architrave, i.e. the horizontal beam which marks the end of the cella *garbha-gṛha* walls, and the beginning of the spire of *śikhara*, on which is constructed the sun-shade or cornice, i.e. eave, called *kapota* (कपोत) since on this projection birds are seen sitting and resting in rows (*kapota* means 'dove');

(iv) the *grīvā* (ग्रीवा): the neck or clerestory, i.e. the upper row of windows or the recessed part of the beginning of the spire or *śikhara*. It is the clerestory over the sanctum (*garbha-gṛha*) terrace and entablature;

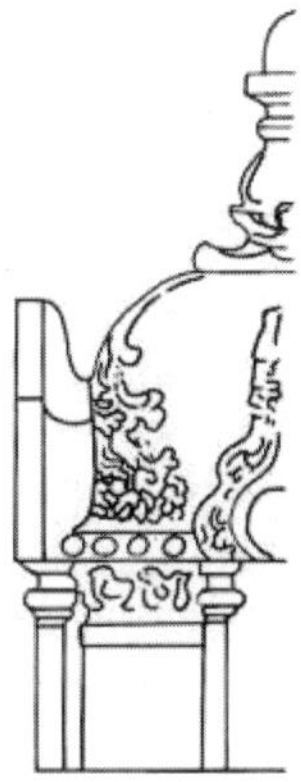

Śikhara of a south Indian Temple (Half)

(v) the *śikhara* (शिखर): the spire or Pyramidal roof covering the top of the clerestory of *grīvā*; and

(vi) the *stūpī* (स्तूपी): the finial in the form of a small *stūpa* or bulbous pot, a *kalaśa* crowning the top of the *śikhara*.

Such a simple construction may be *ekatala* (एकतल) or single storeyed temple or else multi-storeyed type, *bahutala* (बहुतल), each succeeding storey diminishing in dimensions, making the whole structure pointed or pyramidal. Each storey or *tala* (तल) consists of two major parts: (a) *harmya* (हर्म्य), or body, and (b) *prastara*, i.e. architrave. In the south Indian *śilpa* texts we get the mention of as many as sixteen-storeyed *vimāna*, each rising storey called *jāti* (जाति) *vimāna*, the longest one, the first one, the bottom one, is called *mukhya* (मुख्य) *vimāna*.

This makes it clear that a typical south Indian temple is marked by distinctly made storeys or flat floors. In the beginning these storeys were functional, i.e. one could go on them and move around on the roof, but very soon this became only notional, a design of the spire or *śikhara*, a form, a style and no one could actually go to them separately and move about freely.

Kūṭa, Māmallapuram, Tamil Nadu, 7th-8th century CE

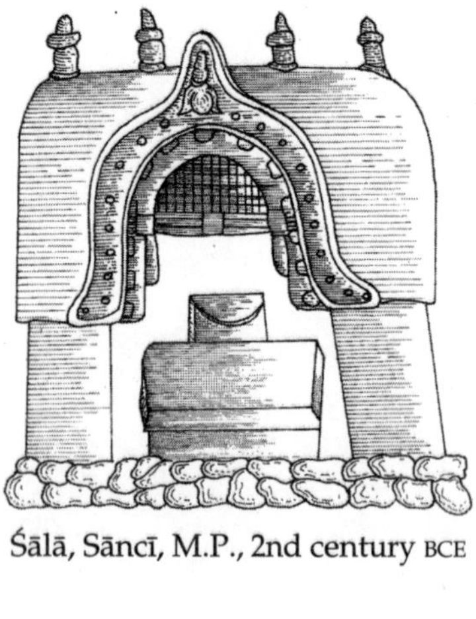

Śālā, Sāncī, M.P., 2nd century BCE

DECORATIVE ELEMENTS

The first thing that attracts our attention in a south Indian temple is the decoration of the flat portion just above the *prastara*, i.e. the horizontal beam, the parapet wall, at each storey. Since it runs round the entire parapet wall in a garland or string-like manner, it is called *hāra* (हार). It contains miniature *vimāna*-like shrines. However, in later temples, from around eleventh century, the *hāra* of the topmost *tala* (तल) or storey is replaced by the *lāñchanas* (लाञ्छन) or *vāhanas* (वाहन) or mounts of the god to whom the temple was dedicated, for example, if it was a Śiva temple, the bull or even *bhūta* (भूत) images were made and placed in a row, and if it was a Viṣṇu temple it could be *garuḍa* (गरुड) or eagle.

KŪṬA VIMĀNA

Many a time one sees the top portion of the *vimāna* of a south Indian temple in the rounded bulbous form, like a dome, plain or faceted and decorated in a variety of designs. It is surmounted by a single finial, the *stūpī* (स्तूपी). This is called *kūṭa vimāna* with *kūṭa* (कूट) *śikhara*; the term *kūṭa* stands for the domed shrine. Where the *śikhara* is not domed, the four corners are decorated with *kūṭa* or domed shrines with square plan.

ŚĀLĀ VIMĀNA

There is yet another absolutely different kind of roof in a south Indian temple and shrines. It is called *śālā* (शाला) type. Here there is absolutely no pyramidal *śikhara*. The roof is like an oblong wagon-top, or vault. It resembles a boat placed upside down leading to a double-sided roof with a central ridge over a rectangular house. Along the central ridge of the longer axis we find a series of *stūpīs* or finials placed at regular intervals to decorate it. It is sometimes called *śālā vimāna* and sometimes *koṣṭha* (कोष्ठ), or even *sabhā* (सभा) *vimāna*, meaning one and the same, rectangular house; *koṣṭha* means room and *sabhā* (सभा) means a large rectangular hall in which meetings take place. A slightly modified form of this double-sided *śālā* type roof is the *gaja* (गज) or *hasti-pṛṣṭha* (हस्ति-पृष्ठ) type roof — here the hind part of the barrel-shaped roof is rounded, hence resembles the back of an elephant. For this category of *śikhara*s the texts use the terms *pañjara*s (पञ्जर) and *nīḍa*s (नीड़) also, the former is more commonly used.

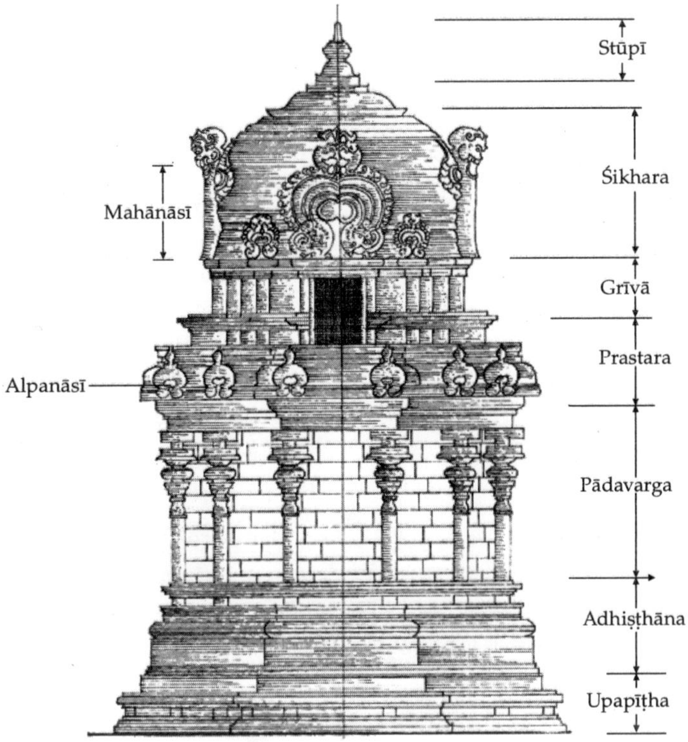

Elements of a south Indian Temple (Elevation)

PAÑJARA VIMĀNA

It is significant to note that the *hāra* (हार) or parapet wall decoration of every *tala* or storey consists of a row of diminutive forms of these three types of shrine-forms: *kūṭa* (domical), *śālā* (barrel-shaped) and *pañjara* (elephant back). At the four corners of the *hāra* we get large *kūṭa*s or domes, called *karṇa-kūṭa*s, *karṇa* (कर्ण) means corner. The *hāra*, i.e. the garland of miniature shrines, has naturally interspaces also amongst all the shrine models; these vacant spaces are called *harantara* (हरन्तर), *antara* (अन्तर) means "space."

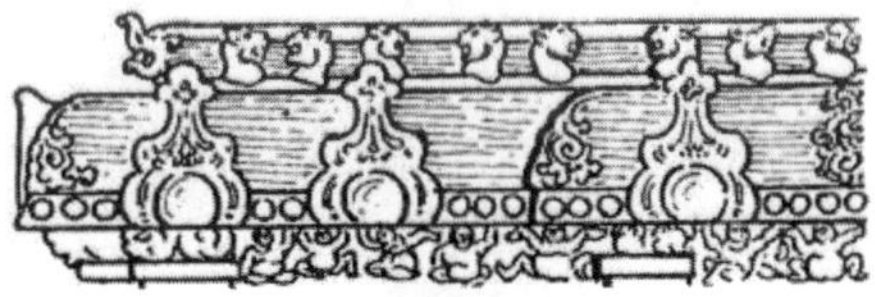
Pañjara Vimāna

BHITTI

The outer face of the walls or *bhitti*s (भित्ति) of the temples are broken by vertical offsets or projections marked by pilasters, or half pillars, at regular intervals. These are called *bhadra*s (भद्र). This is true

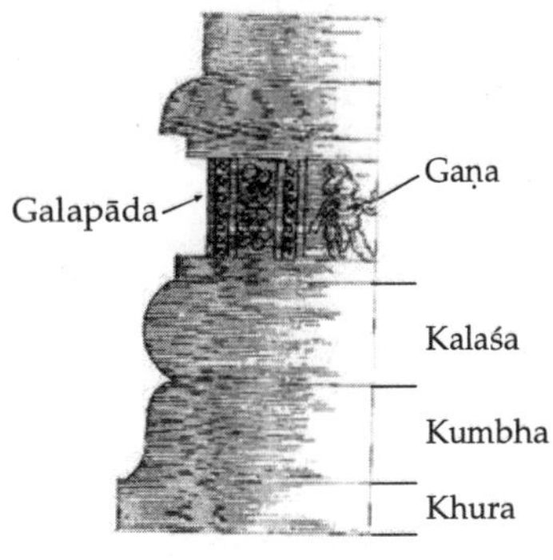

Base of a Temple, Ellorā (Cave 2), 8th century CE

of the north Indian Nāgara style temples also where these offsets are called *ratha* (रथ). Some of these *bhadras* alternate with sunken spaces which are like large vertical niches called *koṣṭhas*, or else *devakoṣṭhas* (देव-कोष्ठक), particularly in which we find images of gods and goddesses carved boldly.

PILLARS

The pillars as well as pilasters of south Indian temples are beautifully decorated. The base or pedestal of the pillar, called *oṁ* (ओम्), is often given the form of a squatting mythical creature with the body of one animal and other part of some other creature. These are called *vyālas* (व्याल), or else a grotesque human figure called *bhūta* (भूत) or else elephant, serpent, lion, etc. The shaft above it, i.e. the middle portion, could be round, square or multi-faceted.

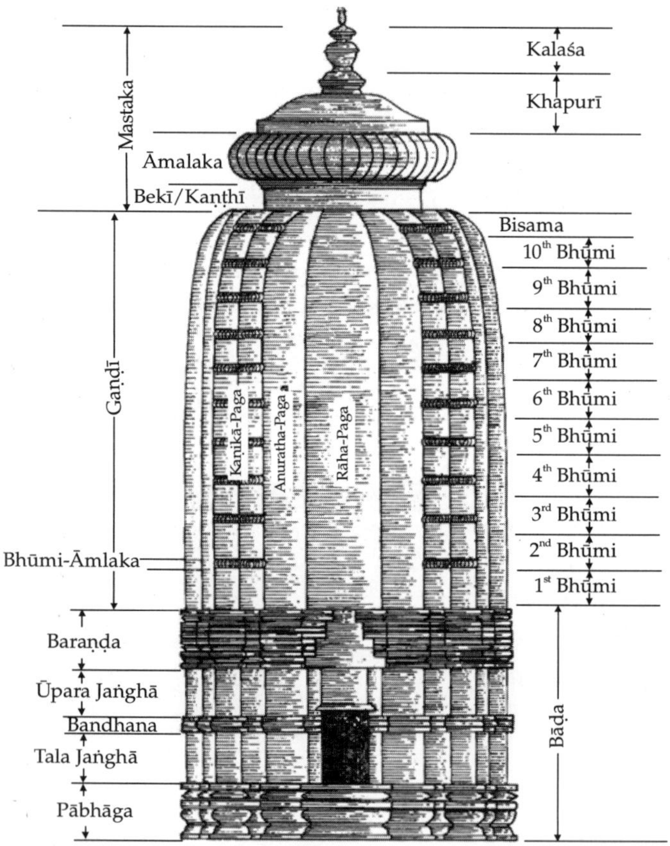

Elements of an Orissan Temple, *after* Liṅgarāja temple of Rekhā Deul type, early 12th century CE

TEMPLES OF ORISSA

Architecturally, Hindu temples are basically the same irrespective of their regional peculiarities and local nomenclature of their body parts. It is true of Orissa also. The lower part of the main temple is *garbha-gṛha* and the upper part is *śikhara* locally called *rekhā* (रेखा). Each one of these two major parts is divided into a number of mouldings. In front of this main structure is a porch or *maṇḍapa*, called *jagamohana* (जगमोहन) in which the devotees stand and face the deity in the *garbha-gṛha*. It has a roof which is slightly different from the porches in north Indian temples. However, in Orissa, as time passed, a couple of more porches were added in the same axis, each one used for a different purpose, *bhoga deul* (भोग देउल) and *nāṭya deul* (नाट्य देउल). In rare examples an independent *toraṇa* was also erected at the entrance. Orissa has given us several texts which governed the temple architecture in the region.

REKHĀ DEUL

Coming to the temple proper, i.e. the structure over the *garbha-gṛha*, i.e. *śikhara*, the Orissan *śikhara* type temple is called *rekhā deul* (रेखा देउल), etymologically, "curvilinear temple" because the *śikhara* here is slightly curvilinear; less in the lower portion but sharp in the upper part. The porch or *maṇḍapa*, on the other hand, is called *pīḍhā deul* (पीढा देउल), etymologically, "flat-seat temple" because the roof here is like a stepped pyramid marked by a series of flat platforms, placed one over the other, in diminishing dimensions, each one representing a storey.

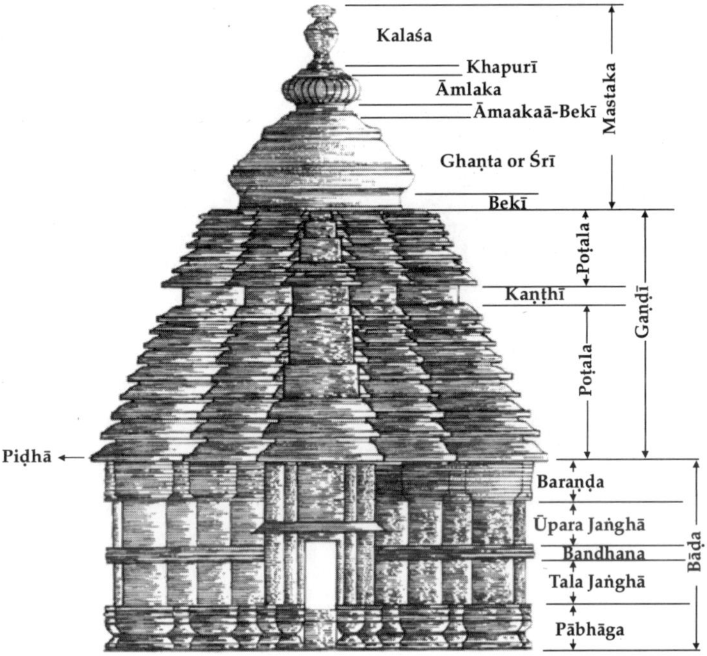

Elements of a storeyed Orissan Temple of Pīḍhā Deul type, *after* Liṅgarāja temple, early 12th century CE

In rare examples, the roof on the *garbha-gṛha* is vaulted with a few *kalaśa*s or *stūpī*s (स्तूपी) placed on the central ridge of the gable roof.

A rekhā deul is broadly divided into three major parts from bottom to top; these are:

(1) *Bāḍa* (बाड) (perpendicular wall)

(2) *Gaṇḍī* (गण्डी) (trunk or *śikhara*)

(3) *Mastaka* (मस्तक) (top).

Each one of these is further sub-divided into many mouldings.

Bāḍa: from bottom upwards, has

(i) *Pābhāga* (पाभाग) (*pā* means feet, i.e. basal part, the low platform)

(ii) *Tala jaṅghā* (तल जंघा) (lower level thigh or shin with vertically laid pillars and walls of the *garbha-gṛha*)

(iii) *Bandhana* (बन्धन) (centre mouldings to divide the vertical wall of the *garbha-gṛha*)

(iv) *Ūpara jaṅghā* (ऊपर जंघा) (upper level thigh)

(v) *Baraṇḍā* (बरण्डा) (entrance mouldings).

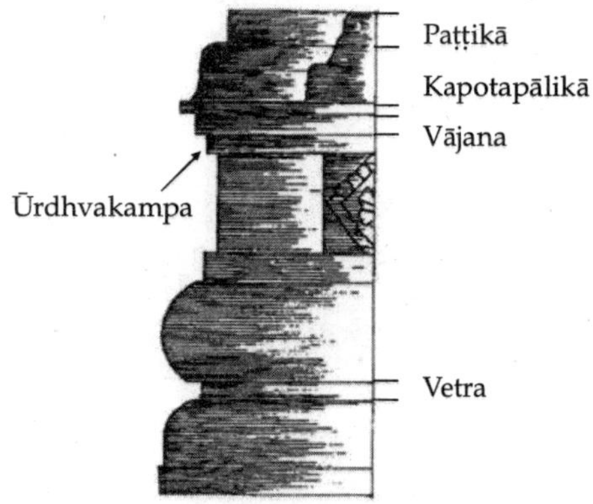

Base of a Temple, Ellorā (Cave 12)
8th century CE

Gaṇḍī: from bottom upwards the sub-divisions are

(i) *Bhūmi* (भूमि) (floor or storey)

(ii) *Bhūmi-āmalaka* (भूमि-आमलक) (*āmalaka* on top of the vertical wall of the floor or storey)

(iii) *Biṣama* (बिषम) (the topmost floor with sharply in-curved profile).

Mastaka: is divided into the following sub-divisions:

(i) *Bekī* (बेकी) (or *kaṇṭhī* (कण्ठी), i.e. neck which is a recessed vertical wall which separates the *gaṇḍī* or *śikhara* from the overhanging *āmalaka* placed on top of it

(ii) *Āmalaka* (आमलक) (or *āmlā* fruit, *Emblic myrobalan*, like cogged wheel)

(iii) *Khapurī* (खपुरी) (etymologically, skull, but shaped like a flat bell)

(iv) *Kalaśa* (कलश) (sacred water pitcher or *pūrṇa kumbha*)

(v) *Āyudha* (आयुध) (on the *kalaśa* may be placed

the *āyudha* of the deity in the *garbha-gṛha* if Śiva, it will be *triśūla*, but if Viṣṇu, it may be a *cakra*).

The *gaṇḍī* (or *śikhara*) of an Orissan temple is divided into a number of vertical parallel facets, anywhere from three to seven, but in odd numbers. The central facet or projection is called *rāha-paga* (राह-पग) with *jālī* (जाली) or screen having window mouldings. The two or more side ones with intricately carved projections are called *anuratha-paga* (अनुरथ-पग) or secondary *rāhas* (राह).

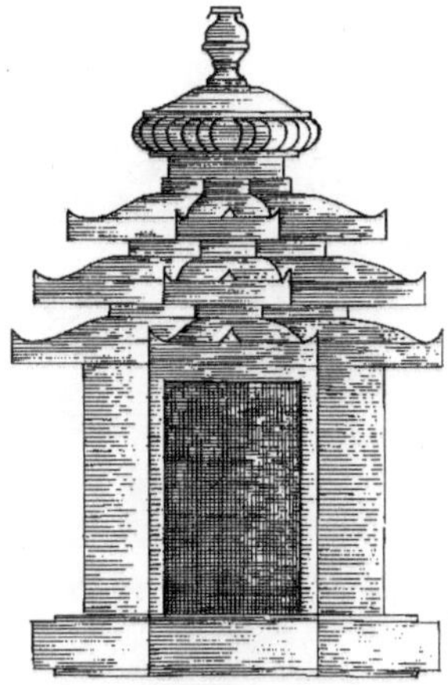

Pīḍhā-muṇḍī, Koṇārka, Orissa, 13th century CE

The four corner *pagas* with *āmalakas* at each floor or storey are called *kaṇikā-paga* (कणिका-पग).

It may be noted that the same divisions and sub-divisions exist in the case of *pīḍhā deul* or the *jagamohana*, except for the fact that here the *bhūmis* are marked by *pīḍhā* or horizontal terraces and there is only one, the central *rāha*: there is neither the *anuratha-paga* or *kaṇikā-paga*.

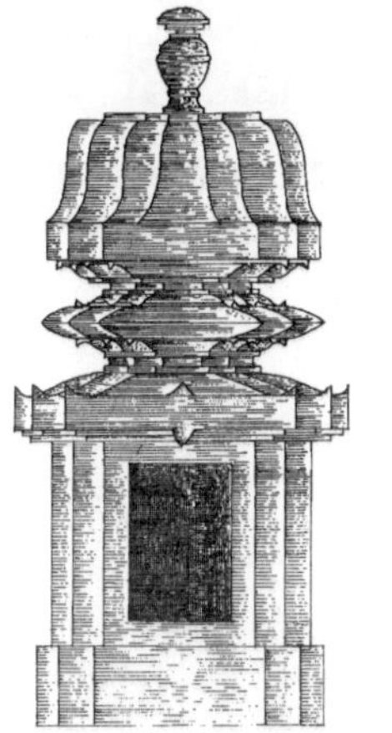

Khakharā-muṇḍī, Koṇārka, Orissa, 13th century CE

MUṆḌĪS

Small shrines, called *muṇḍī* such as *pīḍhā-muṇḍī* (पीढ़ा-मुण्डी) (small terraced shrine), *khakharā-muṇḍī* (खखरा-मुण्डी) (small terraced shrine with *ghaṭa* or *kalaśa* on top), *vajra-muṇḍī* (वज्र-मुण्डी) shrine with *gavākṣa* and floral decoration besides *alasakanyās* (अलसकन्या), loving couples, and *bho* (*kīrttimukha* कीर्त्तिमुख) being garlanded by two men motif inside a niche in *rāha* (very often) and thousands of *nāga-nāgī* (नाग-नागी), floral and faunal motifs decorate the outer surface of the temple. As a matter of fact, the *muṇḍīs* or miniature shrines show in them the images of gods and goddesses. Similarly, on top of the *rāha* and *rathas* are the images in the round of lions with their backs to *bekī* or neck. Such statues are found in the middle of the *rāhas* and *anurathas* also.

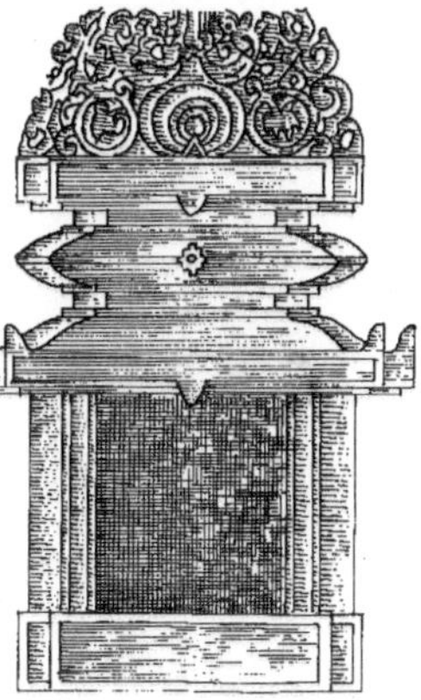

Vajra-muṇḍī, Koṇārka, Orissa, 13th century CE

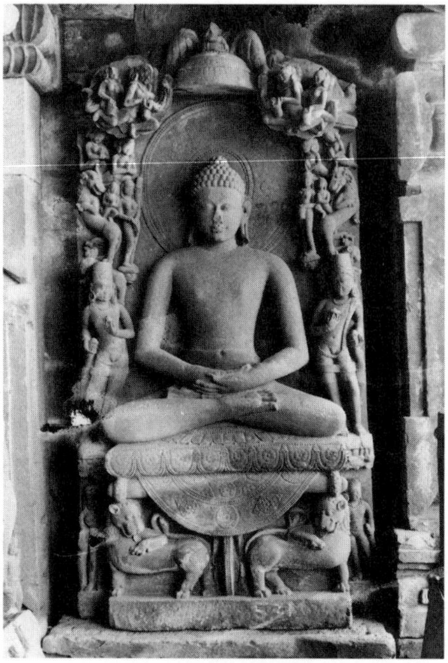

Pārśvanātha, seated, Jaina Temple, early 9th century CE

The Icons

RELIGIOUS DIFFERENCES

Objects through which "worship" is offered to God, the icons, idols and images, are, of course, sectarian. Śiva may be worshipped either through *liṅgam* (लिंगम्), a Sanskrit term which means *cihna* (चिह्न) or sign, even symbol, in this case it is the symbol of cosmic energy, or else through human form, with or without his consort Pārvatī. Viṣṇu may be worshipped either through the form of *śāligrāma* (शालिग्राम), an oval piece of stone, or else through human form, with or without his consort Lakṣmī. Viṣṇu can also be worshipped through any one of his ten incarnations, such as Rāma, Kṛṣṇa, Narasiṁha and others. Brahmā is, however, worshipped only through the human form. Śakti (शक्ति), the female as the goddess supreme, is also generally worshipped through human forms. The Śāktas worship Durgā, Kālī, Yoginīs, and others through different forms of Mothers. Nava Durgā (nine forms of Durgā) worship during the *Navarātra* festival is the biggest event in Śākta or Śakti cult.

Buddha is, however, worshipped either in the form of *stūpa* (स्तूप), a hemispherical or cylindrical structure, often raised on the ashes of the Buddha or a Buddhist saint, or a symbol such as the *pīpala* (पीपल) tree under which he got Enlightenment, or the seat sitting on which he got *nirvāṇa* (निर्वाण), or through the image of his feet bearing auspicious marks, *cakra* (चक्र), *svastika* (स्वस्तिक), etc. or else in the human form. It may be noted that Buddha was against image worship. That is why till about the first century CE Buddhists paid homage to Buddha only through symbols manifesting his life and thought. For a Buddhist the *stūpa*, was, therefore, Buddha himself. Hence worshipping *stūpa* is worshipping Buddha himself. Buddha's image in human form appeared as late as the beginning of the first century CE if not the later half of the first century BCE as now art historians believe.

The Jainas generally worship any or all the 24 *tīrthaṁkaras* (तीर्थंकर), including the last one, Mahāvīra, and a few other deified saints like Bāhubali; the *stūpa*, raised on the cremated remains of the Jaina saints, was worshipped only till the Kuṣāṇa period. However, similar to Bauddha practice, the Jainas also worshipped through symbols, including *stūpa*. The images of *tīrthaṁkaras* in human form started in the first-second centuries CE in case the two Lohānīpur (in Patna) torsos do not belong to *tīrthaṁkaras*. The Sikhs worship only the *Guru Grantha Saheb* (गुरुग्रंथ साहिब), their most sacred book, placed in a temple called *mandira* (मन्दिर). The Ārya Samājīs perform Fire Sacrifice in line with the Vedic traditions, and invoke gods like Agni (अग्नि), Mitra (मित्र), Varuṇa (वरुण) and others. The tāntrics (तान्त्रिक) attach great sacredness to *yantras* (यन्त्र) and *maṇḍalas* (मण्डल), which are diagrams made for ritualistic performances, using *mantras* (मन्त्र) or sacred chants and *tantras* (तन्त्र) or sets of rituals with symbolic meaning, generally confined to the practitioners in great secrecy since these were the parts of *sādhanā* (साधना) which is absolutely personal. The Tantra literature often uses terms which on their face appear to be sex-related but they actually mean something entirely different, connected generally with hands, fingers, gestures, etc. for *sādhanā*.

Symbols

The dictionary meaning of "symbol" is

> something that represents something else by association, resemblance, or convention, especially a material object used to represent

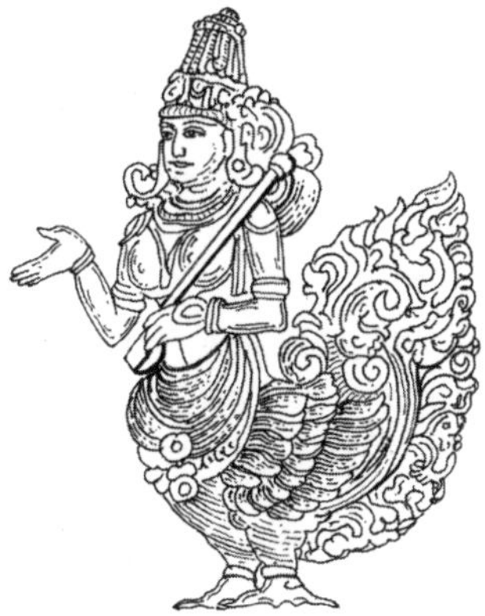

Gandharva, Hoyasaḷa, Karnataka, 13th century CE

something invisible.

For example, lotus represents purity and cross represents crucifixion of Christ. Metaphor, on the other hand, is defined as

> figure [of speech] in which a term is transferred from the object it ordinarily designates to an object it may designate only by implicit comparison or analogy.

For example, *garbha* or womb of mother to the *garbha-gṛha* of temple.

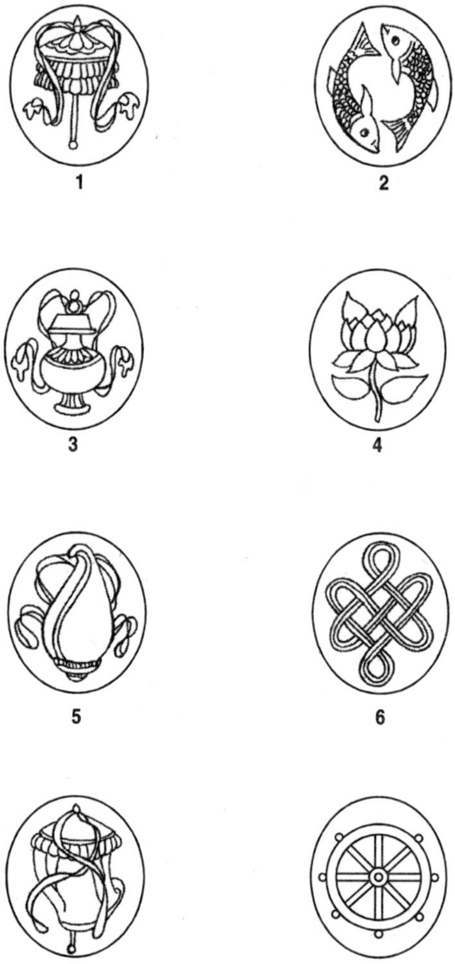

Eight auspicious symbols:

1. Aṣṭamaṅgala: *Chattra* (Umbrella), 2. *Mīna mithuna* (two fish), 3. *Pūrṇa-ghaṭa* (full pot), 4. *Padma* (lotus), 5. *Śaṅkha* (conch-shell), 6. *Anata* (continuous knot) or knot of Life, 7. *Dhvaja* (flag), 8. *Cakra* (wheel)

Every society lives with symbols and metaphors which it creates for the language of its ethos. The national flag, the national anthem, the national bird, the national flower, sacred groves, sacred trees, sacred dates, memorable events, and many others form part of the language of symbols and metaphors. A "symbol" is the shortest form for a whole set of ideas and feelings. The picture of heart stands for one's most intimate love and affection for the other. *Svastika* (स्वस्तिक) symbol denotes the well-being in all human endeavours. A "U" or "V" shaped mark on the forehead is called *viṣṇupāda* (विष्णुपाद) and is enough to inform us that the person is a Vaiṣṇava. The three horizontal lines on the forehead, called *tripuṇḍa*, make him a Śaivite. These are also called *cihna*s (चिह्न) or marks of identification.

NATURE OF SYMBOLS

Indian art embodies a long list of symbols, each with multi-layered meaning developed through ages but generally one or two significant meanings. A Hindu temple is conceived as a lofty mountain with a series of gradually rising peaks and caves. Therefore, a temple is said to represent Mount Meru. It is a metaphor.

Symbols may be in geometric forms and diagrams such as squares and triangles; flowers, fruits and leaves such as the lotus, *śrīphala* (श्रीफल) and *pīpala* leaf; birds and reptiles, animals and insects, such as the peacock, serpent, bull and ant; heavenly bodies like Sun and Moon and other elements of nature such as trees, water, mountains, seas and rivers called Himalaya, Sindhu Sāgara, and Gaṅgā, as well as many man-made items such as the water pitcher or *pūrṇa-ghaṭa* (पूर्ण-घट), sandals or *pādukā* (पादुका), trident or *triśūla* (त्रिशूल), etc. Each one of these denotes something sacred or something specifically meaningful. They together embody the cultural ethos of India.

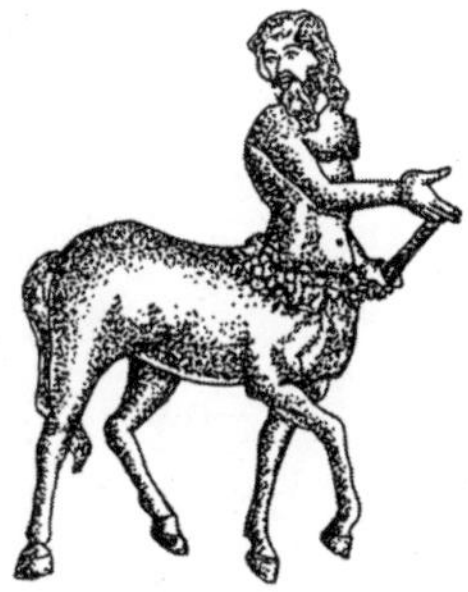

Centaur symbolizes sin of adultery in Christianity

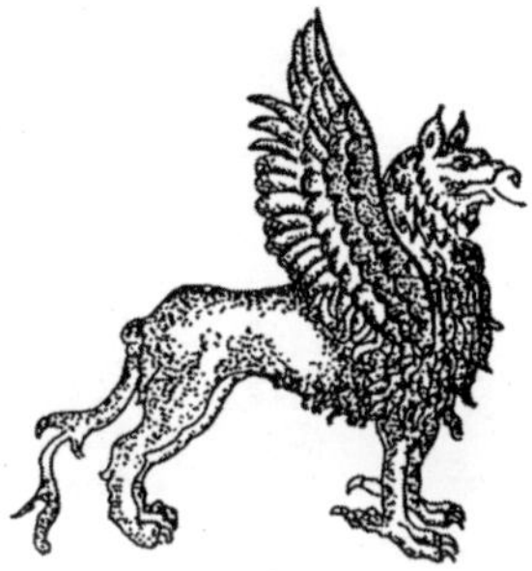

Griffin, the symbol of Saviour as well as of those who persecute Christians

SYMBOLS AND SIGNS IN CHRISTIANITY, ISLAM, ETC.

In Christianity there are two complementary terms, "Sign" and "Symbol," while the former *represents*, as the Cross represents Christ's Crucifixion, the latter *resembled*, for example, Christ resembled the Lamb of God, like lamb he too was sacrificed as an act of atonement. In Christian art the figure of the ape symbolizes sin and malice of man and *śaitāna* (शैतान) and ass symbolizes the entry of Christ in Jerusalem. There are many more of them such as the dove, cock, bat, etc. with their specific symbolism. In Islam also there are a few symbols such as the moon and crescent connected with its calendar based on the appearance of moon. In China a frog with three feet and a coin in mouth is kept on the front-door of the house since it is the symbol of wealth. The pot-bellied Laughing Buddha also represents wealth and well-being for the family.

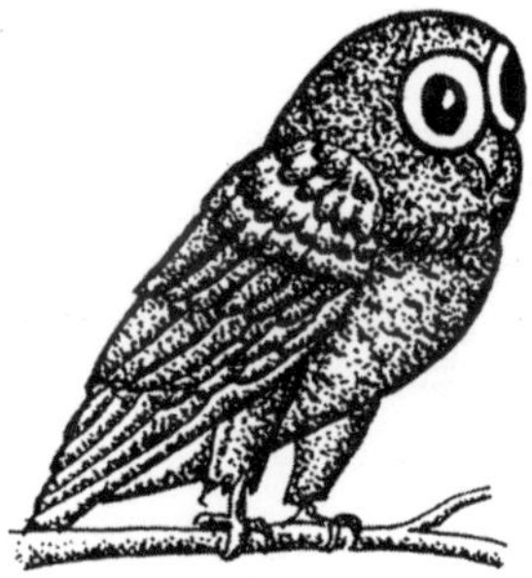

Owl, the symbol of *śaitāna*

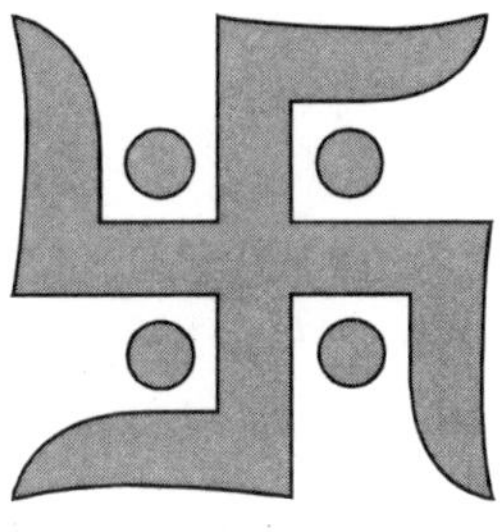

Svastika, symbolizes Good Luck and is solar symbol in Hinduism

UNIVERSALITY OF SYMBOLS IN HINDUISM

Symbols or *pratīka* (प्रतीक) in Hinduism are only rarely

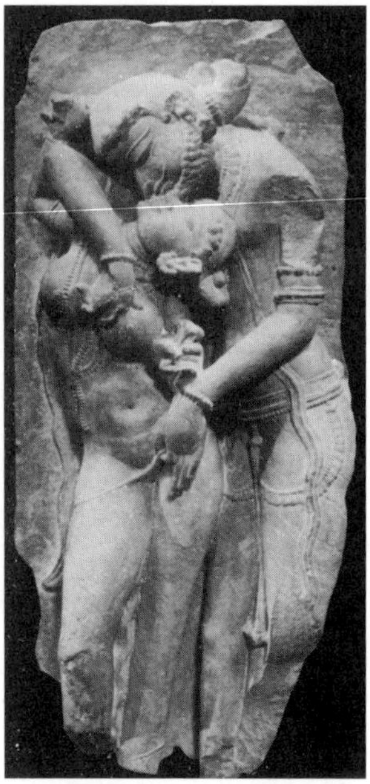

Mithuna or loving couple, Khajurāho, M.P., Candela, 11th century CE

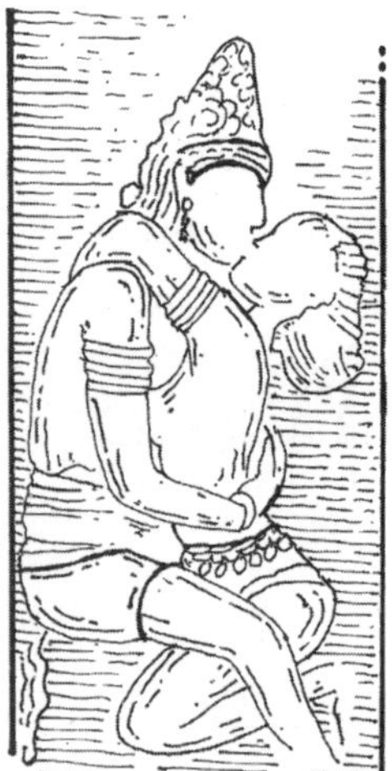

Maithuna, Ellorā, Rāṣṭrakūṭa, Maharashtra, 8th century CE

sectarian; by and large they form the common pool out of which each religion picked up the ones which it thought would represent their ethos best. Lotus, *pīpala*, snake, bull, elephant, crocodile, conch, *svastika, cakra, triśūla*, sun, moon, *chatra* (छत्र) or parasol and several other items formed part of the common gamut of symbols which one finds associated individually and also in combinations in Buddhism, Jainism, Śaivism, Vaiṣṇavism, Śāktism, etc. Lotus, for example, is the most sacred flower for all religions hence all gods and goddesses of all religions are shown sitting or standing on the blossoming lotus. So also the *dhyāna-mudrā* (ध्यान-मुद्रा) or sitting posture of a *yogī* (योगी) which is common to all gods of all religions in India because spiritualism is the core-idea of all religions born in India and this element is manifested in this *mudrā* which is the *mudrā* of perfect concentration of mind-and-body and the long journey within. However, *triśūla* was picked up by the Śaivas, almost exclusively, although Durgā also used it to kill the demon Mahiṣāsura.

It shows the fundamental unity of Hindu civilization, the commonness of the symbols of Indian cultural ethos. It is like one hand with five fingers, each finger is different from the other in every respect but each one is deriving its sustenance from the common hand, if the hand is removed, all fingers lose their very existence. Thus, lotus is common to all religions but *śrīvatsa* (श्रीवत्स) was selected by the Jainas for putting it on the chest of the *tīrthaṁkaras*. Still, Viṣṇu also sports it sometimes. *Svastika*, as an auspicious solar symbol, is also used by all religions and all over India.

MITHUNA AND MAITHUNA SCENES IN ART

From the second century BCE Indian art has

incorporated the symbol of "loving couple," called *mithuna,* as the most auspicious symbol for the health, wealth and progeny, the three basic desires of human beings as spelt out in the Vedic literature. This symbol is found depicted on the walls of the shrines of all religions, including the so-called orthodox religions like Buddhism and Jainism. There was nothing erotic in it. Copulation or *maithuna* (मैथुन) is only the next stage of *mithuna* (मिथुन) — it is the symbol of procreation, a phenomenon without which no one of us could have been born in this world. The birth of a child is, therefore, considered to be the result of meritorious work that the couple may have done in their previous births. This viewpoint is totally opposite to the Christian view of life in which a human being is born of sin, being part of the "Original Sin" that Adam and Eve committed. The symbols of *mithuna* and *maithuna* are, therefore, not erotic and debased.

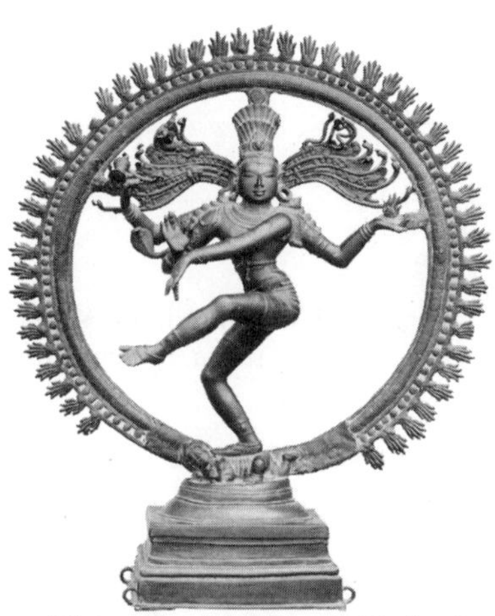

Naṭarāja, Coḷa, Tamil Nadu, 10th century CE

HINDU ICONOGRAPHY

Images and icons are distinguished from each other on the basis of what are generally called the "marks of cognisance" or *cihna*s (चिह्न). These are of various kinds, from hair-do to head-cover, from marks on the chest to marks on the soles, from objects held in hands to objects covering the feet, from *vāhana*s (वाहन), i.e. mounts of gods, or associated men and animals acting as carriers, to objects held in hands often called *āyudha*s (आयुध), meaning weapons, although all of them are not weapons.

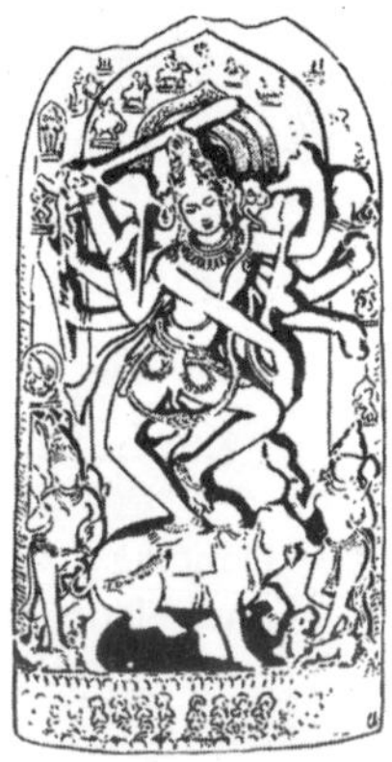

Naṭarāja dancing on bull, Śaṅkarbandha, Bangladesh, Pāla, 10th century CE

ŚIVA

Śiva is supposed to be the Destroyer of the Universe. He is sometimes shown with three heads, and also the third eye, as the symbol of supreme wisdom, on the forehead. One of his popular forms is Naṭarāja

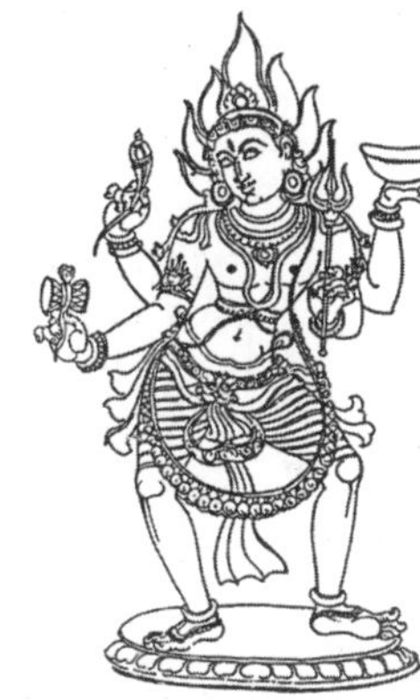

Śiva, Coḷa, Tamil Nadu, 11th century CE

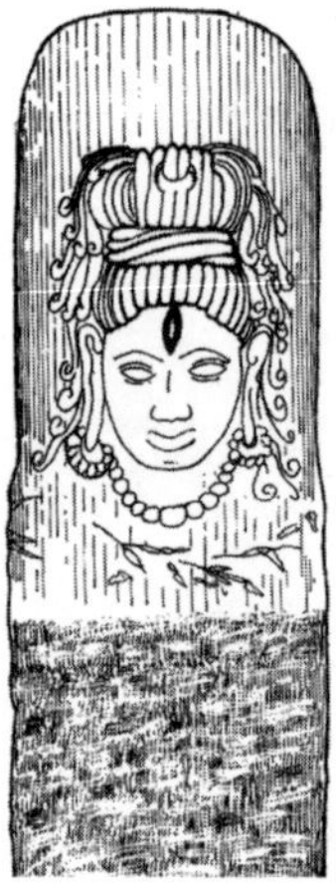

Ekamukhīliṅga, Khoh, M.P., Gupta, 5th century CE

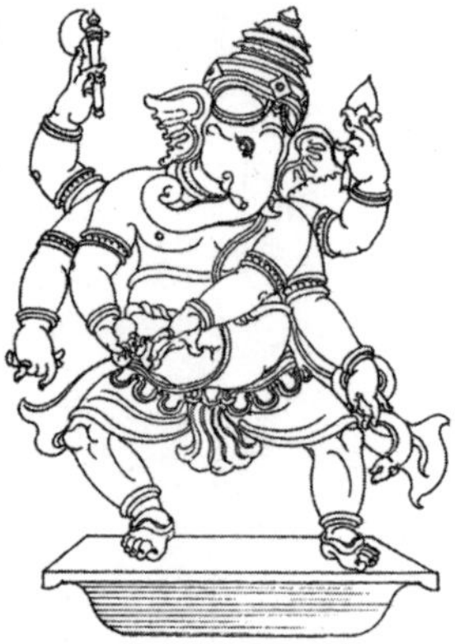

Dancing Gaṇeśa, Nāyaka, Tamil Nadu, 16th century CE

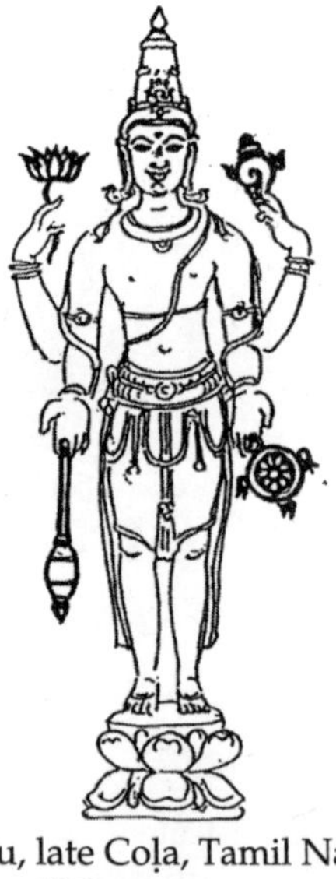

Viṣṇu, late Coḷa, Tamil Nadu, 12th century CE

(नटराज) or master of a dance-form called *tāṇḍava* (ताण्डव) which symbolizes one of the major functions of Śiva — the Destroyer of Evil; the evil is marked by a short deformed human being, called *apasmāra* (अपस्मार), who personifies ignorance and evil, and is, therefore, trampled by Śiva. Śiva's hair is matted, i.e. divided into a number of braids in rope-like manner and wound up in coils, called *jaṭā* (जटा) or *jaṭā-mukuṭa* (जटामुकुट), symbolizing his ascetic character. He has snakes on his body and *tripuṇḍa* (त्रिपुण्ड) on the forehead. On the head he may also be seen sporting half moon and a human skull. His mount is the bull named "Nandī" (नन्दी). Sometimes Śiva is shown ithyphallic or *ūrdhva-retasa* (ऊर्ध्व-रेतस), which symbolizes his greatest asceticism in which sexual passion and the lust of different senses are fully controlled, to the extent no human being can ever hope to control once the erection takes place. All the forms of *Śivaliṅga*s (शिवलिंग) are, therefore, in a sense represent the yogic form of Śiva or the highest spiritual form of Śiva. His consort is Pārvatī.

In Śaivism there are a few gods who too are worshipped. For example, Gaṇeśa, the son of Śiva and Pārvatī, who has the elephant head and is considered by all religions, including Buddhism, as the one who removes all obstacles in the way of performing any good action, Vighna-Vināyaka. Kārttikeya, with peacock as his mount or *vāhana*, is also worshipped as the second son of Śiva and Pārvatī; Nandī, Śivaliṅga in *yoni-pīṭha* (योनि-पीठ), etc. are commonly found items of worship in Śiva temples.

VIṢṆU

Viṣṇu, on the other hand, is the Preserver of the Universe. His role is that of a king. Hence, he wears a cylindrical crown studded with jewels, called *kirīṭa mukuṭa* (किरीट मुकुट). He wears a *vanamālā* (वनमाला),

or a long garland of flowers, sometimes studded with five jewels, hence in that form it is called *vaijayantī-mālā* (वैजयन्ती-माला). He generally holds in his four hands *śaṅkha* (शंख) (conch), *cakra* (चक्र) (wheel), *gadā* (गदा) (mace) and *padma* (पद्म) (lotus). His mount is Garuḍa (eagle) and his consort is Lakṣmī.

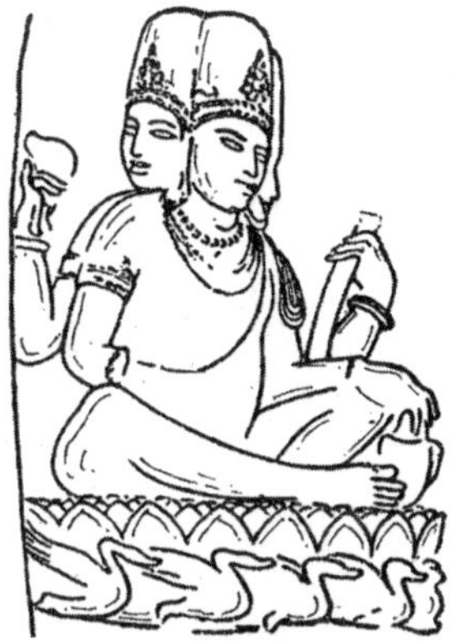

Brahmā, Aihoḷe, Karnataka, 7th century CE

In Vaiṣṇava religion there are many forms of Viṣṇu which are not covered in the "Incarnations of Viṣṇu" category but are worshipped in independent temples, for example Viṣṇu lying on Śeṣanāga, or Raṅganātha, Keśava, etc. However, Sūrya was the most popular god of the Vaiṣṇava category. He is usually shown with full boots on legs and lotus flower in hands. He is also shown riding on a chariot drawn by four or seven horses. He, like Viṣṇu, wears a *kirīṭa-mukuṭa.*

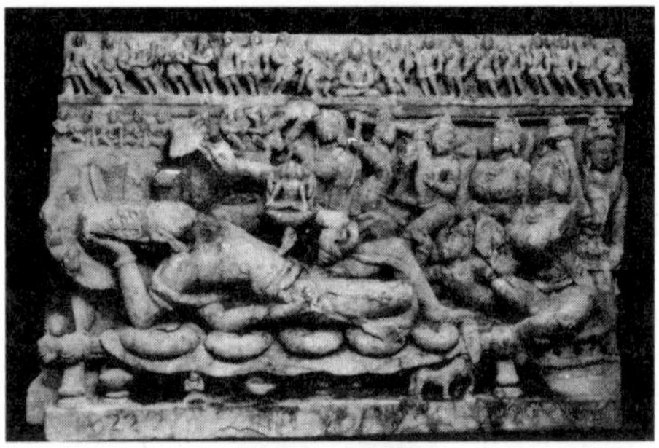

Brahmā emerging from the navel of Viṣṇu, Behaṭā Bujurga, Ghātampur, Kanpur, U.P., 10th century CE

BRAHMĀ

Brahmā is the Creator of the Universe. He is old and wise, hence shown with a beard. He holds a *pothī* (पोथी), i.e. book of wisdom, Vedas in particular, a rosary, a *kamaṇḍalu* (कमण्डलु), i.e. water pot, and lotus. His mount is swan, i.e. *haṁsa* (हंस), (sometimes Garuḍa) which symbolizes the highest wisdom in separating milk from water or virtue from evil. His consort is Brāhmī but he is only rarely shown with her.

The three principal gods of Hinduism had, therefore, three major functions to perform which are partly reflected in their iconography as described above. However, sometimes they are seen interchanging their function: Śiva becomes the preserver and Viṣṇu the humbler of the pride of human beings.

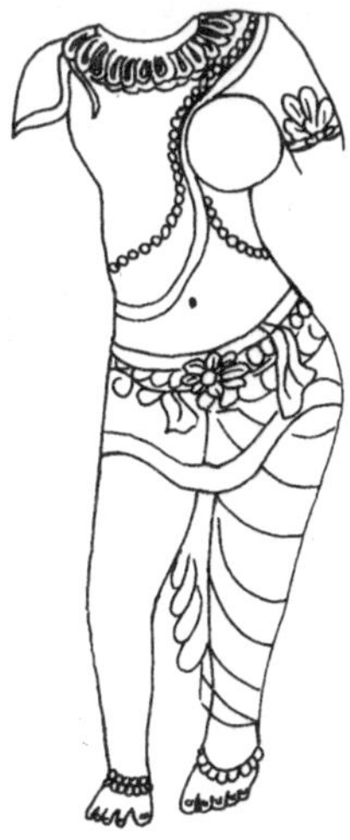

Ardhanārīśvara, M.P., 13th century CE

THE ŚĀKTA

Amongst all the forces of *maithunī saṁsāra* (मैथुनी संसार) or the world born of copulation, according to the Purāṇas, the mother occupies the prime position of creative as well as sustaining force, hence divine. Divinity, even otherwise, has these two major roles to play in human life. Mother is, therefore, all powerful, the Śakti (शक्ति), hence Goddess. With her inherent power she is capable of vanquishing all forms of evil to protect her children, the humans.

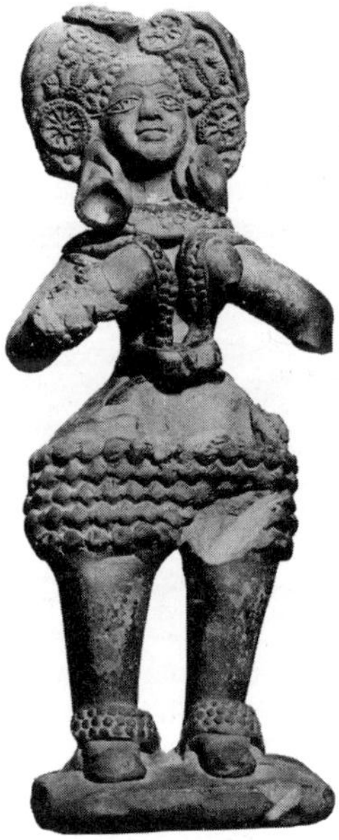

Mother-goddess, terracotta, Mathurā, 3rd century BCE

She, in another sense, also provides to her consort, the male god, the "power" to do what is expected of him — Śiva, Viṣṇu or Brahmā — thereby becoming his Śakti or Energy. This concept is best epitomized in the iconography of Ardhanārīśvara (अर्धनारीश्वर) where Pārvatī occupies the half of Śiva's body. The underlying idea is, which we get to know from various narratives in the Purāṇas, that she, besides power, also supplies to her consort wisdom (*prajñā* प्रज्ञा), intelligence (*buddhi* बुद्धि), consciousness (*cetanā* चेतना), mind (*citi* चिति), compassion (*karuṇa* करुणा), and faith (*śraddhā* श्रद्धा).

The roots of Mother Goddess or Devī (देवी) concept, of course, goes back to the Vedic times, for example, Rākā (राका) and Sinīvalī (सिनीवली) are the two prominent ones who later on find mention in *Rudrayāmala* (रुद्रयामल) with their iconographic details. However, the concept of Mother Goddess as Śakti developed in stages and pervaded Buddhism and Jainism as well in which there are now so many female deities many of them are the same as in Śaiva, Vaiṣṇava and Tāntrika cults although they may have assumed new names.

From the Mauryan period at least we start getting the glimpses of the Mother Goddess through her terracotta images, but by the Kuṣāṇa period we get her definite form, to begin with, as Mahiṣāsuramardinī (महिषासुरमर्दिनी), an image in which she is shown killing the demon Mahiṣāsura using her hands as well as *triśūla* (त्रिशूल) or trident. From Soṅkh, near Mathurā, and other places we have several terracotta images of this Goddess. This form is over and above many simple forms of Mother Goddess in which she is shown highly bejewelled and sitting or standing, sometimes on lotus, as we find from Mauryan through Śuṅga times. In one of the most popular forms, the Mother Goddess, found depicted in Buddhist and Jaina contexts as well, she is shown standing on a lotus and being bathed with water flowing out of water pitcher (*kalaśa*), held high overhead by two elephants, one on each side. In this form she is called Gaja-Lakṣmī (गजलक्ष्मी).

Śakti, or Ādiśakti (आदिशक्ति), i.e. primordial power, took various forms from the Gupta period onwards all over the country of which the following ones are important:

(1) Durgā and her nine forms (Nava Durgās) (दुर्गा)

(2) Ten Mahāvidyās (महाविद्या)

(3) Pīṭha-Devīs (पीठ-देवी)

(4) Asuramardinī (असुरमर्दिनी)

(5) Mātṛkā (मातृका) and her seven (or eight) forms (Sapta or Aṣṭa-Mātṛkās)

(6) Yoginīs (योगिनी), 64 of them (Cauṅsaṭha Yoginīs)

The sources of our knowledge about them are the Purāṇas, Tantras and the Āgamas. Some of the prominent texts are *Mānasāra* (मानसार) (seventh century), *Mayamata* (मयमत) (eighth century), *Samarāṅgaṇasūtradhāra* (समरांगणसूत्रधार) of King Bhoja (eleventh century), *Abhilāṣitārthacintāmaṇi* (अभिलाषितार्थचिंतामणि) of Someśvaradeva III (twelfth century), *Aparājitapṛcchā* (अपराजितपृच्छा) of Bhuvanadeva (twelfth-thirteenth century), *Caturvargacintāmaṇi* (चतुर्वर्गचिंतामणि) of Hemādri (thirteenth century), *Rūpamaṇḍana* (रूपमण्डन) and *Devatāmūrtiprakaraṇa* (देवतामूर्तिप्रकरण) of Sūtradhāra Maṇḍana (early sixteenth century) and *Śilparatna* (शिल्परत्न) of Kumāra (late sixteenth century).

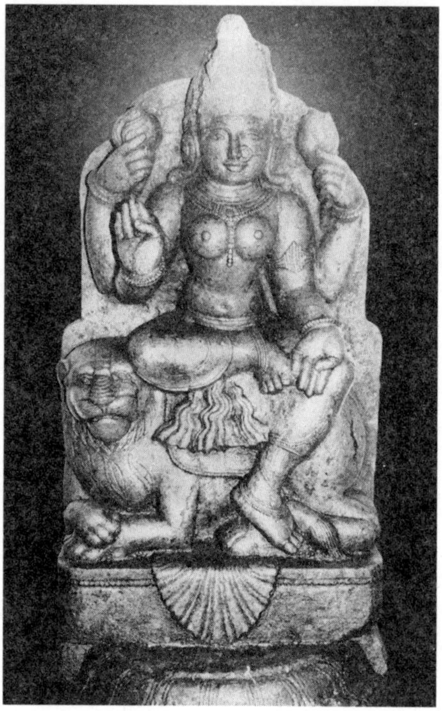

Simhavāhinī Durgā, Suvarṇeśvara temple, Śākuntalapura, Orissa. 15th–16th century CE

DURGĀ (दुर्गा)

Literally meaning "Beyond Reach," impregnable, terrible, invincible, the destroyer of all difficulties and afflictions. She as Pārvatī is said to have killed the demon Durgā (दुर्ग). She is equated with Mahiṣā-suramardinī. She created Kālī and other female goddesses to kill the Mahiṣāsura.

The world has two opposed phenomena such as the Good and Evil, the *devatā* and the *dānava*, and Light and Darkness, both existing side by side, both influencing each other's conduct. Hence the world is constantly at war and shall remain so till eternity. Yet, if the world has to survive with all its life, the Good has to keep on winning. But, who will win the war against the Evil? Śakti, the invincible force that keeps on killing the Evil in whichever form it may appear and in the process sustaining the world of life. Everytime a *dānava*, like Śumbha (शुम्भ) and Niśumbha (निशुम्भ), strikes she kills him.

The nine forms of Durgā (दुर्गा) are:

(i) Śailaputrī (शैलपुत्री), (ii) Brahmacāriṇī (ब्रह्मचारिणी), (iii) Candrakhaṇḍa (चन्द्रखण्डा) or Candraghaṇṭā (चन्द्रघंटा), (iv) Skandadurgā (स्कन्ददुर्गा) or Skandamātā (स्कन्दमाता), (v) Kuṣmāṇḍā (कुष्माण्डा) or Kuṣmāṇḍī (कुष्माण्डी), (vi) Kātyāyanī (कात्यायनी), (vii) Kālarātri

(कालरात्रि), (viii) Mahāgaurī (महागौरी), and (ix) Siddhidāyinī (सिद्धिदायिनी).

The south Indian Āgamas have, however, a few different names but that does not matter much.

TEN MAHĀVIDYĀS (महाविद्या)

The Tāntrikas have special favour for the worship of Mahāvidyās since according to them they are the Ultimate Sources of all that is to be known in the world. These are (i) Kālī or Śyāmā (काली अथवा श्यामा), (ii) Tārā (तारा), (iii) Chinnamastā (छिन्नमस्ता), (iv) Sundarī (सुन्दरी), (v) Bagalā (बगला), (vi) Mātaṅgī (मातंगी), (vii) Bhuvaneśānī or Bhuvaneśvarī (भुवनेशानी अथवा भुवनेश्वरी), (viii) Siddhavidyā (सिद्धविद्या), (ix) Bhairavī (भैरवी), and (x) Dhūmāvatī (धूमा वती). Each one of these has different iconographic feat ures most of

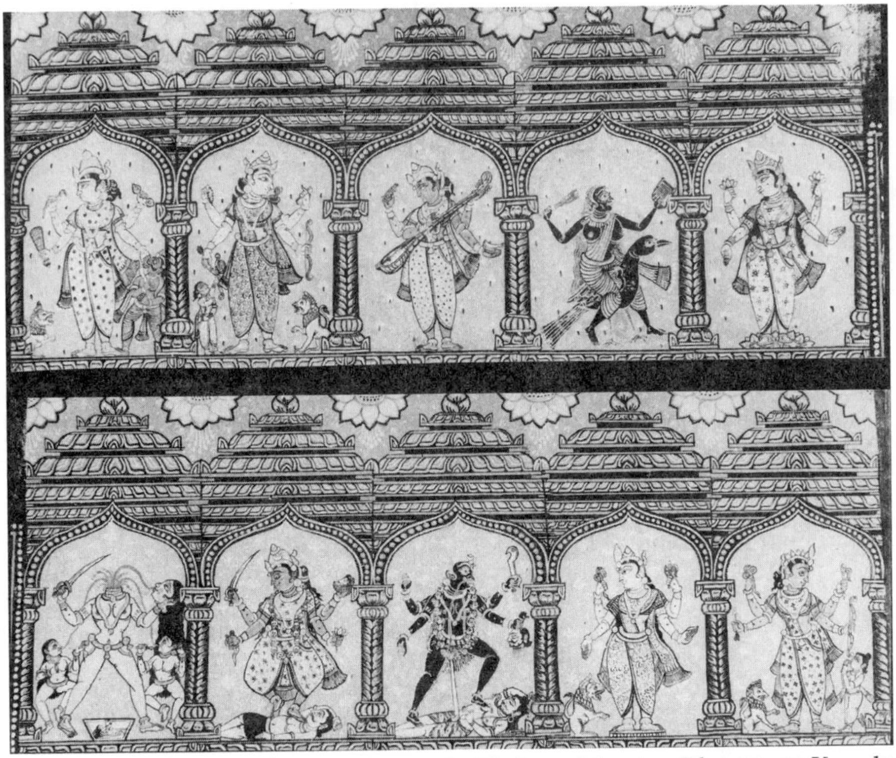

Ten Mahāvidyās (from top left) Bagalā, Bhairavī, Mātaṅgī, Dhūmāvatī, Kamalā (from bottom left) Chinnamastā, Tārā, Kālī, Bhuvaneśvarī and Ṣoḍaśī; Paṭṭanaikiā; modern wall painting

which are mentioned in the *Śrītattvanidhi.*

The temple-complexes of these Tāntric deities are, in fact, the centres of all kinds of esoteric practices which the initiated ones alone know: Datiā in Madhya Pradesh is known for such centres.

PĪṬHEŚVARĪS OR PĪṬHADEVĪS (पीठेश्वरी अथवा पीठदेवी)

There are many Śāktapīṭhas (शाक्तपीठ), said to have been formed out of the limbs of Pārvatī, in the country, each one presided over by one Śakti. The Tāntrika texts give various figures for them, ranging from 7 to 8, 10, 18, 42 and 50 to 108. They are mentioned in texts like *Pīṭhanirṇaya* (पीठनिर्णय) or *Mahāpīṭhanirūpaṇa* (महापीठनिरूपण). It may, however, be noted that some of these Śāktapīṭha Devīs occur in Mahāvidyā lists and other lists given in other texts, such as the *Devībhāgavata Purāṇa* (देवीभागवत पुराण).

Some of these Śāktapīṭhas are:

(i) Karavīra (करवीर), (ii) Vidyānātha (विद्यानाथ) or Kālīghāṭa (कालीघाट), (iii) Ujjayinī (उज्जयिनी), (iv) Gaṇḍakī (गण्डकी), (v) Tripura (त्रिपुर), (vi) Kāmagiri (कामगिरि), (vii) Kurukṣetra (कुरुक्षेत्र), (viii) Vṛndāvana (वृंदावन), (ix) Prayāga (प्रयाग), (x) Nāsik (नासिक), (xi) Varanasi (वाराणसी), (xii) Vindhyagaṅgā Saṅgam (विन्ध्यगंगा संगम), etc.

Their presiding deities are respectively:

(i) Mahiṣamardinī (महिषमर्दिनी), (ii) Jayadurgā (जयदुर्गा), (iii) Maṅgalā (मंगला), (iv) Caṇḍī (चण्डी), (v) Tripurasundarī (त्रिपुरसुन्दरी), (vi) Kāmākhyā (कामाख्या), (vii) Sāvitrī (सावित्री), (viii) Kātyāyanī (कात्यायनी), (ix) Kamalā (कमला), (x) Mahāvidyā (महाविद्या), (xi) Annapūrṇā (अन्नपूर्णा), (xii) Vindhyavāsinī (विन्ध्यवासिनी), etc.

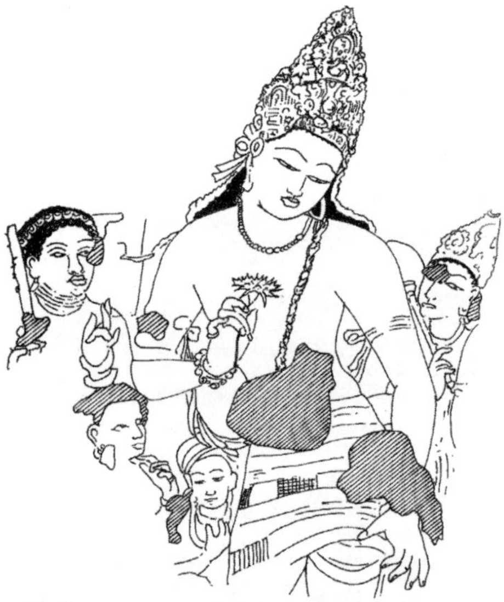

Bodhisattva Padmapāṇi, in perspective, Painting, Ajantā, Maharashtra, Gupta, 5th century CE

In fact, the Śākta cults are most prominently practised at these Śāktapīṭhas where people go to worship the presiding Mother Goddess.

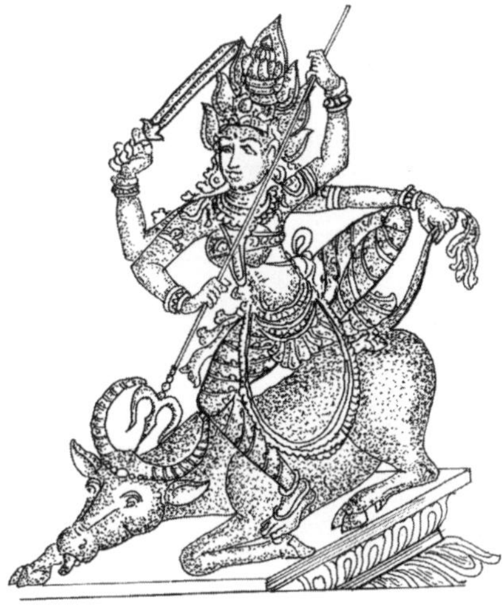

Asuramardinī, Bengal, 16th century CE

ASURAMARDINĪ (असुरमर्दिनी)

It may be noted that She is the mother of both, the *devas* (देव) and the *dānavas* (दानव), but she has to kill the latter, her own sons, because of their acts of wickedness, according to various Purāṇas. The *Mārkaṇḍeya Purāṇa*, for example, gives detailed accounts of her battles against demons or *asuras* in three phases or *caritas*. In the *Pūrvacarita* she battled against Madhu and Kaiṭabha; in the *Madhyama-carita*, she kills Mahiṣāsura; and in the *Uttaracarita* she vanquishes five *asuras*, viz. Śumbha, Niśumbha, Caṇḍa, Muṇḍa and Raktabīja. The *Devī Māhātmya* of *Mārkaṇḍeya Purāṇa*, and *Vāmana Purāṇa* give details of these exploits of the Goddess Durgā who is often shown as Siṁhavāhinī or one riding a lion. In the Mahiṣamardinī form she may or may not be shown with a lion but the buffalo or else buffalohead, symbolizing demon Mahiṣa, has to be there.

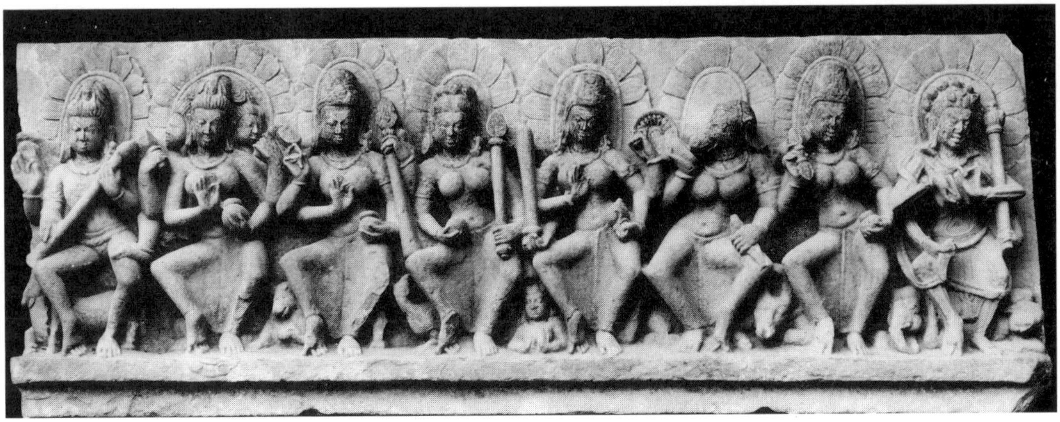

Aṣṭamātṛkās (Mother Goddesses), Sandstone, Pratihāra, Allahabad, U.P., 10th century CE

SAPTAMĀTṚKĀS (सप्तमातृका) OR SEVEN DIVINE MOTHERS

In the *Varāha Purāṇa* there is a story according to which Śiva had to create Mātṛkās to lick the blood of Andhakāsura, (अन्धकासुर) a demon, who tried to kill Śiva since everytime the *asura*'s blood fell on the ground a new *asura* or demon was created out of that blood. First he created Yogeśvarī, and then Māheśvarī to do this job. When the *deva*s found that this was not sufficient, Brahmā, Indra, Varāha, Viṣṇu, Kumāra and Yama also sent their own Śaktis to help Śiva in doing this job. In some texts, instead of seven, eight Śaktis are mentioned, as in *Varāha Purāṇa*. These are:

(i) Brahmāṇī (ब्रह्माणी) (ii) Māheśvarī (माहेश्वरी), (iii) Kaumārī (कौमारी), (iv) Vaiṣṇavī (वैष्णवी), (v) Vārāhī (वाराही), (vi) Indrāṇī (इन्द्राणी), and (vii) Cāmuṇḍā (चामुण्डा).

The name of Narasiṁhī (नरसिंही) replaces Yogeśvarī (योगेश्वरी) in some texts. In some texts these are replaced by Mahālakṣmī (महालक्ष्मी).

The Mātṛkās are shown in art either collectively in a row or else individually and can be identified with the iconography which they often share with the iconography of their male counterparts. They are shown sitting or standing or even in dance pose.

Sometimes Sarasvatī sporting a swan as the emblem, sharing Brahmā's emblem, is also included in the Mātṛkās. Lakṣmī, as the consort of Viṣṇu, also assumes the forms of Annapūrṇā and Tulasī, and included in the Mātṛkās. So also Śrī and Bhūmi. Gaurī, also named Pārvatī, Umā, Kālī, Ambikā, etc., is included amongst the Mātṛkās but mainly as the consort of Śiva.

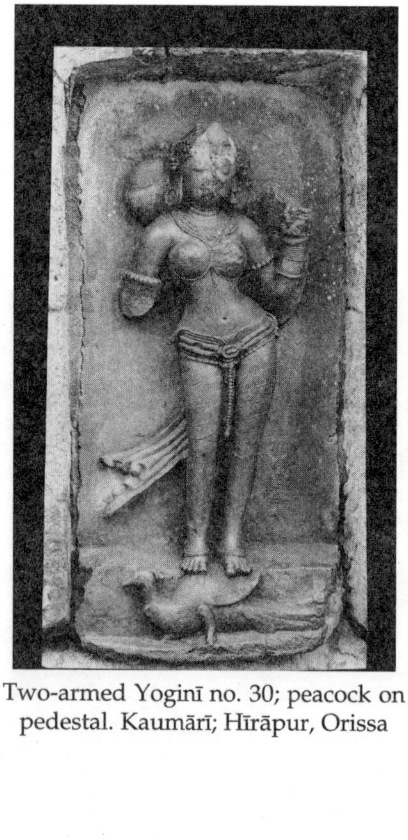

Two-armed Yoginī no. 30; peacock on pedestal. Kaumārī; Hīrāpur, Orissa

YOGINĪ (योगिनी)

Yoginīs are generally considered to be the attendants of Durgā or Kālī to help her in various jobs. Their names, however, suggest that they represent human passions, feelings and other mental faculties, such as the *kāma, buddhi,* etc., as well. They kill demons also, bestow favour, fulfil desires and remove distress. Although they are more than 200, generally 64 of them are found in temples which are mostly round in shape and are found at places like Bherāghāṭa in Madhya Pradesh and Hīrāpur in Orissa. Views differ on their cultic associations which range from Kaula-Kāpālikas, a *vāmamārgī* Śaiva cult, through Sahaja cult and Nātha Sampradāya. These goddesses are many a time found naked with *yoni* fully opened for worship. And it is for this reason also they are called "Yoginīs." Many of them are also fearful to look at sharing the features of Durgā. These are found either sitting or standing or else dancing. Each of them has her own individual iconographic features.

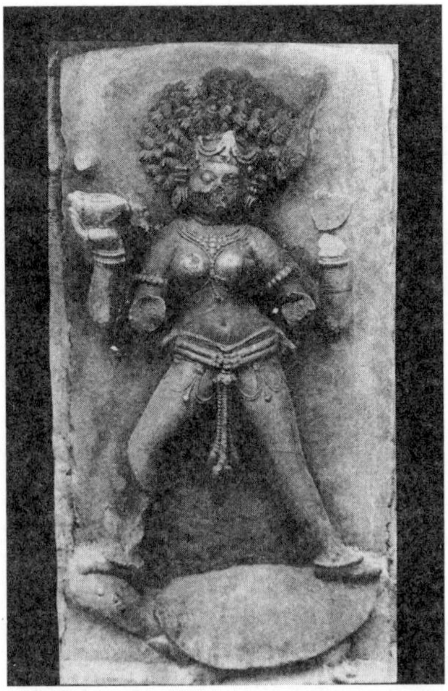

Four-armed Yoginī no. 4 with *jaṭā-maṇḍala;* tortoise, Yamunā; Hīrāpur, Orissa

The Śakti, symbolizing the Female Energy, does not represent a single cult, it is a concept which took various forms in various sects but she figures prominently in Śaiva and Tāntric contexts throughout the country, particularly at Śaktipīṭhas.

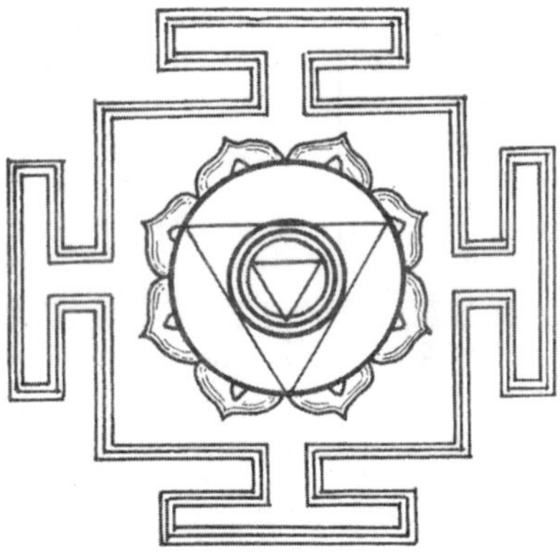

Chinnamastā Yantra, contemporary

THE TANTRA

Indian religious thought and practice has one major component, that of Tantra. Tantra has been defined differently by various ancient authors but by and large it means a science through which we come to know the powers lying hidden in the human body itself. However, now it stands for a system of esoteric practices involving mental and physical faculties in which Śakti is worshipped through Yogic exercises which completely control sexual passion and make the act of copulation, a test for the Tāntrika, redundant since the real *yoga* will make semen flow upwards through different *cakra*s up to the *sahasrāra*, same as the point of *uṣṇīṣa* (उष्णीष) of the Buddha. The Tāntrics in Mediaeval period introduced the practice of *pañca-makāra* or taking *madya* (मद्य), *mīna* (मीन), *maithuna* (मैथुन), etc. It is found in one form or the other in Śaiva, Vaiṣṇava and Bauddha systems of late medieval times.

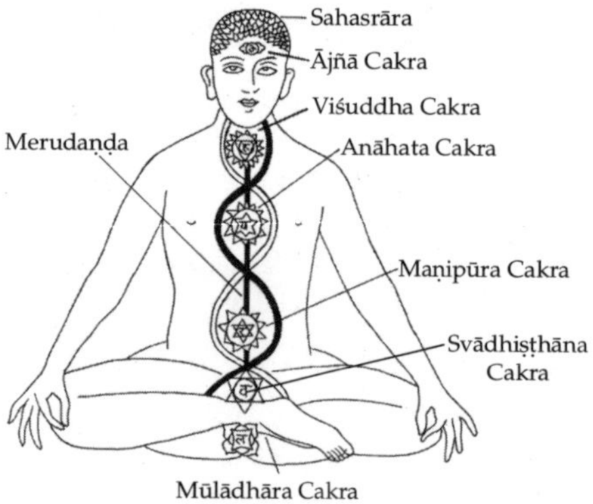

Positions of six *cakra*s in the body

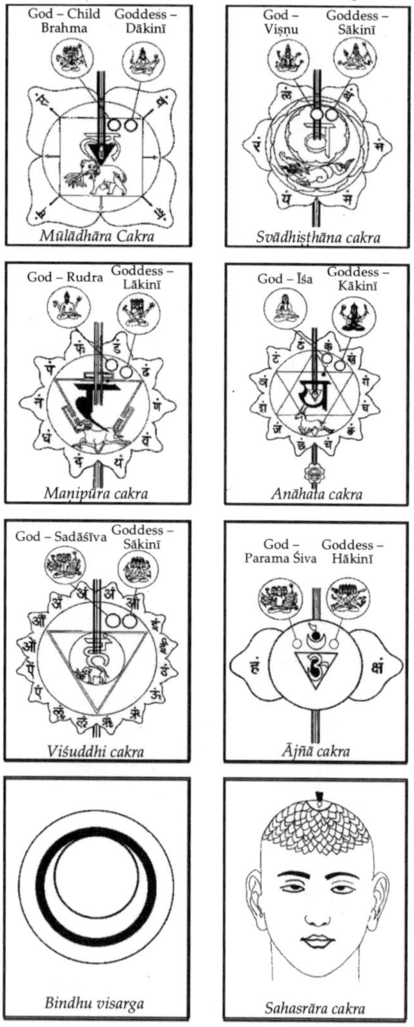

Contemporary

Tantrism, both in Hinduism and Buddhism, is closely related to *yoga* in terms of body-mind control exercises, eight of them, viz. *yama, niyama, āsana, prāṇāyāma, pratyāhāra, dhāraṇā, dhyāna* and *samādhi.* Tantra gives importance to *mantra, yantra, pratibhā* and *siddhi.* However, Tantra and Yoga both lay special emphasis on *ṣaṭacakra, kuṇḍalinī, yoga* and *kuṇḍalinī-siddhi*. The *ṣaṭa* (or six) *cakra*s are common to all Yoga and Tantra concepts. At the base is *mūlādhāra,* located between the anus and the genital, in the form of a coiled serpent, and supports the *merudaṇḍa* or spine. Over this is located the *svādhiṣṭhāna-cakra* which is above the genital. Over this is the *maṇipūra-cakra,* located at the navel. Then follows the *anāhata-cakra,* located in the heart. Over this is the *viśuddhi-cakra,* located at the base of the throat. The sixth *cakra* is called *ājñā-cakra* which is located between the eyebrows. The seventh *cakra* is called *sahasrāra* which resides in the centre of the skull, called *brahmarandhra*; this is the highest centre of vitality. Each one of these seven *cakra*s is like a lotus flower but each with a different number and series of petals as we see in Indian art. Men and women are shown in art with these *cakra*s. Tantra therefore, is not debased as it is taken to be; the roots of Tantra go deep into the *Atharvaveda* and are found even in China in Taoism. In Himalayan

Buddhism, the term *Tantra-Yoga* is, therefore, very popular.

In the *tantra-vidyā*, *yantra*s and *maṇḍala*s also play important roles. A *yantra*, also called *cakra*, is a geometric diagram, formed by lines, dots, deities, human forms, animals, plants, etc. A *yantra* is, according to Tantra Śāstra, angular, consisting of triangles cutting each other, producing rectangles in the process, and ending up in trident-like projections. These figures are filled at specific places with *bījākṣara*s or seed-letters. These letters belong to *mantra*s or spells invoking the power of the god or goddess to which it is addressed. It is a technique of manifestation of a deity and his or her power. The Buddhist Tantras use *dhāriṇī*s which are like the Hindu *mantra*s meant to be recited since "power" is inherent in them. *Maṇḍala* is a circular diagram containing symmetrical configurations of Tāntrika

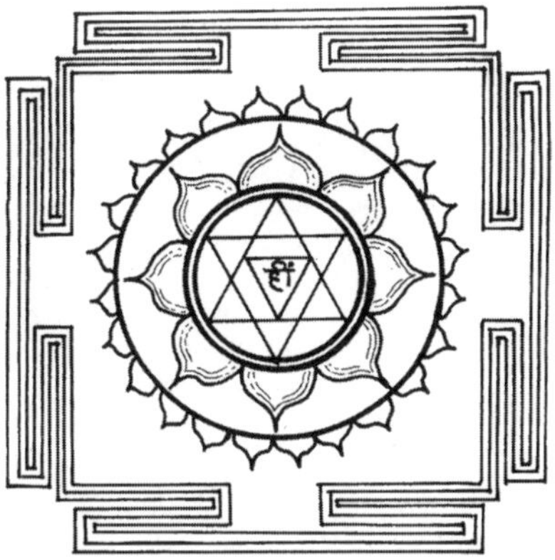

Durgā-Yantra, contemporary

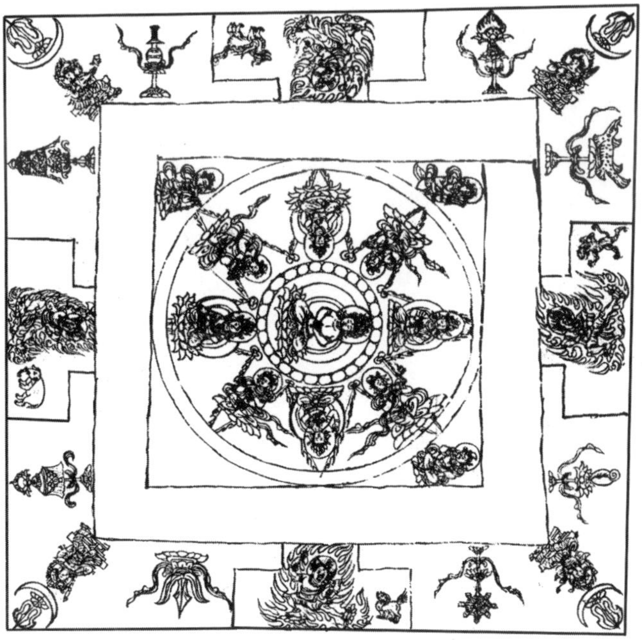

Maṇḍala of five Dhyānī Buddhas, Central Asia, Dun-huang, China, Late 9th century CE

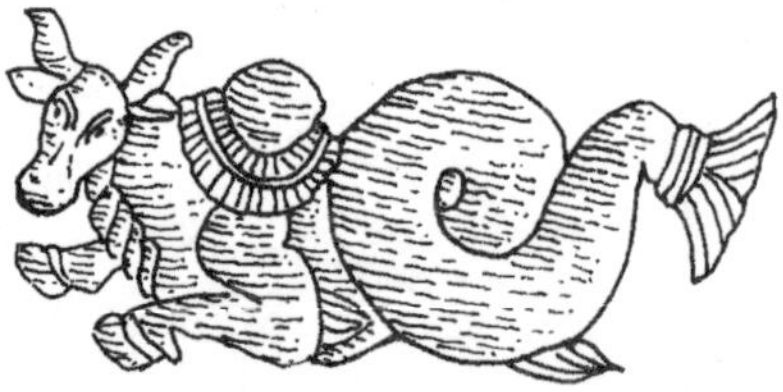

Fish-bull Īhāmṛga, Bharhut, Śuṅga, 2nd century BCE

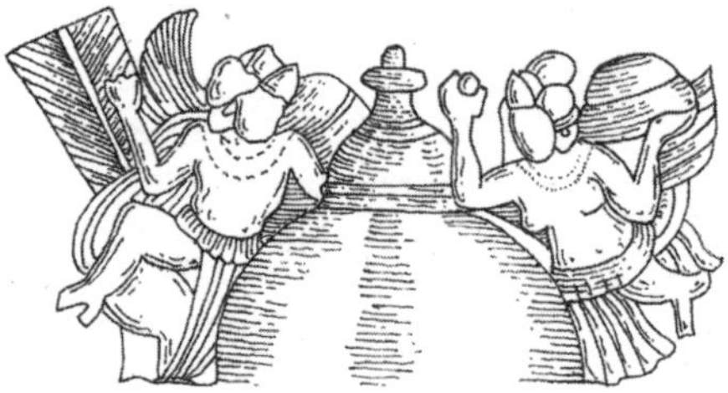

Gandharvas worshipping *stūpa*, Mathurā, U.P., Śuṅga, 1st century BCE

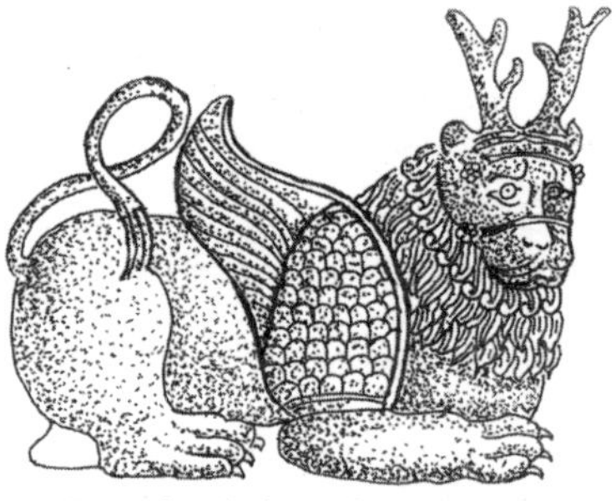

Lion-bird-deer, Sāñcī, M.P., Śuṅga, 1st century BCE

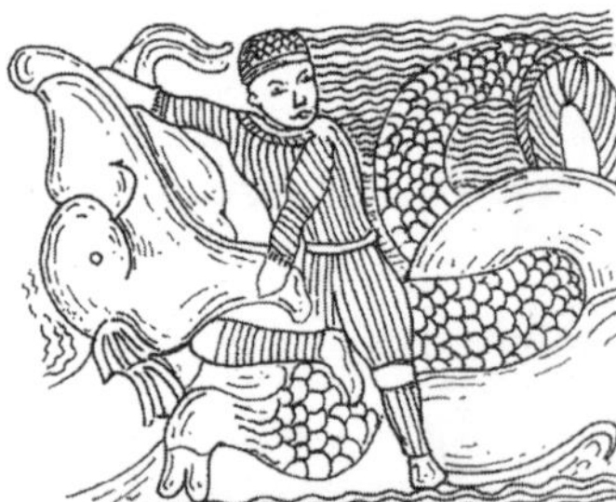

Crocodile-fish, Mathurā, U.P., Kuṣāṇa, 1st century CE

deities and symbols. Buddhist Tāntrikas used it widely by making them on cloth banners. The most popular *yantra* is *śrīyantra* and practically all Śākta Tantras mention it since it is considered to be the unified *yantra* of Śiva and Śakti. This and many other *yantra*s are formed round open-petalled lotuses.

There are many other *yantra*s such as *rakṣā-yantra, durgā-yantra, chinnamastā-yantra, sarvato-bhadra-yantra,* besides the *yantra*s of all the Mahāvidyās and of Brahmā, Viṣṇu and Śiva as well as of Buddhist gods. These *yantra*s, engraved on metallic sheets, are found even inside the Śāktapīṭha shrines in south India. The illustrations of many of these forms are found in the famous text of *Rudrayāmala Tantra.* The Tantra texts have some common topics such as the origin and dissolution of the Universe, ascertainment of *mantra*, installation of deities, description of places of pilgrimage, the duties attached to different stages or *āśrama*s of life, survey of traditional history similar to the Purāṇic approach, *kālacakra*s or cycles of existence, duties of kings, signs of masculinity and femininity, spiritual elevation, etc., which have been classified into four *pada*s or groups of subjects: (i) *jñāna* (philosophical doctrine), (ii) *yoga* (meditation), (iii) *kriyā* (temple building and idol-worship), and (iv) *caryā* (observances and rites).

ĪHĀMṚGA

Somewhat closely related to the *devavāda* is the concept of composite figures called in our texts *īhāmṛga*, a term which normally stands for the mixed human and animal forms. For example Mahiṣāsura has the trunk of human being but the head is of buffalo. Narasiṁha has human body and lion head. Gaṇeśa, Vārāhī, Hayagrīva have the same features. In Greek art there are centaurs with horse's body and male or female human heads. In India similar images are called *kinnara* and *kinnarī* who are heavenly beings. In Indian art there are also *vyāla* figures in which two images from the animal world are crossed — lion's body but parrot's face. In the *Ṛgveda* such images are called *yatu*. In the epics and the Purāṇas the terms *īhāmṛga* and *vyāla* are found occurring together, often interchanging themselves. Kālidāsa also uses these terms which stand for mythical and fabulous forms.

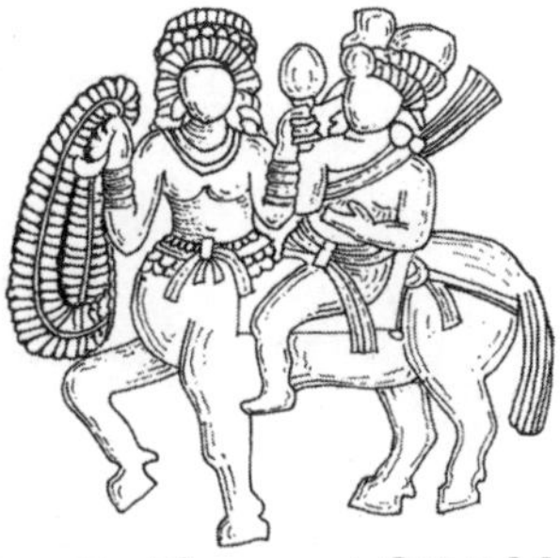

Kinnarī with consort, Sāñcī, M.P., Śuṅga, 2nd century BCE

In Indian art we get *īhāmṛgas* in the form of winged lions, beaked lions, horned lions, winged bulls, bull with elephant face, crocodile with fish-tail, stag with fish-tail, sea-monsters, etc. from the Śuṅga–Sātavāhana–Bactrian Period itself, starting in the second century BCE. Such fabulous figures were earlier found in the Greek, Persian and Assyrian art from the seventh-sixth century BCE. As the decorative elements of pillars, copings, beams, etc., we find them repeatedly occurring all the time in the Śaiva, Vaiṣṇava, Bauddha and Jain contexts.

Mythology: What it is in Hinduism?

The mythologies connected with these gods have been the subject matter for most of the narrative scenes in temples and shrines. Hence, Purāṇas are repeatedly referred to identify them. Mythology, it may be noted, is the product of the collective wisdom of a people grown over a long period of time; it is not a story or novel written by a single author at a single point of time. A mythological story has a moral to convey, one has only to read it in between the lines. Mythology is, therefore, not a fantasy created by an author to entertain people.

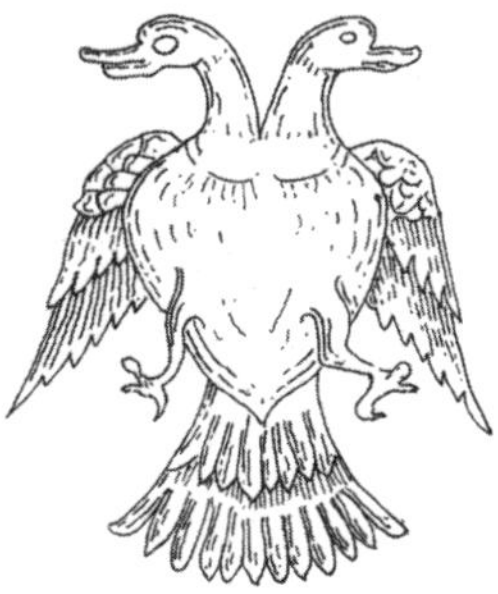

Double Eagle, Taxila, 1st century CE

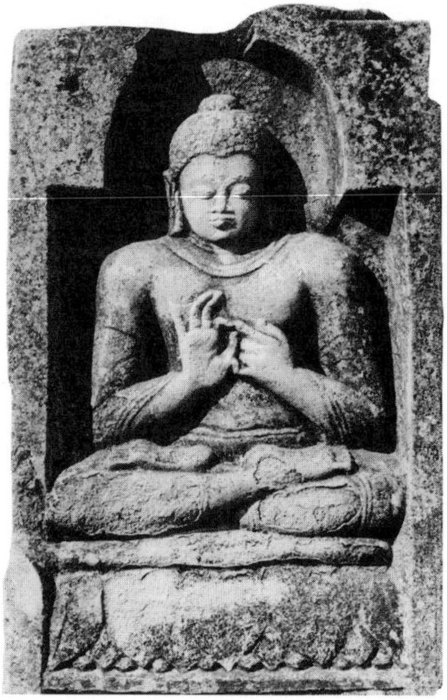

Buddha, Sārnāth, U.P., Gupta, 5th century CE

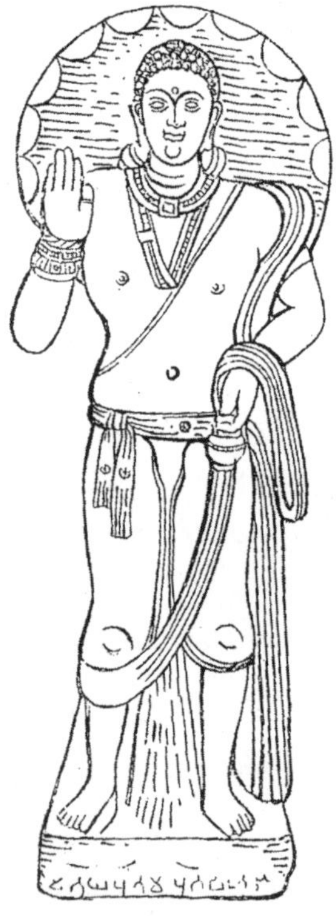

Bodhisattva Maitreya, Mathurā, U.P., Kuṣāṇa, 1st century CE

BUDDHA

Buddha is shown either as shaven-headed, like an ascetic, or else with small curls of hair or with wavy hair with a round bump on the top of the head covered either with locks of hair or else a piece of cloth, called *uṣṇīṣa* (उष्णीष). Very often he is shown with a round *tilaka*-(तिलक) like mark on the forehead. It is called *ūrṇā* (ऊर्णा) formed out of a piece of curled hair. It represents his super-knowledge. His ears are long and on his soles there are several auspicious marks. These are the marks of *mahāpuruṣa*, great or extraordinary human being, called *mahāpuruṣa lakṣaṇa*s (महापुरुष लक्षण).

These normally number 32 though 64 also occur in texts.

Buddha sits on a lotus in *padmāsana* or lotus-posture. He sometimes sits on a *siṁhāsana* (सिंहासन), i.e. a chair with two lions, one on either side, generally front legs or hands shaped as lions. Below the seat is *dharmacakra* (धर्मचक्र) or the Wheel of Dharma, sometimes flanked with two stags representing the forest of stags, called *mṛgadāva* (मृगदाव), at Sārnāth, where he gave his first Sermon. Since Buddha belonged to the *śramaṇa paramparā* (श्रमण परम्परा) or ascetic tradition, he was never shown with his consort although he was married.

BODHISATTVA

In Buddhism, besides Buddha, *bodhisattva*s (बोधिसत्त्व) are also worshipped. In China and Japan very often *bodhisattva*s are independently worshipped. These images are usually shown with crown on the head, ornaments in the neck and pensive in mood, representing his period of princehood. The *bodhisattva*s, according to Buddhism, were the personages who refused *nirvāṇa* (निर्वाण) or salvation for themselves although they were capable of achieving it. They also refused to leave the worldly affairs, instead assumed the role of the Saviour of the Humanity for serving the suffering human beings who are in fact suffering due to ignorance.

BUDDHIST TRIRATNA

In Buddhism three things are most important — Buddha (बुद्ध) himself, his *dhamma* (धम्म) or religious teachings and the *saṁgha* (संघ), i.e. the monastic order; all human beings are asked to take refuge in them. It is called *triratna* (त्रिरत्न) or Three Jewels representing Buddha, Dharma and Saṁgha.

In Buddhist art scenes from the life of the Buddha and the *Jātaka* (जातक) stories, i.e. stories connected with the previous lives of the Buddha, around 500 of them are very popular. There are other stories also, called *avadāna*s (अवदान), which also form the themes of art.

JINA

*Jina*s (जिन) or *tīrthaṁkara*s (तीर्थंकर) may be naked or wearing a white dress. When naked they represent the Digambara (दिगम्बर) sect but when wearing cloth they represent Śvetāmbara (श्वेताम्बर) sect. *Jina*'s seat is lotus as that of the Buddha and other gods. However, each of the 24 *tīrthaṁkara*s, i.e. deified saints, has one mark of cognisance, often on the seat, like *śaṅkha* on the seat represents the 22nd Tīrthaṁkara Neminātha, while tortoise on the seat represents the 20th Tīrthaṁkara Muni Subrata. *Tīrthaṁkara*s are also distinguished by their own pairs of *yakṣa*s (यक्ष) and *yakṣī*s, called *śāsana-devatās* (शासनदेवता), the protectors of *jina*. Since the *tīrthaṁkara*s, like Buddha, also belonged to the *muni* or *yati* or *tapasvī* (तपस्वी), i.e. *śramaṇa paramparā* (श्रमण परम्परा), i.e. the ascetic tradition starting from the

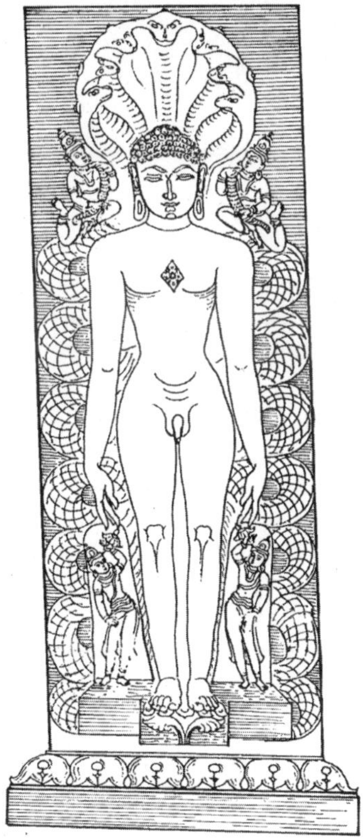

Jain Tīrthaṁkara Ṛṣabhadeva, Mathurā, U.P., Gupta, 5th century CE

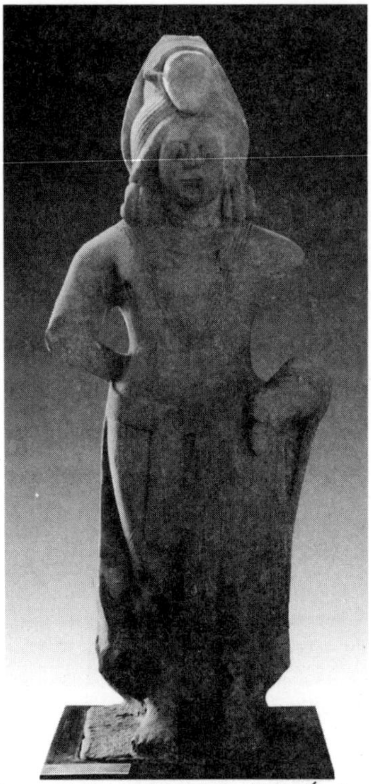

Agni Yakṣa, Mathurā, U.P., Śuṅga, 2nd century BCE

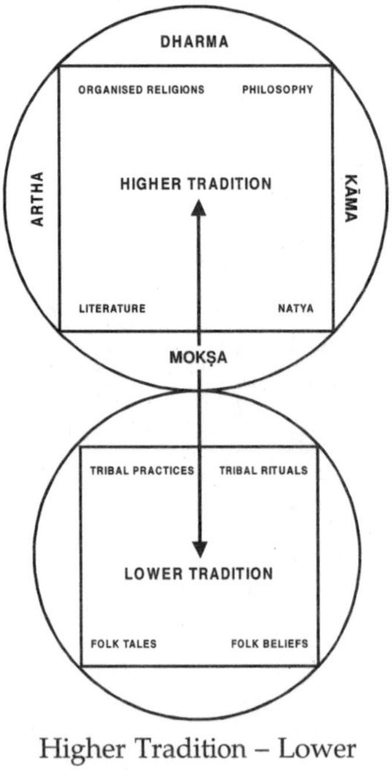

Higher Tradition – Lower Tradition Interaction

Ṛgvedic times, they were also not shown with consorts.

It may be noted that while the images of the Digambara sect are naked and with no ornaments to adorn them, the images of the Śvetāmbara sect are decked with a variety of ornaments, including *kirīṭa mukuṭa*. All these were, of course, the later developments. In the second and first centuries BCE even the Jainas offered prayers through eight auspicious symbols, called *aṣṭa māṅgalika cihnas* (अष्ट मांगलिक चिह्न), generally engraved on stone tablets or *āyāga-paṭṭas*, i.e. *phalakas*. These are *svastika* (स्वस्तिक), *divyamāna* (दिव्यमान), *śrīvatsa* (श्रीवत्स), *ratna-bhāṇḍa* (रत्नभाण्ड), *padma* (पद्म), *bhadrapīṭha* (भद्रपीठ) or *indrayaṣṭi* (इन्द्रयष्टि), *pūrṇa-kumbha* (पूर्णकुम्भ) and *matsya* (मत्स्य). We find them on a stone tablet from Kaṅkālī Ṭīlā at Mathurā.

Basic Nature of Indian Art

Indian art has been the product of Indian culture as the Greek art has been the product of Greek culture or the Roman art has been the product of Roman culture. Indian culture, however, has been the product of two streams of thoughts and practices, one, the folk, belonging to the oral traditions operating at the folk level in the villages, and the other, classical, belonging to the sophisticated literary traditions; the former is sometimes called "Lower Tradition" and the latter "Higher Tradition."

"LOWER TRADITION" AND "HIGHER TRADITION" INTERACTION

The two traditions are not exclusive to each other; the roots of the Higher Tradition lay in the Lower Tradition or Little Tradition, as anthropologists name it. In other words, items like snake worship, tree worship, water worship, spirit worship, mother goddess worship, etc. which usually characterize the Lower Tradition, are picked up by the practitioners of the Higher Tradition and assimilated in their own belief-systems by inventing mythologies. Thus, *yakṣas* (यक्ष) and *yakṣīs* (यक्षी) characterize all religions from the Vedic times. A snake was called "Mucalinda" and incorporated in the life-history of Buddha as his saviour against heavy rains. Another snake was called "Śeṣanāga" (शेषनाग) on whose coils Viṣṇu was shown reclining. Pārśvanātha, the 23rd *tīrthaṁkara*, had the snake with open hoods at his back. There was thus an upward mobility in the case of gods and goddesses of the Lower Tradition. The two traditions were, thus, complementary to each other.

SOME TECHNICAL ASPECTS

Engraving, Relief and In-the-round

The Indian art had many technical aspects. Some are engravings and etchings, some are peckings, while others are sculptures in low or high relief. Some are also images in-the-round. One category is pseudo-round, i.e. although the back is also carved it is flattish and schematic in comparison to the frontal part of the body even though garments and ornaments are carved on them. Most of the *yakṣa* and *yakṣī* images belonging to the third century BCE to first century CE time-bracket fall in the category of "pseudo-round."

Many of the high-relief sculptures show deep undercutting, particularly when the figures are shown in partial or three-fourth profile filled with the element of animation. Such figures give false impression or illusion of figures in-the-round. However, by casting light and shadow in the day-time due to the changing positions of sunlight, this

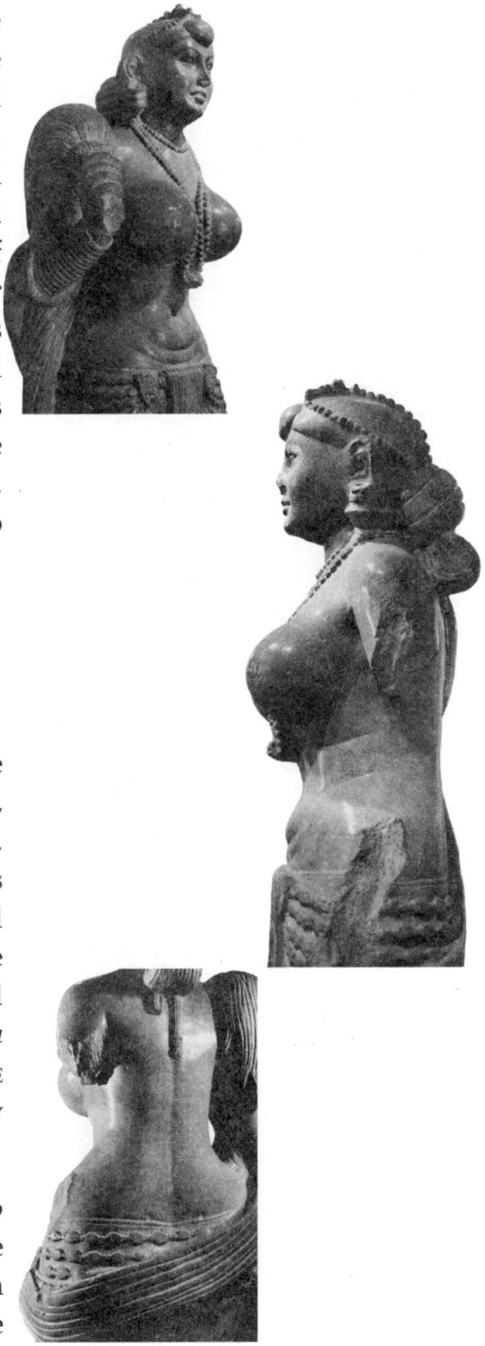

Yakṣī, sculpture in the round Didārgañj, Patna, Bihar, Mauryan, 3rd century BCE

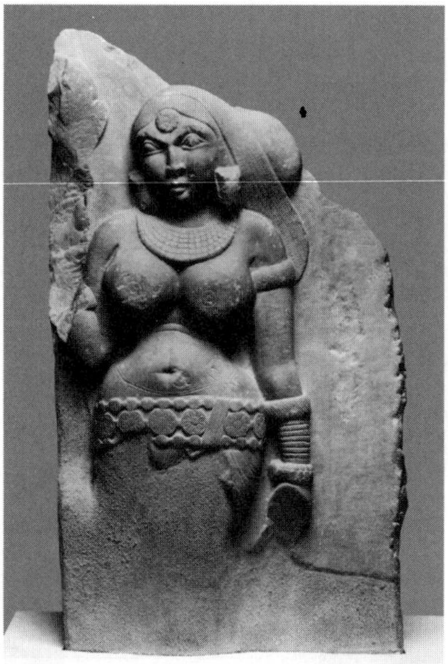

Yakṣī in low relief, Amarāvatī, A.P., 2nd century BCE

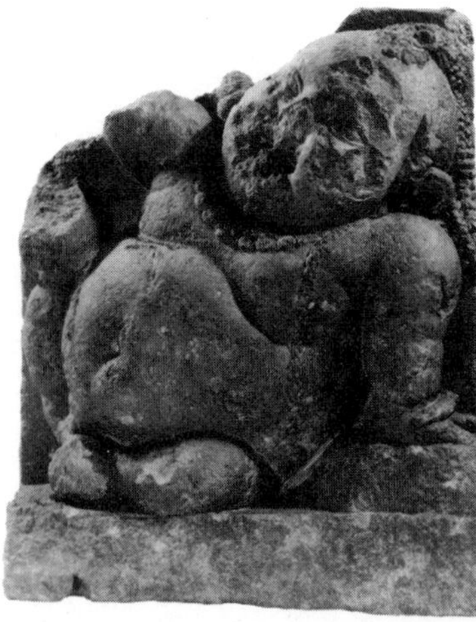

Gaṇa (weightlessness), Nagardan, Maharashtra, Vākāṭaka, 5th century CE

technique created extremely enchanting figures.

Stencil Style

Carving on temples has one more style, called "Stencil Style." In this technique the entire surface remains plain but the cutting of figures and designs is done deep into the stone. The carvings on the *śikhara*s of the Hindu temples are done in this style. Later day Islamic art used this technique in abundance, as one can see in the carvings of Qutab Minar.

Perspective and Weightlessness in Body

When figures are composed in groups some consideration to perspective and depth (things in the background are shorter in size than the things in the foreground even though they may be of equal size, because of optical illusion), poise and gaiety (standing at an angle with the hips a lot thinner than the chest), visual weight and weightlessness (heavy body *versus* light body) is given. But most of these elements of great art developed slowly and gradually, over a period of 800 years, from the Mauryas of the third century BCE to the Guptas of CE 500. Further refinement of details took 500 years more, around CE 1100 the Candelas of Madhya Pradesh at Khajurāho and the Coḷas at Thañjāvur and Gaṅgaikoṇḍacoḷapuram developed the sculptural art in stone and bronze to its greatest height. For 300 years this graph continued to rise but after CE 1300 craftsmanship started replacing the virtues of artistic creations with spirituality reflecting itself in the face which the onlooker himself or herself experiences. The Vijayanagar (fourteenth century) and the Nāyaka (sixteenth century) schools of art are more or less the examples of highly stylized art.

PAINTINGS

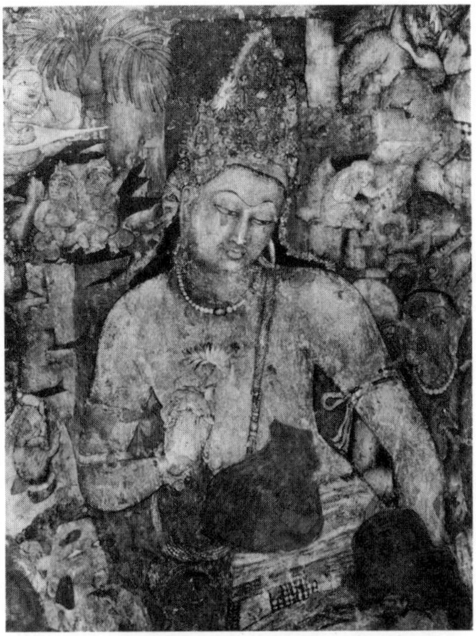

Wall painting of Bodhisattva Padmapāṇi in a cave-shrine, Ajantā, Maharashtra, Gupta, 5th century CE

Painting has all along been a very powerful medium of art in India as in most of the countries of the world. It is easier to execute a painting than to carve a sculpture. That is why even the Stone Age men in France, Spain and India decorated their caves and rock-shelters and also expressed their beliefs with paintings done in a variety of colours made out of the local earths and minerals applied directly on the rock surface. Madhya Pradesh is the paradise of these rock-shelter paintings depicting animals as well as scenes of everyday life, such as hunting, dancing and cooking. There are also scenes of worship of natural objects and animals. The most famous group of painted rock-shelters is located at Bhīmbeṭkā in Raisen District. However, such shelters are found in most of the Indian states, including Uttar Pradesh, Bihar, Tamil Nadu, Karnataka and Kerala.

There are three terms used in Sanskrit literature for pictures: *citra* (चित्र) = image in the round; *ardha-citra* (अर्धचित्र) = image in relief, low relief (French: Bas relief) and high relief; and *citrābhāsa* (चित्राभास) = painting in which some attempt is made to create an impression of third dimension through the use of light and shade of colours in a picture drawn by line-sketch.

In commentory of Yaśodhara on Kāmasūtra of Vātsyāyana six limbs or *ṣaḍāṅga* (षडांग) have been described which make a painting beautiful. These are:

1. *Pramāṇam* (प्रमाणम्) = Correct perception of the objects being painted in terms of overall structure of anatomy of men, women, animals, etc. and their measurements. It includes even the element of perspective.

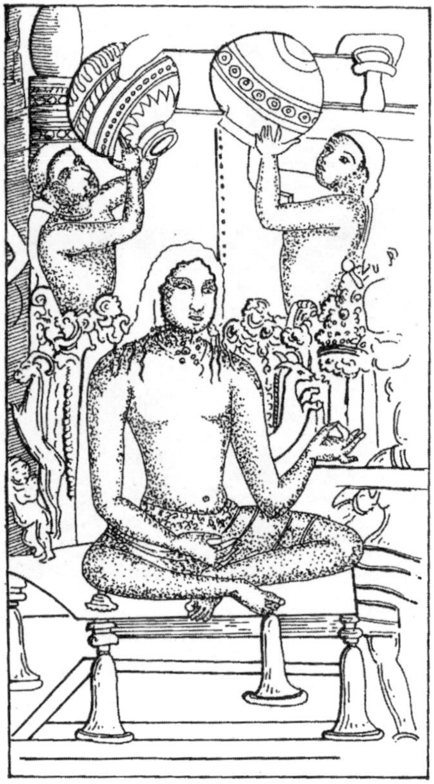

Snāna, Painting, Ajantā, Maharashtra, 5th century CE

2. *Rūpabheda* (रूपभेद) = The perfect knowledge of all the differences in the appearances of figures, natural and man-made, or subject matter which constitute the picture to be drawn and painted.

3. *Sādṛśyam* (सादृश्यम्) = It is the element of similitude, i.e. faithfully copying the items of painting.

4. *Bhāva* (भाव) = It stands for the faithful and effective depiction of the inner feeling of all the living creatures being painted; if it is a narrative painting, then as the situation demands from an actor of the play at a particular moment being caught in the picture. It, therefore, also relates to all doings in the world.

5. *Lāvaṇya yojanam* (लावण्य योजनम्) = Infusion of gracefulness, beauty and charm in the figures.

6. *Varṇikābhaṅga* (वर्णिकाभंग) = Artistic manner of using the brush and colours. It relates to the perfection in techniques being used by the painter artist.

Citralakṣaṇa (चित्रलक्षण), another treatise on painting, gives us precise rules for making pictures of divine beings and kings, and also general rules for others. For example, it tells us that the standard faces should be quadrangular, sharply outlined, beautifully finished with shining and splendid attributes.

> It should not be made triangular, or crooked, nor should it be made oval or round. Whosoever has painted a face accordingly will constantly possess blessings. For ordinary

men a face longing after peace, lengthy or round, or triangular, etc. may be used . . . the hair on the head of a lord of men or of the gods should be fine and curly, and painted a heavenly blue.

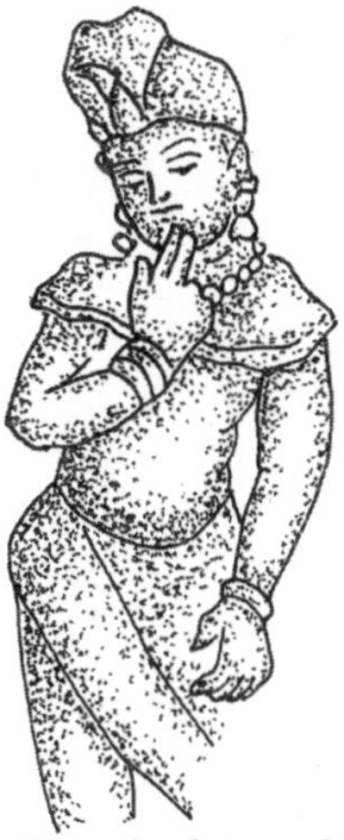

Adbhuta Rasa, Sculpture, Mathurā, 1st century CE

Nine Rasas (नव रस)

*Rasaśāstra*s talk about nine *rasa*s or juices, i.e. emotional status in *kāvya*s (काव्य) which apply to all forms of artistic creations. These are: (i) *śṛṅgāra* (शृंगार) or love-making sentiment. It includes *vātsalya* (वात्सल्य) also, (ii) *hāsya* (हास्य) or comic sentiment, (iii) *karuṇa* (करुण) or sentiment of pathos, (iv) *raudra* (रौद्र) or ferocious sentiment, (v) *vīra* (वीर) or heroic sentiment, (vi) *bhayānaka* (भयानक) or terrible sentiment, (viii) *bībhatsya* (बीभत्स्य) or odious sentiment, (viii) *adbhuta* (अद्‌भुत) or marvellous sentiment, (ix) *śānta* (शांत) or quiescent sentiment.

It may, therefore, be seen that in ancient India proper guidelines were worked out by experts for the newcomers in the profession.

Tempera and Fresco Techniques

During the second and first centuries BCE, organized religions, such as Buddhism, employed the medium of painting to propagate their belief-systems. In Ajantā caves Nos. 9 and 10, for example, there are the remains of paintings depicting scenes of the *Chadanta Jātaka* (छदन्त जातक) done in a style which reflects the style of stone sculptures of the Śuṅga–Sātavāhana period seen in the caves of Pītalkhorā in Maharashtra and other sites in northern India. Other cave paintings at Ajantā, Bāgh, etc. belong to Gupta–Vākāṭaka period of fifth century CE. And the third series belongs to the Early Cāḷukya period of sixth-seventh centuries. The

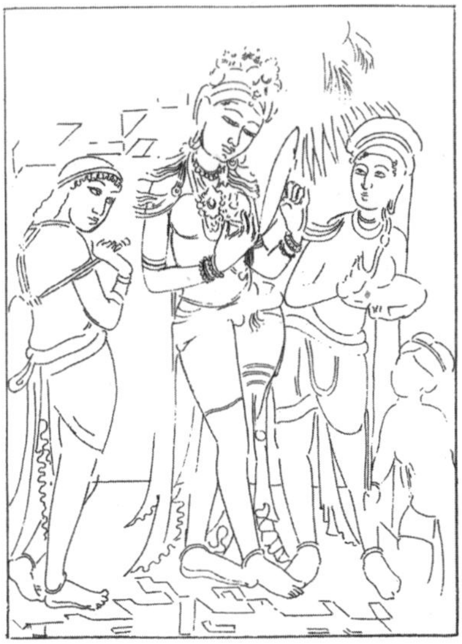

Śṛṅgāra, Painting, Ajantā, Maharashtra, Gupta, 5th century CE

tradition of Buddhist cave paintings continues even in the Hindu temples as well as the palaces of kings in all the major subsequent periods, the remains of which are still preserved in south India.

The Ajantā paintings done in tempera technique in which paints are applied on the dry clay or lime plaster covering the rock-surface, depict men, women, animals, floral motifs and geometric patterns in a variety of colours and in a variety of moods from sacred to profane. The strong points of these paintings are the use of free flowing lines for delineating beautiful figures and their delicate inner feelings, the use of shading different parts of the body to produce three-dimensional effect in images, and the use of proper colours, sometimes contrasting and sometimes matching to create magical effect. It is called "chiaroscuro."

Ajantā, near the village called Ajinṭhā (अजिन्ठा), is the ideal-most place for the proper study of the classical art and architecture of India — painting and sculpture, as well as monasteries, temples and caves, all at one place. Not too far from Ajantā is the site of Ellorā (एलोरा) where rock-cut art and architecture of Buddhist, Jain and Hindu origin, belonging to the period of eighth-ninth centuries, excelled. The huge rock-cut Kailāsa Temple is the marvel of the world.

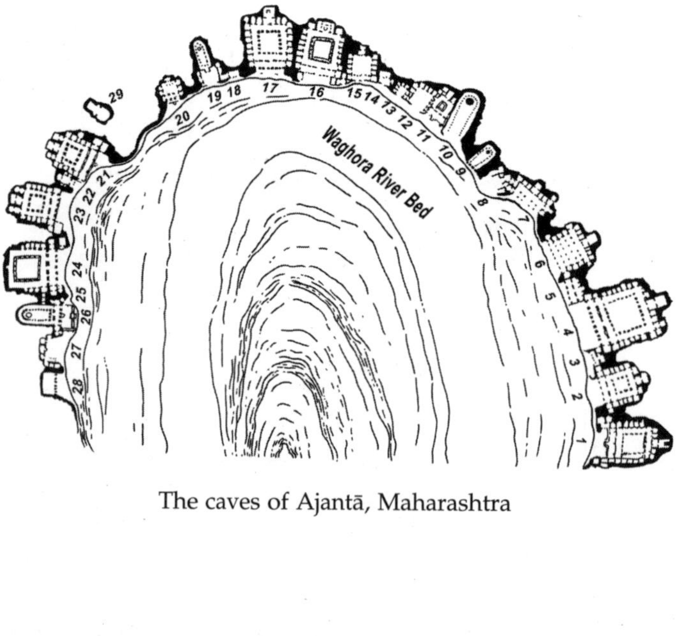

The caves of Ajantā, Maharashtra

The tradition of wall paintings continued in post-Gupta–Cāḷukya periods both in the south and the north in caves, temples and dwelling houses. In Coḷa temples there are many fresco paintings.

From the twelfth-century manuscripts on palm leaf as well as on paper were also beautifully illustrated with paintings, particularly those belonging to Jainism and found in western India, mainly in Gujarat. Cloth was also used for making paintings.

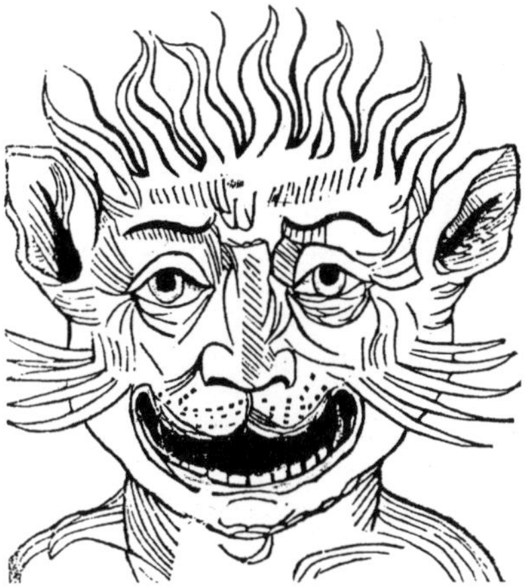

Devil's head in 1484 German edition of Mandeville (courtesy: Partha Mitter)

Differing Attitudes Towards Indian Art

THE LOVE AND HATE OF THE WEST

One should not think that the Indian art and architecture had favourable appreciation in the West from the times the Europeans started coming to India. In fact, for centuries together, almost from thirteenth century when Marco Polo came to India on his way to China, through the early twentieth century, the West was most uncharitable to Indian art in spite of the fact that from the eighteenth century itself Sanskrit classics were translated in English and greatly appreciated, such as the *Abhijñānaśākuntalam* (अभिज्ञान-शाकुन्तलम्) of Kālidāsa. Even *Bhagavad Gītā* (भगवद् गीता) was translated and greatly appreciated. Even scholars like Ruskin and Goethe abhorred Indian art. This *internal contradiction* in the Western attitude towards the Indian culture in which Sanskrit literature is superb in quality but its product, the Indian art, is debased, was resolved only from the 1920s when scholars like Havell, Bachhofer, Coomaraswamy, Stella Kramrisch and others started looking at the Indian art from Indian point of view and discarding the yardstick of Greek art to measure the quality of Indian art. In the beginning Indian art of Hindu and Buddhist idols was considered "monstrous" depicting "devils" with many heads, many hands and awfully looking countenance but now these are taken to be very gracious and highly meaningful in terms of

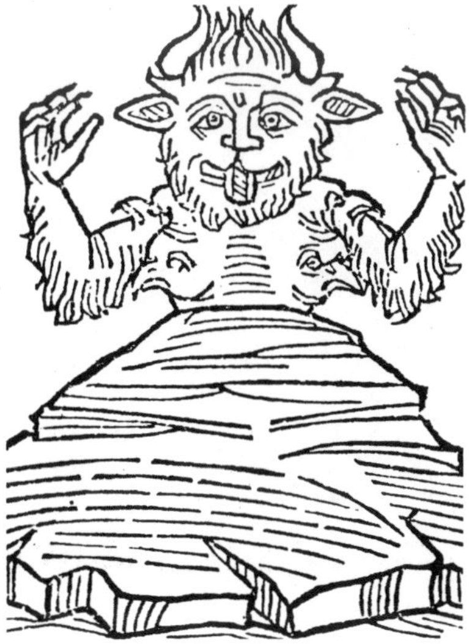

Devil's head in 1482 German edition of Mandeville (courtesy: Partha Mitter)

humanity and spiritualism because it has been realized that the techniques applied to demonstrate the superhuman qualities of god should not be at all be confused with the "form" of god himself and the meaning that the "form" is intended to convey.

The Role of European Travellers Coming with Christian Bias

This change in attitude has not been sudden. Earlier, for almost 500 years European travellers to India, who were Christians, judged the Indian art from the Christian point of view in which the concept of hell and *śaitāna* (शैतान) was predominant. Those who were scholars tried the Greek classical model to judge the Indian art.

Both the approaches failed because a culture is a unique creation of its originators and practitioners, hence the art that a culture produces has necessarily to be evaluated within the parameters of its own cultural norms. Once this was realized, things became easy for the serious scholars of Indian art all over the world. It became clear to all of them that for the Hindu the image or *mūrti* (मूर्ति) is not God at all, it is just a *bimba* (बिम्ब) or reflection of the real, hence unreal, the image has a very small and limited purpose to serve — to concentrate on the Godhood behind the idol. It is, thus, temporary. It is transitory. And, therefore, an image when judged aesthetically is an entirely different matter, it has to be completely dissociated from the religious aspects which the images are supposed to be portraying.

Indian approach

A.K. Coomaraswamy, the greatest exponent of the virtue of Indian art in the West, aptly observes:

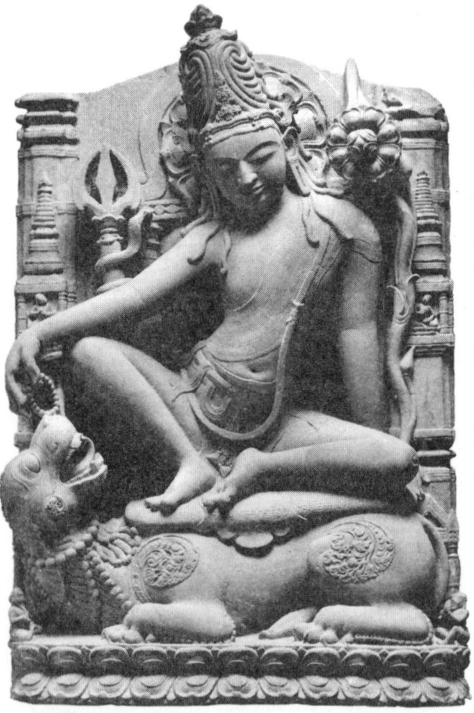

Siṁhanāda, Nālandā, Bihar, 10th century CE

> The immediate purpose of Indian civilization is not *nirvāṇa* or *mokṣa* (मोक्ष), but *dharma;* not a desertion of the household life, but the fulfilment of functions. And here, in *karmayoga* (कर्मयोग), the spiritual support is found, not in pure knowledge, but in devotion to higher powers, personally conceived, and directly approached by appropriate offerings (*pūjā*) (पूजा) and means (*sādhanā*) (साधना).

However, it must be clearly understood that ancient Indian art combined in its personality both the mind and the matter, that is, ideas and forms merged into one, often supported by technical excellence. This is called "stone turned into image, image that stirs your heart as well as mind and takes them together to the eternal bliss" *saccidānanda* (सच्चिदानन्द).

That is why it is said that in ancient India art was just not for art's sake, the urge to carve or paint emerged from the deep sense of spirituality combined happily with the intense desire to live a life of fulfilment in terms of materialistic enjoyments. Other-worldliness was the ultimate goal but worldliness was the immediate concern. *Preyaṣ* (प्रेयष्) and *śreyaṣ* (श्रेयष्) co-exist.

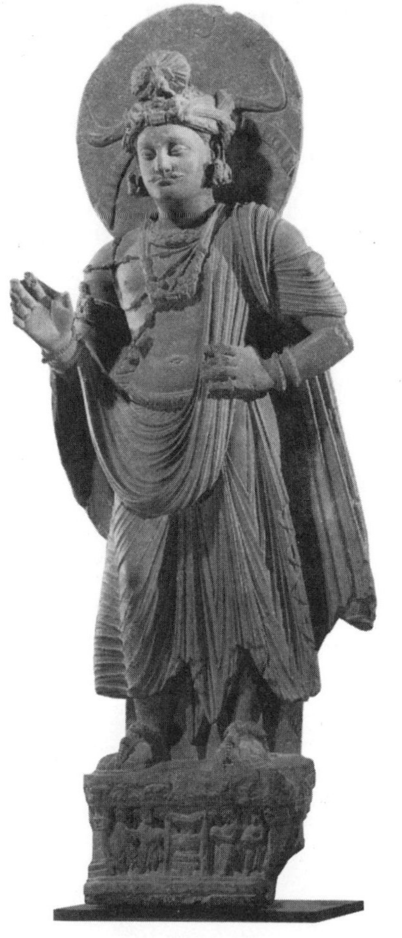

Bodhisattva, schist, Gandhāra,
2nd century CE

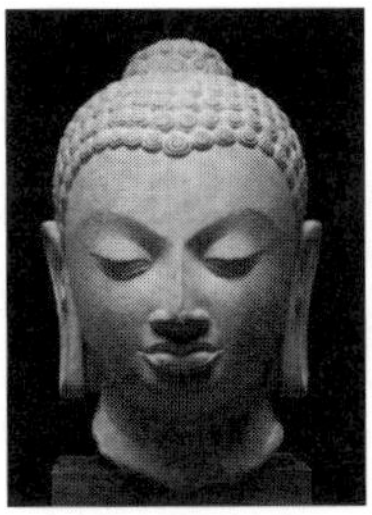

4

Indian Art in Historical Perspective

The Terminology

"ICON," "Image" and "Idol" are the three commonly used terms in English language for the objects of ritualistic worship and spiritual experience in Hinduism. These are also freely used in the context of other religions. But in fact these are not inter-changeable, *image* or *pratimā* alone is basic to the concept of God as one sees Him since it alone means the "true mental picture" of "an object of desire." *Idol*, on the other hand, stands for a kind of object which only "represents" god. *Icon* (which comes from Greek word *eikon*) means any "sign" which "resembles" the god it represents. For a Hindu, the object of worship is neither God, nor a "god," nor it "represents" or else "resembles" god. Instead, it is the true "image" of his god, it is *bimba* (बिम्ब), complete reflection, it is *pratimā* (प्रतिमा) or *mūrti* or image, it is the full-fledged or complete reflection of the moon in clear water and it is the concrete form of the mental image of his *iṣṭa-devatā* (इष्ट-देवता). It is the god of his desire. But it itself is not God or god. This is precisely the reason why *iconography* is only an apology for the term *mūrti-vijñāna* (मूर्ति-विज्ञान) since "icon" is not *mūrti*, it is only symbol. The term, however, now stands for the scientific or systematic study of the images or *pratimā* so often conceived in ancient Indian religions. We, therefore, prefer the

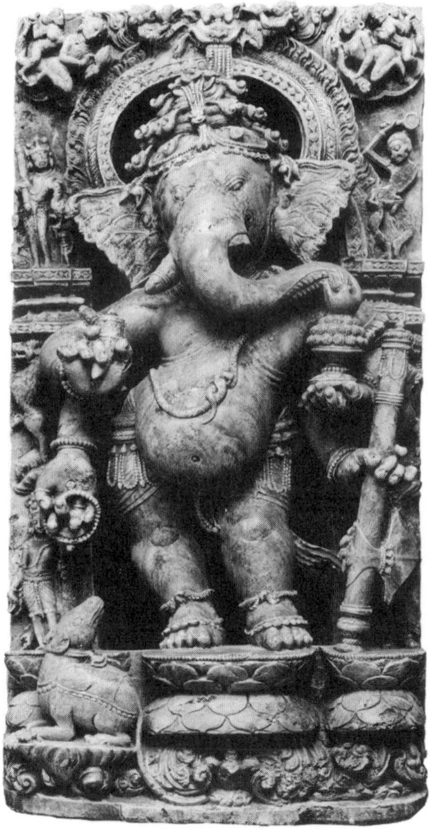

Gaṇeśa, Bhubaneswar, Orissa, 11th century CE

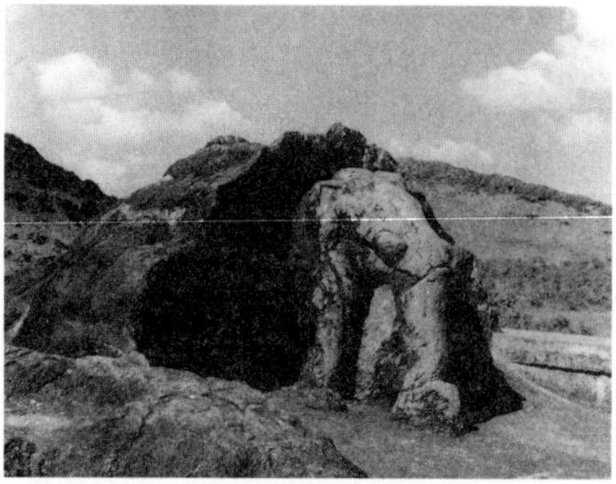

Rock-cut Elephant, Dhaulī, Orissa, Mauryan, 3rd century BCE

term *pratimā* or "image" for our use here keeping in mind that for a devotee of his or her personal god it is the *bimba* or reflection of that god. As we as individuals cannot see and identify ourselves except through the image or reflection that we see in the mirror so do we identify our gods through the images we ultimately start worshipping. Iconography further particularizes these gods.

Vedic Heritage

"Images" in India, in the sense of complete reflections of conceptual entities, undoubtedly existed in the Early Vedic period. But from the times of the *Ṛgveda* to the times of Pāṇini of 500 BCE we have hardly any archaeological evidence to prove that the images described therein were translated into any material medium — the gods Indra, Mitra, Varuṇa, etc. remain in verbal pictures. Similarly, not that the mother goddesses like Aditi (अदिति) and Pṛthvī (पृथ्वी) were not conceived by the Vedic seers, these are in fact graphically described in the Vedas — in fact the Vedas give us a very long list of the *devatās* (देवता), Candra, Sūrya, Agni, Soma, Vāyu, Jala, etc. and many natural items of environment which directly support human and animal life on the earth, a system of beliefs sometimes called Paganism in Western parlance but they are doubtfully represented in sculpture and painting during this period.

The earliest material remains of imagery are terracottas. Terracottas have their own story to tell in the entire history of Indian imagery both content-wise and form-wise. The interaction of this tradition with other traditions of plastic art starts only when from the Mauryan period the tradition of stone sculptures emerges as its most powerful competitor, at least in the elite. It is precisely at that point that

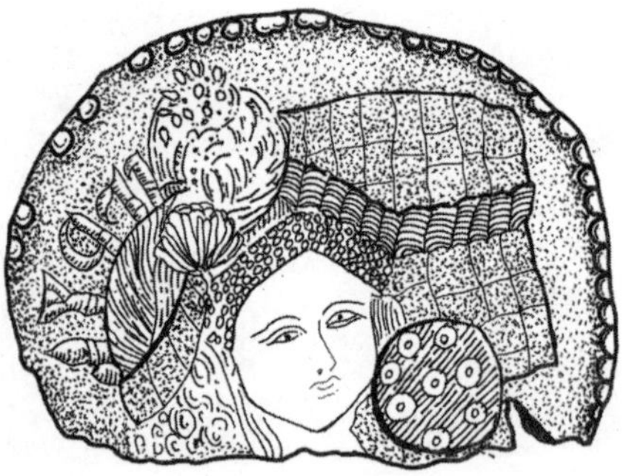

Sinīvalī, terracotta, Śuṅga, 2nd century BCE

the concepts and forms popular with the terracotta makers enter into the tradition of stone sculptures and vice versa. But, and this is very significant, neither all the concepts and forms popular with the terracotta makers entered into the *ateliers* (workshops) of stone sculptors nor all the concepts and forms popular in the workshops of the stone sculptors entered into the potters' houses. The interaction was two-way but limited and selective on the part of both the groups of artistes, the folk and the elite.

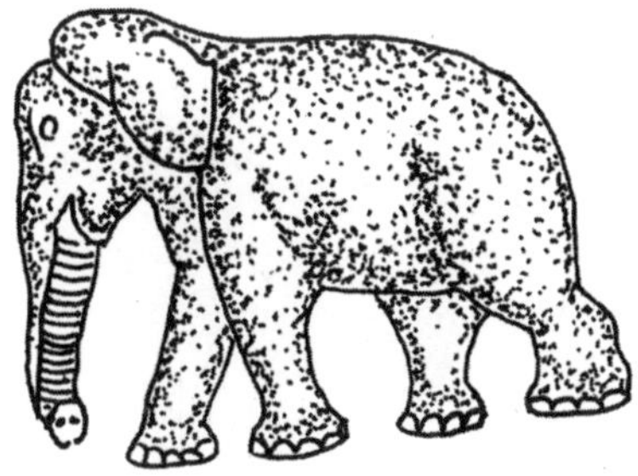

Elephant on abacus of a Mauryan pillar, Sārnāth, 3rd century BCE

MAURYAN ART (Fourth-Third Centuries BCE)

Aśoka's own efforts to articulate his preference in stone was not of the Vedic order although it was not totally devoid of the Vedic cultural heritage just as Buddhism, his favourite religion, was not devoid of Vedic cultural heritage; in the origins of Buddhism, the later Vedic heritage of the Upaniṣads had a significant role to play. Thus, although Aśoka did not initiate the stone sculptures of Indra, Agni, Sūrya, and others, he did cause the *dharma-stambha*s (धर्म-स्तम्भ) or the pillars of piety, with four *mahāpaśu*s (महापशु) or sacred animals (the bull, the horse, the lion and the elephant), *dharmacakra* or wheel representing *dharma*, *haṁsa* (हंस) (goose), *pīpala* leaf *aśvattha* (अश्वत्थ) and lotus (*padma*) depicted on them in a variety of combinations. As we know, each of these was traditionally sacred to the Indian people, the Vedic as well as non-Vedic. What is to be noted in this context, is, however, something else: the Vedic gods were conceived in human form, the Buddha himself was a human being, the terracotta tradition had human forms, but with Aśoka it did not appear to have found much favour. The reason for the comparative absence of anthropomorphic

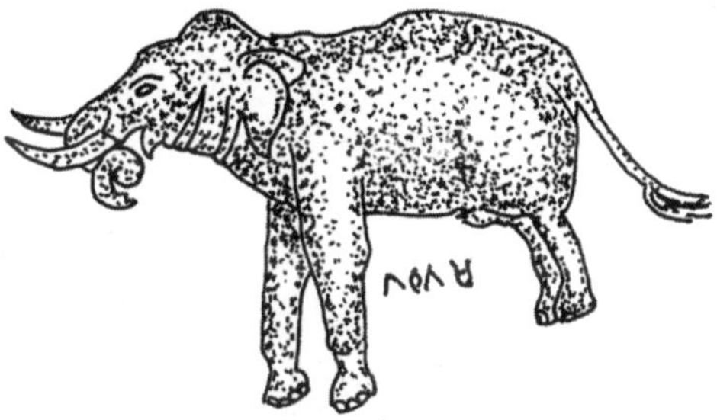

Elephant bearing "gajatame" inscription, Kalsī rock-engraving, U.P., 3rd century BCE

Nāgapuṣpa on Mauryan pillar abacus, 3rd century BCE

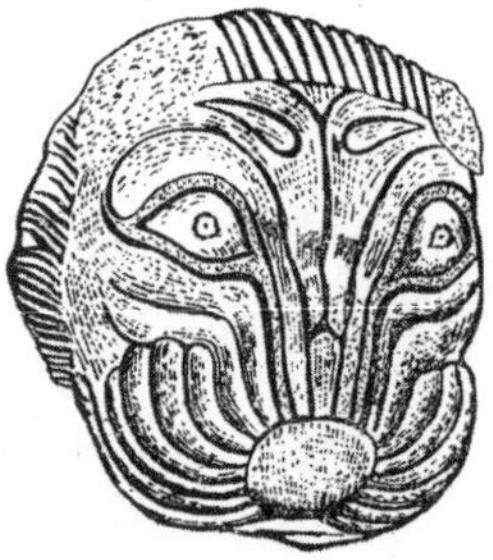

Lion-face, Pāṭaliputra, Bihar, 3rd century BCE

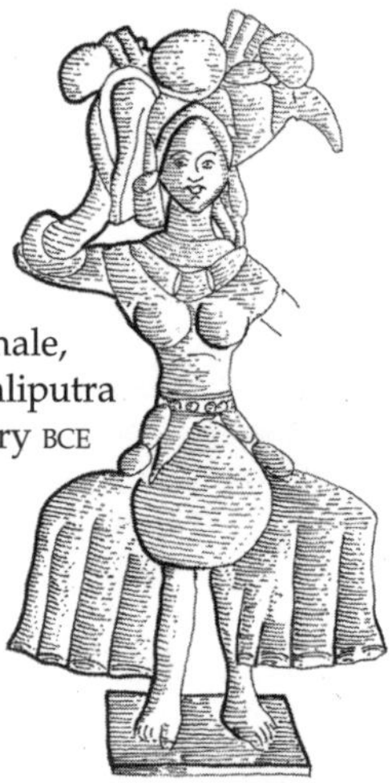

Terracotta, female, Bulandībāgh, Pāṭaliputra Bihar, 3rd century BCE

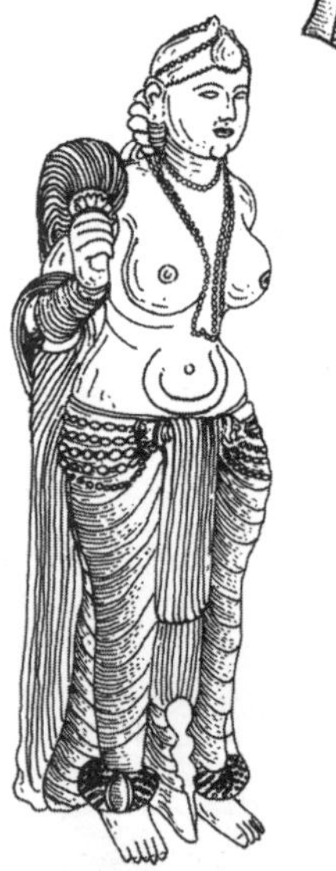

Yakṣī, from Dīdārgañj, Pāṭaliputra, Bihar, 3rd century BCE

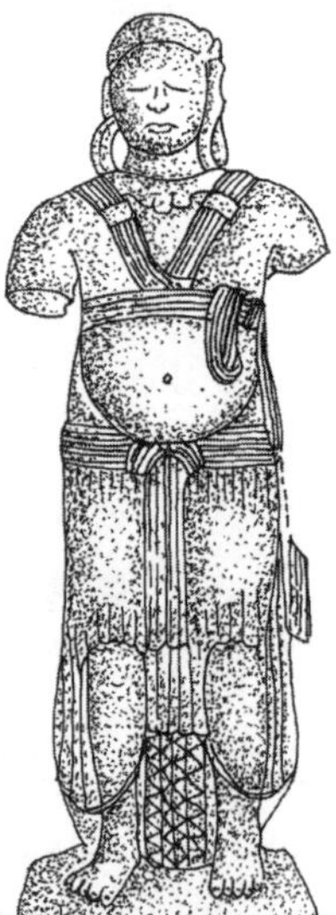

Yakṣa from Parkham, Mathurā Distt., U.P. 3rd century BCE

gods in stone during this period appears to be Buddha's own instructions to his disciples against imagery. Aśoka, who, through his so-called "schism edicts," appears to have assumed the *de facto* role of the Protector of the *dhamma*, the Pāli form of *dharma*, could hardly be expected to flout the specific instructions against imagery.

FROM WOOD TO STONE

But Aśoka possibly never realized that by adopting stone as the medium of sculpture, he had opened a floodgate through which one day the water will be gushing out in such a forceful manner that his successors will not be able to withhold the prohibitory orders of Buddha which he himself had so zealously honoured and guarded. For example, a Viṣṇu image, with a dedicatory inscription in late Mauryan or early Śuṅga characters, has been unearthed at Malhār in Chhatisgarh. Then we have a large number of more than life-size *yakṣa* and *yakṣī* images in stone, from northern India (Mathurā, Kauśāmbī, Pratāpgaṛh, Vidiśā, Pāṭaliputra, etc.) belonging to the second century BCE, if not the late third. Some of them are inscribed such as that from Parkham, near Mathurā and those from Pāṭaliputra in Patna city.

WORKS OF ART: MAURYAN AND EARLY POST-MAURYAN

There are two nude male torsos from Lohānīpur locality of the Patna city, one with the mirror like (Mauryan) polish, and the other not so brightly polished, both housed in the Patna Museum, and both are sometimes identified as *jina* images. Then we have also the famous Dīdārgañj (Patna city) *yakṣī* in this museum which too bears the highest quality of Mauryan polish.

At Guḍimallam, Andhra Pradesh, there is the *śivaliṅga* with the standing Śiva trampling the *apasmāra* (अपस्मार), "ignorance" personified. There is a large-sized stone sculpture in high relief of Balarāma in the Lucknow Museum which is from Mathurā and is datable to second century BCE. Significantly, the Ghosuṇḍī (Rajasthan) inscription mentions Saṁkarṣaṇa and Vāsudeva also but their actual images have not been so far found at the site. Thus, the 86 years" period which elapsed between 236 BCE, when Aśoka died, and 150 BCE when the Garuḍadhvaja of Heliodoros was erected at Vidiśā, witnessed a kind of sculptural activity the like of which India had not witnessed before. From the north to the south the flood of anthropomorphic gods swept all major religions, except Buddhism.

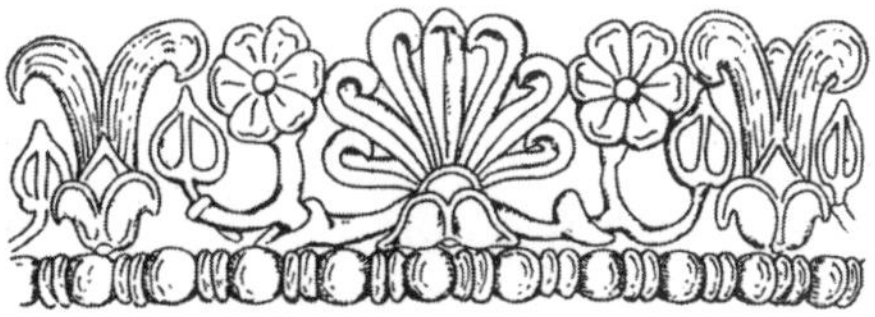

Saṅkisā

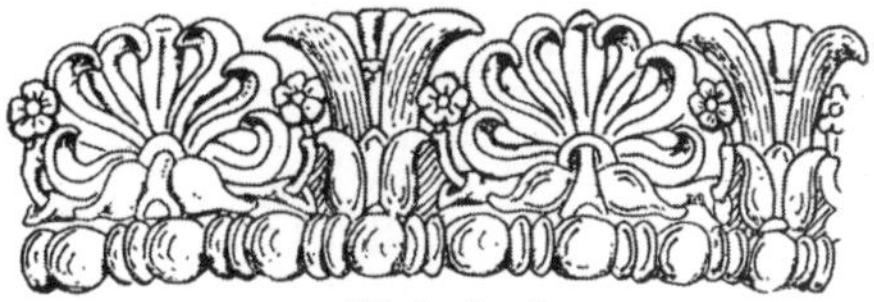

Allahabad

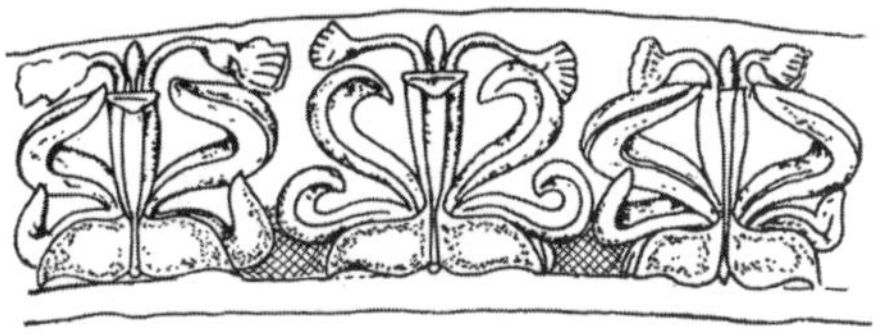

Bansī, Bastī

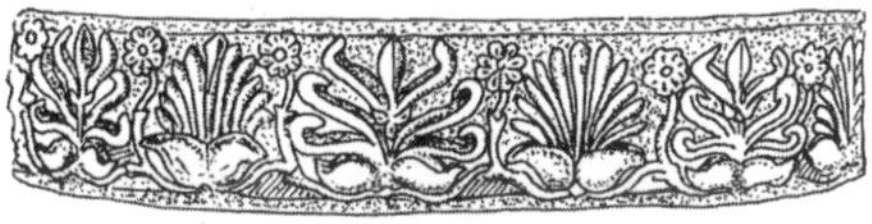

Rāmpurvā

Floral motifs on abacus of Mauryan capitals, 3rd century BCE

BUDDHA IMAGE

But how long the puritanism of Buddhism could last when the Buddhist zealots saw the people flocking around these anthropomorphic gods of the non-Buddhist faiths. By the latter half of the first century BCE they killed the instructions of their own Master by flouting his instructions and made him reborn as a young handsome *yogī*, sitting on a pedestal and wearing a single piece of the upper garment covering one shoulder called Saṁghāti. A full group of such images in high relief, on life-size stone tablets, has been found at Butkara and Saidu Sharif in the Swāt Valley, Pakistan. J.E. Van Lohuizen-de Leeuw, who has made a detailed study on them, is of the opinion that they belong to the Mathurā style, although at Mathurā we do not have any exact parallel of it, and they are pre-Gandhāran i.e. pre-first century. There is, however, a small sitting figure in a medallion of a cross-bar of first century BCE at Mathurā, in local style, which, acording to

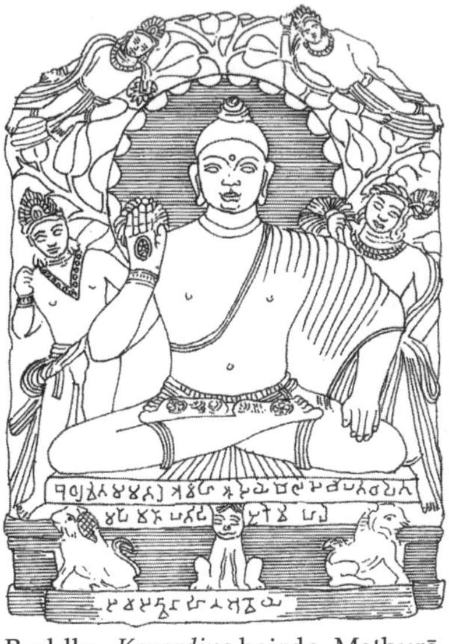

Buddha, *Kapardina* hairdo, Mathurā, U.P., Kuṣāṇa, 1st century CE

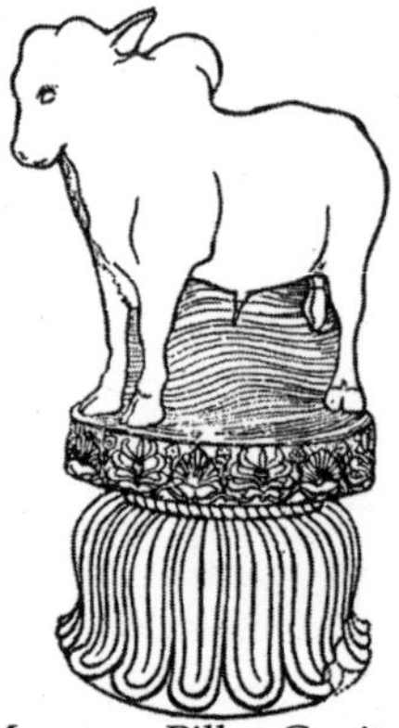

Mauryan Pillar Capital (bull) Rāmpurvā, Bihar, 3rd century BCE

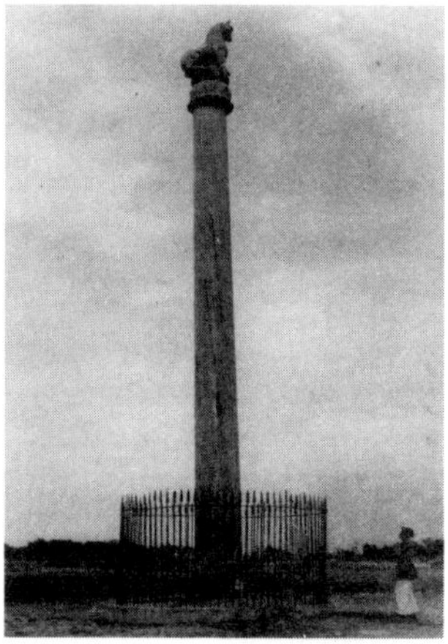

Aśokan Pillar, Lauriā–Nandangaṛh, Bihar, 3rd century BCE

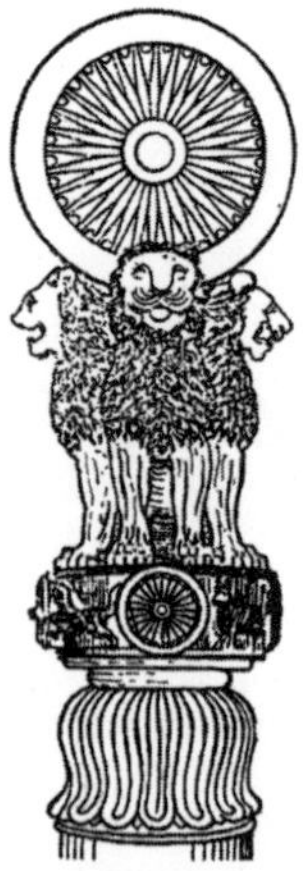

Sārnāth

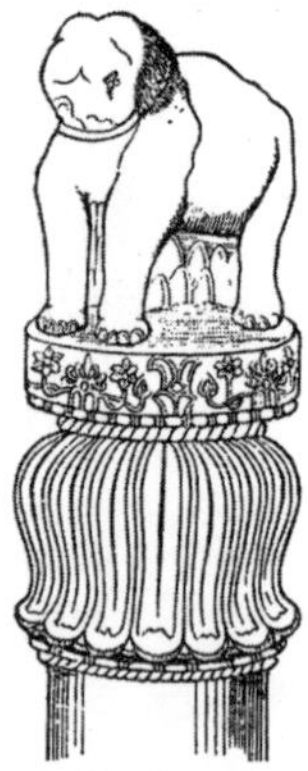

Saṅkīsā

Mauryan Pillar capitals, 3rd century BCE

R.C. Sharma, may be the representation of the Buddha.

Our knowledge about the Mauryan art comes from the (i) Capital decorations of the Mauryan Pillars, (ii) Rock-cut caves and Sculptures, (iii) Images, (iv) Palace and Pavilion, and (v) Ringstones and Discstones.

PILLARS

A Mauryan pillar is carved out of pinkish buff fine grained sandstone which is abundantly found in the Gaṅgā Valley at a place called Chunar, near Mirzapur and Varanasi in Uttar Pradesh. So far two dozens of them have been found, but only a few of them still standing for example, at Vaiśālī, Lauriā–Nandangaṛh and Kauśāmbī. It is made of two parts: (i) the monolithic or single piece tapering shaft, round in section, and often bearing Aśokan edicts, and (ii) the monolithic capital, depicting in high relief on inverted lotus, followed by a rope design, capped by the abacus on which one can see in low relief panels of floral and faunal designs in running order. On the abacus sits one or more images of lions or bulls or elephants, and perhaps of the horse since Hieun-Tsang mentions that he had seen such a pillar at Śrāvastī but it has since disappeared. At Sārnāth, where four lions are shown sitting on haunches back-to-back the capital was topped by a free-standing stone *dharmacakra*, some surviving pieces of which are preserved in the Sarnath Museum. As we know this capital is now our nation's emblem. The symbolism of these four animals in Buddhism perhaps relates to the Buddha's own life. The elephant represents his nativity since he entered the womb of his mother as a white elephant. The bull represents the *rāśi* and *nakṣatra* in which he was born. The horse represents his departure from his palace in search of Truth, called *mahābhiniṣkramaṇa.* The lion, on the other hand, represents his social status, he is called "Śākya-Siṁha," i.e. lion of the Śākya clan. The pillar and the capital in all examples are highly polished, the shine was produced mechanically by rubbing the surface repeatedly with sand, cloth and hide for a long time and not by applying any outside substance over it.

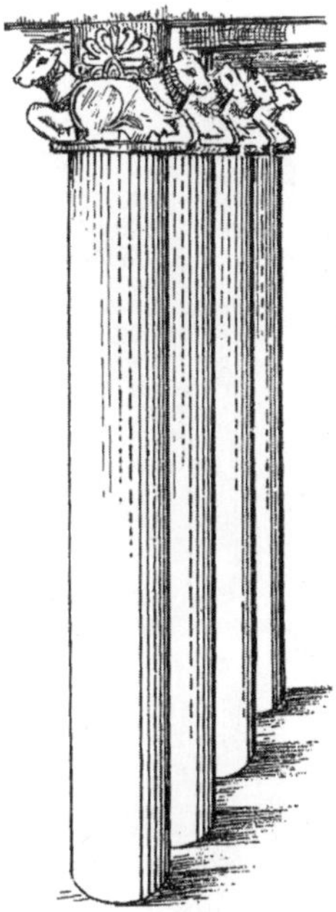

Pillars with double bull capitals, Pāṭaliputra, Bihar, 3rd century BCE (Reconstruction)

It may be noted that the abacus was the area in which a variety of representations are found depicted — *nāgapuṣpa, haṁsa,* leaves, flowers, etc.

ROCK-CUT CAVES AND SCULPTURES

Barābar and Nāgārjunī are the twin granitic hills near Bodh-Gayā, only 40 km away. In them are scooped eight caves with walls bearing typical Mauryan polish. Some of them were got carved by Aśoka and some by his grandson Daśaratha. In cave called "Sudāmā" one finds a beautifully carved round hut while Lomas Ṛṣi cave has an arched gateway showing low-relief carvings in panels with pictures of *stūpa*s being worshipped by elephants. Rock-cut sculpture of monumental size in pure indigenous style was carved on the Dhauli hill near Bhuban-eshwar in Orissa. It is the front part of the elephant only, as if the animal is emerging from the depths of a cave in hills.

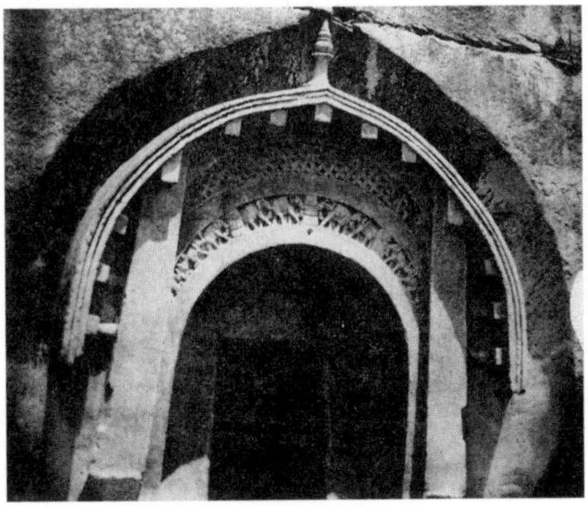

Lomas Ṛṣi Cave Sculptures, Barābar Hill, Bihar, 3rd century BCE

The images in-the-round bearing typical Mauryan polish include the world-famous fine sandstone Dīdārgañj *yakṣī* with a *caurī* (चौरी or चंवर) held in the right hand and two black stone torsos of nude males from Lohānīpur. These places are located in Patna, the ancient Pāṭaliputra, the capital city of the Mauryas. There are a number of terracotta female figurines from Bulandībāgh, the palace-area of the kings. Mathurā and other places,

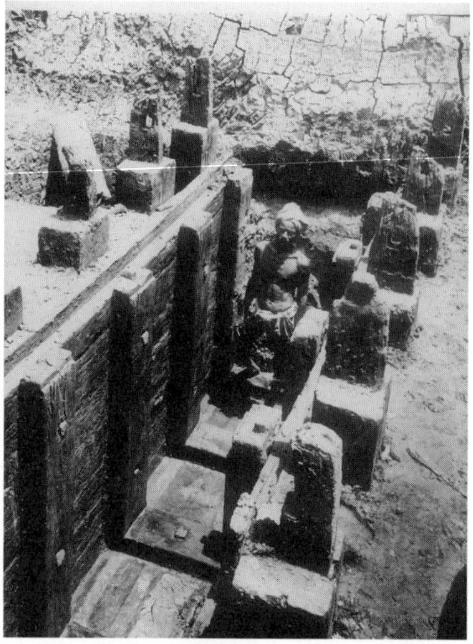

Mauryan Wooden Palace, Bulandībāgh, Patna, Bihar, 3rd century BCE

such as Buxar, have yielded several examples of terracotta mother goddesses.

PALACE AND PAVILION

The Mauryan palace of Bulandībāgh in Pāṭaliputra was made of plain wood whose remains have been found in excavations. At Kumrahār, near the palace area, there was a pavilion in which sandstone pillars were used. The beam-bearing capitals has two bulls sitting back-to-back.

RINGSTONES AND DISCSTONES

Along with these monumental works of art and architecture produced under the royal patronage, there were some works of art depicting folk beliefs of nude mother goddesses and faunal and floral worship. These are carved very minutely in ringstones, i.e. round polished stones, less than three inches in diameter, having a central hole. There are also many examples without hole, hence called "discstones," which depict lotus, palm tree, birds and animals.

It may be noted that the tradition of Mauryan art and architecture continued for all time to come although the polishing technique initiated by Aśoka was abandoned around the beginning of the Kuṣāṇa era.

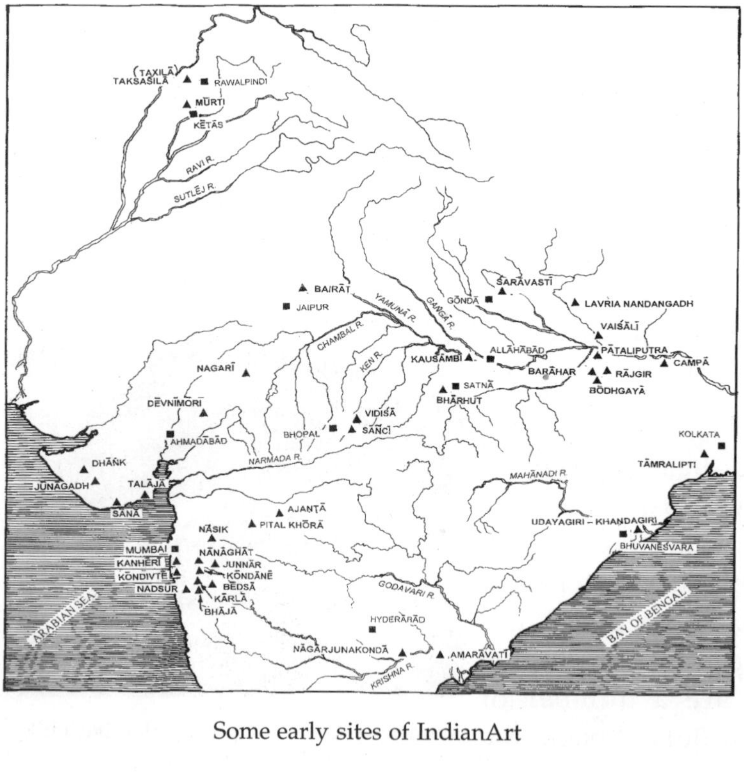

Some early sites of IndianArt

ŚUṄGA–SĀTAVĀHANA ART
(Second–First Centuries BCE)

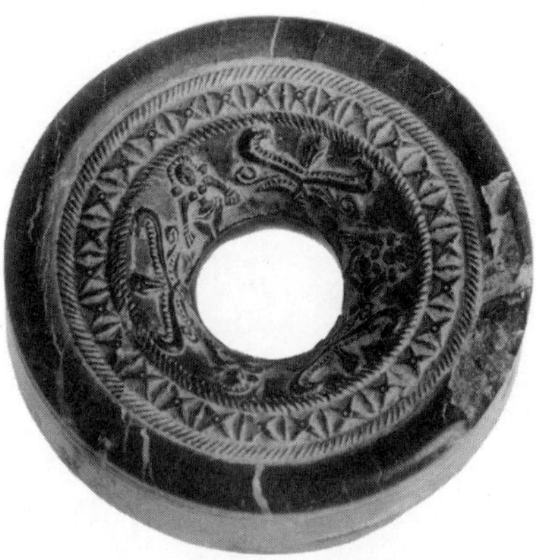

Ringstone, Taxila, 3rd century BCE

INDIGENOUS GROWTH VS. FOREIGN IMPACT

The second and first centuries BCE also witnessed the growth of earlier forms and birth of many new anthropomorphic forms of gods of Śaiva and Vaiṣṇava religions. Our main source of information on this front is numismatics although rock engravings on Karākoram Highway, at places such as Chilas, also depict them. Strangely though it may look, these gods appear on the coins of foreign rulers of north-western India, maybe they did it for political reasons, to become acceptable to the Indian population; nevertheless, they, in the process, emerged as the rulers in whose times several new anthropomorphic forms in plastic art took birth. Thus, on the reverse of the coins of Plato we have the Sūrya in the form of a radiating deity, driving a chariot drawn by four horses, a familiar feature of the early north Indian Sūryas as at Bodh-Gayā. The coins of Greek rulers like Hippostratus, Pantaleon and Peucolus show a goddess with lotus or cornucopia in the right hand, which appears to be Lakṣmī. Some Ujjainī coins, in the hinterland of India, bear Gaja-Lakṣmī. On the reverse of the coins of Agathocles we have the Aśvamukhī Yakṣiṇī. Maues had on his coins Śiva standing to front with a long trident in the left hand. On another series of his coins Śiva is shown with a club and a trident on shoulder, striding to the left. On a few coins of Agathocles (second century BCE) from Ai-Khanum in northern Afghanistan, we have the beautiful representations of Balarāma with a plough or *hala* (हल), and a corn-beater or *mūsala* (मूसल), and Vāsudeva with a spoked wheel or *cakra* (चक्र) and a conch-shell or *śaṅkha* (शंख). A.K. Narain and A.N.

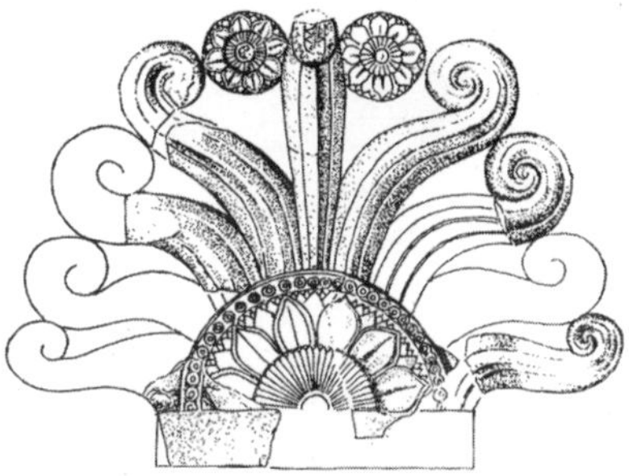

Lotus and Nāgapuṣpa Top of the Gateway, Bharhut, M.P., 2nd century BCE

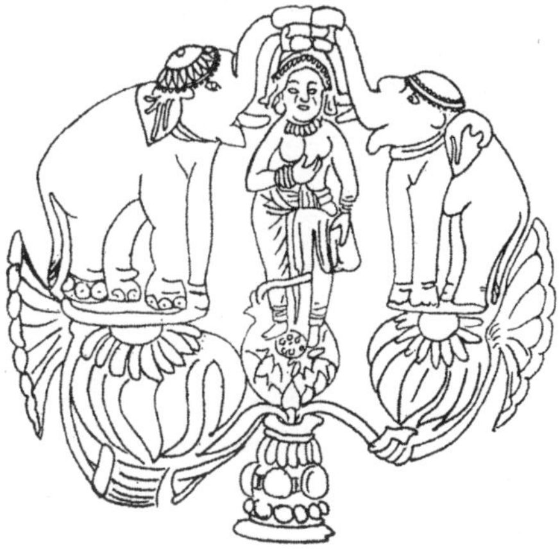

Gaja-Lakṣmī, Khaṇḍagiri, Orissa, 2nd century BCE

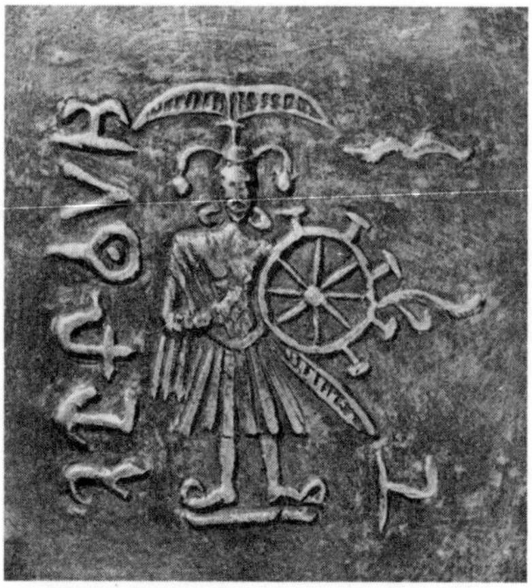

Kṛṣṇa Vāsudeva, on copper coin of Agathocles, 2nd century BCE

Lahiri identify even a sitting Gaṇeśa on a coin of one of these kings. Maues also issued a series of coins with Lakṣmī sitting on lotus but dressed in somewhat Greek style of clothes. Azilises introduced the *abhiṣeka* (अभिषेक) or *gajalakṣmī* type silver coin in which the standing goddess is being bathed by two elephants.

NEO-VEDIC TRENDS

One may, therefore, clearly notice that in the second and first centuries BCE, under the impact of the Neo-Vedic trends, in Śaiva and Vaiṣṇava sects, gods in anthropomorphic forms were introduced in plastic media both in the hinterland and the peripheral regions of India. Those found in the mainland are purely indigenous in physical features, dress, ornaments, posture, etc. but those found in north-western India and Afghanistan show strong undercurrents of Hellenistic features in all these respects. This historical situation, it is extremely significant to note, existed in the following four centuries: in the hinterland there developed again and again pure indigenous forms while on the north-western frontier there developed hybrid forms in which hinterland forms crossed with the Hellenistic forms both in physical features and dress.

GREEK AND INDIGENOUS ELEMENTS IN ART

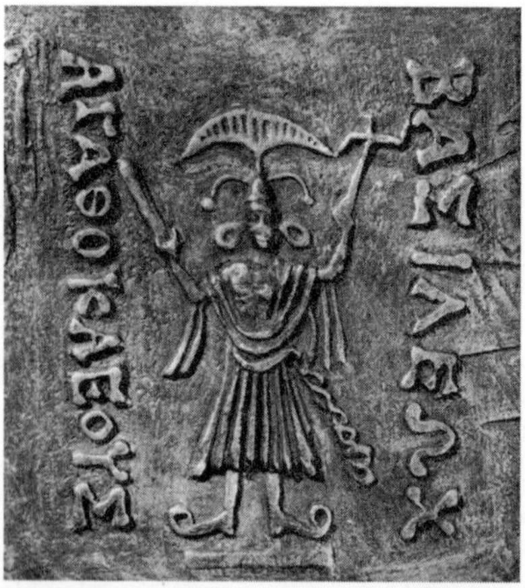

Balarāma on copper coin of Agathocles, Greek ruler of Bactria, 2nd century BCE

On conceptual grounds, it should be clearly understood that except for Sūrya or sun, none of the gods and goddesses had its origin outside the country. The image, the *bimba* or the *mūrti* with all its *āyudhas*, was the product of an Indian mind. Similarities between Indian and Hellenistic forms have sometimes been noted by scholars but these are only incidental; they exist even without these similarities. In other words, the image of, say,

Balarāma or Vāsudeva or Lakṣmī or Śiva or Gaṇeśa was not conceived by any foreigner in north-western India on the basis of the Greek gods and goddesses with whom he was familiar from birth. Conceiving these images or *bimbas*, with all their attributes was the outcome of inheritance of a long tradition or *paramparā*, the acquisition of supreme knowledge or *jñāna*, and an act of intense devotion or *bhakti*, all of which came naturally to an Indian mind.

GREEK AND HINDU INTERACTION

It is extremely doubtful if in the second and first centuries BCE the Greeks, who had hardly two centuries of history of stay in Bactria and Afghanistan, and that too under the pressure of constant threat of risings and counter-risings, and the actual wars which broke very often, were favourably placed for this kind of job. As noted earlier, none of these Hindu gods was conceived *after* a Greek god; it was just not a question of effecting certain modifications in the existing forms of Greek gods and goddesses in order to get the forms of these Hindu gods and goddesses, it was a matter of original ideas; in fact, it was a matter of sheer revelation, i.e. dawning upon effortlessly.

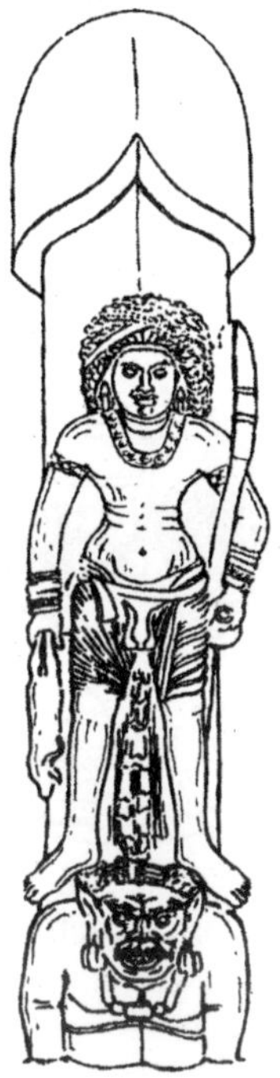

Śiva, standing on a *kīcaka*, shown against *liṅgam*, Guḍimallam, Andhra Pradesh, Sātavāhana, 2nd century BCE

THE BIRTH OF IMAGE-WORSHIP: BHAKTI AND PERSONAL GOD

The birth of an image is a matter of self-creation in the mind of a *bhakta*, a devotee of the highest order to whom god reveals himself or herself. We feel that at that point of time, only a Hindu mind had that kind of ploughed and manured mental field for the proper germination of the images of Śaiva and Vaiṣṇava gods and goddesses. Bhandarkar's brilliant exposition of *bhakti* movements of the second and

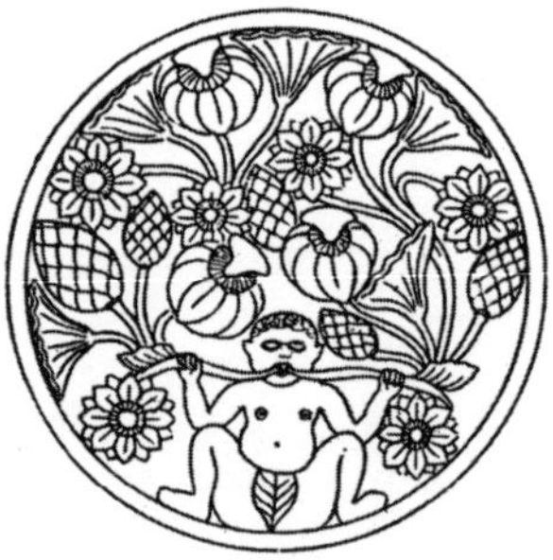

Lotus stalks emerging from the mouth of Yakṣa, Sāñcī, M.P., Śuṅga, 1st century BCE

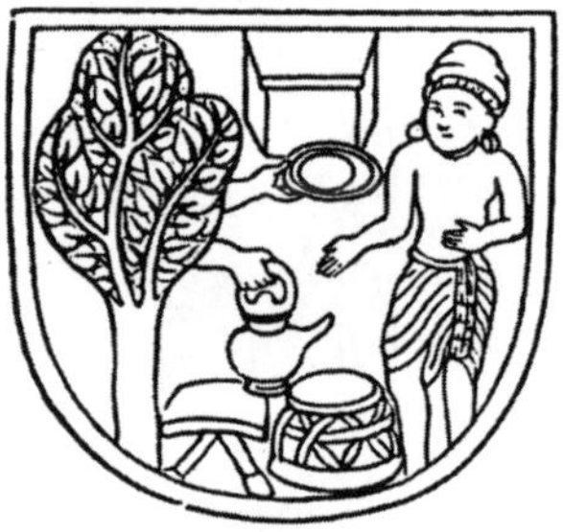

Tree-Yakṣa, Sāñcī, M.P., Śuṅga, 1st century BCE

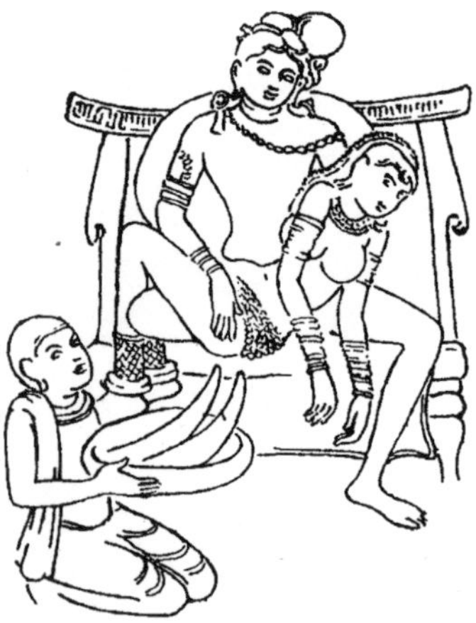

Dying queen, Goli, Sātavāhana, 3rd century CE

first centuries BCE in the Indian hinterland of Rajasthan, Madhya Pradesh and Uttar Pradesh does not leave any doubt in our mind that the Śaiva and Vaiṣṇava images were originally conceived in this part of the world, their occurrence in north-western India was a matter of diffusion of ideas, quick diffusion, of course, through trade-routes connecting them with the north-western regions. The differences in some costumes, postures and physical features were the natural outcome of culture-interaction between the East and the West, and the mixed nature of population of north-western India. Ideas always precede art. Theories always precede practice.

PAN-INDIANISM IN ART

The Śuṅga–Sātavāhana art had the pan-Indian dimension in which Buddhist system of monastic life played the major role because of two reasons. First, attention to embellish the architecture of the monasteries with sculptures and paintings was given in the framework of the concept "Art is Worship." Therefore, many inmates, who were bachelors, devoted themselves to the pursuits of carving and painting. Second, mobility of the lay-disciples and workmen, going from one monastery to another, sometimes as part of pilgrimage, but often for getting better education, created commonality in art styles. Thus, if we take, for example, the *yakṣī* images from Mathurā, Bodh-Gayā, Bharhut, Sāñcī, Udaigiri–Khaṇḍagiri, Pītalkhorā, Amarāvatī, Guḍimallam, Sannati, etc. their idiom and style remain the same, the difference was confined to the colour, nature and texture of the stone, for example, in Bharhut it was red and granular sandstone while at Amarāvatī it was greenish and smooth soapstone or limestone.

WORKS OF ART AND ARCHITECTURE

The earliest examples of works of art come from Bharhut, a Buddhist *stūpa* site in Madhya Pradesh, near Satanā. Here a large brick *stūpa* with a huge railing and a gateway, both of red sandstone, existed in the second century BCE. At Sāñcī also the *mahāstūpa* and several smaller *stūpa*s with railings and gateways were erected. At Pītalkhorā there was a rock-cut monastery. There was at Bhaja, near Pune, a rock-cut monastery. All these four centres of fine art and architecture were Buddhist. The Udaigiri–Khaṇḍagiri cave monastery was, however, Jaina. At Mathurā also there was a Jaina monastery.

THE SUBJECT MATTER

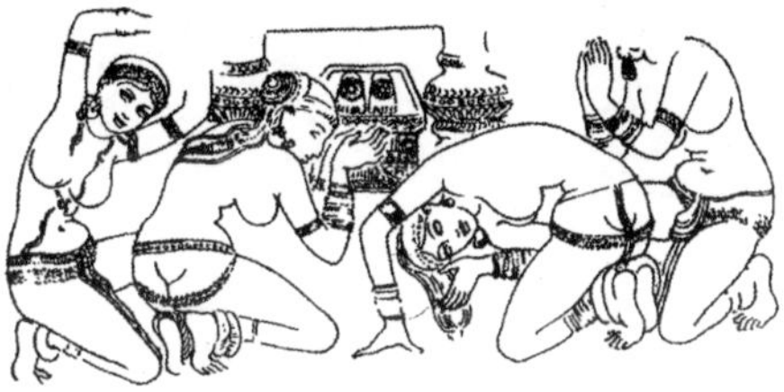

Worship of Buddha's feet, Amarāvatī, A.P., 2nd century CE

The *yakṣas*, *yakṣīs*, ordinary men and women, royal couples, all kinds of animals, birds and reptiles, various narrative scenes from the life of Buddha as well as from the *Jātakas*, stories of the 500 and odd known previous births of Buddha, besides Buddhist symbols of *dharmacakra, triratna, stūpa, buddha-pada,* etc. provided the subject matter of art. It may be noted that in Udayagiri, Pītalkhorā, Amarāvatī, etc. we see foreigners clad in high boots and short tunic, and carrying lances guarding the caves. It is repeatedly mentioned in texts and notices of the foreigners that Indian kings from the Mauryan times employed West Asian men and women for guarding their palaces.

THE ART STYLE

The style of the works of art of human beings was folkish, since the models before the artists during this period of time included village headman and village woman, many of them coming from the tribal background. The faces, therefore, have been treated

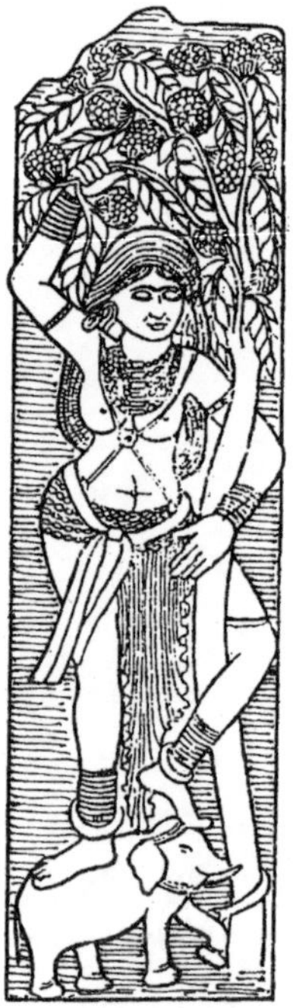

Chulakokā Devatā standing on elephant, Bharhut, M.P., 2nd century BCE

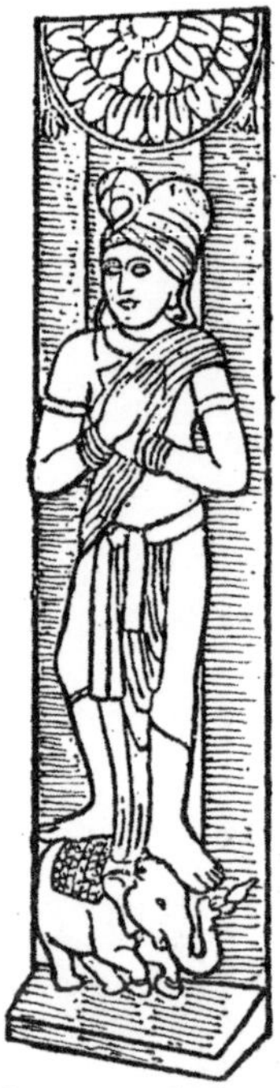

Supavāso Yakṣa standing on elephant, Bharhut, M.P., 2nd century BCE

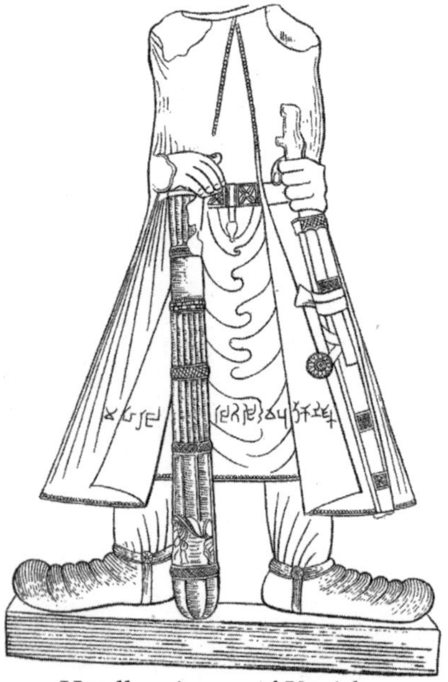

Headless image of Kaniṣka, Mathurā, U.P., 1st century CE

as heavy and bold with fully open eyes, thick nose, thick lips, high jaw-bone, and short neck. The headgear or turban in men and large scarf on the head of women, is also very heavy. Nudity is through transparent *dhotī*.

The trunk is equally very heavy. There are tatoo marks in many examples on the face and the rest of the body of women. The *dhotī* with folds is also not tied with any sophistication. The figures are mostly frontally portrayed with legs oddly crossed while standing. These figures are heavy and earth-bound. The hands and legs are awkwardly portrayed. The ornaments, with which the men and women adorned themselves, and these were many, were very heavy, whether these were neck-ornaments or hand, hip and leg ornaments.

KUṢĀṆA ART
(First–Third Centuries)

The Kuṣāṇas were as much foreigners as the Indo-Greeks but they were thoroughly naturalised, at least the successors of Kaniṣka at Mathurā and Peshawar. The process of Indianization of foreign rulers, as shown earlier, had started in the third century BCE itself as a by-product of peculiar socio-political situation in north-western India where intense cultural interaction between Indian and Hellenistic traditions was taking place. The Greeks in Bactria were now rulers, but in the first century BCE they lived in hopeless minority and more or less completely cut-off from their mainland. It may have been a painful realization on their part that they had to seek their fortune in an alien land and live there permanently, the homeland promised little to them. Once it dawns on someone that he has to live and die in a foreign country amongst the foreigners, even as a ruler, it changes radically his entire attitude towards life, his own and those of the local people. He starts accepting many cultural items of the local people in order to get himself acceptable to them. This is generally called "Historical Process." This historical process, which was initiated by the Indo-Greeks in the second century BCE, continued during the Śaka and Pahalava times in the first century BCE and first half of the first century CE.

When the Kuṣāṇas come on the political scene in late first century BCE and early first century CE they had hardly any other choice except continuing the wise policy of their predecessors. In fact, they not only continued this policy and helped the growth of the historical process we have outlined above, but they also accelerated it to its maximum.

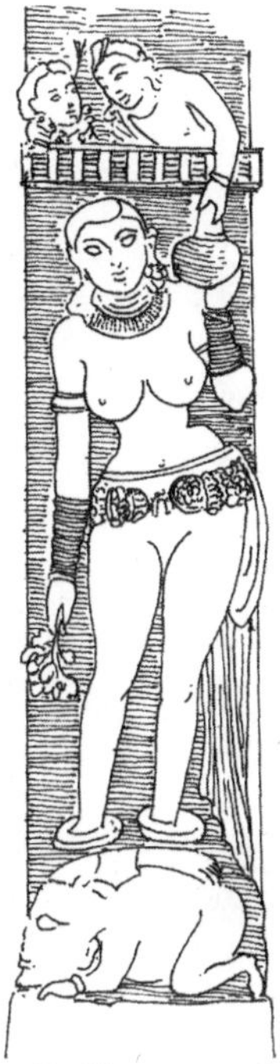

Yakṣī on Railing-post, Sanghol, Punjab, Kuṣāṇa, 1st century CE

ACCULTURATION AND POLITICAL EXPEDIENCY MARKED THE KUṢĀṆA HISTORY

What were the underlying reasons which prompted the Kuṣāṇas to accelerate the historical process? These were mainly two: first and foremost was the fact that while the Indo-Greeks had come to India with a long tradition of their own gods and goddesses, the Kuṣāṇas, a branch of the Yu chi tribe from Chinese Central Asia, came to India without any developed religion and imagery of their own. For them the Indian religions offered the first choice in the non-mundane world and they accepted it wholeheartedly, perhaps partly as a political expediency and partly as a cultural mission, although they did not neglect the strong element of Greco-Roman imagery of the local population.

The second is the tremendous growth during this period in the field of religious experiences and image formulations on the part of all the Indian religions because two factors, first: all of them — Buddhism,

3.4

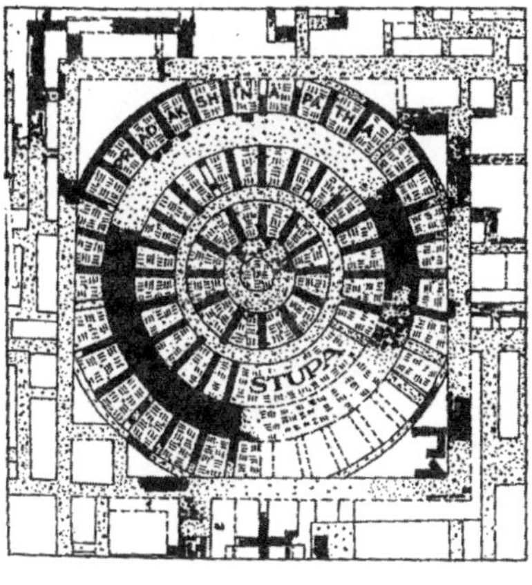

Stūpa, plan, Sanghol, Punjab, Kuṣāṇa, 1st century CE

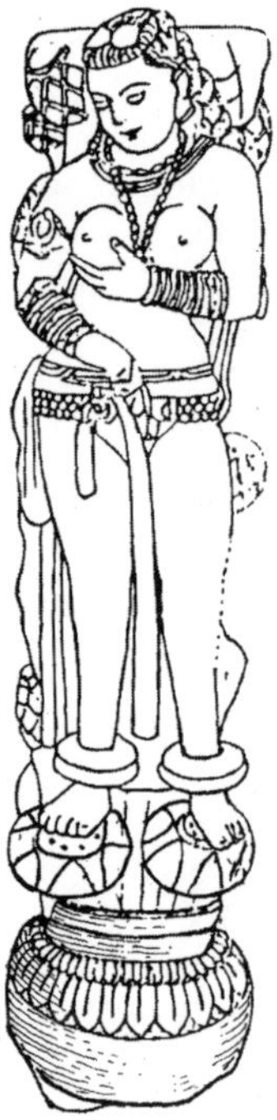

Lakṣmī, Mathurā, U.P., Kuṣāṇa, 1st century CE

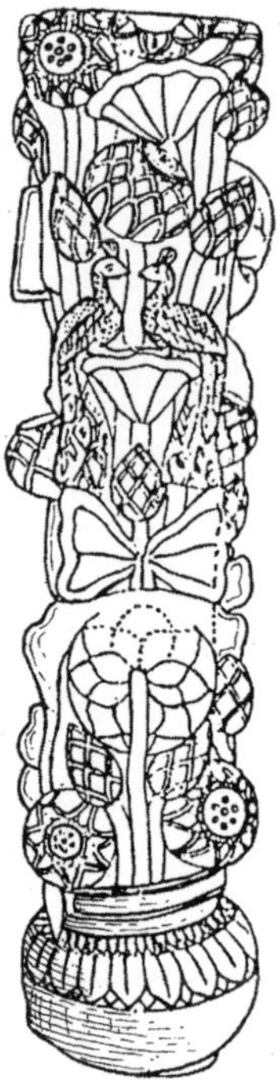

Backside of Lakṣmī

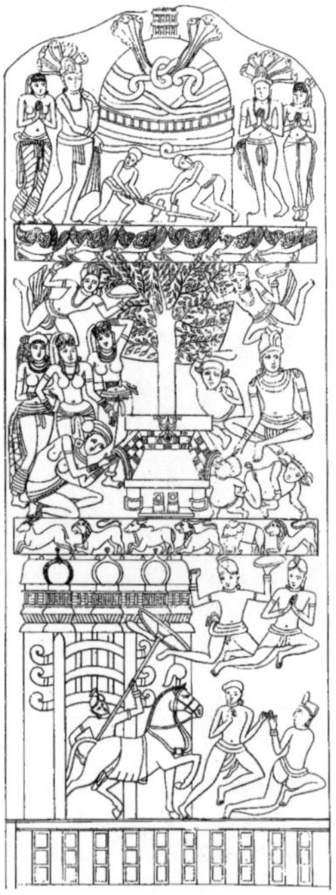

Scenes from the Life of Buddha (narrative style), U.P., 1st century, BCE

Jainism, Śaiva, Vaiṣṇava, etc. assumed "all India' character — by this time they had developed deep roots in Maharashtra, Karnataka, Andhra Pradesh and Tamil Nadu besides the north Indian states, and secondly, the fierce competition which had developed in each one of them to outdo the popularity of the other, even at the cost of adopting the philosophical thoughts and formal imagery of the others.

The birth of Mahāyānism and image worship in Buddhism, through as many forms, numerically speaking, as the Śaiva and the Vaiṣṇavas had, is a case in point. Similarly, the Buddhist love for symbols and *mudrā*s or hand gestures had its singular effect on Śaivism, Vaiṣṇavism and Jainism.

THE ART OF NARRATION

The perceptible results of mutual borrowings was astonishing on imagery in the major Indian religions. A large body of *ākhyāna*s (आख्यान) or religious stories developed in each one of them, and that too often sharing similar characters — the *Jātaka*s (जातक), Purāṇas and Āgamas started swelling. And, hand in hand with this, another trait developed: in order to present the gods and their deeds to the common people, for their easy comprehension as well as to stabilize their devotion, rituals round the gods were multiplied and their superhuman actions narrated through the media of plastic art in stone, terracotta, metal, bone and ivory.

SYMBOLS AND MUDRĀS FORMED THE COMMON POOL FOR ALL RELIGIONS

As a matter of fact, there was nothing sectarian in individual symbols and *mudrā*s, they formed the common pool of Indian art language; sectarianism developed only in their combinations reflected in iconography. For example, *śaṅkha, cakra, gadā* and *padma* as well as *dhyāna-mudrā, sukhāsana* (सुखासन), etc. were common to all; only their combinations made them Vaiṣṇava or Buddhist or Jaina.

ROYAL PATRONAGE AND PUBLIC PARTICIPATION

This brings us to another ticklish problem: how far the royal patronage was responsible for the phenomenal growth of imagery in the Kuṣāṇa period?

We have several series of Kuṣāṇa coins of each Kuṣāṇa ruler. They depict various Indian deities — Śaiva, Vaiṣṇava and Bauddha, obviously under the direct orders of the kings. There are a few public buildings, such as temples, both Vaiṣṇava and Buddhist, in and around Mathurā, such as Soṅkh and Bhūteśvara, which have yielded folk deities in stone, like *nāgadeva* (नागदेव), and important cult deity in terracotta, like Mahiṣāsuramardinī (महिषासुरमर्दिनी). None of them was made under the patronage of a Kuṣāṇa king. On the other hand, at Mathurā we have a number of structures for, and sculptures of, these deities which were made under the patronage of Kuṣāṇa kings and queens. It is not surprising when we see their epithets, and even their names, like Vāsudeva, which clearly show that they were completely Indianized. Besides Mathurā, we have a large number of sites in northern India, such as Kauśāmbī, Ahicchatra and Rājaghāṭa which have yielded sculptures and temples of the *yakṣas*, *nāgas*, Śaiva, Vaiṣṇava and Bauddha deities.

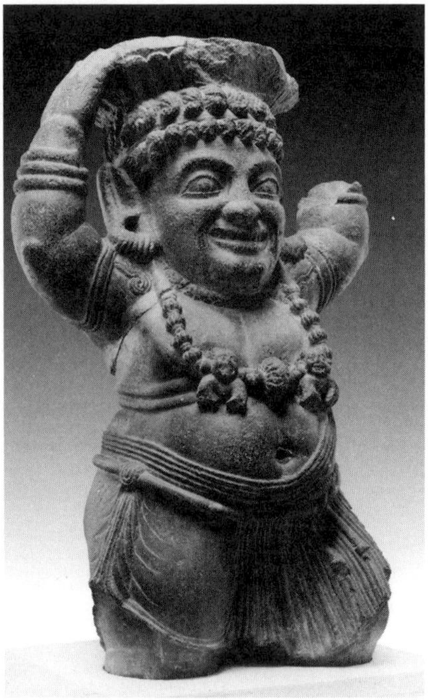

Yakṣa, Pītalkhorā, Maharashtra, Sātavāhana, 2nd century BCE

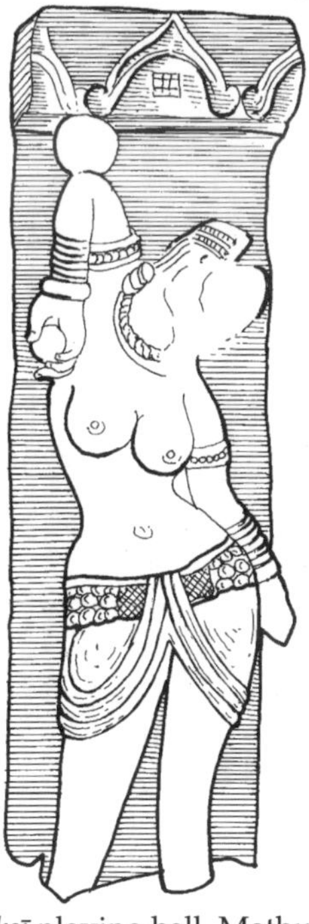

Yakṣī playing ball, Mathurā, U.P., Kuṣāṇa, 1st century CE

DYNASTIC ART AND COMMON MAN'S ART

Amongst the terracottas, a series of crudely made heads of *devatās* with tenons to fit into big statues

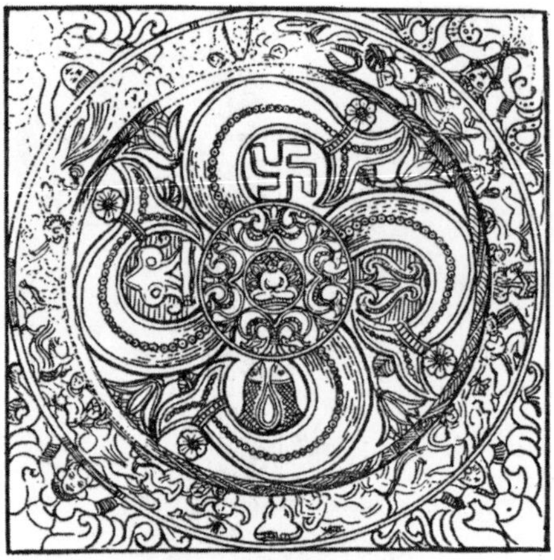

Āyāgapaṭṭa, Mathurā, U.P., Kuṣāṇa, 1st century CE

have been found. And they exist along with another series of beautiful plaques depicting various semi-divine female figures with voluptuous features comparable only with the Bhūteśvara (Mathurā) *yakṣīs* on stone railings. Besides these, we have a more than life-size *bodhisattva* in red sandstone with a large halo and decorated umbrella or *chatra* in the Sarnath Museum. In the National Museum another somewhat similar *bodhisattva* with robust body exists. In the National Museum, an inscribed sitting *bodhisattva* with prominent top-knot and terse attitude, from Kaṭarā (Mathurā), is housed. There are two large pieces of Jaina *āyāgapaṭṭa*s (आयागपट्ट) or stone tablets, with auspicious marks for worship from Mathurā. Most of these sculptures were donatory and caused by the laity in the Śuṅga–Sātavāhana tradition. All these facts show that although the Kuṣāṇa kings and queens extended royal patronage to imagery, there are many images of Kuṣāṇa royalty in and around Mathurā, such as those of Kaniṣka, Masṭana or Chasṭana; they were neither solely nor largely responsible for the unprecedented growth in imagery; their contribution in this respect was of a different kind.

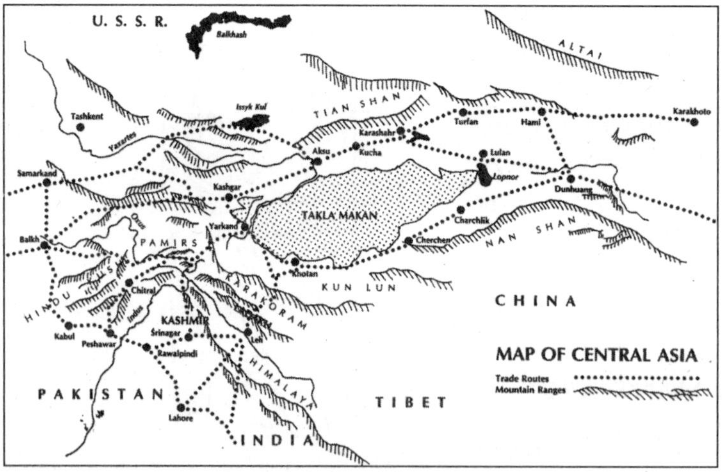

Map showing Silk Routes

THE KUṢĀṆAS AND THE SILK ROUTES

First of all they ushered in a long era of peace and prosperity in the country by their stable rule over a vast empire and the tremendous success they achieved in opening long-distance trade routes connecting Indian mainland with Central Asia. The bridges over the Oxus allowed Indian goods to reach the famous Silk Routes which connected China with Egypt through Syria, Assyria, Iran, Uzbekistan and Khotan. Indian colonies were established in Bactria as well as around Taklamakan desert in Chinese Central Asia, such as in the Khotan Oasis, Niya, Miran, etc. And secondly, consciously and purposely, they adopted the most liberal attitude towards all religions prevalent in their empire. In fact, they gave us a perfect secular state in spite of the fact that each one of the Kuṣāṇa rulers had his own personal preferences in matters of religion.

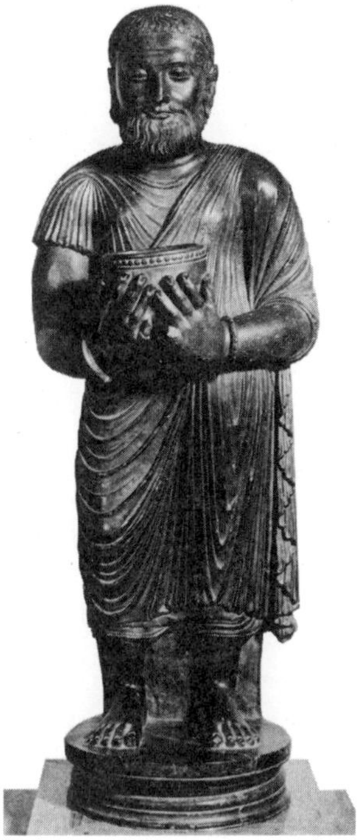

A Greek person, Gandhāra, 1st century CE

THE SOCIO-POLITICAL BACKGROUND OF ART

In such a congenial politico-economic situation, the social condition was equally free from major strains, a fact which is reflected in the somewhat non-conflictness of the religious sects — establishments of all religions existed side by side. Mathurā, a capital city of the Kuṣāṇas, presents us all the best that the era gave us. The Swat Valley and the Gandhāra region shared their artistic beauty with Bactria. Their combined echo is present in the Kṛṣṇā basin, at Amarāvatī and Nāgārjunakoṇḍa, as well as in the Gaṅgā basin at Kauśāmbī and Sārnāth. The Indo-Gangetic divide had so many townships, like Kurukṣetra and Shugh, to support the Kuṣāṇa ethos in every field of life, including art and literature, both religious and non-religious. There was all round progress and innovations without oppressive constraints of organized churches and well-laid canons. The field was free for individual artists to evolve his own style of art and method of work. The image was still simple with limited number of icons and iconographic features. The religious art, as opposed to the "dynastic art" of the Kuṣāṇas, in which portraits of kings and nobility were carved in large numbers, as noted above, was extremely free and dynamic.

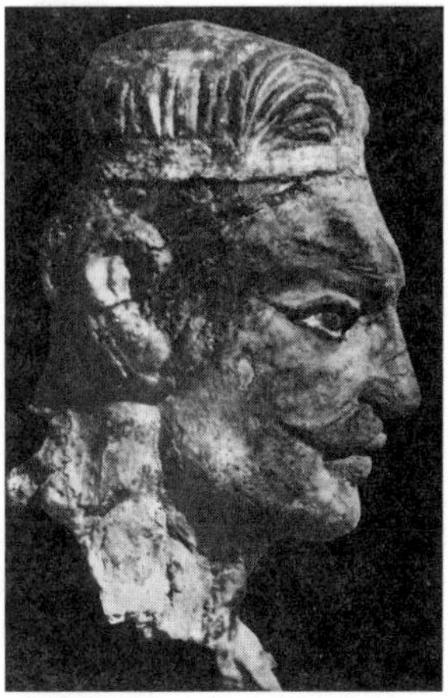

Profile of a Bactrian person, 1st century CE

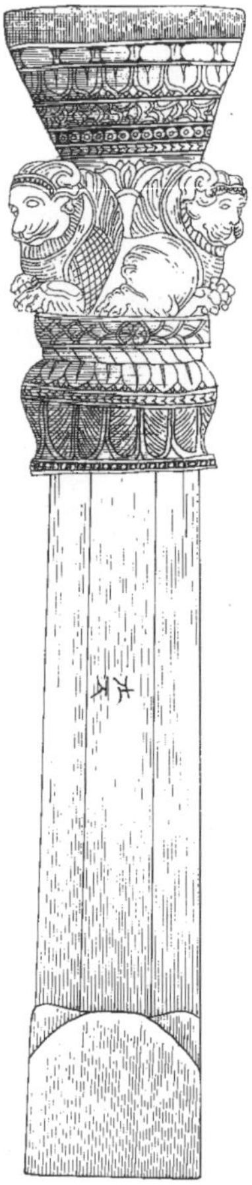

Pillar, Mathurā, U.P., Kuṣāṇa, 1st century CE

The Kuṣāṇa art, therefore, was both a logical outcome of the Śuṅga–Indo–Bactrian art and a great improvement on its heritage. It was the flowering of the buds which burst forth in the period immediately preceding it. Under the cool shadows of the liberality of the kings, the Kuṣāṇa artist worked with full vigour sharing the ideals of the men of all religions and the aspiration of the folk with whom he shared his joys and sorrows of everyday life. Still, the culmination had not reached and perfection was not achieved. Possibly, the necessary discipline of body and mind was still lacking on the part of the artist. Long periods of labour and apprenticeship coupled with conscious search for new idioms and technical perfection was yet to become the order of the day in every field of art.

THE PROCESS OF INDIANIZATION OF ART OF FOREIGN ORIGIN

The process of Indianization was yet not complete; we have still the curious mixture of indigenous and foreign elements. Images were beautiful to look at but the Indian ethos of spiritualism could not penetrate the figures to reveal their godliness. It was a great progress indeed, nevertheless a halting

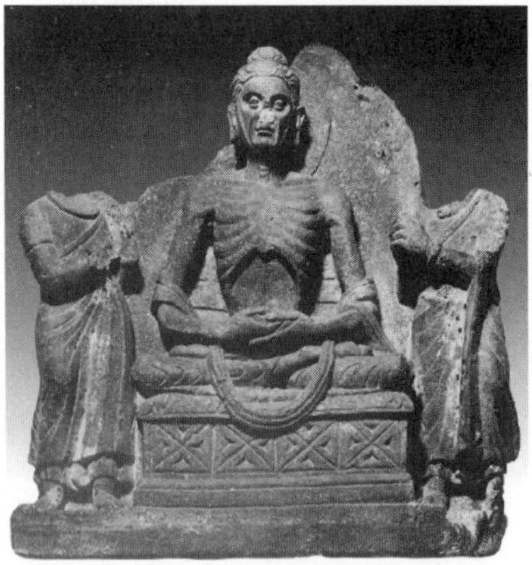

Fasting Buddha, Gandhāra, 1st century CE

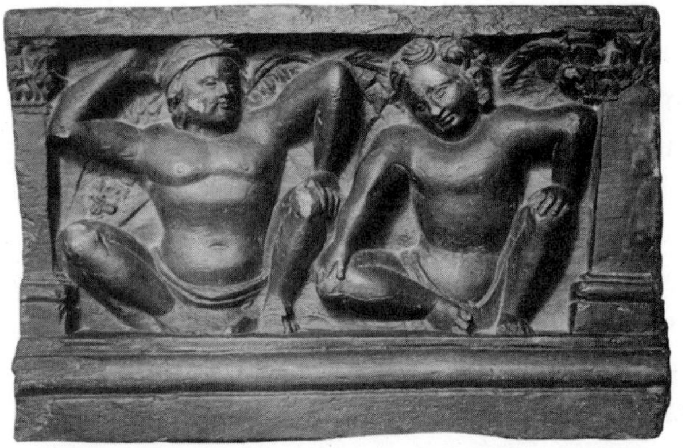

Atlantic figures of Greek origin in Gandhāra, 1st century CE

progress as far as art was concerned. But India had not to wait for long to achieve full success in these fields. It happened in the period immediately following it. The Gupta period undoubtedly witnessed the art of India to its culmination. Hence classical. Hence golden.

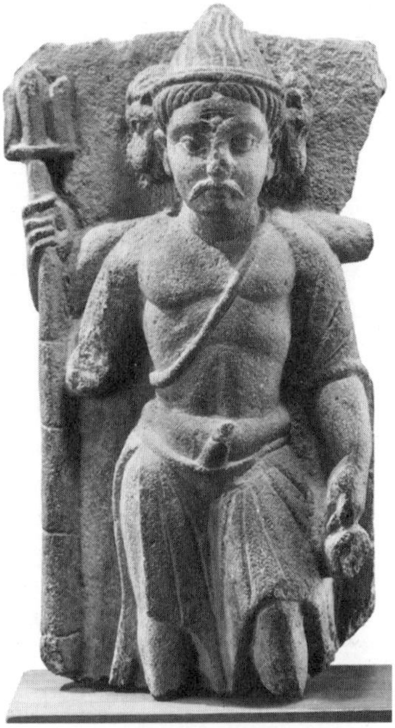

Śiva, Gandhāra, 1st century CE

BACTRIAN, MATHURĀ AND GĀNDHĀRA SCHOOLS OF KUṢĀṆA ART

The Kuṣāṇas had at least three capital cities — Ai-Khanum in Bactria, Purushapur (Peshawar) in NW Pakistan, and Mathurā in India. At all these three places excavations have revealed the existence of several temples and works of art. At each, however, a style developed which was peculiar to that region even though there was a common thread running amongst them and binding them together.

Thus, the art of Ai-Khanum has many Bactrian elements, the art of Gandhāra has many classical (Greco-Roman) elements while the art of Mathurā has been predominantly indigenous.

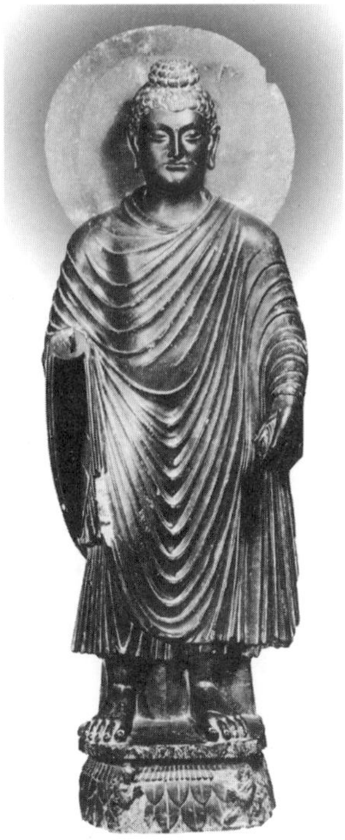

Buddha, Gandhāra, 2nd century CE

BACTRIAN SCHOOL

The image of Kaniṣka found at Ai-Khanum shows in its dress typical Bactrian motifs. The design of the *pāyjāmā* and tunic also show the same chracteristic features. Here was found a Greek temple with a Greek inscription.

GĀNDHĀRA SCHOOL

Gandhāra region was a great centre of Mahāyāna Buddhist art and architecture. The Buddha and *bodhisattva* images and narrative scenes in low and high relief show that while the subject matter was by and large Buddhist, there are very few Śaiva and Vaiṣṇava images, the costumes and coiffure were

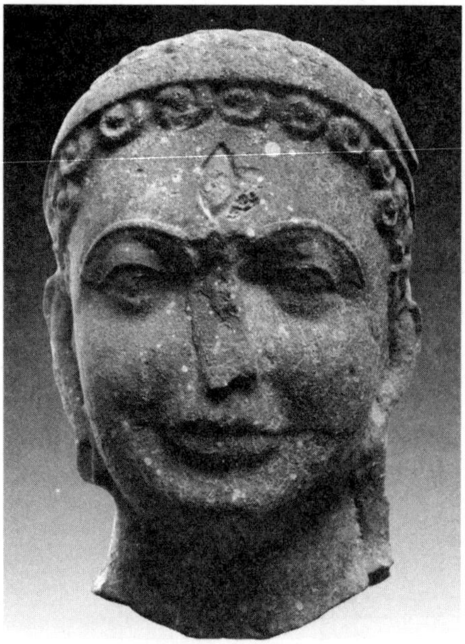

Śiva Head, Greek style, Mathurā, U.P., Kuṣāṇa, 1st century CE

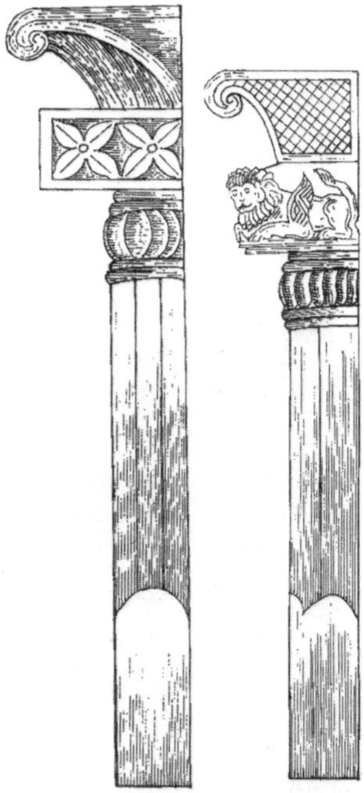

Pillars of Kuṣāṇa period, Mathurā, U.P., 1st century CE

mixed: Indian, classical and Bactrian. The Buddha head is marked by curly hair, wavy hair, flame-like hair, etc. which characterized classical art. The upper garment, i.e. *saṁghāti,* shows heavy folds which remind us of the toga, a loose outer garment worn by men in ancient Rome. The sandals are also classical in form. Buddha in the beginning was shown sporting prominently a moustache, which also reminds us of the Greeks and the Romans. According to one view, even the clean-shaved oval face with youthful countenance of the Buddha was modelled after the image of sun-god Apollo. However, after the works of Coomaraswamy, it is now generally agreed that the radiant face with spiritual element in it could be produced only in India, perhaps at Mathurā where there was a long tradition of carving out *yakṣa* images and where the philosophical background of Buddhism of Mahāsāṁghika School was prevalent.

The Gāndhāra School of art was largely done on bluish schistose stone and slate, particularly up to the third century CE. The Gāndhāra School of the post-Kuṣāṇa period, i.e. of the Gupta period (fifth-sixth century CE), was mostly done in clay and stucco, particularly in the Kabul Valley and beyond.

MATHURĀ SCHOOL

The Mathurā School of Kuṣāṇa art, done on red blotchy sandstone, on the other hand, shows Indian *dhotī* generally covering only the left shoulder, hair arranged in small curls, or else in a *kapardina* top-knot, like that of a *sādhu*, left hand held on hip, heavily built, open eyes, thick lips, eyes partly closed and face round or oval. *Abhaya-mudrā* and *yoga-mudrā* have been most popular although *bhūmi-sparśa-mudrā* was not wanting.

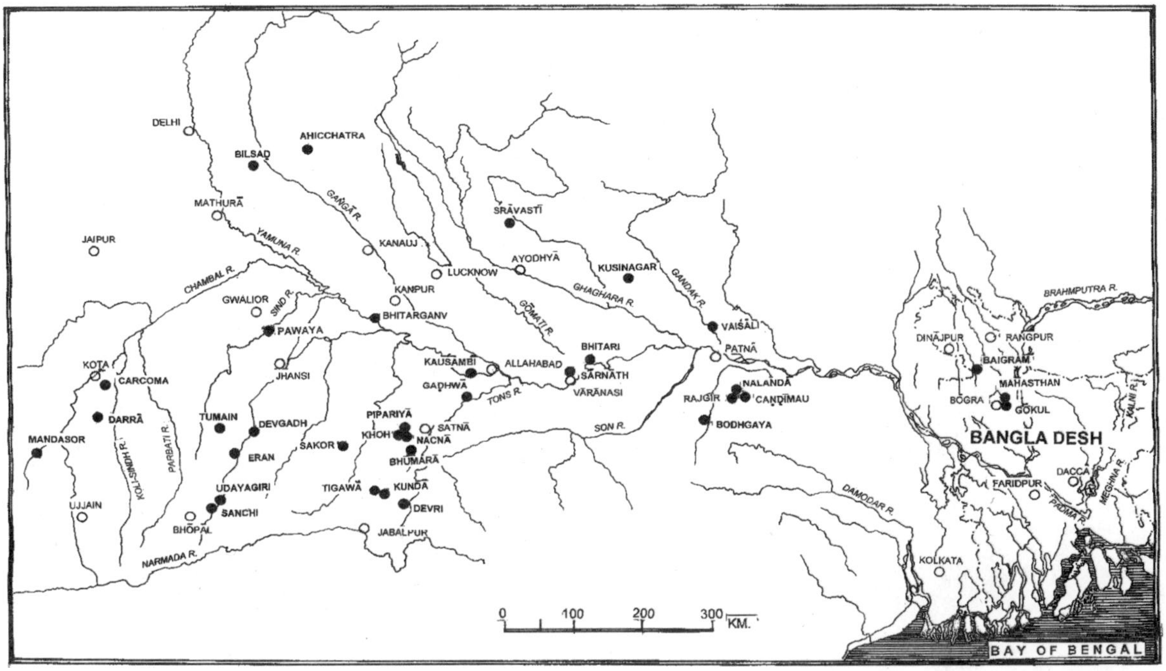

Some Gupta Period Sites

The plants, leaves, animals and birds were drawn realistically and handled delicately. So also the female figures which are marked by semi-nudity, transparent *dhotī*, full breasts, fish-like eyes, *tribhaṅga* posture, a variety of ornaments, and sitting or standing in full and half profile.

The Kuṣāṇa art of Mathurā was the culmination of the Śuṅga art where also we see many *yakṣa* and *yakṣī* figures marked by voluptuous elements.

GUPTA ART
(Fourth–Sixth Centuries)

The Guptas had absolutely no foreign moorings. They had no foreign blood in them. They originated in India's mainland. Their empire also did not extend beyond the Hindu Kush. They had no particular love for foreign dress, ornaments and mannerism

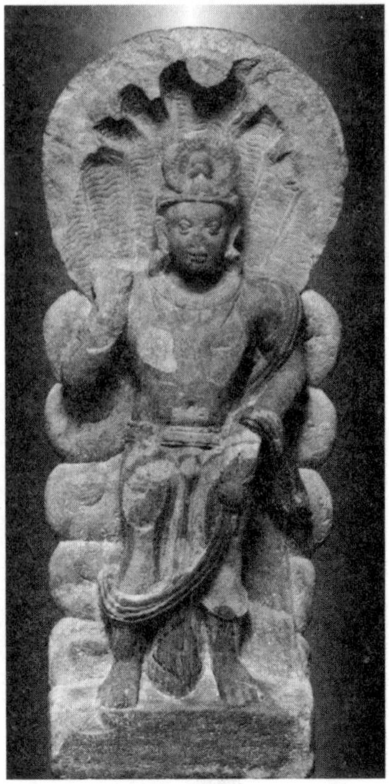

Nāga Devatā, Mathurā, U.P., Kuṣāṇa, 1st century CE

save perhaps a couple of first kings, Candragupta, for example, who is seen in the Kuṣāṇa trousers and tunic in his coins, which is natural for a king who steps into the shoes of a ruler whose preferences had a long history behind them. Significantly enough, they, like the Kuṣāṇas, also gave the country a long period of peace and prosperity — political, social, economic and religious. Thus, under them, the civilization marched ahead, practically by leaps and bounds.

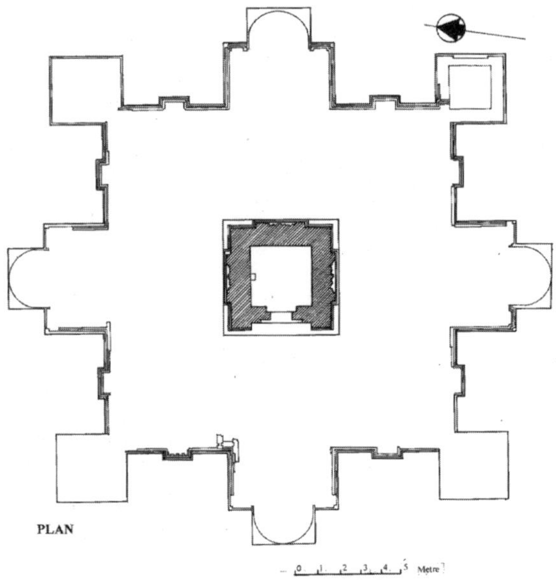

Plan of a Deogaṛh *pañcāyatana* type temple, M.P., Gupta, 5th century CE

ALL ROUND DEVELOPMENT DURING THE GUPTA PERIOD

There was all round development, particularly in fine arts — literature, both religious and non-religious, sculpture and painting, music, dance and drama; nothing lagged behind. In fact, each one of these worked in such close collaboration that their mutual interaction is more than clear from their actual products. Kālidāsa's literary metaphors, lyrics and norms of beauty are found translated in stone as much as the softness and suppleness of limbs of sculpture are found translated in painting. Bharata's *Nāṭyaśāstra* (नाट्यशास्त्र) is completely

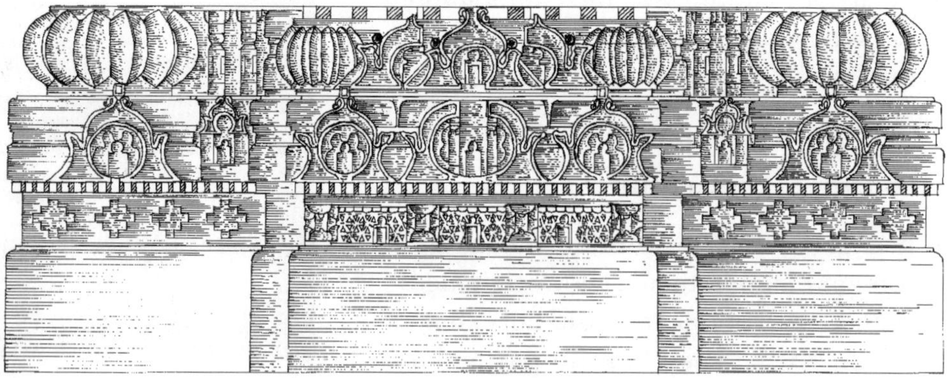

Deogaṛh temple lintel, Gupta, 5th century CE

reflected in the dance and drama scenes of not only the sculpture and painting but also in the notes of music, both vocal and instrumental. The *Viṣṇu-dharmottara* (विष्णुधर्मोत्तर) is articulated in the iconic art and architecture of this period. The epics, Purāṇas and Āgamas provided most of the themes to artists and litterateurs. India in this way achieved the orchestral harmony in different arts which beautify human life and make it worth living.

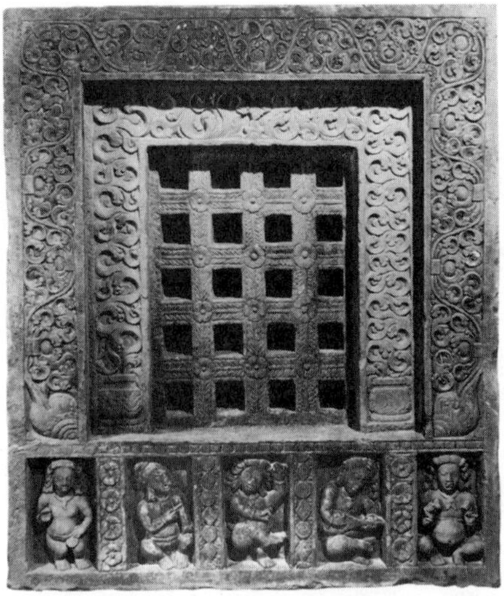

Sculptured windows, Nacanā temple, M.P., Gupta, 5th century CE

CREATIVITY AND SPIRITUALISM IN ART

The Gupta art, in spite of the constraints of implied discipline of "the orchestra," offered full liberty to the artist to beautify his own creations. This beautification was real and not the product of imposed sophistication with the help of excessive ornamentation or some other method. It was "real" because it completely harmonized the mind with matter. The "idea" and the "image" became inseparable, thanks both to the technical excellence that the Gupta artist achieved in the arts of sculpture and painting and the idiom that he chose for himself. All this is completely reflected in the famous Sārnāth Buddha head housed in the National Museum, New Delhi. This is often described as the best example of "spiritual content in stone." In other words, now a new value-system was attached to human life, the value which we still cherish in India — spiritual attainment is the highest form of joy.

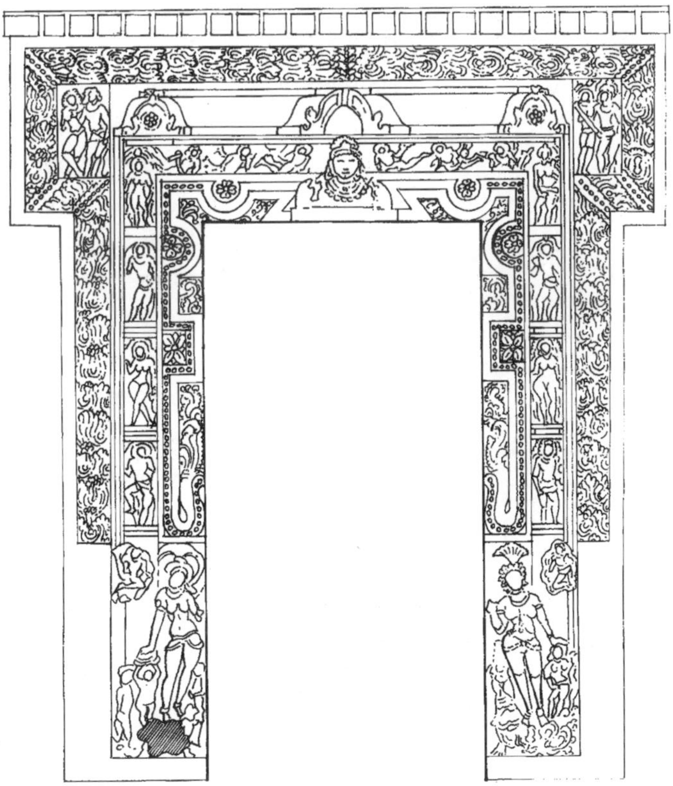

Dvāra of Śiva Temple, Bhūmarā, Gupta, 5th century CE

It is called *ānanda* (आनन्द) or "bliss." The ideal of bliss is the triumph of extra-mundane over mundane.

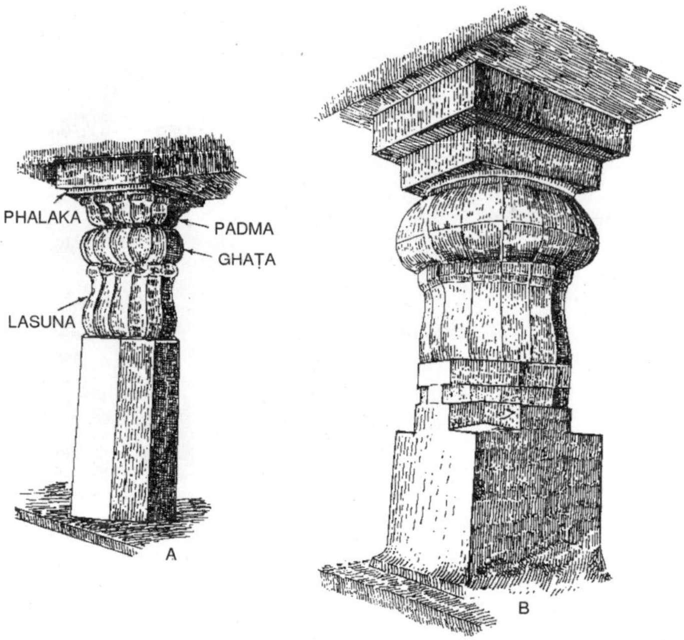

Pillars: (A) Ajantā Cave 7, 5th century CE
(B) Kānherī, Cave 1, 6th century CE

FORM (रूप) AND IDEA (भाव) IN GUPTA ART

Religious revitalism spelt out the Vedāntic ideal through numerous writings, literary as well as ecclesiastical. It was now held that only that remains the best which leads you to spirituality and not to gross, although gross is as real as the subtle and cannot be ignored. Still the path that leads to spirituality is the path of beauty in form and content both. The form was, therefore, as important to the Gupta artist as the content. What is not formally beautiful, cannot hope to lead you to spirituality or bliss, according to a new approach in art. The description of the formal beauty of Pārvatī by Kālidāsa is not incidental — it is the outcome of the new idealism. Similarly, the captivating beauty of the female forms in the Ajantā painting, the charming faces of Lakṣmī, Sītā, Pārvatī in terracottas and stone from Ahicchatra, Sārnāth and Kauśāmbī, and the soft and flowing contours as well as the posture of self-assured ease in the Nara-Nārāyaṇa and Gajendramokṣa panels of Deogaṛh temple, the Varāha with Bhūdevī panel of Eraṇ and the Sārnāth style Buddhas in stone and bronze in various museums of the world and the figures of kings, queens and Lakṣmī on Gupta gold coins present the eloquent testimony for this idealism articulated in sculpture and painting.

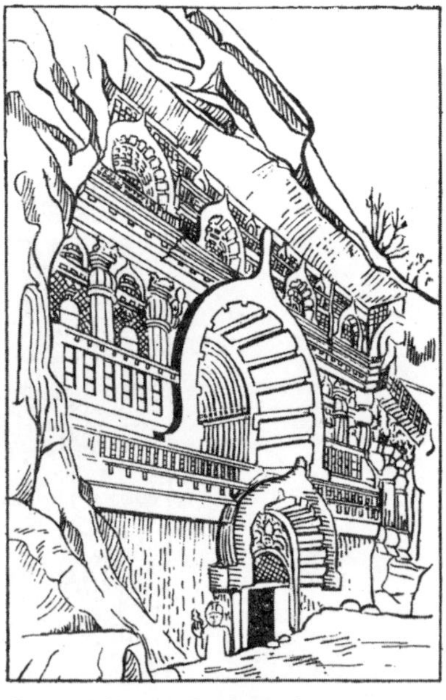

Caves, Ajantā, Maharashtra, Gupta, Vākāṭaka, 5th century CE

ARTISTIC ELEMENTS IN GUPTA ART

The Gupta figures are large in proportion but extremely light in visual weight even when they are carved in crude stone, which, of course, they generally avoided. The figures just float in air. They are marked by the sense of weightlessness. They are not at all heavy and earth-bound, and, therefore, present a sharp contrast with the Śuṅga *yakṣa* and Kuṣāṇa *bodhisattvas*. In narrative panels, the compositions are not only perfectly balanced but also each one forms an unbreakable unit. This is quite clear from the biographical scenes of Buddha in a Sārnāth panel housed in the National Museum as well as from the scenes in the Deogaṛh panels. By and large, they use very few ornaments, and the dress is scanty. Their eyes are often very beautifully shaped and somewhat half-closed, looking slightly downwards, as if in contemplation. It is often called "yogic posture with eyes fixed on the tip of the nose." The faces are generally oval with sharp features. The anatomical proportions are true to life although the overall treatment of physical features is highly idealized, evoking serenity in mind and admiration in heart. The drapery clings to the body as if it is wet and transparent exposing the softness of flesh and contours of the body in partial concealment.

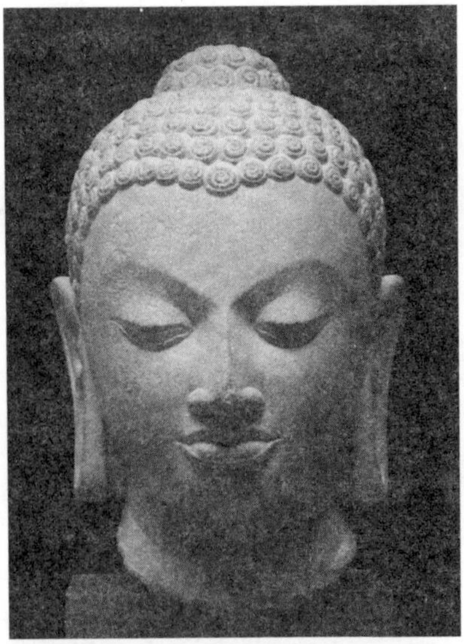

Buddha Head, Sārnāth, Gupta, 5th century CE

THE IDEALS OF GUPTA ART

Thus, the figures are not nude but the youthfulness of body is also not concealed under heavy drapery. In fact, for this very purpose the drapery is generally transparent as if it is made of fine thin silk. Buddha images from Mathurā and Sārnāth bear out this fact very clearly. These are, therefore, unlike the Gandhāran figures and Mathurā images of the Kuṣāṇa period where they are either nude or dressed heavily. The Gupta and the Vākāṭaka figures of the

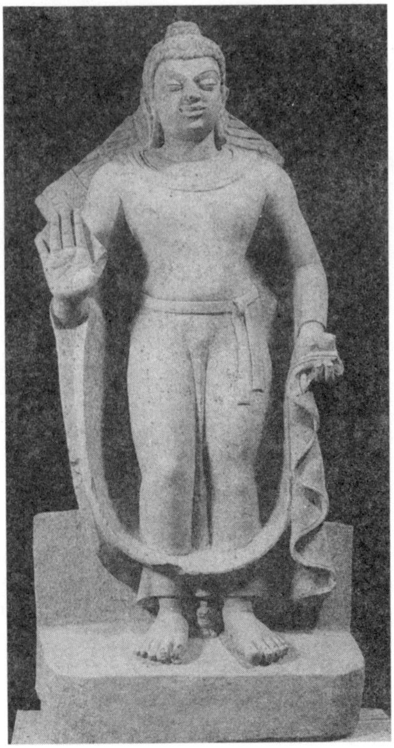

Buddha, Early Gupta period (Sārnāth style), Govindnagar, Mathurā, 5th century CE

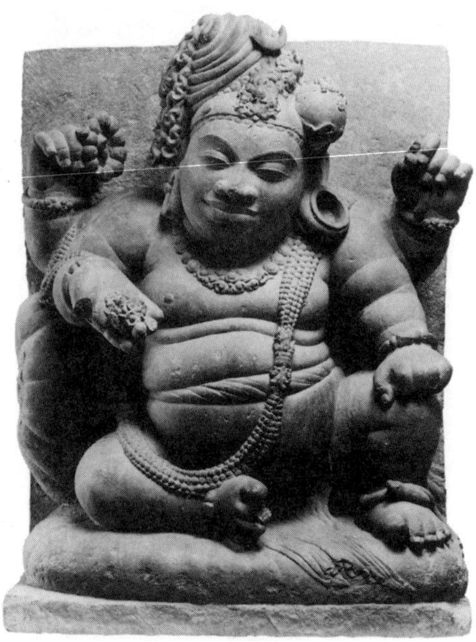

Śiva-Vāmana, Mansar, Maharashtra, (Vākāṭaka), 6th century CE

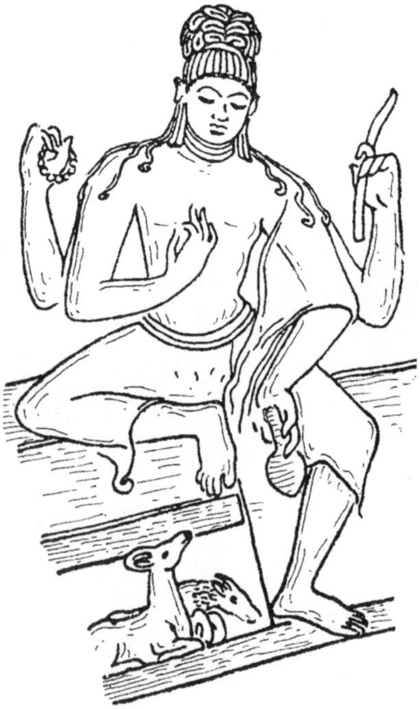

Image of Nārāyaṇa, Deogaṛh, Gupta, 5th century CE

fifth-sixth centuries CE also present a great contrast to the Greek norms of beauty even though anatomical precision is emphasized in both the arts. The contrast lies in the norms of beauty. The Greek norm was based on Olympic beauty, i.e. the beauty of the male atheletes who participate in Olympic games, while the Gupta norm is based on the beauty of a youthful *yogī*, calm and composed not showing off his developed muscles but expressing his bliss. Some adherence to *iconometry* (प्रतिमा-विज्ञान), as given in *Viṣṇudharmottara*, etc. is equally visible although the iconographic canons were still not meticulously followed.

THE CLASSICAL ART OF THE GOLDEN AGE

The Gupta art was, therefore, the culmination of the developmental process that started in the Śuṅga times. The apex was now reached. It was, therefore, classical which provided model for the later periods. But after attaining this height, some stagnation set in, in the quality of art in northern India after the sixth century. Although there occurred a marked prolification in artistic activity that spirit could not be recaptured. The quality was sacrificed at the altar of quantity and technical achievements. Slowly and gradually spirituality or bliss gave way to draftmanship and craftmanship. In short, art in north India was replaced by craft, technically excellent, canonically perfect but artistically a bit poor from the ninth century onwards.

But the decline in spirituality in the works of art did not occur instantly. It passed through a long period of slow and gradual process of change. The art of late sixth, seventh and eighth centuries are still having a large amount of classical Gupta style and feeling. The happenings of this period are fascinating and may now be recounted.

THE BIRTH OF REGIONAL STYLES IN ART AND ARCHITECTURE

The last phase of the Guptas in Bihar and Uttar Pradesh and the Vākāṭakas in Maharashtra coincided with the emergence of a number of powerful dynasties in different parts of the country. The Cāḷukyas in Karnataka, the Pallavas in Tamil Nadu, the Vallabhīs in Gujarat, the Maitrakas in Rajasthan and Gujarat borderlands, the Pālas in Bengal and parts of Bihar, and the Gurjara–Pratihāras in northern India are known for their architectural and artistic achievements. This was the period, it may be noted, in which the canonical texts and the Purāṇas and the Āgamas, which started taking concrete shape in the Gupta period, got completely crystallized and started throwing their weight all round.

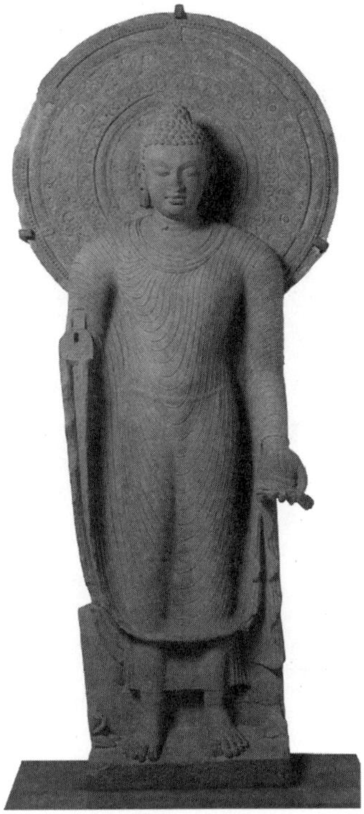

Buddha, Gupta period, Jamālpur mound, Mathurā, 5th century CE

POST-GUPTA ART — PHASE I (Sixth–Eighth Centuries)

The post-Gupta periods in India are marked by prolification of regional styles both in art and temple architecture. This period is marked by great religious strides which simultaneously witnessed the birth of a plethora of cults in each religion. The net result of this phenomenon was the multiplication of cult-gods and goddesses.

MAITRAKAS ART (Sixth–seventh centuries)

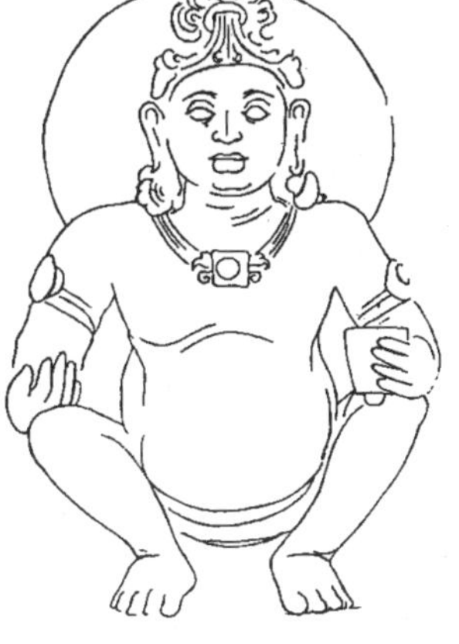

Jambhala, Deccan, 8th century CE

The Maitrakas of Vallabhī in Saurashtra embodied the Gupta tradition in a remarkable manner with most of its sensitivity. The finest examples of sculptures of this school come from the Sun Temple of Gopā as well as from Shāmalājī. Akoṭā, on the outskirts of Vaḍodarā, has also yielded a large number of beautiful bronzes. Works of art in stone are equally of superb quality. In the National

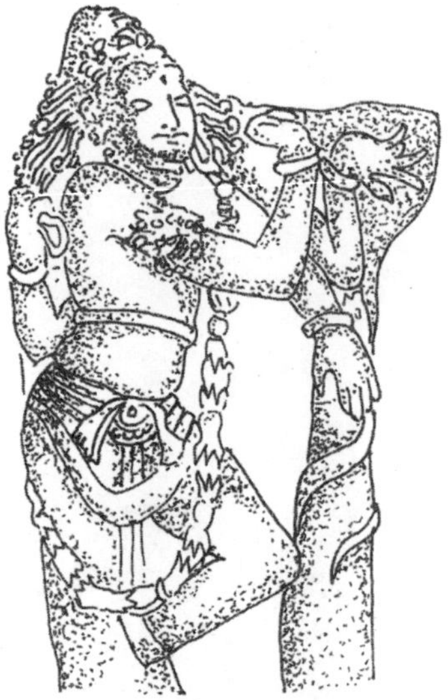

Dvārapāla, Eastern Cāḷukyan, Vijayawāḍā, A.P., late 7th century CE

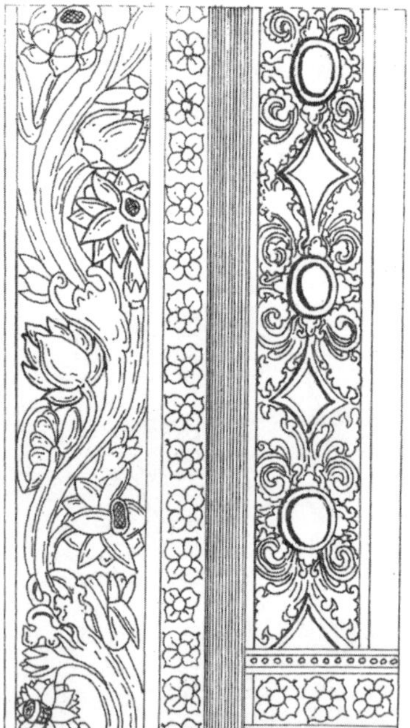

Rāṣṭrakūṭa art-motifs, Ellorā, Cave 2, 8th century CE

Museum there is a beautiful figure of a lady in greenish soft stone belonging to this school of art.

EARLY CĀḶUKYAN ART (Sixth–seventh centuries)

Bādāmī and Aihoḷe in Karnataka give us the best examples of early Cāḷukya art and architecture. They clearly show two dominant features: (i) in architecture there is the coexistence of Drāviḍa and Nāgara *śikhara* styles, and (ii) trend towards exhuberance of ornamentation, both in architectural members, such as pillars with triple brackets, and in art in the figures of Brahmā, Śiva and Viṣṇu. The famous Anantaśāyinī Viṣṇu in Aihoḷe temple shows the same trend although the trend is incipient. The Rāmeśvara cave temple of Ellorā also shows the same.

In the eighth century these trends became well marked since now the Cāḷukyas were receiving cultural waves from the Pallavas of Kāñcīpuram in Tamil Nadu. The Kailāsanāth temple of Kāñcī offered the model for the Virūpākṣa temple of Paṭṭaḍakal, near Bādāmī.

RĀṢṬRAKŪṬA ART (Eighth–ninth centuries)

The Rāṣṭrakūṭas succeeded the Cāḷukyas in the Deccan in CE 753. Kṛṣṇa II, their greatest ruler, caused the world famous 100 ft tall, Kailāsa temple at Ellorā since it represents all the features of an architectural temple in rock-cut monument — *gopuram, nandī-maṇḍapam, mahāmaṇḍapam, garbha-gṛha*, etc.

In the second half of the eighth century, their rulers made another world-famous rock-cut temple — at Elephaṇṭā — with superb sculptures, such as that of Maheśa or Sadāśiva (erroneously called *trimūrti*) form.

This art still retains the basic qualities of the Gupta Art — serenity, spirituality and excellence in balance, poise and gaiety. However, compositions now become a bit crowded and ornamentation moved towards multiplication.

PALLAVA ART (Sixth–eighth centuries)

The Pallavas start their career in the sixth century at Veṅgī, with a still earlier beginning, but it is in the seventh century that Mahāmalla created some of the most magnificent rock-cut temples at Mahābalipuram or Māmallapuram. The Pallavas gave us three types of monuments. The first includes five rock-cut *ratha* (रथ) temples, each one free-standing. These are the textbook examples of Indian rock-cut temple art and architecture. The Dharmarāja Ratha at Mahābalipuram is the highest and is known for the second example of a Hindu king getting his portrait sculptured; earlier to this only his father Mahendravarman (CE 600-25) had his and his two queens' effigies carved in Ādivarāha cave. They were in the position of devotees. The Draupadī Ratha is known for its roof being merely single cell of *parṇaśālā* (पर्णशाला) type where the roof is a copy of thatched hut.

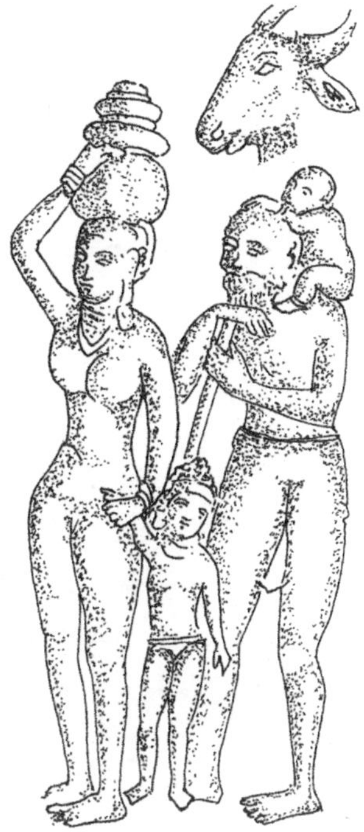

Family scene, Pallava, Māmallapuram, Tamil Nadu, 7th century CE

The second type is *maṇḍapa*s, or rock-cut caves, such as the Ādivarāha cave.

The third type is called *tīrtham* or open-air carving on the face of a rock. At Mahābalipuram, we have the famous *Gaṅgāvataraṇa* (गंगावतरण) scene, sometimes called "Arjuna's Penance" (अर्जुन-तपस), carved in this style.

However, the Pallava art of the seventh century differs form the Gupta art in the following ways:

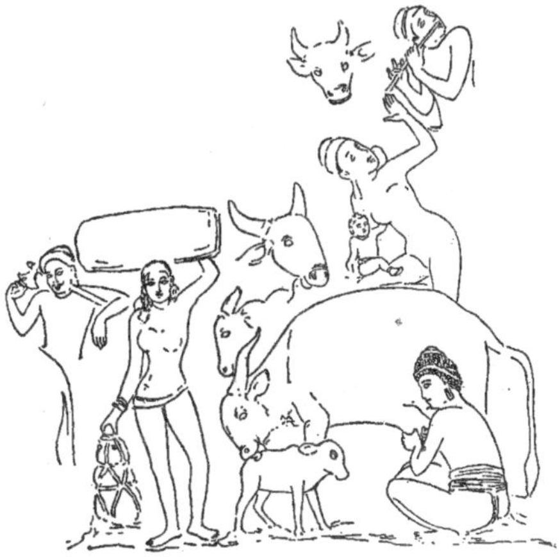

Cowherd scene, Māmallapuram, Tamil Nadu, Pallava art, 7th century CE

the forms of human bodies in the Pallava art

show greater slenderness; the faces are near oval; the faces have high cheek-bones; the humans are infinitely gracious; the animals excel the rest of the figures.

Rājasiṁha, however, wanted structural temples as well and, therefore, caused the Kailāsanātha temple built at Kāñcī; the figures, their dresses and ornaments, countenance and lightweightness, are simple and gracious.

On the whole, the Pallava art is nearer to Gupta art tradition, just as the Early Cāḷukyan and Maitraka arts were, than to the later art traditions either of the north or of the south.

That brings us to the last eighth-twelfth-century bracket.

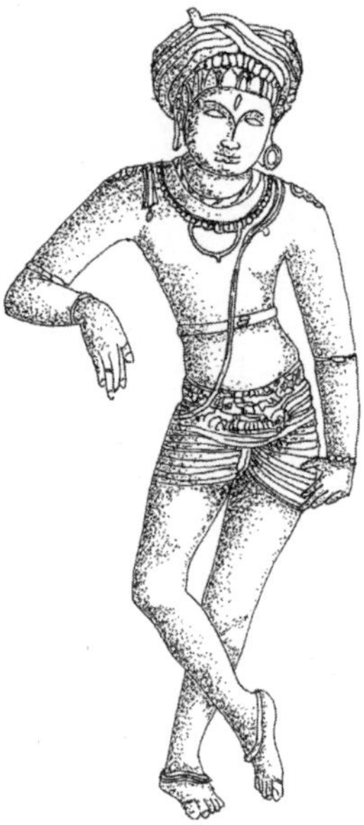

Vr̥ṣabhavāhana Śiva, bronze, Coḷa, Thañjāvur, Tamil Nadu, 10th century CE

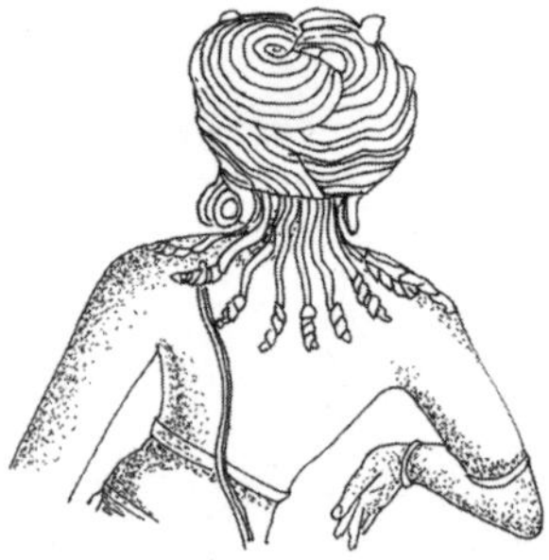

Back of Śiva showing *jaṭā-bhāra*

POST-GUPTA ART — PHASE II (Ninth–Twelfth Centuries)

GURJARA-PRATIHĀRA ART (Eighth–tenth centuries)

In the north the Guptas were succeeded by the Vardhanas whose greatest king was Harṣavardhana, and after him the Gurjara-Pratihāras came to power. They, under Nāgabhaṭṭa and Mihirbhoja, produced some of the great works of art and architecture marked by elaboration in jewellery and craftsmanship in figure carving. The brick temple of Lakṣmaṇa with great elaboration found at Sirpur in Chhatisgarh, and Temple 18 at Sāñcī belonged to the Vardhana period.

COḶA ART (Ninth–twelfth centuries)

The Pallavas were succeeded by the Coḷas in Tamil Nadu. They were the most powerful dynasty of the south Indian history since their two kings, Rājarāja (CE 985-1018) and Rājendra (CE 1018-33) had a vast empire with intimate political, cultural and economic contacts with South-East Asian countries and Sri Lanka. The art that flourished in this period, both in stone and bronze, as well as in painting, represents the mature phase of Indian art. The Coḷa art indeed marks the culmination in the south Indian art, which started in the early Cāḷukyan and Pallava times, just as the Gupta art marked the culmination in the north Indian art which had started in the Śuṅga times. In both the cases it involved the period of five centuries — from the Śuṅga to Gupta it was from the second century BCE to the fifth century CE and from the Pallavas to Coḷas, it was from the sixth to the twelfth century.

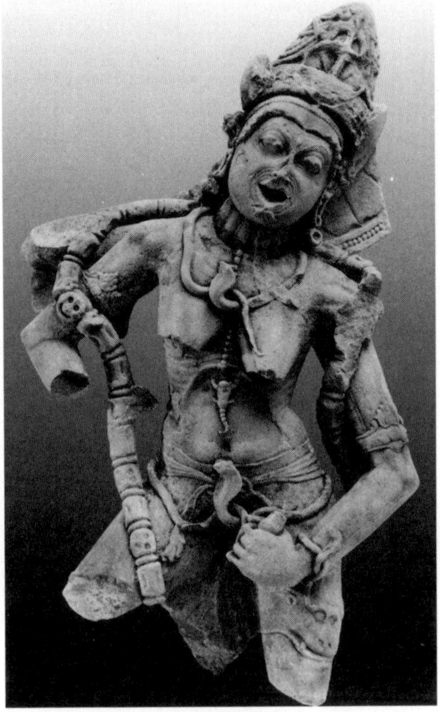

Cāmuṇḍā, Hiṅgalājgaṛh, M.P., 10th century CE

The two temples which represent the highest water mark of the Coḷa art and architecture are Bṛhadīśvara temple (CE 1000) of Thañjāvur (Tañjor) and the Gaṅgaikoṇḍacoḷapuram temple, near Kumbakoṇam (CE 1025). The former temple is marked by a huge and tall *vimāna* (विमान), with thirteen diminishing storeys, over the *garbha-gṛha*, with the *gopurams* comparatively lower in height, while in the latter temple these positions interchange themselves, the *vimāna* on the *sanctum sanctorum* or *garbha-gṛha* becomes smaller than the *gopurams* (गोपुरम्) on the four gateways. It is significant to note that in the subsequent periods, the temples of south India follow the latter tradition. In Kāñcīpuram the Coḷas built what is called the "town of temples," indeed we get the temples here in the largest concentration.

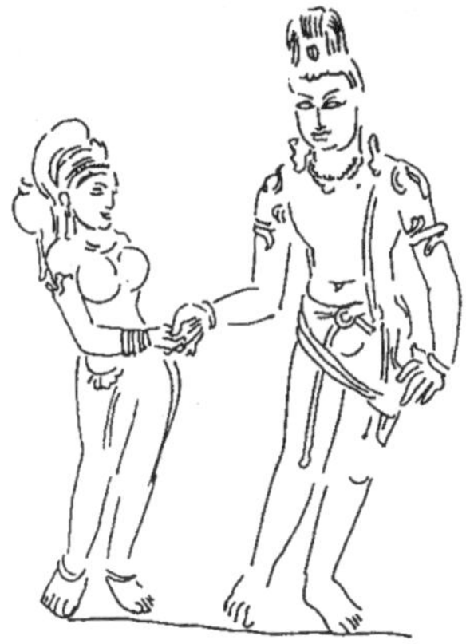

Śiva-Pārvatī, Tamil Nadu, 10th century CE

The Gaṅgaikoṇḍacoḷapuram temple is possibly the only example in which all the 108 forms of dance, as mentioned in the *Nāṭyaśāstra*, are depicted through various panels of dancing Śiva. The Thañjāvur temple, on the other hand, is famous not only for various Śiva images on the walls of the

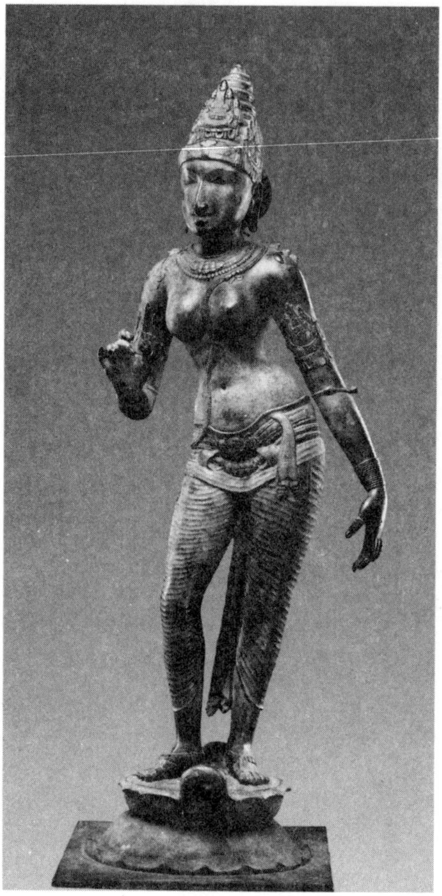

Devī, bronze, Coḷa, 11th century CE

Bṛhadīśvara temple, modelled on Āgamic texts, but it is also known for a very powerful school of painting done under the patronage of the kings.

The Bronzes

The Coḷa art is, however, best represented through bronzes, mostly housed in temples and the State Museum, Chennai but found in small numbers all over the world; some beautiful examples are in the National Museum, New Delhi. They produced the best Śiva-Naṭarājas. The best of all, of the eleventh century, is from Tiruvālangāḍu, district Chittor. Rāma, Sītā and Hanumān group in the State Museum Chennai is another important collection of superb castings in bronze. "Bharat with Rāma's sandals" is a unique piece in the National Museum, New Delhi. In the same collection is the famous *Caturatāṇḍava* (चतुरताण्डव) form of Naṭarāja of the Pallava–Coḷa transition period, ninth century.

The Coḷa Naṭarāja images solved one of the greatest problems facing Indian art: how to express the cosmic metaphysical concept of *Motion and Rest* which lies under the very foundation of creation myths. The Coḷa art is also known for perfecting the technique of *cire-perdue* or lost-wax process of bronze casting, which, of course, was first initiated in India in the Indus–Sarasvatī times, some 5000 years ago, but then lost to us for over a millennium. In this technique the image is first made in wax; it is then coated in several fine clay coats and dried in shade; followed by making two holes, one on the top and the other on the bottom. It is then put into fire; due to heat the wax runs off through the holes. Thus was created a hollow mould. Just fill it up with molten metal. Allow it to cool down and then break the mould. The metal image can be filed for final dressing. It reappeared in the Maurya–Śuṅga times.

Belonging to this period, we have the unique image of a woman playing on *vīṇā* (वीणा) from the excavations at Ropaṛ, now Rūpa Nagar, near Ambālā, in Punjab.

Coḷa bronzes are marked by not only soft modelling, graceful flowing contours and tasteful ornaments but also by serenity which goes with the inner "bliss" of the gods and goddesses transmitted to the *bhakta*s or devotees. Poise and gaiety are also marked in them. That is why these are so very delicate, sophisticated and charming to look at. And this applies not only to Devī images but also the male images, such as those of *go-pālaka* Kṛṣṇa.

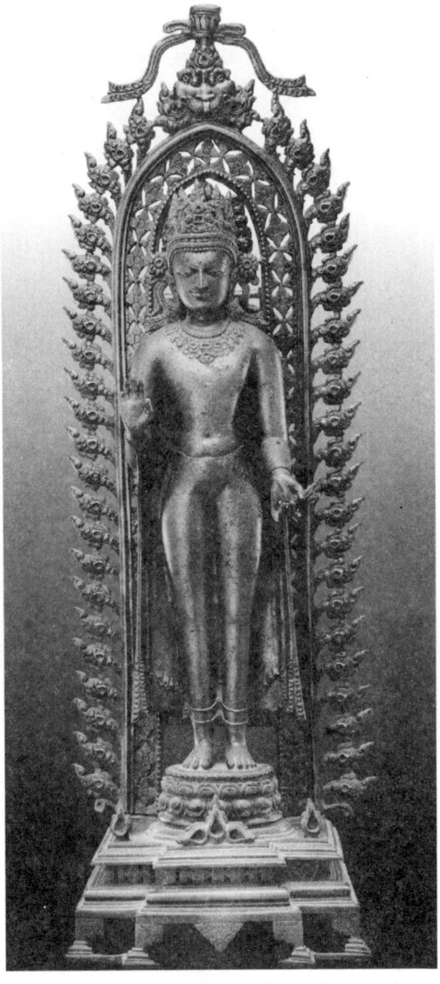

Crowned Buddha, Kurkihāra, Bihar, 10th century CE

PĀLA ART (Eighth–eleventh centuries)

Contemporary with the Late Pallavas and Coḷas, i.e. from the eighth to the eleventh century, we have the early Pāla kings patronizing stone sculptures and bronzes, both. Nālandā was the greatest centre of Pāla art of the ninth and tenth centuries, maintaining close contacts with South-East Asia.

South-East Asian countries of Indonesia, Thailand, Cambodia, etc. show strong Indian currents of art and architectural traditions and created in history what was once called "Greater Indian Art" with active support from the Coḷa art and architecture — somewhat similar situation in the context of European art the roots of which lie in the classical art of Greeks and Romans.

The Pāla art of Nālandā, iconographically, passed through three different stages:

(i) *Early Mahāyāna* (महायान) *phase* with Buddha and *bodhisattva* images, both in stone and bronze.

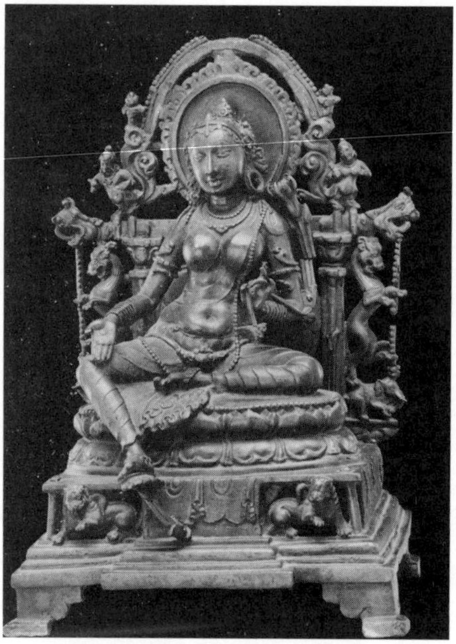

Tārā, Kurkihāra, Bihar, 9th century CE

(ii) *Sahajayāna* (सहजयान) *phase* with images, mostly bronzes, of various new Buddhist deities, both male and female.

(iii) *Kāpālika* (कापालिक) *phase* during which *kālacakra* images, mostly of bronze, were made, and even exported.

The Pāla bronzes of highest quality, however, come from the Kurkihāra hoard in Bihar, although such bronzes have been found at Vikramaśilā and other places also. The Pāla stone sculptures, mainly Buddhist, and secondarily Vaiṣṇava, have been discovered at Nālandā, Bodh-Gayā, Rajashāhī, and Khiciṅga in Mayūrbhañja. They are generally in schistose black stone of Rājamahal type with very smooth and oily touch. These are marked by large proportions, poses or *mudrā*s of ease, and iconographic details, particularly those which belong to the Late Pāla period. Like the post-Coḷa art examples they also started becoming stereotyped, more important as examples of iconographical details of complex esoteric nature, than as works of great art — technically excellent, aesthetically pleasing but artistically slightly less expressive.

HOYASAḶA ART (Eleventh–thirteenth centuries)

Contemporary with the late Pāla and early post-Coḷa period (eleventh-thirteenth centuries) we have in the southern region of Karnataka the rule of the Hoyasaḷas who developed their own characteristic style of art and architecture. First of all, they chose a very fine textured soft stone, bluish-black chlorite schist, which could yield to lathe work as well as initiate the minute carvings of the carpenters and goldsmiths. The figures are simply loaded with intricately carved ornaments from top to bottom. The Halebiḍ temple in district Hasan, about 85 km from Mysore, presents the best examples of the Hoyasaḷa art. On it is portrayed the entire heaven of Indra. Men, women and gods on the walls of this temple present the climax of workmanship, though with less degree of spirituality. The nose is sharp, the eyes are long, narrow and idealized, the poses have various twists, although the legs are rather heavy and the body proportions squatish.

Another group of important Hoyasaḷa temples is in Beḷur, in the same Hasan district. The Keśava temple of Somnāthpur, around 32 km from Śrīraṅgapaṭṭanam, is another outstanding example of Hoyasaḷa School of art and architecture.

ORISSA SCHOOL (Eighth–thirteenth centuries)

Contemporary with the Pāla–Sena School (eighth–thirteenth centuries), we have in Orissa some of the finest examples of art and architecture of another style.

(i) Paraśurāmeśvara (CE 750).

(ii) Mukteśvara (CE 950).

(iii) Liṅgarāja (CE 1000).

(iv) Rāja-Rānī (CE 1150).

(v) Sūrya temple of Koṇārka (CE 1250).

On the one hand, these intricately carved temples show the gradual development of basically Nāgara style of architecture, from the simple *śikhara* on the *garbha-gṛha* of Paraśurāmeśvara through the addition of front *maṇḍapa*, called *pīḍhā deula* (पीढा देउल), of the Rāja-Rānī, to the chariot on twelve wheels, run by seven horses, and a separate *nāṭya-maṇḍapa* (नाट्य-मण्डप) or pavilion for dance of

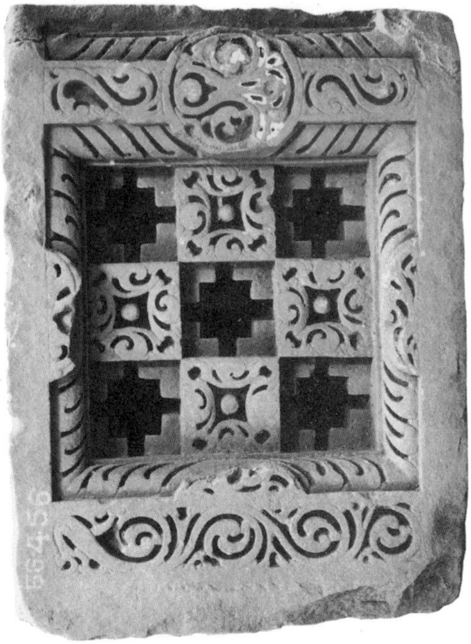

Temple *jālī*. Astabhya Hills, U.P., 10th century CE

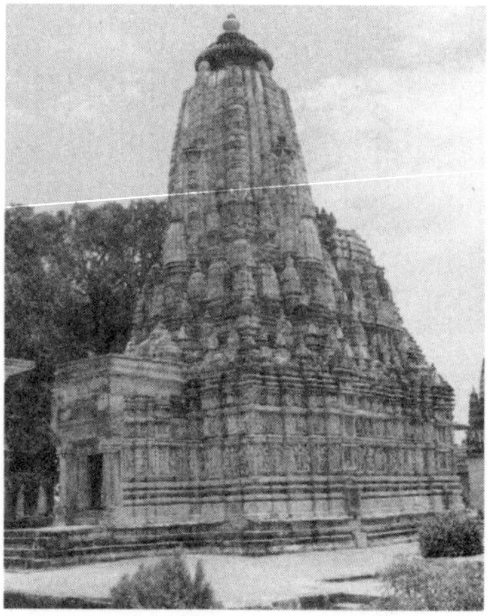

Pārśvanātha Temple, Khajurāho, M.P., 10th century CE

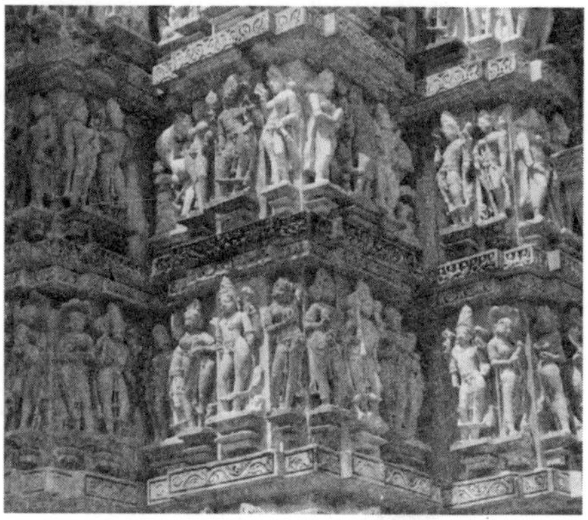

Khajurāho, M.P., Candela, 10th century CE

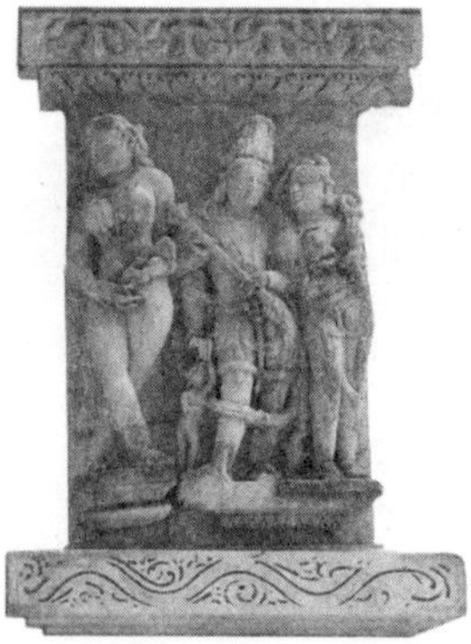

Close-up of a pillar, Khajurāho, M.P., Candela, 10th century CE

Koṇārka. The sculptures present exuberance of a rare kind — enormous, multiplying but not crowding. The emphasis, in the post-CE 1000 sculptures, is on craftsmanship as was the case in south India as a whole. In temple architecture the emphasis was on monumentality, largeness and expansiveness, leading to what is called the birth of "Temple Complexes." But the conception, both in art and architecture, was absolutely fresh. In fact, with the passage of time tastes also keep on changing and no value judgement should be given either with regard to the changing styles of art and architecture in Orissa or elsewhere.

CANDELA ART (Tenth–eleventh centuries)

Khajurāho in Madhya Pradesh was the capital town and temple town of the Candela rulers. About 30 temples, mostly Śaiva and Vaiṣṇava, but some Jaina also, were erected within 100 years time CE 950-1050. Of these, the Kandarīya Mahādeva is superb both in quality of architecture and quantity of sculptures. Beside the Vaiṣṇava and Śaiva gods and goddesses these temples are known for *devakanyā*s (देवकन्या) some of whom may have acted as *prekṣaṇikā*s (प्रेक्षणिका) or actresses in the dance-dramas with which the royal courts were enter-tained regularly. The Śaiva temples were mostly made under the patronage of Kaula-Kāpālikas and they exhibit many forms and scenes which go with the rituals of their sects.

These sculptures are marked by superior craftsmanship which was the order of the day, both in the south and the east. The facial features are very sharp — the nose and the eyes are angular, the chin is short, often with bifurcation line, and the preference is for tall figures. They are imbued with great movement, flexibility and animation as well as undercutting and high relief.

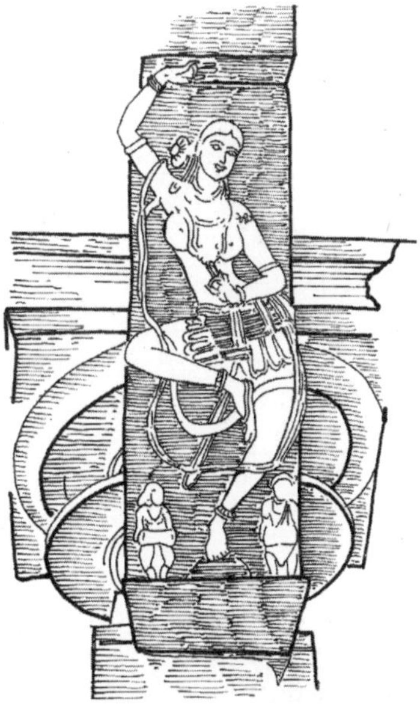

Yakṣī, bracket figure, Hanamkoṇḍa, A.P., Kākatīya, 12th century CE

Other Mediaeval Monuments and Art Traditions

NORTH INDIA

Belonging to the Mediaeval tradition of art and architecture, we have in northern India the following important monuments:

(i) The Sun Temple at Moḍherā, near Vaḍodarā, Gujarat (eleventh century).

(ii) Udayeśvara temple, near Gwalior (eleventh century).

(iii) Vimalā, Tejpāla and Vastupāla temples of the Jainas at Mt. Ābu (twelfth–thirteenth centuries).

(iv) Jayastambha (twelfth century), and Kīrtistambha of the Jainas (fifteenth century) at Chittor, in Rajasthan.

The outstanding image of this period is the famous Jaina Sarasvatī in white marble from Pāli in Bikaner, now in the National Museum, New Delhi. It is the best example of craftsmanship and ideal female forms as well as perfect example of iconographic texts. The only comparable example, perhaps better, is from Fatehpur Sīkrī, near Agra excavated recently by D.V. Sharma. It is of sandstone and painted.

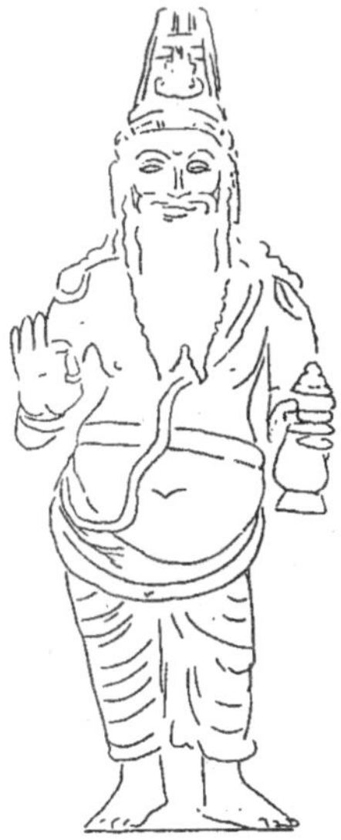

Ṛṣī, Tamil Nadu, 16th century CE

SOUTH INDIA

The Vijayanagar monumets of Hāmpī (fourteenth century) and the Nāyaka temples of Śrīraṅgapaṭṭanam as well as the Mīnākṣī temple of Madurai (sixteenth century) present us the largest panorama of sculptures in stone, metal and stucco of such a large number of gods and goddesses whose identity is possible only in terms of the *Mānasāra* (मानसार) and Āgamas (आगम). As said earlier, they represent the practically last phase of ancient Indian art — technically superb, aesthetically enchanting but spiritually somewhat poor. It was the birth of a new taste.

And it is this taste which dominated the Indian art traditions for another two to three hundred years in south India. North India unfortunately witnessed repeated waves of wholesale destruction of Hindu temples from twelfth century CE at the hands of barbarous Muslim invaders.

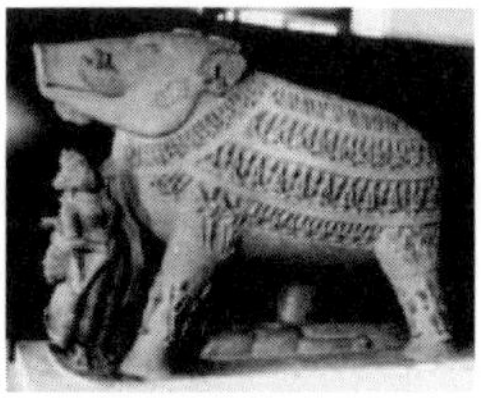

5

Iconography: The Making of Cult Images

THE first grammar of image-making was possibly written in the late Gupta period; before that there were only the descriptions of images and some attempts to create well-proportionate figures. This grammar was elaborated and perfected in the subsequent periods. Commensurate with the differences in the language of art of the north and the south, we have the grammar of the north and the grammar of the south which differ not so much on vital points as on details and variations in contours.

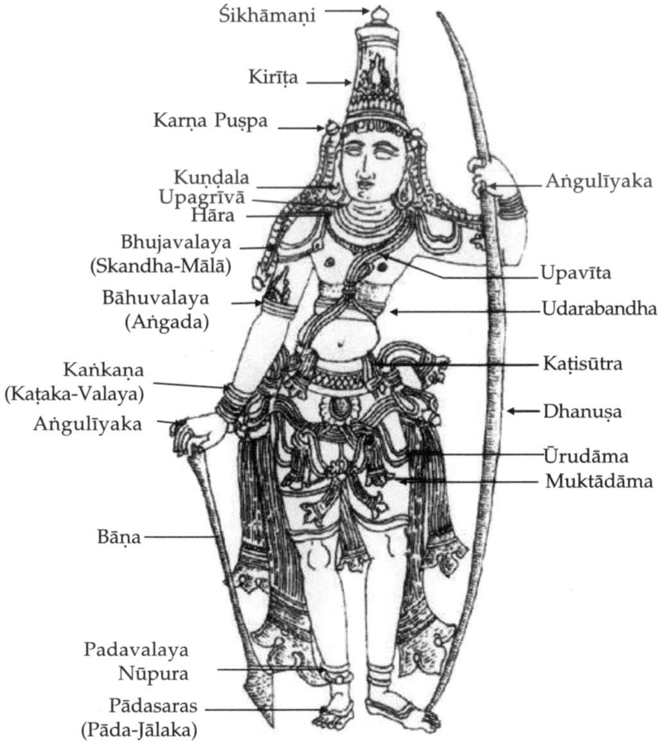

The Image of Rāma

The grammar of image-making is called "iconography" which literally means "detailed des-cription of icons." There is another term used by art historians, the scope of which is precise but wider and comprehensive. It is "iconology" which literally means "the science of icons." The scientific study of icons obviously is not the mere description of the attributes, postures and positions of icons for their correct identification and labelling, it has necessarily to take into account the various social factors, religious injunctions, literary works and personal experiences besides narratives of *bhaktas* and saints as well as measurements, etc. In other words, while iconography describes an image in its own terms, iconology takes into consideration different contextual materials which formed the proper background of the image required to be described. Here we shall confine ourselves to Indian iconography which is largely based on canons of image-making, i.e. iconometry of material for icons exists in the non-iconometric texts also.

Iconometric Sources

The important iconometric texts are the following:

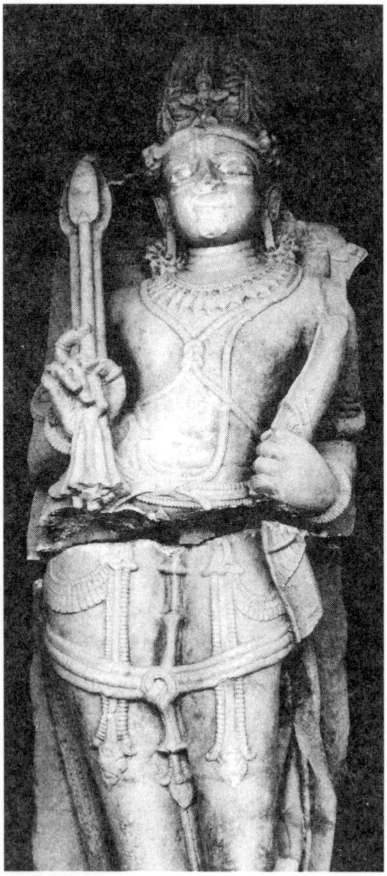

Rāma, Gaṛhwā, U.P., 10th century CE

TEXTS GOVERNING THE NORTHERN SCHOOLS

(i) Maṇḍana's *Vāstuśāstra* (मण्डन का 'वास्तु-शास्त्र')
(ii) Bhuvanadeva's *Aparājitapṛcchā* (भुवनदेव का 'अपराजितपृच्छा')
(iii) *Samarāṅgaṇa Sūtradhāra* of Mahārāja Bhoja (महाराज भोज का 'समरांगण सूत्रधार')
(iv) *Viśvakarmā Prakāśa* (विश्वकर्मा प्रकाश)

The second is dated to the eleventh century while the third is dated to the thirteenth century. About others the dates are not precise but they all belong to the time bracket of tenth to fifteenth century.

TEXTS GOVERNING THE SOUTHERN SCHOOLS

(i) *Mānasāra* (मानसार)
(ii) *Mayamata* of Mayāsura (मयासुर का 'मयमत')
(iii) *Sakalādhikāra* of Agastya (अगस्त्य का 'सकलाधिकार')
(iv) *Aṁśumadbheda* of Kaśyapa (कश्यप का 'अंशुमद्भेद')

NON-ICONOMETRIC OR ŚĀSTRĪYA SOURCES

Purāṇas, mainly for northern tradition

(i) *Viṣṇudharmottara* (Khaṇḍa III) of *Viṣṇu Purāṇa* (विष्णु पुराण का विष्णुधर्मोत्तर – खण्ड 3)

(ii) *Matsya Purāṇa* (मत्स्य पुराण)

(iii) *Agni Purāṇa* (अग्नि पुराण)

(iv) *Bṛhat-saṁhitā* of Varāhamihir (वराहमिहिर का 'बृहत्-संहिता')

Besides these, *Garuḍa* (गरुड़), *Liṅga* (लिंग), *Skanda* (स्कंद) and *Bhaviṣya* (भविष्य) Purāṇas also contain passages on iconography and iconometry.

Viṣṇu Purāṇa (विष्णु पुराण) and *Bṛhat-Saṁhitā* (बृहत्संहिता) are of the Gupta period.

Āgamas, mainly for southern tradition:

(i) *Kāmikāgama* (कामिकागम)

(ii) *Karṇāgama* (कर्णागम)

(iii) *Vaikhānasāgama* (वैखानसागम)

(iv) *Aṁśumadbhedāgama* (अंशुमद्भेदागम)

(v) *Suprabhedāgama* (सुप्रभेदागम)

It may be significant to note that the Āgamas contain *Liṅgodbhava-mūrtis* (लिंगोद्भव-मूर्ति), the feature which is only casually present in the Purāṇas. Similarly, the *dhruvabera* (ध्रुवबेर) images of Viṣṇu are common in the Āgamas, and, therefore, in the south, but not in the Purāṇas and the north. That is precisely the reason why one has to be a master of these Āgamas before he or she can hope to identify the south Indian images.

The Āgamas have three major schools — Śaiva, Vaiṣṇava and Śākta. The Vaiṣṇava school has two major branches: the Pañcarātra (पञ्चरात्र), and the Vaikhānasa (वैखानस).

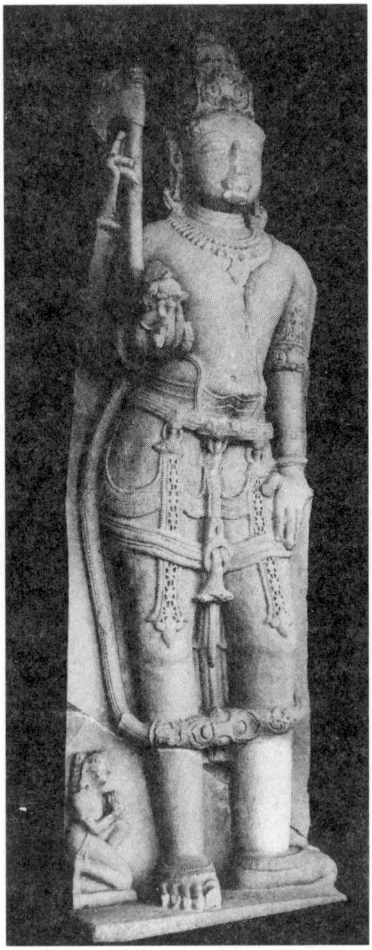

Paraśurāma, Gaṛhwā, U.P., 10th century CE

TANTRAS

In common parlance, Śaiva Tantras are called

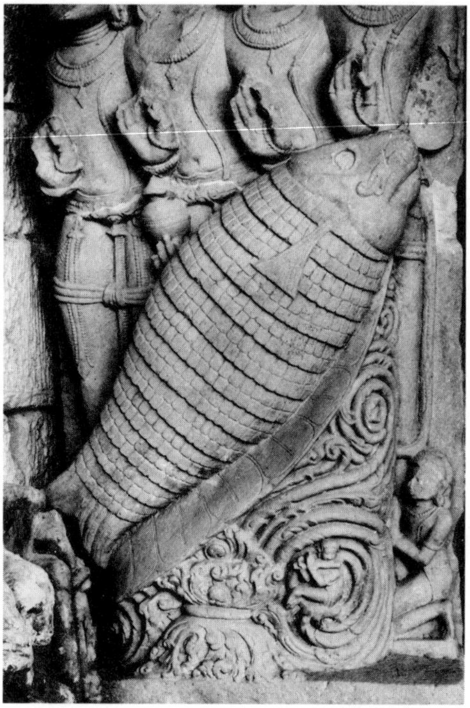

Matsyāvatāra of Viṣṇu, 9th century CE

"Āgamas" and Vaiṣṇava Tantras are called "Pañcarātras" but strictly speaking the term Tantra (तन्त्र) is to be applied only to those texts in which Śaivite and Śakti-devīs have been enumerated. Buddhist Tantras are also excluded here.

The important Tantras are as follows:

(i) *Gautamī Tantra* (गौतमी तन्त्र)

(ii) *Kālī Tantra* (काली तन्त्र)

(iii) *Mahānirvāṇa Tantra* (महानिर्वाण तन्त्र)

(iv) *Hayaśīrṣa-pañcarātra Tantra* (हयशीर्ष-पञ्चरात्र तन्त्र)

OTHER WORKS

Besides these important texts we have the following selected works which have ample material on iconography:

(a) *Abhilāṣitārthacintāmaṇi* or *Mānasollāsa* (अभिलाषितार्थ-चिंतामणि अथवा मानसोल्लास)

(b) *Haribhakti-vilāsa* (हरिभक्ति-विलास)

(c) *Īśānaśivagurudeva Paddhati* (ईशानशिवगुरुदेव पद्धति)

It is not easy to date all these texts and those for which agreed dates are available have been mentioned. But circumstantial evidence shows that although a few scholars of iconometry, like Nagnadeva, mentioned in the *Viṣṇudharmottara*, may have belonged to the Kuṣāṇa period, majority of them belonged to the period bracketed between CE 500 and CE 1300; those coming later than this period, like the writer(s) of *Śukranītisāra* (शुक्रनीतिसार) depended mainly on the existing texts for description and classification of the images, their postures, pedestals, attributes, etc.

There is one other point worth noting: it should not be imagined that all the available images can be identified on the basis of *śilpa*-texts. J.N. Banerjea has quoted a number of examples which are not mentioned in them. Similarly, the texts often give a very large number of forms of Śiva, Viṣṇu, Liṅgas and Śaktis but all of them are not found in plastic art and painting. This appears to be due to the personal images, dreams, literary descriptions, etc. which were not always accepted or incorporated by the canon writers.

SOME CLASSIFICATIONS OF IMAGES

The classification of images in India has been done by various scholars and differently, such as northern and southern, or Hindu, Śākta, Bauddha and Jaina, or as Gandhāra, Mathurā, Sārnāth, Amarāvatī, or else as Śuṅga, Kuṣāṇa, Gupta, Pallava and Coḷa, i.e. on the basis of dynastic names. There is, however, one other but very important Āgamic classification of Hindu images. It is as follows:

(a) *Cala* and *acala* ('चल' एवं 'अचल'), i.e. portable and non-portable or fixed.

(b) *Pūrṇa* and *apūrṇa* ('पूर्ण' एवं 'अपूर्ण')

(c) *Śāminta* and *aśāminta* ('शामिंत' एवं 'अशामिंत')

The *cala* or portable images are generally made of metal or wood or light stone, and in proportion these are small for obvious reasons — these are to be carried on chariots through the town or village as the case may be on certain festive occasions. The *acala* or non-portable images are generally large in size and heavy in weight, usually made of stone or metal. These are permanently installed in the temples, some as the main deity in the *garbha-gṛha* or *sanctum sanctorum*, some as *parivāra devatā*s or family gods of the main deity, and some in the subsidiary temples, such as those in the *pañcāyatana* form of temples.

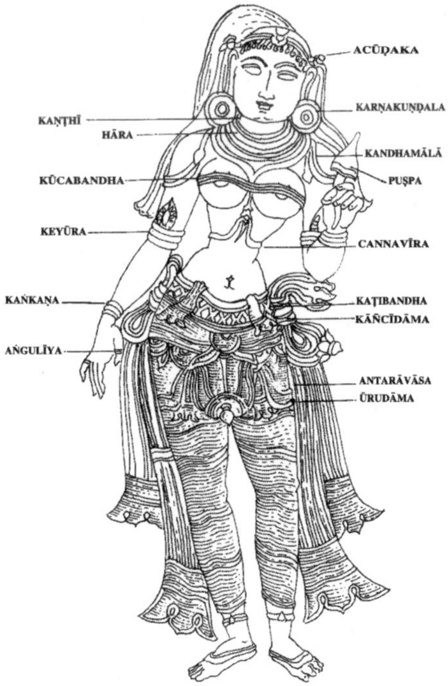

Female decorations

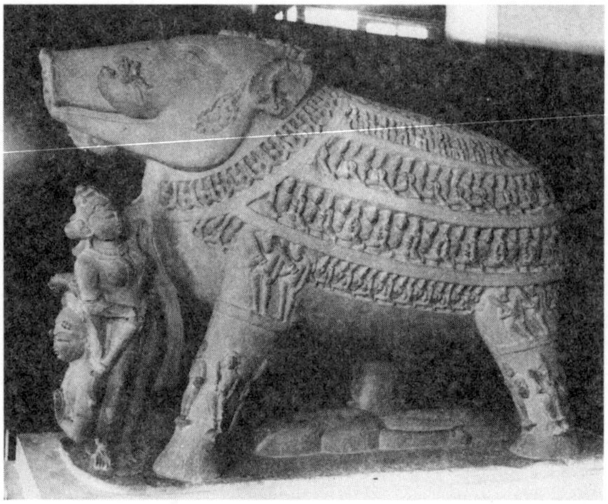

Varāhāvatāra of Viṣṇu, Dudhai, U.P., 11th century CE

According to *Bhṛgu Vaikhānasāgama* (भृगु वैखानसागम) these two kinds of images are further divisible as follows:

CALA (चल) OR PORTABLE IMAGES

These images could be :

(a) *Kautuka bera* (कौतुक बेर), meant for *pūjā* or worship. The term *bera* used for image is popular in south Indian texts.

(b) *Utsava bera* (उत्सव बेर), those meant for festive occasions.

(c) *Bali bera* (बलि बेर), those meant for votive offerings in daily *pūjā*.

(d) *Snapana bera* (स्नपन बेर), meant for bathing the image with sacred water or milk or honey or all put together.

ACALA (अचल) OR STATIONARY IMAGES

These images could be :

(a) *Sthānaka* (स्थानक), standing.

(b) *Āśanīya* (आशनीय), lying stretch in rest. Meant only for Viṣṇu and Buddha.

There are several other categories of sub-classification, but that is a matter of details.

PŪRṆA (पूर्ण) OR COMPLETE IMAGES

These are the images carved fully in-the-round with all hands, legs, attributes, face, hair-do, etc. These are also called, "manifest images."

APŪRṆA (अपूर्ण) OR INCOMPLETE IMAGES

These images are not full, they are sculptured and often only up to the bust. These are sometimes combined with another cognate form. These are also called "partially manifest," even "non-manifest." *Mukhaliṅga*, the so-called *trimūrti*, i.e. Sadāśiva image of Elephaṇṭā, and *bāṇa-liṅgas* are the examples of this category.

ŚĀNTA (शांत) IMAGES OR IMAGES WITH PLEASING COUNTENANCE

These images portray serenity, spirituality and bliss, such as Viṣṇu in Nara-Nārāyaṇa panel of Deogaṛh.

AŚĀNTA (अशांत) IMAGES OR IMAGES WITH AGITATED COUNTENANCE

These images show anger and are in aggressive mood and posture, such as those of Narasiṁha, Tripurāntaka and Mahiṣāsuramardinī.

As mentioned earlier, there are various other classifications, for example, one can classify them on the basis of *rasas* (रस), nine or ten of them mentioned in the Rasa Śāstras, but that is again a matter of details.

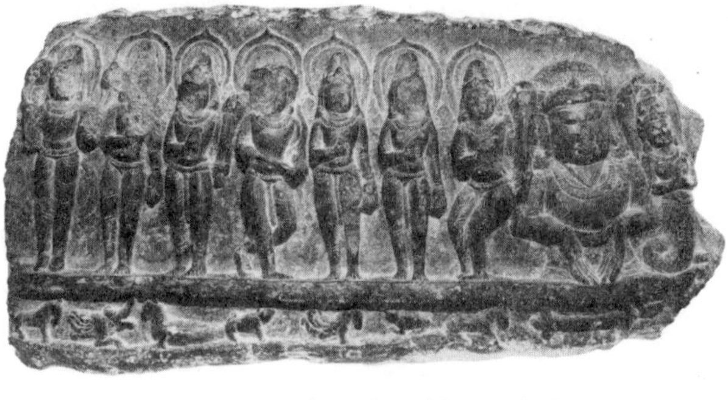

Nava-grahas, Gorakhpur, U.P., 12th century CE

Mudrās

In Hindu iconography, *mudrās* (मुद्रा) or body poses supported by hand poses and gestures created by fingers and palm, play a very important role simply because it is through them that the images speak all about themselves, and the worshipper makes a perfect rapport with his or her *iṣṭa-devatā* (इष्ट-देवता) or the image of the god of his choice. A thing made of non-living matter, such as stone and metal, is after all dead and mute but once it is given a recognizable form through specific marks of cognisance, man comprehends that. Give it a combination of specific poses and attributes and it starts speaking which is understandable to those who know the language of these poses and gestures of the whole body or *mudrās*. This language of poses and gestures, i.e. *mudrā-śāstra*, is to be learnt from the iconographic texts (canons, epigraphs, devotional poems, etc.) since it is embodied in them.

In the *Nāṭyaśāstra* and the *Abhinaya Darpaṇa* we have a long list of these *mudrās*. R.K. Poduval has divided them into Vedic *mudrās* (45), *laukika mudrās* (64) and *tāntric mudrās* (108). In total 217. According to *Tantraśāstra* Viṣṇu has 19 *mudrās* which here actually means attributes (*śaṅkha, cakra, gadā,* etc.), Śiva has 10 (*yoni, triśūla, liṅga,* etc.), Gaṇeśa has 7 (goad, elephant tooth, sweet-balls, etc.), Sarasvatī has 7 (rosary or *akṣamālā, vīṇā,* sacred book Veda, etc.), Sūrya has 1 (*padma* or lotus), Agni has 7 (flames, etc.), and so on. In the *tāntric mudrās* or attributes we have *tilaka, jaṭā, bhasma,* etc. In the *Viṣṇudharmottara, nṛtya* or dance is also included in the list of *mudrās*. The *Samarāṅgaṇa Sūtradhāra* gives a list of 64 hand poses, 6 poses of legs, and 9 poses of body.

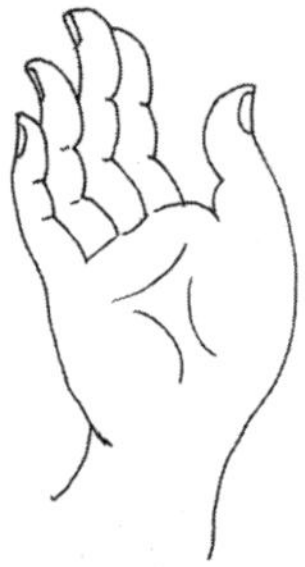

Abhaya-mudrā

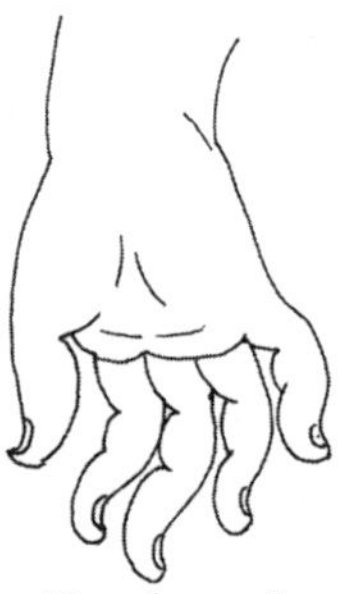

Varada-mudrā

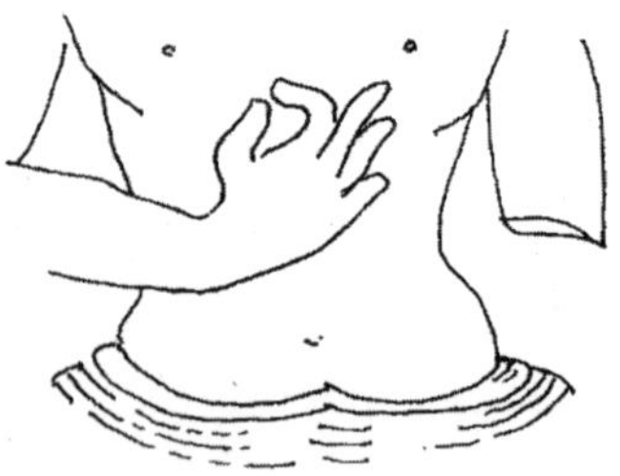

Jñāna-mudra

HASTA MUDRĀS (हस्त-मुद्रा) OR HAND POSES

***Abhaya-mudrā* (अभय-मुद्रा)** : In it the right hand is raised to the shoulder with palm facing the viewer in a manner of protection. The idea conveyed here is that the deity protects you from all evils. "Move fearlessly, I am here to protect you," is the message conveyed.

***Varada-mudrā* (वरद-मुद्रा)** : In it the right hand is generally hanging down with palm facing the viewer. The idea conveyed is that the god gives boon to his devotee, the boon is that no harm could be done to him.

***Jñāna-mudrā* (ज्ञान-मुद्रा)** : In it thumb and the index finger of the right hand meet each other and touch the heart. The hand faces inwards. The idea conveyed is that the knowledge comes from within.

***Vyākhyāna-mudrā* (व्याख्यान-मुद्रा)** : In it the thumb and the index finger join but they face the viewer. It is also called *cin-mudrā* (चिन्-मुद्रा), the idea conveyed is that the knowledge is given to others as was done by Buddha at Sārnāth and as is done while one delivers a lecture or makes a speech. In a cognate form the other hand is also raised and held against the chest almost touching the right palm. It is called *dharmacakra-mudrā* (धर्मचक्र-मुद्रा) for the same reason since it is in this pose that Buddha is said to have delivered his First Sermon.

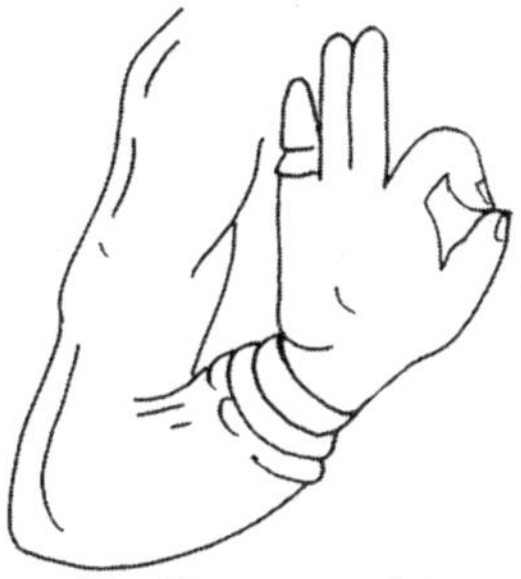

Vyākhyāna-mudrā

Sometimes *jñāna* and *vyākhyāna mudrā*s are mentioned together since the two are closely related like the two sides of the same coin.

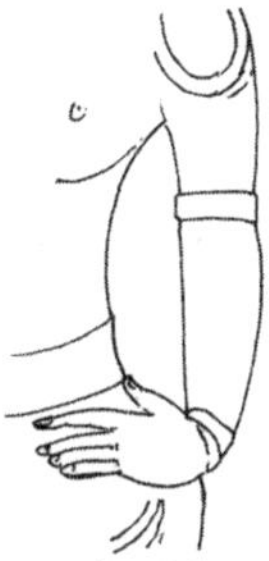

Kaṭyāvalaṁbita-mudrā

***Kaṭyāvalaṁbita-mudrā* (कट्यावलंबित मुद्रा)** : In it the hand, generally left, is half-raised at ease and kept on the hip. It is also called *kaṭi-hasta* (कटि-हस्त) (hip-hand) *mudrā*.

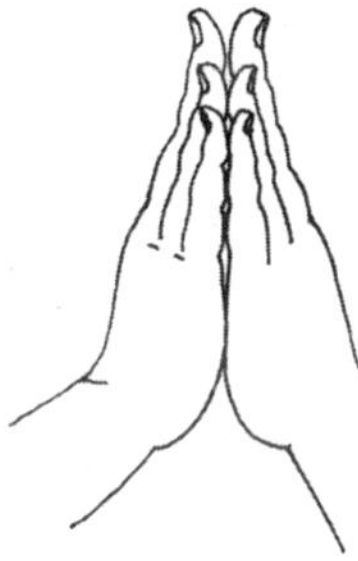

Namaskāra-mudrā

***Namaskāra-mudrā* (नमस्कार-मुद्रा)** : In it the two palms facing and joining each other are raised to the chest. The idea conveyed is that of salute and reverence. It is normally used by the devotees and the *bhakta*s.

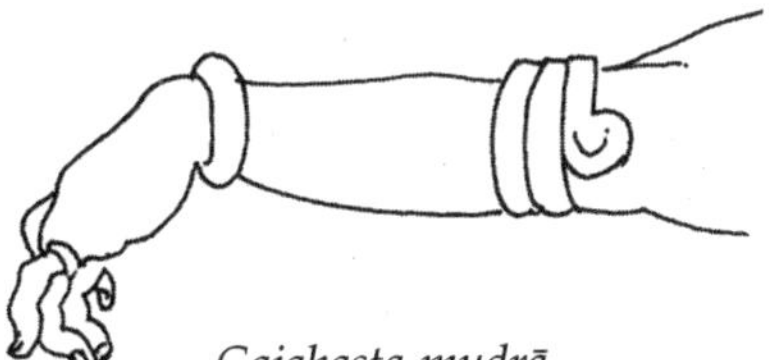

Gajahasta-mudrā

***Gajahasta-mudrā* (गजहस्त-मुद्रा)** : In it the hand is stretched like a staff or the trunk of an elephant, half-raised up to the chest and then taken across the body with palm facing downwards. It is generally seen in the Naṭarāja *mūrti*s. It is also called *lola-hasta* **(लोल-हस्त)** as well as *daṇḍa-hasta* (दण्ड-हस्त).

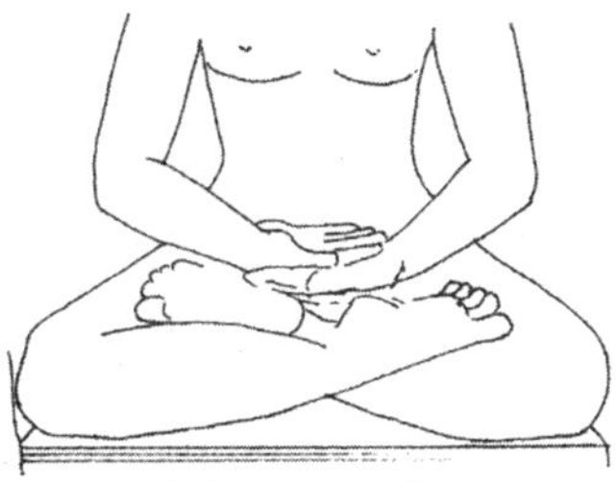

Dhyāna-mudrā

***Dhyāna-mudrā* (ध्यान-मुद्रा)** : A posture of *yoga* (योग) or *samādhi* (समाधि), i.e. meditation. In this pose the

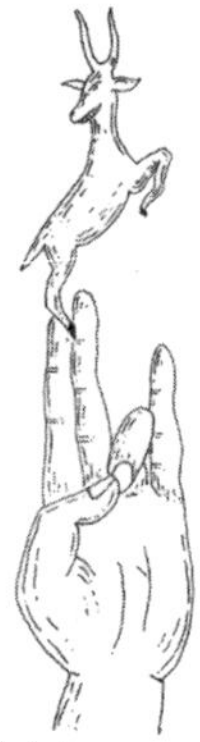

Hariṇi (stag or deer)-*mudrā*

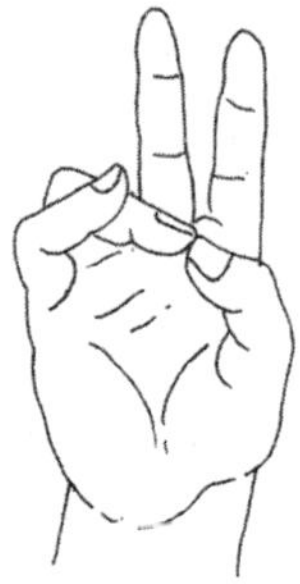

Kartarī-mudrā

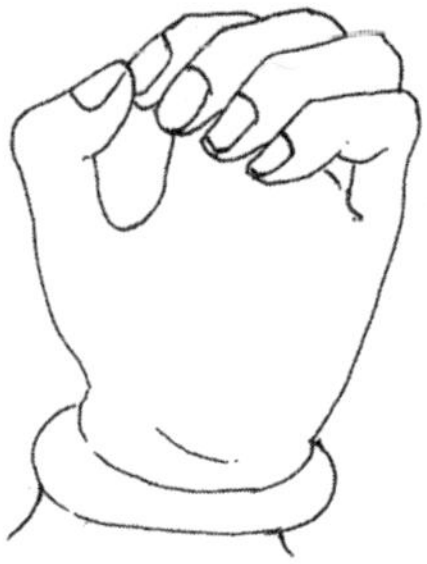

Kaṭaka-mudrā

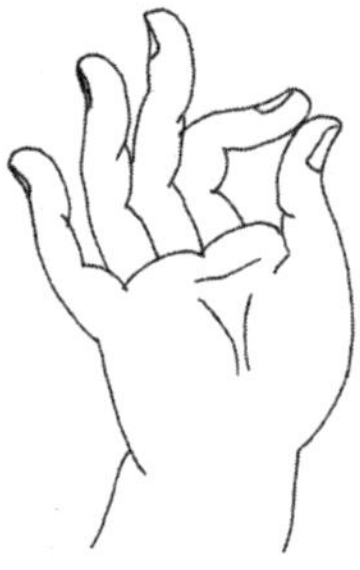

Vitarka-mudrā

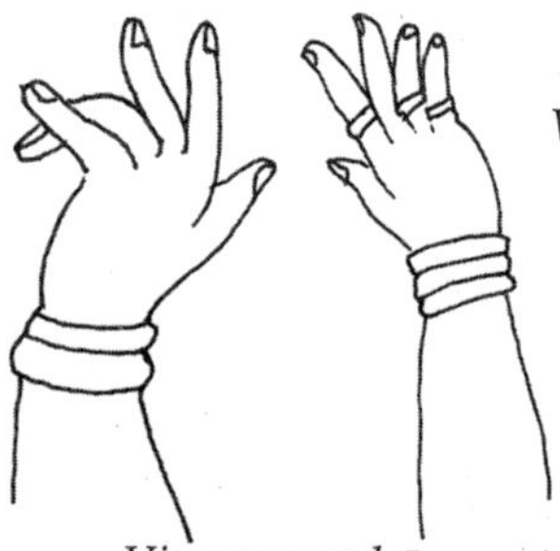

Vismaya-mudrā

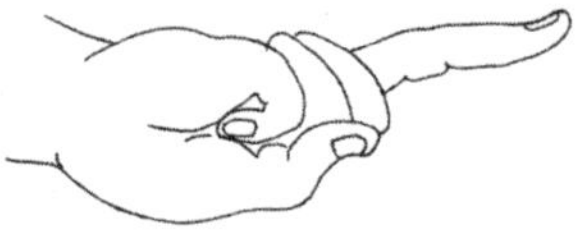

Tarjanī-mudrā

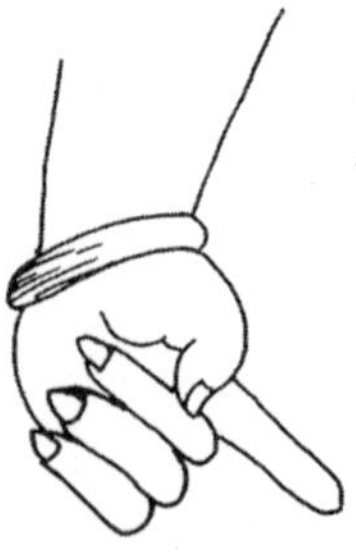

Sūcī-mudrā

figure sits in the *padmāsana* (पद्मासन) and the palms of the two hands, one over the other, generally right on the left, sometimes vice versa also, are kept at ease. In Chinese Turkestan, the palms are sometimes seen open with extended fingers. The palms face upwards.

***Hariṇi* (*stag or deer*)*-mudrā* (हरिणि-मुद्रा)** : In it the form of the hands form the shape of the head of a stag, the thumb touching the middle and ring fingers, resembling ring or circle, the little and the index fingers are straight and held upwards.

***Kartarī-mudrā* (कर्तरी-मुद्रा)** : Here the index and middle fingers are held straight upwards to form a "V," to hold an emblem. The thumb and the ring fingers, however, touch each other and form a ring. The hand is kept at the level of the shoulder.

***Kaṭaka-mudrā* (कटक-मुद्रा)** : It is also called *siṁhakarṇa-mudrā* (सिंहकर्ण-मुद्रा) and is meant to hold a flower, generally offered and inserted everyday. In this *mudrā* the tips of the fingers are loosely joined to the thumb to create a ring.

***Vitarka-mudrā* (वितर्क-मुद्रा)** : *Vitarka* means argumentation. In this the thumb and the index finger join to form a ring while rest of the fingers are slightly twisted and face upwards.

***Vismaya-mudrā* (विस्मय-मुद्रा)** : In this posture astonishment, coupled with the sense of enquiry, is indicated. The hand is raised up to the shoulder, the palm is turned inward, while the fingers are spread out in a circular manner.

***Tarjanī-mudrā* (तर्जनी-मुद्रा)** : As the term suggests, in it the forefinger is held out straight while the others are closed. The idea conveyed is that the other person is scolded, admonished or warned to behave.

***Sūcī-mudrā* (सूची-मुद्रा)** : It is exactly like the *tarjanī*-

mudrā with the only difference that the raised forefinger in this *mudrā* points to an object below.

***Tarpaṇa-mudrā* (तर्पण-मुद्रा)** : In this *mudrā* the hand is raised up to the shoulder and the palm, open with joint fingers, face downwards. The idea conveyed is that of paying homage.

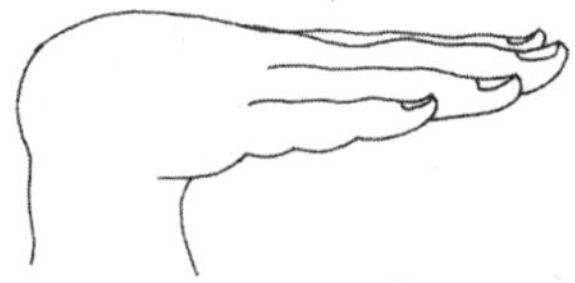

Tarpaṇa-mudrā

***Kṣepaṇa-mudrā* (क्षेपण-मुद्रा)** : This is the posture of showing the pot of *amṛta* or nectar taken to achieve immortality. In it the two palms are joined, the forefingers stretch out, touching each other intimately, while the other fingers are locked strongly. The joined hands are then turned downwards pointing towards the vase of nectar.

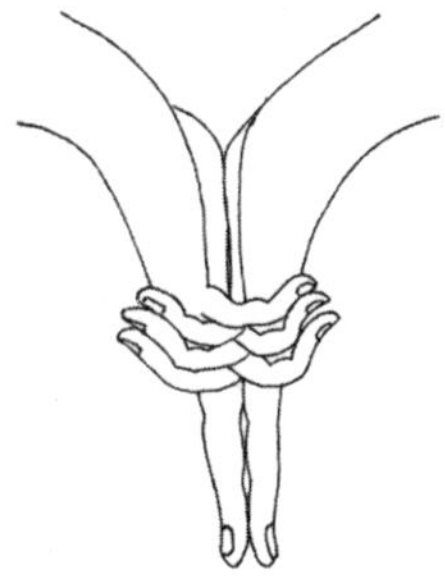

Kṣepaṇa-mudrā

***Uttarabodhi-mudrā* (उत्तरबोधि-मुद्रा)** : The hands in this pose are held exactly like *kṣepaṇa* with the only difference that in this case the outstretched forefingers point upwards and the crossed thumbs are also seen by the viewer. It denotes perfection and goes with the Buddha.

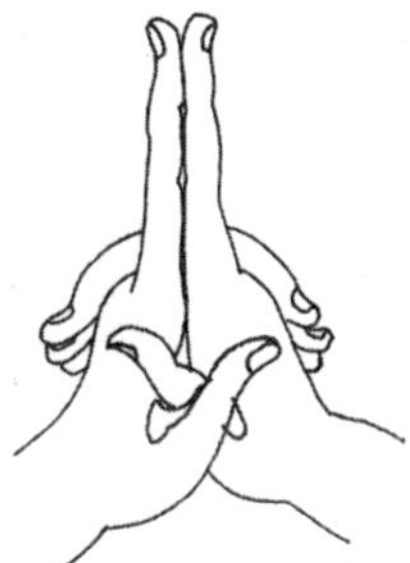

Uttarabodhi-mudrā

***Buddhaśramaṇa-mudrā* (बुद्धश्रमण-मुद्रा)** : As the term suggests, it is a pose meant mainly to denote the important Buddhist *śramaṇa*s or wandering mendicants and is found with Uṣṇīṣavijayā and Vasudhārā. In it, the hand is raised up to the level of the head, with palm facing up and fingers joined and extended.

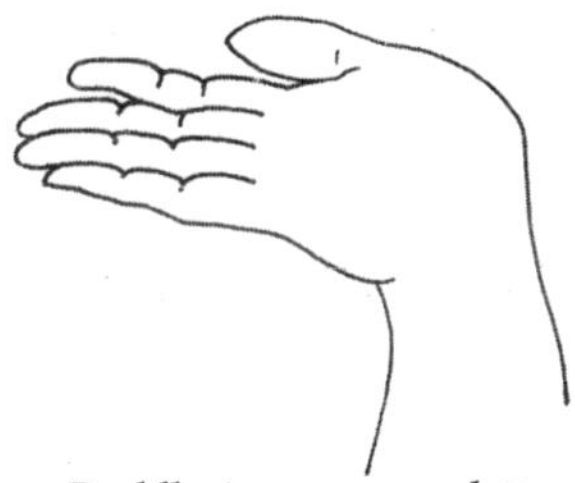

Buddhaśramaṇa-mudrā

***Bhūmisparśa-mudrā* (भूमिस्पर्श-मुद्रा)** : Literally it means "touching-the-earth pose." It denotes that incident in the life of Buddha in which he called the Mother Earth as witness to his virtues due to which he remained unmoved even when the wicked Māra and his beautiful heavenly damsels, the daughters of Māra, tried to disturb his resolve when he was meditating under the *bodhi* tree. In this posture his right hand dangles in front of his right crossed leg

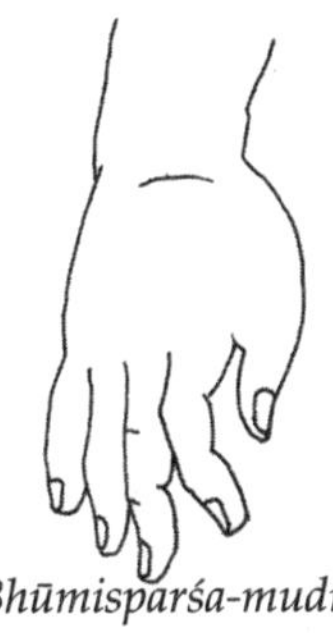

Bhūmisparśa-mudrā

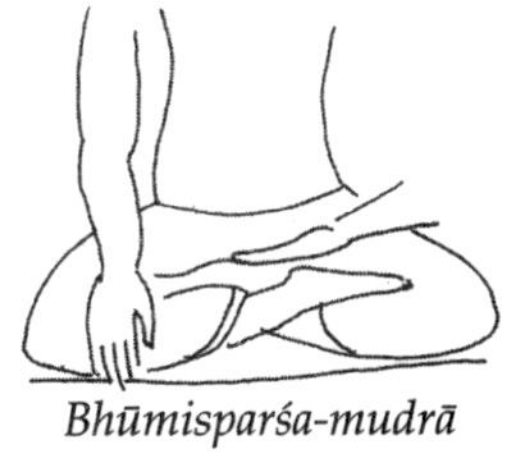

Bhūmisparśa-mudrā

and touches the lotus seat *padmāsana* or the earth with palm open and facing inward. Akṣobhaya, one of the Dhyānī Buddhas, is also shown in this *mudrā*.

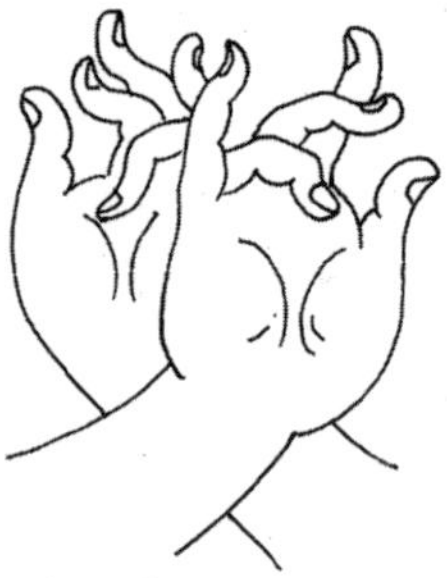

Bhūtaḍāmara-mudrā

***Bhūtaḍāmara-mudrā* (भूतडामर-मुद्रा)** : In this *mudrā* two hands at the wrist cross each other at the level of the chest. The palms open outward with fingers twisted at different angles. It is meant to create awe and fear in the minds of the viewers. Vajrapāṇi is often shown in this *mudrā*.

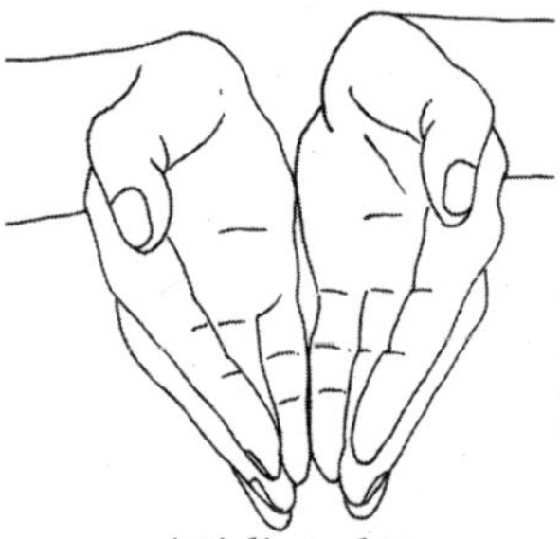

Añjali-mudrā

***Añjali-mudrā* (अञ्जलि-मुद्रा)** : This is the pose of offering flowers, grains, money, etc. to god. In it, with palm open and facing the viewer, the two hands join each other and are held at the chest or below it.

***Vajrahuṁkāra-mudrā* (वज्रहुंकार-मुद्रा)** : As the term suggests, it has a *vajra* or thunderbolt in one hand and a *ghaṇṭā* or bell in the other to sound loudly. It

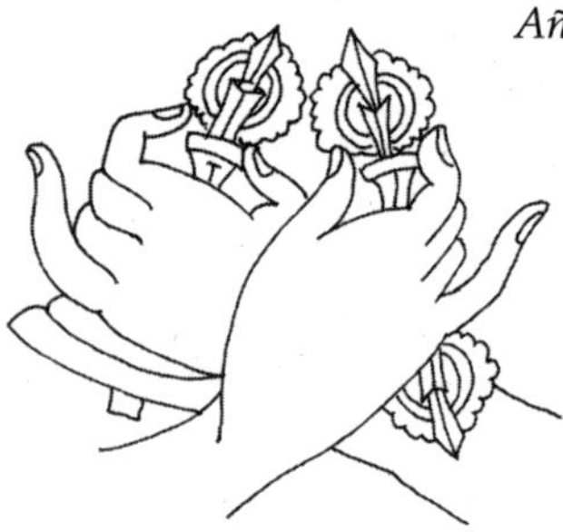

Vajrahuṁkāra-mudrā

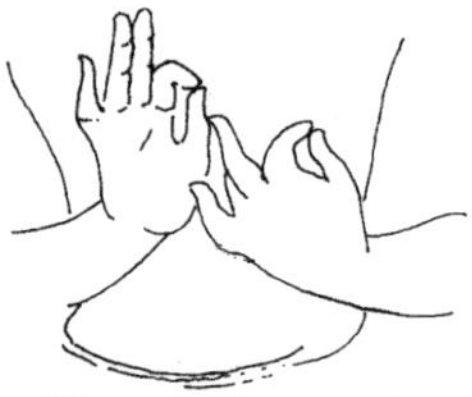

Dharmacakra-mudrā

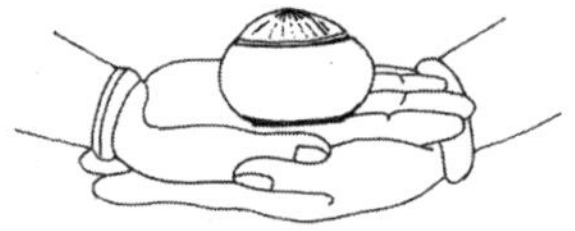

Dhyāna-mudrā

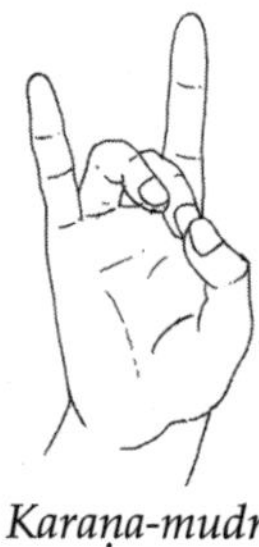

Karaṇa-mudrā

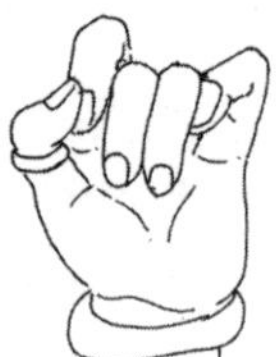

Siṁhakarṇa-mudrā

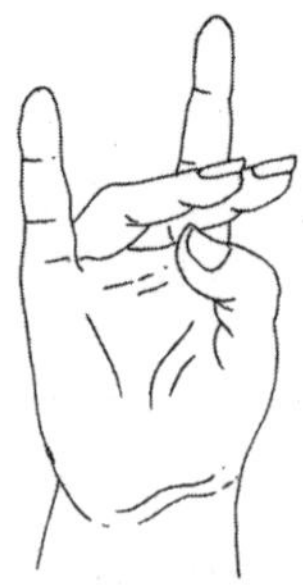

Hariṇa-mudrā

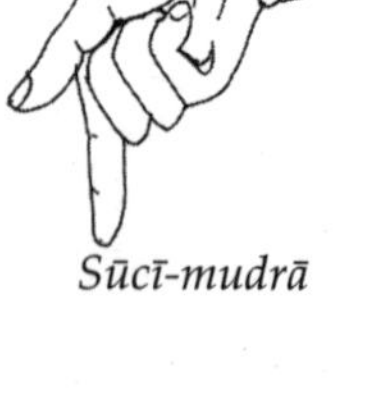

Sūcī-mudrā

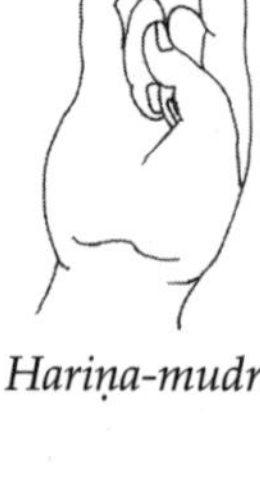

Hariṇa-mudrā

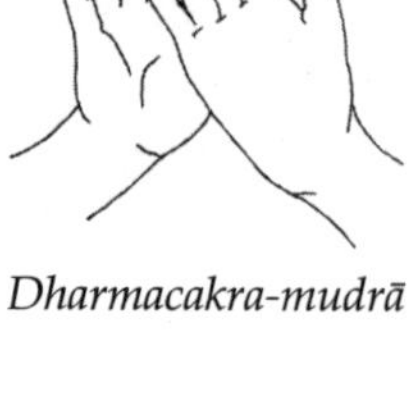

Dharmacakra-mudrā

symbolizes the eternal Buddha. In it two hands cross each other from the wrist at the chest, in one hand a *vajra* is held and in the other a *ghaṇṭā.*

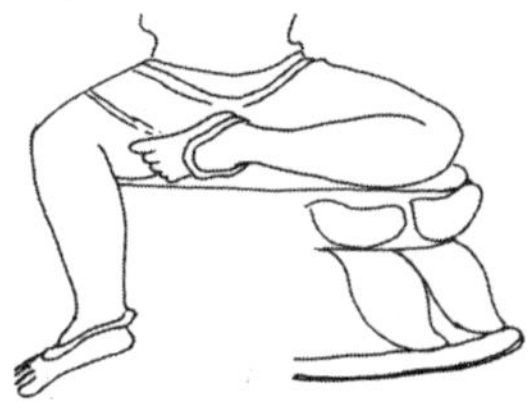

Vaiṣṇavam

PĀDA MUDRĀS (पाद मुद्राएं)

In Hindu iconography the *pāda mudrā* or the posture of legs is equally important if not more. In fact, it is the *pāda mudrā* which makes the figures action-packed by infusing animation in them. The six *pāda mudrā*s, according to the *Samarāṅgaṇa Sūtradhāra,* are as follows:

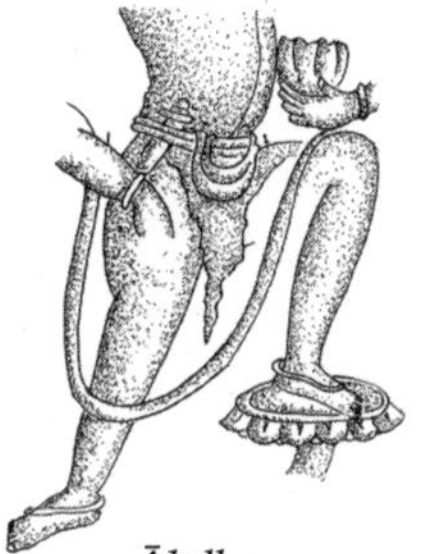

Ālīḍham

***Vaiṣṇavam* (वैष्णवम्)** : In it one of the legs is straight but the other one is slightly curved at an angle. The thighs are, however, a little bent. This is the *ādhidaivatya* form of Viṣṇu.

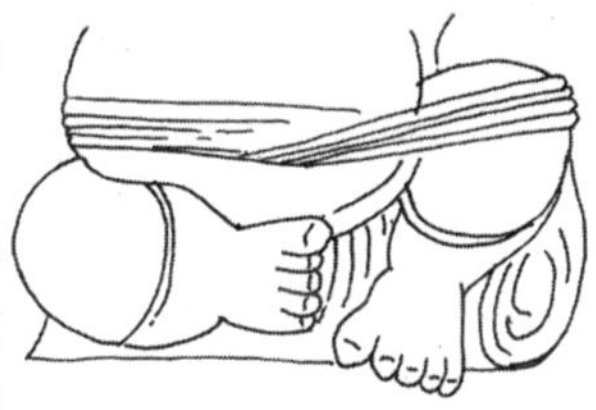

Udarabandha

***Sampādam* (सम्पादम्)** : In it the god stands erect with both the legs joined, hands straight and touching the sides with face fully towards the viewer. Here the weight is distributed equally on both legs. Brahmā is often shown in this posture.

***Ālīḍham* (आलीढ़म्)** : In it the posture is that of an archer with right leg brought forward and left backwards. Arjuna is shown in this posture.

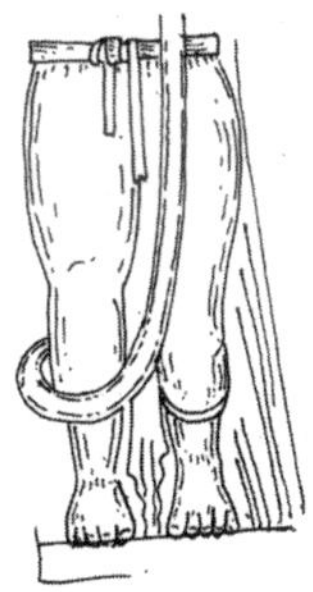

Sampādam

***Pratyālīḍham* (प्रत्यालीढ़म्)** : It is the opposite of *ālīḍham* — the left leg is brought forward while the right leg is pushed backward.

***Vaiśākham* (वैशाखम्)** : In it while one leg is thrown out the other remains stable. Viśākhadeva images are made in this style, hence this term.

***Maṇḍalam* (मण्डलम्)** : In this case also one leg is outstretched and the other remains stable. Indra is shown in this posture.

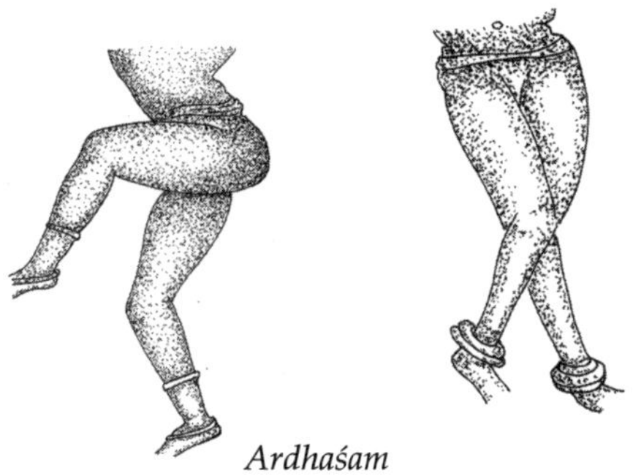

Ardhaśam

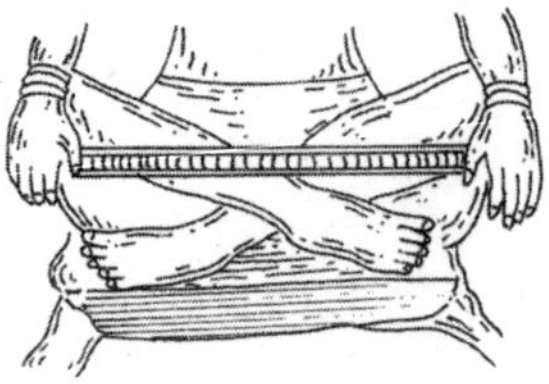

Pāda-paṭṭa or *yoga-paṭṭa*

ŚARĪRA MUDRĀS (शरीर मुद्राएं)

The body as a whole is also having its posture irrespective of the postures of the hands and legs. These are four in number :

Samabhaṅga **(समभंग)** : In it the whole body, sitting or standing, remains perpendicular to the horizontal axis of the earth — the body remains straight, divisible in two equal parts, with weight divided equally on its own axis. Jaina *tīrthaṁkaras* are often shown in this posture.

Abhaṅga **(अभंग)** : In it the body is slightly bent forward or backward, as the kings are shown in many Gupta gold coins, e.g. in the Candragupta-Kumāradevī type coin.

Tribhaṅga **(त्रिभंग)** : In it the vertical axis of the body is broken at two points to give three bends in the body — one is at the hip and the other is at the neck. "Kṛṣṇa playing on flute" images are often shown in this pose. Vyantara *devatā*s are also shown likewise.

Atibhaṅga **(अतिभंग)** : In it the body of the god is bent at various places, sometimes even twisted. Śiva Naṭarāja is mostly shown in this posture.

In the *Viṣṇudharmottara* we have one more category of *śarīra mudrā* which is based on the different views of the body. It is of nine types:

Ṛjvāgata **(ऋज्वागत)** : This is the front view of the body.

Anruju **(अनृजु)** : This is the back view of the body.

Sācīkṛta śarīra **(साचीकृत शरीर)** : It is the bent position in profile.

Ardhavilocana **(अर्द्धविलोचन)** : It is the three quarter profile of body and full profile of the face.

***Pārśvāgata* (पार्श्वागत)** : It is the side view proper.

***Parivitta* (परिवित्त)** : In it the head and shoulder are bent and turned backwards.

***Parivṛta* (परिवृत)** : In it the body is sharply turned back from the waist upwards.

***Pṛṣṭhāgata* (पृष्ठागत)** : This is the back view with the upper part of the body partly visible in profile view.

***Samanata* (समनत)** : This is the back view in sitting posture with body bent.

With the help of perspective these positions have been extended to twelve but that is a matter of details.

Besides these major postures, there are the following other postures of images :

(a) Flying figures, as the *gandharva*s (गंधर्व) are often shown.

(b) Figures with wings, often flying like Garuḍa (गरुड़), but sometimes standing like the Śuṅga female figures on plaques from Kauśāmbī, Vaiśālī, etc. whose identification is doubtful.

(c) Figures in dance pose. According to Śaiva Āgamas there are 108 forms of dance *mudrā*s. Śiva and Kṛṣṇa are often in dance pose.

(d) Figures shown lying and resting, *śayana*, as Śeṣaśāyī Viṣṇu (शेषशायी विष्णु).

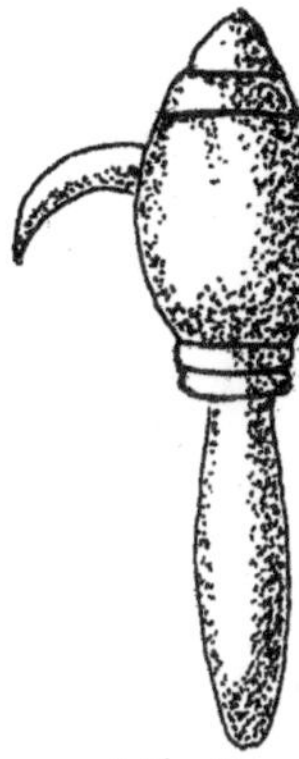

Aṅkuśa

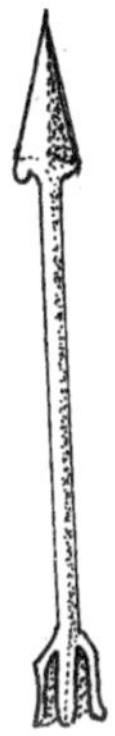

Bāṇa

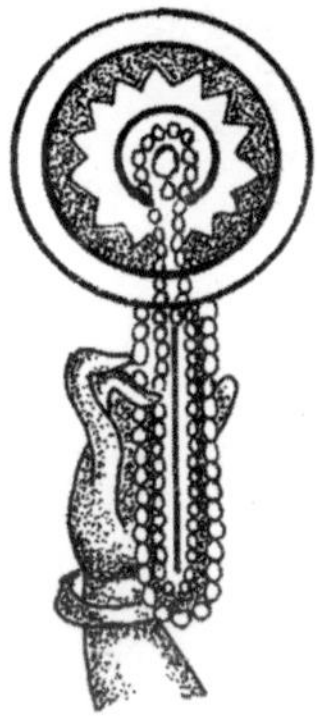

Cakra

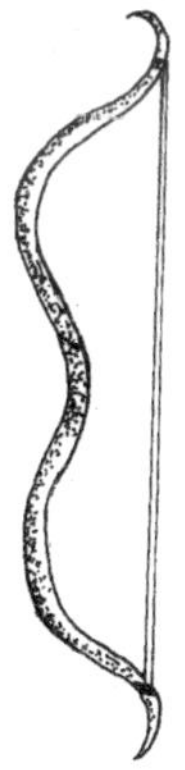

Dhanuṣa

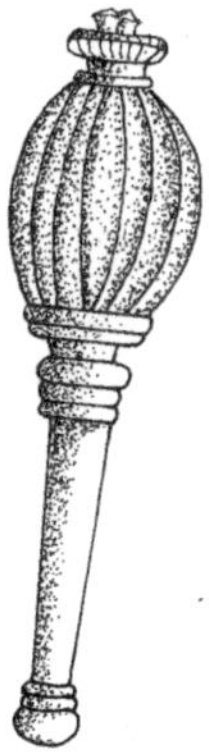

Gadā

Attributes or objects held in hands

WEAPONS OF WAR AND CHASE

Aṅkuśa (अंकुश) = Goad

Bāṇa (बाण) = Arrow

Cakra (चक्र) = Wheel

Dhanuṣa (धनुष)	=	Bow
Gadā (गदा)	=	Club
Khaḍga (खड्ग)	=	Sword
Khaṭvāṅga (खट्वांग)	=	Club of bone with skull(s)
Kheṭaka (खेटक)	=	Shield
Paraśu (परशु)	=	Battleaxe
Pāśa (पाश)	=	Noose
Śakti (शक्ति)	=	Spear
Śūla (शूल)	=	Javelin
Triśūla (त्रिशूल)	=	Trident
Vajra (वज्र)	=	Thunderbolt
Viśva-vajra (विश्ववज्र)	=	Double thunderbolt

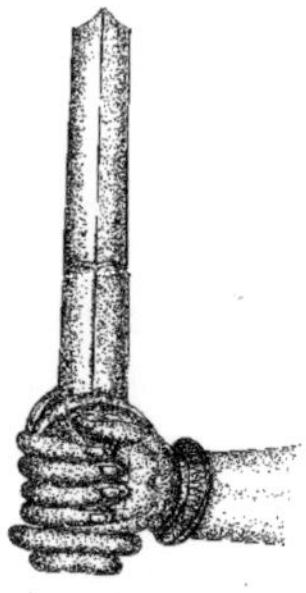

Khaḍga

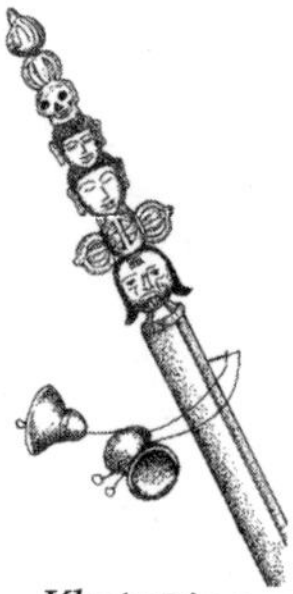

Khaṭvāṅga

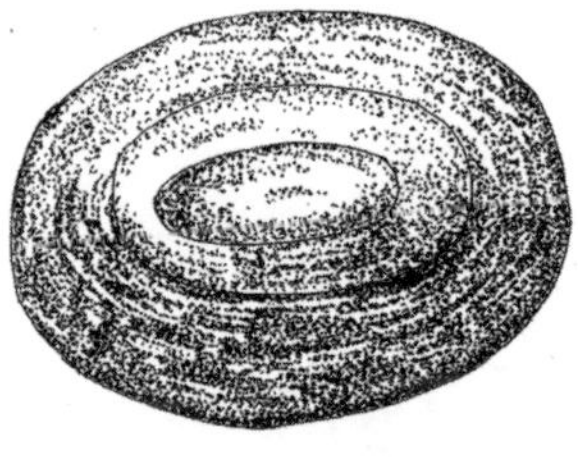

Kheṭaka

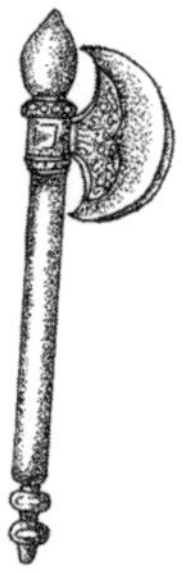

Paraśu

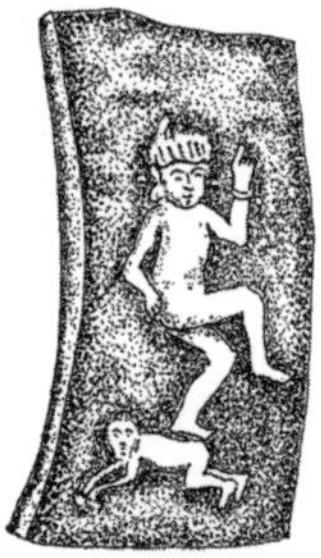

Kheṭaka

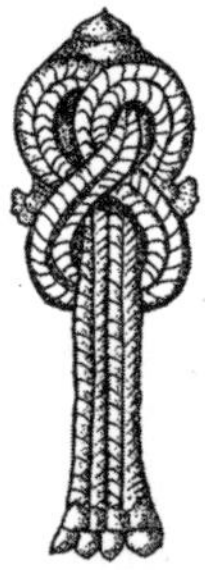

Pāśa

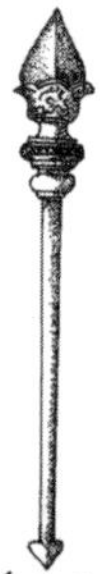

Śakti

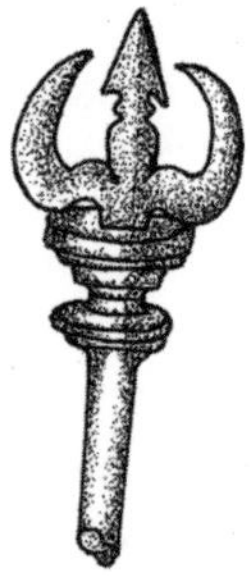

Triśūla

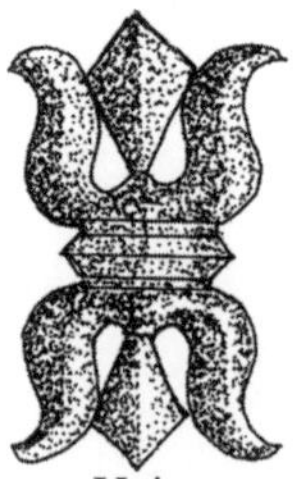

Vajra

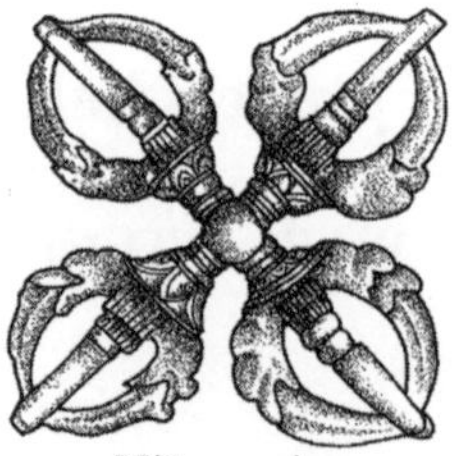

Viśva-vajra

HOUSEHOLD AND AGRICULTURAL OBJECTS AND IMPLEMENTS

Agni (अग्नि)	=	Fire
Darpaṇa (दर्पण)	=	Mirror
Hala (हल)	=	Plough
Kalaśa (कलश)	=	Vessel. Also *Amṛta-ghaṭa* (अमृत-घट)
Kātri (कात्रि)	=	Knife
Kamaṇḍalu (कमण्डलु)	=	Spouted vessel
Kartṛkā (कर्त्रृका)	=	Chopper
Mudgara (मुद्गर)	=	Wooden pestle with round flat end
Mūsala (मूसल)	=	Wooden pestle with rounded end
Pātra (पात्र)	=	Bowl
Ṭaṅka (टंक)	=	Chisel or stone cutter

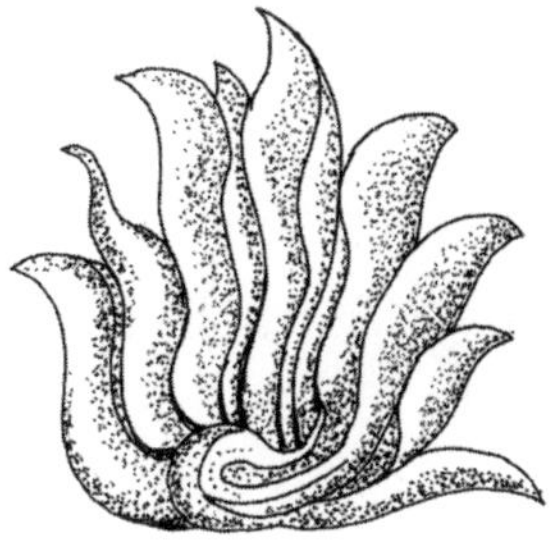

Agni

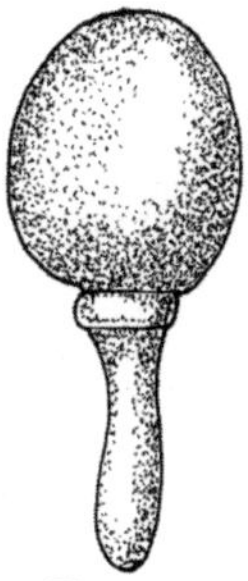

Darpaṇa

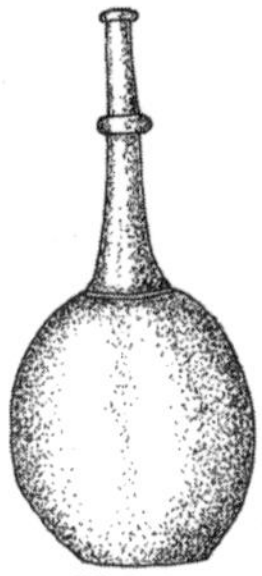

Kalaśa

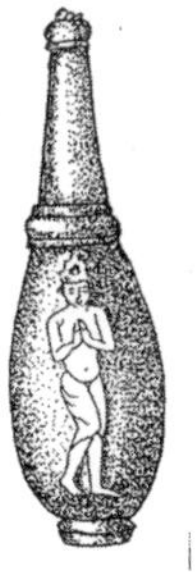

Gadā

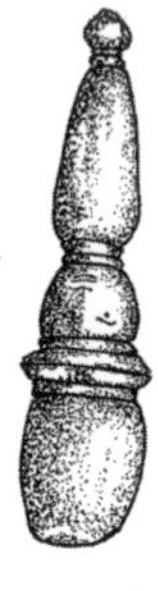

Mūsala

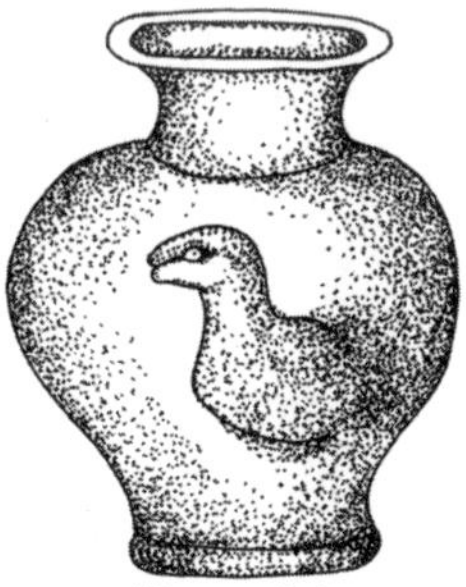

Kamaṇḍalu

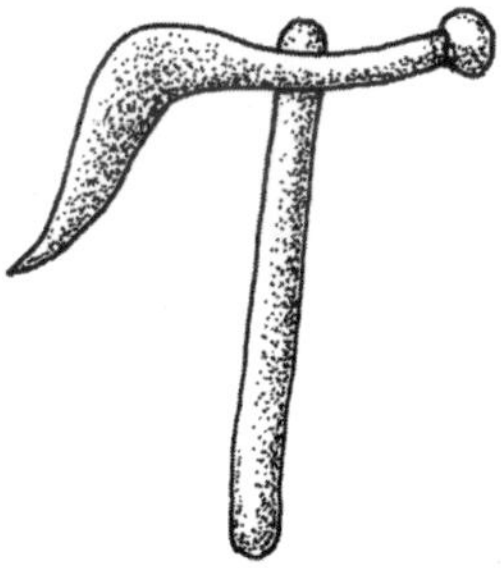

Hala

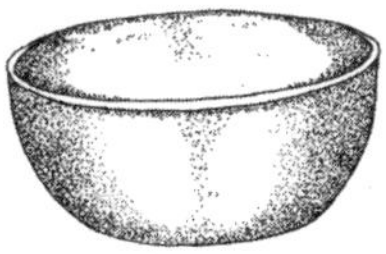

Pātra

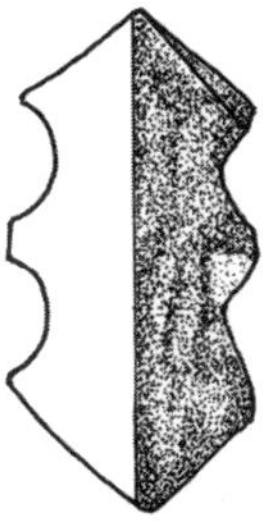

Ṭaṅka

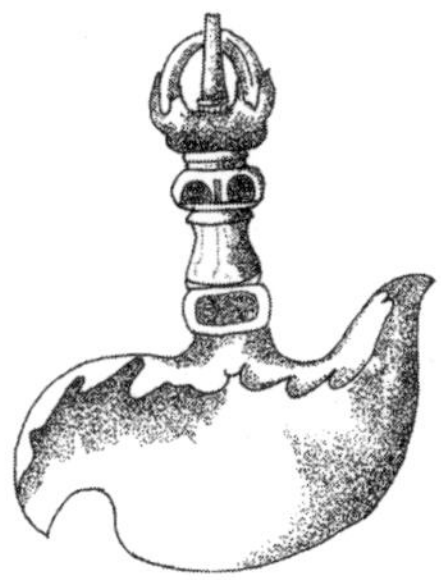

Kartṛkā

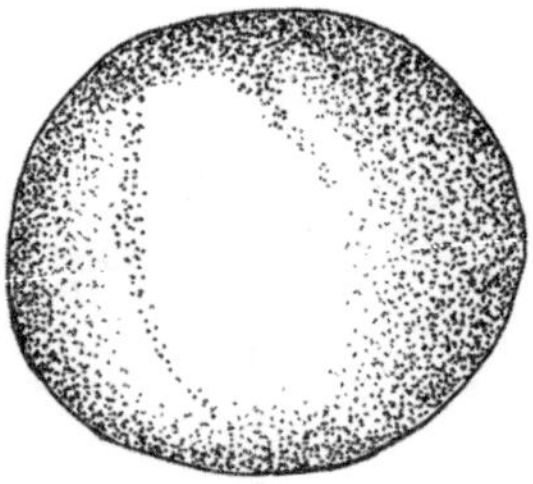
Bilvaphala

FRUITS

Bilvaphala (बिल्वफल)	=	Woodapple
Jambhāra (जंभार)	=	Lemon
Āmlaka (आमलक)	=	Emblie, Myrobalan
Śrīphala (श्रीफल)	=	Coconut

FLOWERS

Nalinī (नलिनी)	=	Lily. Same as *kamalinī* (कमलिनी)
Padma (पद्म)	=	Indian Lotus with broad petals

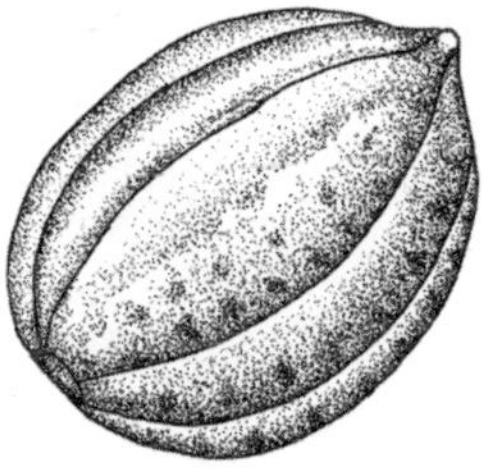
(*Āmlaka*) Myrobalan

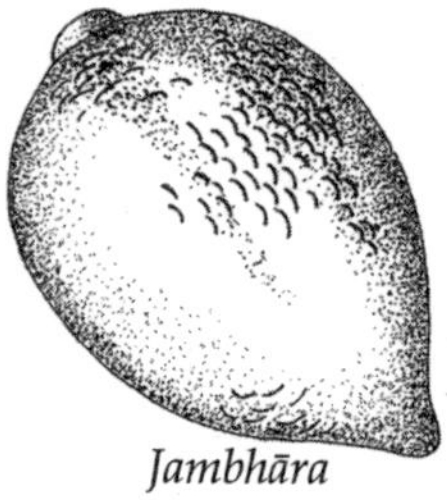
Jambhāra

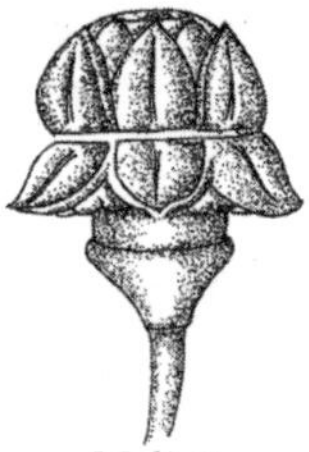
Nalinī

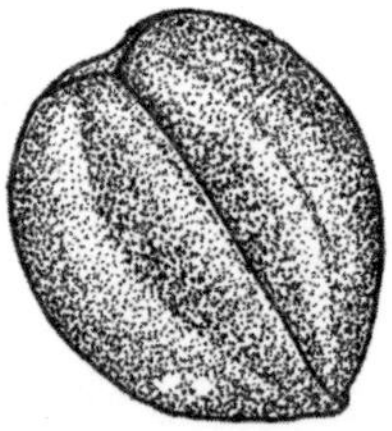
Śrīphala

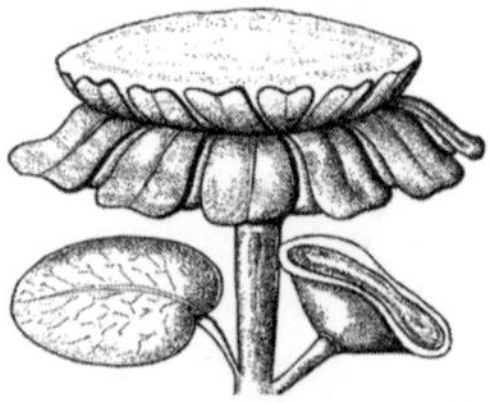
Padma

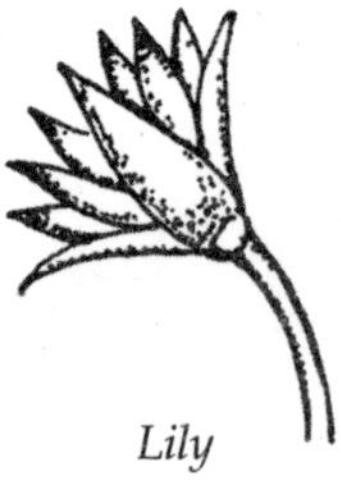
Lily

ANIMAL WORLD

Aja (अज)	=	Goat
Kukkuṭa (कुक्कुट)	=	Cock
Mayūrapiccha (मयूरपिच्छ)	=	Peacock feather
Meṣa (मेष)	=	Ram
Mṛga (मृग)	=	Deer
Nakula (नकुल)	=	Mongoose
Śaśa (शश)	=	Rabbit
Śaṅkha (शंख)	=	Conch-shell

MUSICAL INSTRUMENTS

Ḍamarū (डमरू)	=	Small drum, hour-glass shaped
Ghaṇṭā (घण्टा)	=	Bell
Karatala (करतल)	=	Cymbals
Mṛdaṅgam (मृदङ्गम्)	=	Drum, tubular
Muralī (मुरली)	=	Flute. Same as *veṇu* (वेणु)
Vīṇā (वीणा)	=	String instrument held against the chest

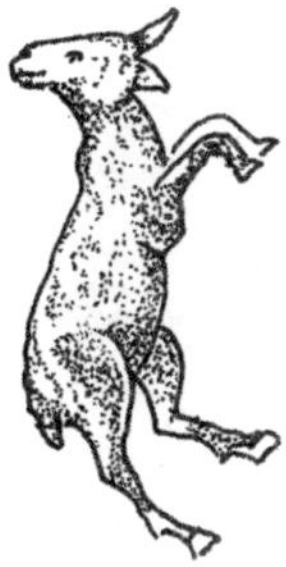
Aja

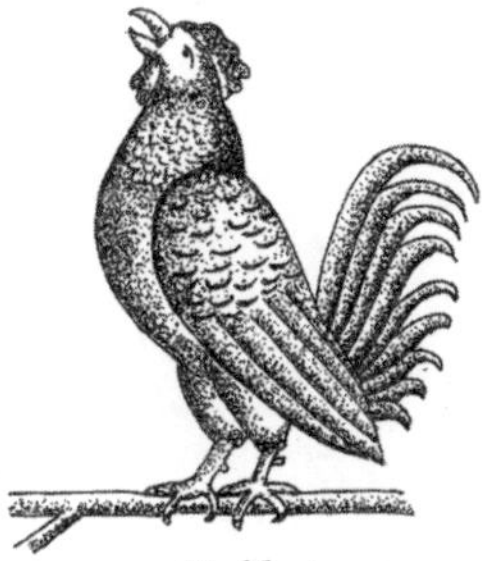
Kukkuṭa

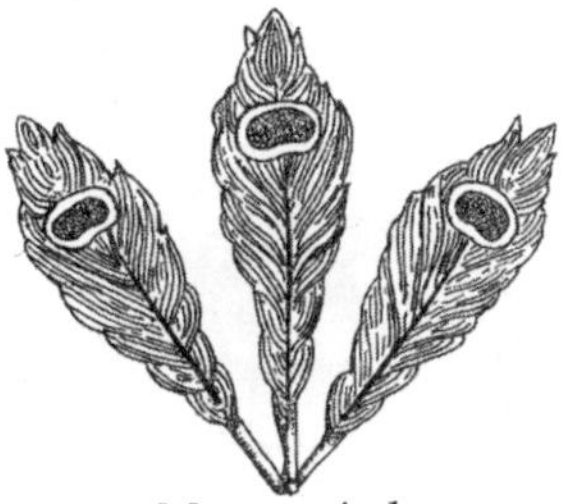
Mayūrapiccha

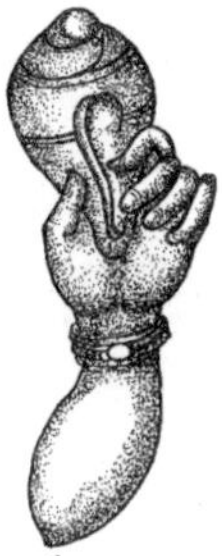
Śaṅkha

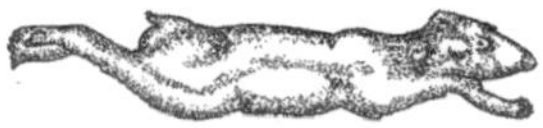
Meṣa

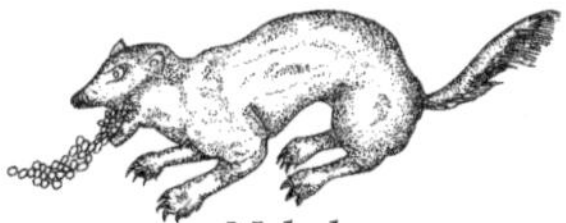
Nakula

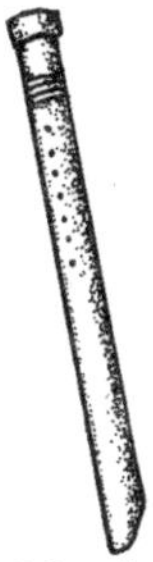
Muralī

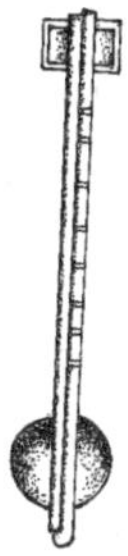
Vīṇā

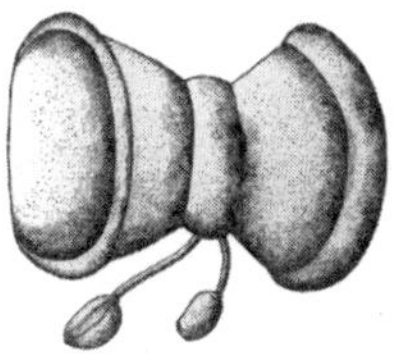
Ḍamarū

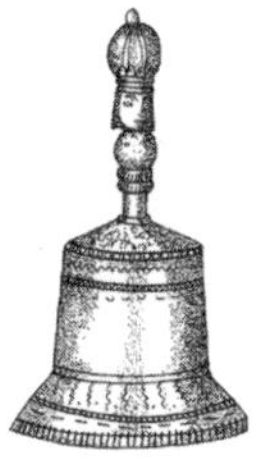
Ghaṇṭā

OTHERS

Akṣamālā (अक्षमाला)	=	Rosary
Aṭapātra (अटपात्र)	=	Parasol
Caitya (चैत्य)	=	Stūpa
Caurī (चौरी)	=	Flywhisk
Dhvaja (ध्वज)	=	Flag
Kapāla (कपाल)	=	Skull Cup
Kaumudī (कौमुदी)	=	Half-moon
Khakkar (खक्कर)	=	Alms staff. If without rings on the top it is simply *daṇḍa* (दण्ड) or staff
Laḍḍū (लड्डू)	=	Sweet balls
Patra-kuṇḍala (पत्र-कुण्डल)	=	Disc or leaf-shaped earring
Pustaka (पुस्तक)	=	Book
Śaṅkha-patra (शंख-पत्र)	=	A slice of conch-shell used as ear-ring
Śruka (श्रुक)	=	Sacrificial spoon. *śruva* (श्रुव) also
Triratna (त्रिरत्न)	=	Three jewels of Buddhist creed — symbolizing Buddha, Dharma and Saṁgha. The term is used by the Jainas also in which context the three jewels.
Upavīta (उपवीत)	=	Deer skin; also sacred thread.

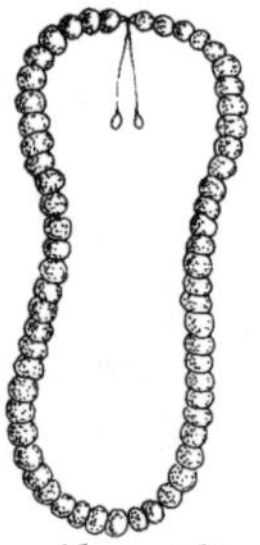
Akṣamālā

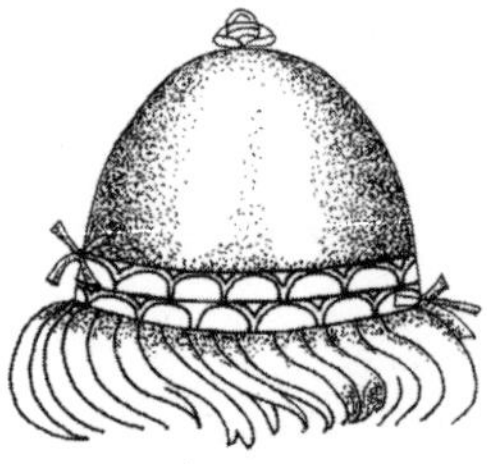
Aṭapātra

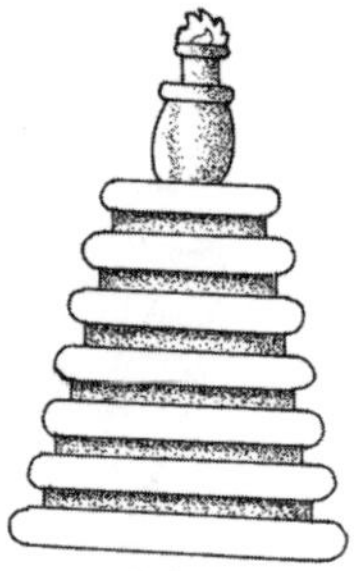
Caitya

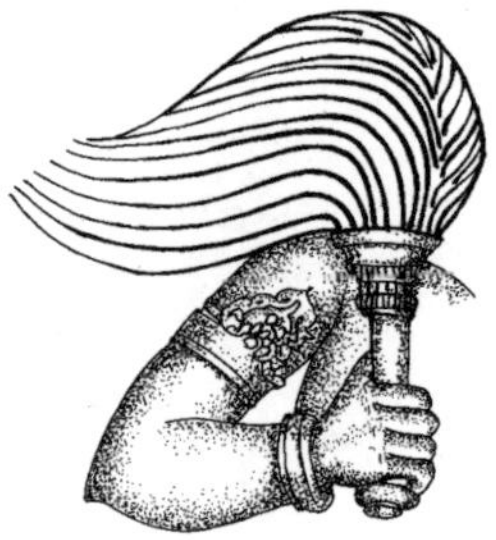
Caurī

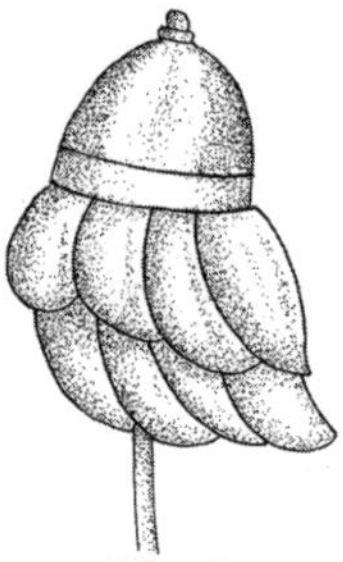
Dhvaja

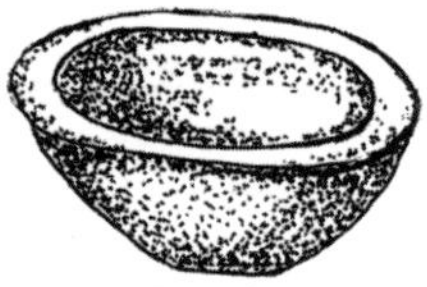
Kapāla

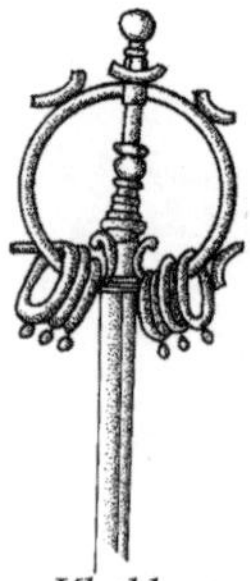
Khakkar

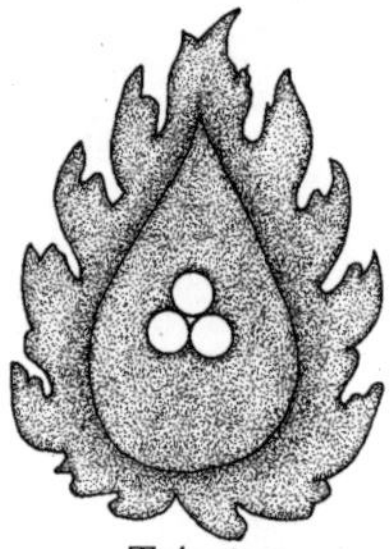
Triratna

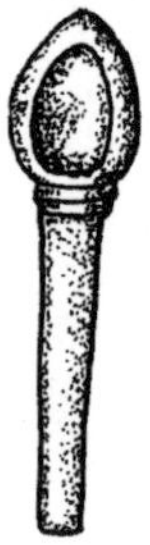
Śruka

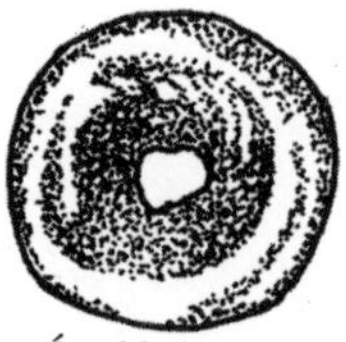
Śaṅkha-patra

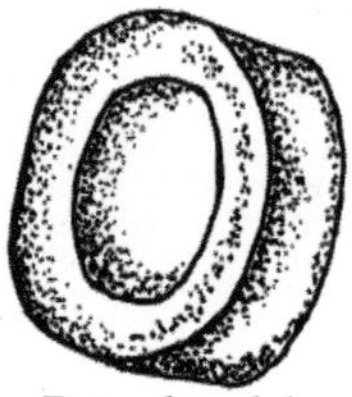
Patra-kuṇḍala

Āsanas (आसन) or Sitting Postures

The gods and goddesses are often shown sitting on pedestals. There are various ways in which they have been shown sitting in sculpture and painting. This may be enumerated as follows:

***Ardhaparyaṅka* (अर्द्धपर्यंक)** : It is also called *mahārājalīlā* (महाराजलीला). In it one leg is folded at the hip, touching the thigh of the other, which hangs, with the heels slightly raised above the pedestal which is touched only by the toe or a few fingers.

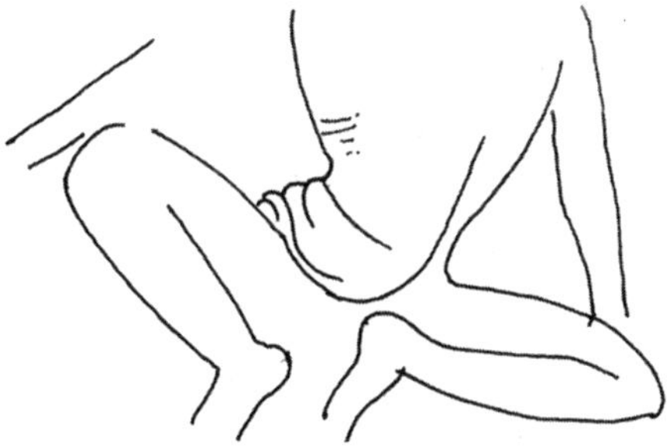

Ardhaparyaṅka Āsana

***Paryaṅka* (पर्यंक)** : In it the god sits in *padmāsana* **(पद्मासन)**, i.e. both legs crossed with soles looking up.

***Bhadra* (भद्र)** : Sitting with legs crossed as in *kūrmāsana*, with soles touching pedestal but holding the two toes with hands.

Dhyāna (ध्यान) : Like *paryaṅka* and *padmāsana*, sitting cross-legged with soles upwards, in meditation. Same as *yogāsana* (योगासन) and *padmāsana* (पद्मासन).

***Kūrma* (कूर्म)** : In it the god sits cross-legged with the soles of the feet touching the pedestal.

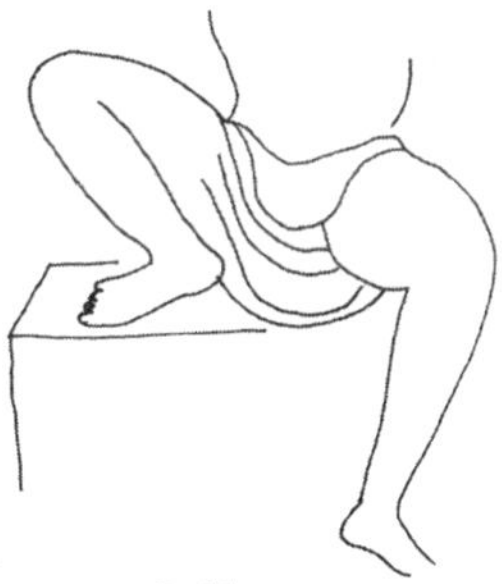

Sukhāsana

***Lalita* (ललित)** : It is also called *sukhāsana* (सुखासन) or *savya-lalitāsana* (सव्य-ललितासन). In it the god is generally shown sitting on a high pedestal with right leg folded and resting on a cushion or a small pedestal, while the left leg is hanging.

***Vāma lalita* (वाम ललित)** : It is the opposite of *lalitāsana* in the sense that the left leg is folded and the right leg hangs down.

***Pralambapāda* (प्रलम्बपाद)** : In it the god is shown sitting in the European style, i.e. with both legs hanging down.

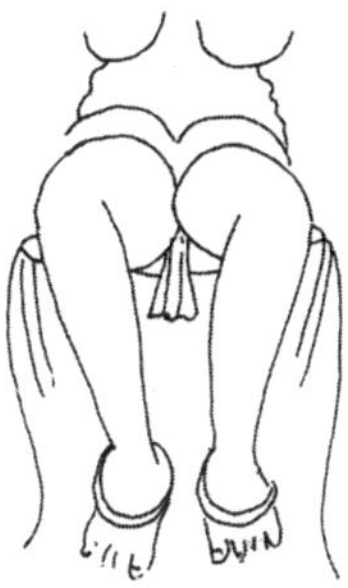

Pralambapāda Āsana

***Siṁha* (सिंह)** : In it the god is shown sitting in *kūrmāsana* with the palms, having stretched fingers, kept on the thighs. The eyes remain in *yogāsana*, i.e. fixed on the tip of the nose, but mouth open.

***Sopāśraya* (सोपाश्रय)** : In it the god is shown sitting with legs locked loosely and soles resting in front.

***Svastika* (स्वस्तिक)** : It is the posture in which the god is sitting cross-legged with the toes touching the opposite knees.

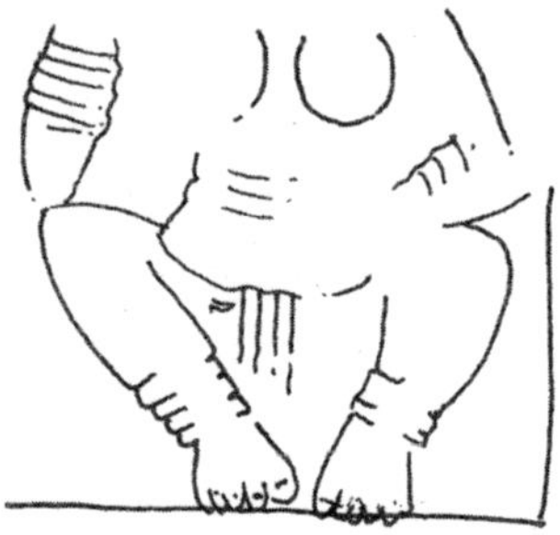

Utkuṭika Āsana

***Utkuṭika* (उत्कुटिक)** : It is the posture in which the god is shown sitting with the heels brought together and kept close to the bottom. The legs which are obviously bent inwards are kept in position with the help of a *yoga-paṭṭa* (योग-पट्ट) or a band of cloth. The back of the deity is slightly bent in comfort.

***Vajra* (वज्र)** : It is the sitting pose in which the legs are crossed with the soles turned upwards, as in *padmāsana*, but with the specific provision that the hands are placed on the knees.

***Vīra* (वीर)** : In it the god is shown sitting with the left leg resting on the right thigh.

***Yoga* (योग)** : It is sitting in *padmāsana* with two hands on the lap, palms one over the other, both in upward position.

Āsanas or Pīṭhas (आसन अथवा पीठ) (Pedestals)

The term *āsana* is also used for the pedestals or seats (पीठ) on which gods sit or stand.

***Anantāsana* (अनन्तासन)** : It is a triangular seat or stool and is used usually when one views sports.

***Bhadrapīṭha* (भद्रपीठ)** : It is a seat, rectangular or circular in form.

***Kūrmāsana* (कूर्मासन)** : The seat, oval in shape, is in the form of a tortoise.

Makarāsana **(मकरासन)** : It is a pedestal shaped like the crocodile.

Simhāsana **(सिंहासन)** : It is a rectangular seat with four legs shaped like lions. Often it has a back, making it a modern chair used for kings and gods alike.

Vimalāsana **(विमलासन)** : It is hexagonal in shape and is generally used as a low stool kept before the god for placing offerings.

Viśva-padmāsana **(विश्व-पद्मासन)** : *Padmāsana* is the seat of lotus while *viśva-padmāsana* is the seat of double lotus.

Yogāsana **(योगासन)** : The seat is octagonal and is used in the ritual of worship, sometimes for placing offerings.

Pretāsana **(प्रेतासन)** : It is rare. It is the *āsana* of a dead hardened corpse.

Śayana-pīṭha **(शयन-पीठ)** : It is a long seat, oval or rectangular, meant for deities shown in lying position.

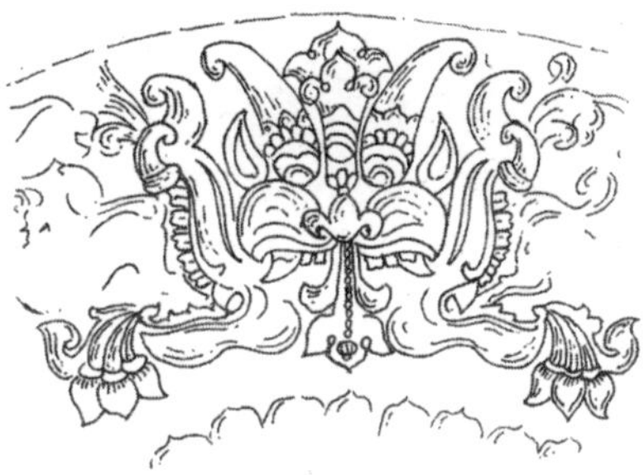

Kīrtimukha

Vāhanas (वाहन) or Mounts

A number of gods and goddesses are shown with their *vāhana*s or mounts, generally, one with one, but not always, and they identify the god or goddess very closely. These *vāhana*s are generally animals and birds but sometimes humans also.

Gaja **(गज)** : Elephant. It is the mount of Indra.

Gardabha **(गर्दभ)** : Donkey. This is the mount of Śītalā Devī.

Garuḍa **(गरुड़)** : Eagle. This is the mount of Viṣṇu.

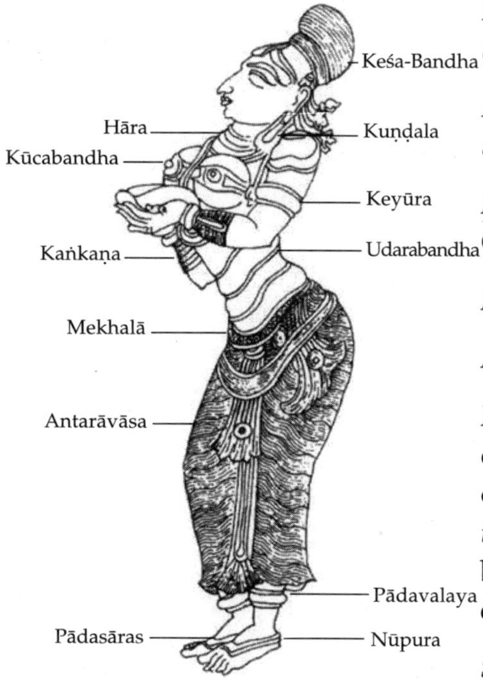

Female decoration

***Haṁsa* (हंस)** : Swan. This is the mount of Brahmā and Sarasvatī.

***Kūrma* (कूर्म)** : Tortoise. This is the mount of Yamunā, a river goddess.

***Makara* (मकर)** : Crocodile. This is the mount of Gaṅgā, another river goddess.

***Mayūra* (मयूर)** : Peacock. It is the mount of Kārttikeya.

***Mūṣaka* (मूषक)** : Rat. It is the mount of Gaṇeśa.

***Nandī* (नन्दी) *or* *Vṛṣabha* (वृषभ)** : Bull. It is the mount of Śiva and Pārvatī and the identification mark, put on the pedestal, of Ṛṣabhanātha or Ādinatha, Jaina *tīrthaṁkara*. Nandī, of course, is the name of that bull which serves as the mount of Śiva and Pārvatī exclusively.

***Siṁha* (सिंह)** : Lion. This is the mount of goddess Durgā.

***Ulūka* (उलूक)** : Owl. This is the mount of Lakṣmī.

Mukuṭas or Hair-Do and Headgears (मुकुट एवं केश-विन्यास)

In the *Mānasāra* twelve kinds of *mukuṭa*s have been enumerated, and they also distinguish one category of gods from the other.

***Alakacūḍa* (अलकचूड़)** : Or simply *cūḍā,* hair-do of the *devī*s.

***Dhammila* (धम्मिल)** : A particular hair-do for *devī*s.

***Jaṭāmukuṭa* (जटामुकुट)** : Hair arranged in long braids and then tied around. Hair-do for Śiva and Brahmā. It has no *mukuṭa* as such, it is hair-do.

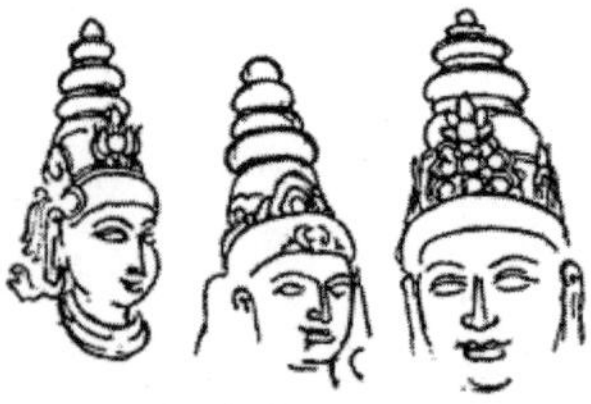
Karaṇḍa mukuṭa

***Karaṇḍa* (करण्ड)** : A tall conical headgear or *mukuṭa,* often with a series of diminishing tiers of roundels used mostly in the south for *deva*s and *devī*s, other than Vāsudeva and Nārāyaṇa.

***Keśabandha* (केशबन्ध)** : It is a band that holds up the hair-do in position. Used by *devī*s.

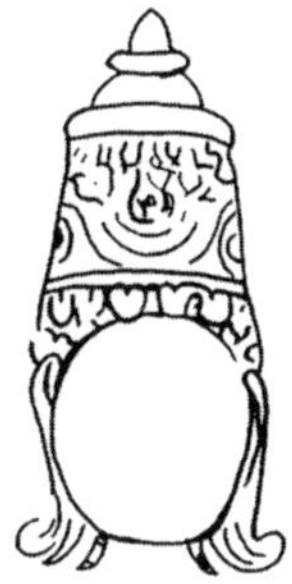

Kirīṭa mukuṭa

***Kirīṭa* (किरीट)** : It is also a conical headgear but short and with tiered rounds. It is cap-like, beautifully decorated; kings, Kubera, Viṣṇu, Sūrya, and other Vaiṣṇava *deva*s and *devī*s are shown in it.

***Kuntala* (कुन्तल)** : Locks of hair used by *devī*s in particular.

***Maulimukuṭa* (मौलिमुकुट)** : It is a form of hair-do of *jaṭā*s. In it the tubular braids of hair are tied in the form of a round sea-shell. Used by *devī*s.

***Mukuṭa* (मुकुट)** : Headgear, caps of various forms. Used by *deva*s, kings and emperors.

***Śirastraka* (शिरस्त्रक)** : Same as *śirastrāṇa* (शिरस्त्राण). It is a heavy but loosely tied turban twisted on the left. It is a kind of turban, popular from Śuṅga times. Used by *yakṣas*, *nāgas*, *vidyādharas*.

Ābhūṣaṇa (आभूषण) or Ornaments

Gods like human beings are shown wearing various kinds of ornaments (आभूषण); sometimes these are also helpful in identifying the deities.

KARṆĀBHŪṢAṆA (कर्णाभूषण) OR EAR-ORNAMENTS

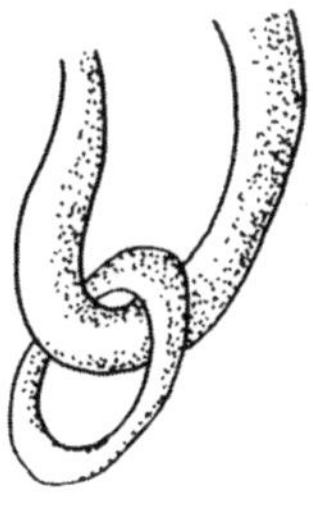

Karṇāvalī

These are also called *kuṇḍala*s (कुण्डल) and have been classified as follows:

Karṇāvalī (कर्णावली)	=	Beaded earring, used by Pārvatī
Karṇāpūra (कर्णापूर)	=	Used by Sarasvatī
Karṇikā (कर्णिका)	=	Used by Kālī

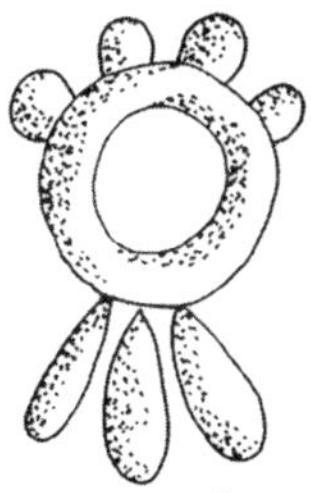

Karṇāvalī

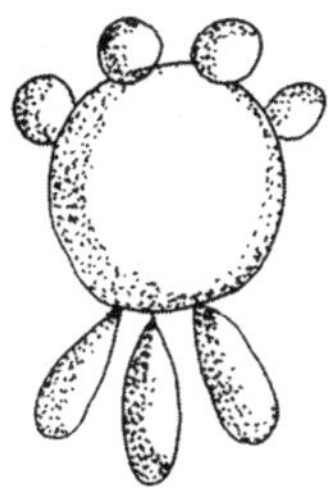

Karṇāpūra

Maṇi-kuṇḍala (मणि-कुण्डल) = Jewelled earring used by Lakṣmī

Patra-kuṇḍala (पत्र-कुण्डल) = Leaf earring used by Umā

Śaṅkha-kuṇḍala (शंख-कुण्डल) = Conch-shell earring used by Umā

Sarpa-kuṇḍala (सर्प-कुण्डल) = Serpent earring used by Śiva

KAṆṬHĀBHŪṢAṆA (कण्ठाभूषण) OR NECK-ORNAMENTS

Vaiṣṇava deities and *devī*s are more fond of these ornaments than the others.

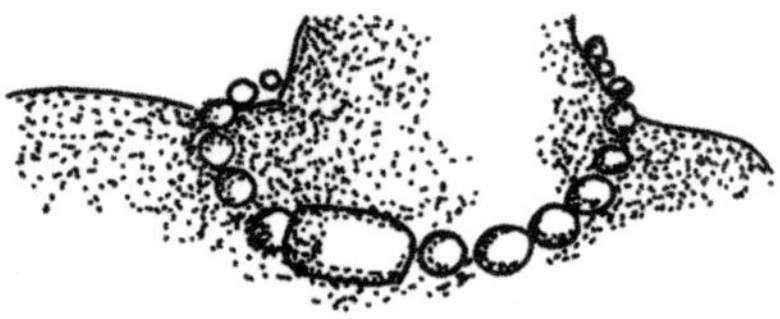

Kaustubha

Graiveyaka (ग्रैवेयक) : Broad necklace covering the whole upper part of the chest. Used by Śaiva deities.

Hāra (हार) : Necklace.

Kaustubha (कौस्तुभ) : It is a *maṇi* or gem recovered during *samudra-manthana* and worn on chest by Viṣṇu.

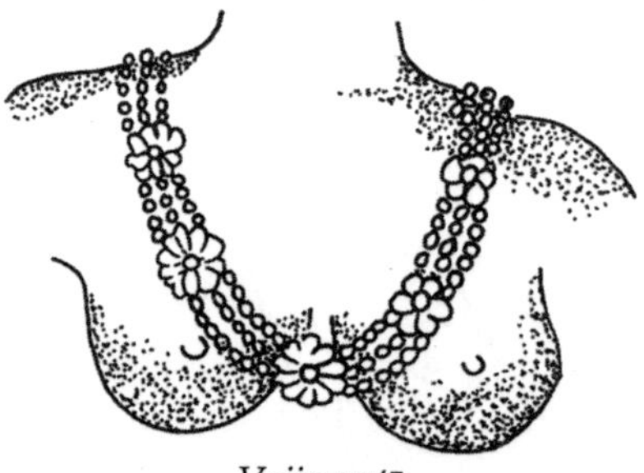

Vaijayantī

Niṣka (निष्क) : Necklace of coins.

Vaijayantī (वैजयन्ती) : Same as *vanamālā* (वनमाला) in form which is a long necklace, going up to the knees, and made of flowers. It is, however, studded with five sacred jewels worn by Viṣṇu as against *vanamālā* which has no jewel, only flowers.

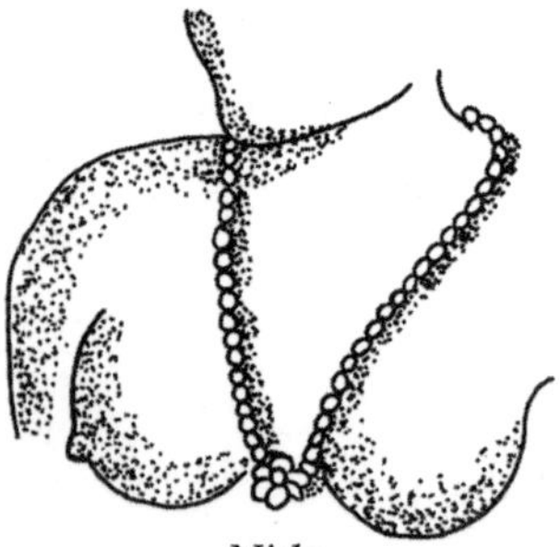

Niṣka

VAKṢĀBHŪṢAṆA (वक्षाभूषण) OR CHEST ORNAMENTS

Some ornaments were particularly meant for the chest.

Channavīra (छन्नवीर) : Cross-belt. Basically it denotes valour. Used by Viṣṇu. Others also sport it.

Kūcabandha **(कूचबन्ध)** : Breast-band. Used by *devīs*.

Śrīvatsa **(श्रीवत्स)** : A sacred stylized human form. On the chest of Viṣṇu. Jina's chest also often bears this mark. Its form is like a stylized babe with hands and legs twisted. When stylized it is like the bud of a flower.

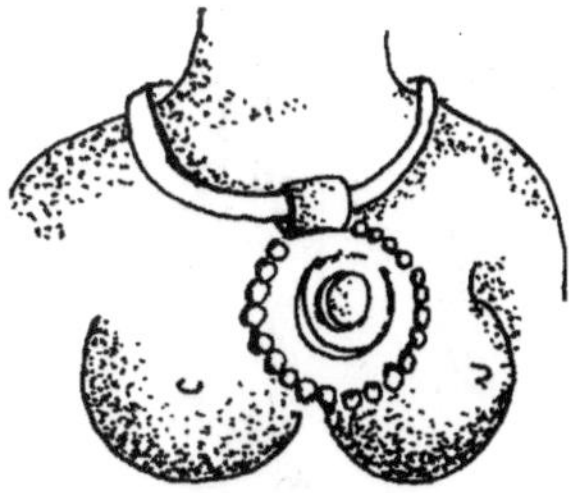

Kaṇṭhābhūṣaṇa

Yajñopavīta **(यज्ञोपवीत)** : Sacred thread. Single, goes across the chest.

KAṬI-ĀBHŪṢAṆA (कटि-आभूषण) OR HIP ORNAMENTS

Ornaments on hip have been of special interest to sculptors.

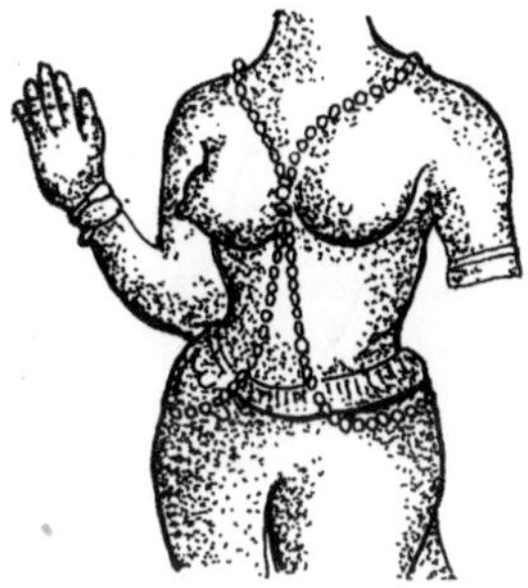

Channavīra necklace

Kāñcīdāma **(काञ्चीदाम)** : Strings with small bells.

Kaṭibandha **(कटिबन्ध)** : Any girdle.

Mekhalā **(मेखला)** : Girdle with strings.

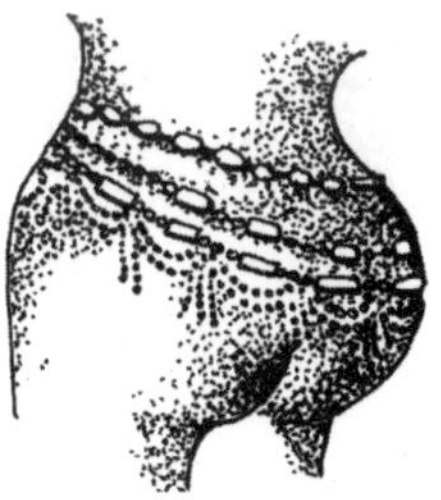

Girdle

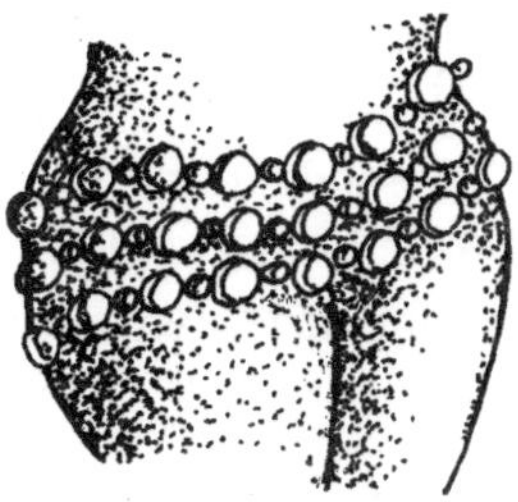

Mekhalā

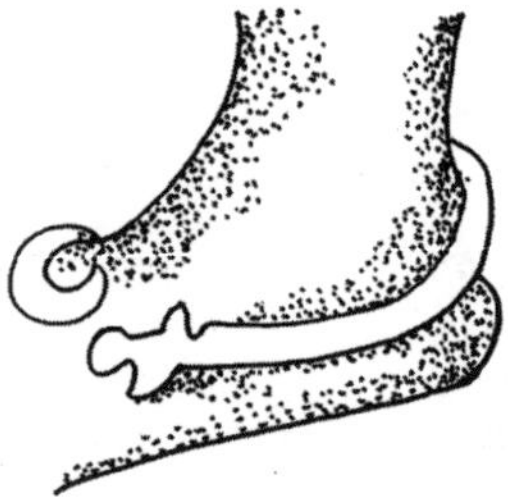

Foot-ring

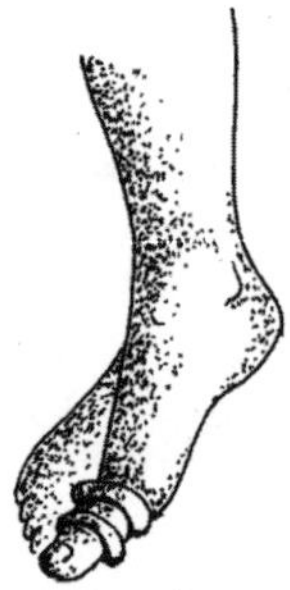

Mundarī

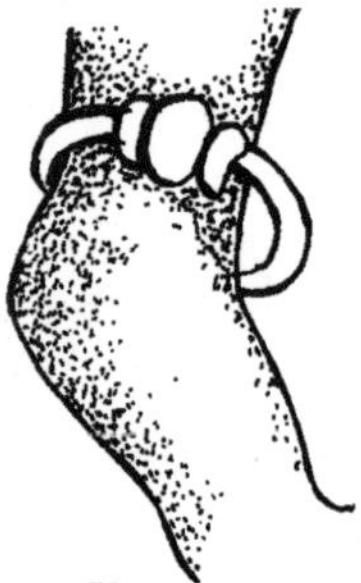

Keyūra

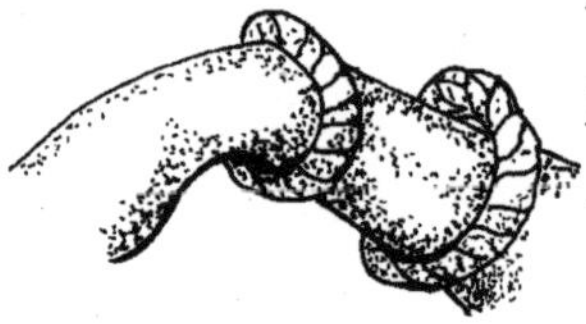

Kaṅkaṇa

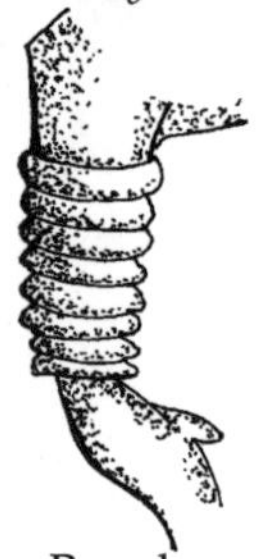

Bangles

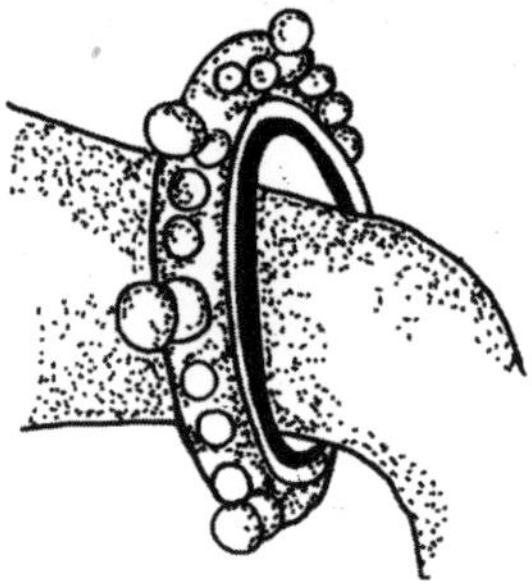

Aṅgada

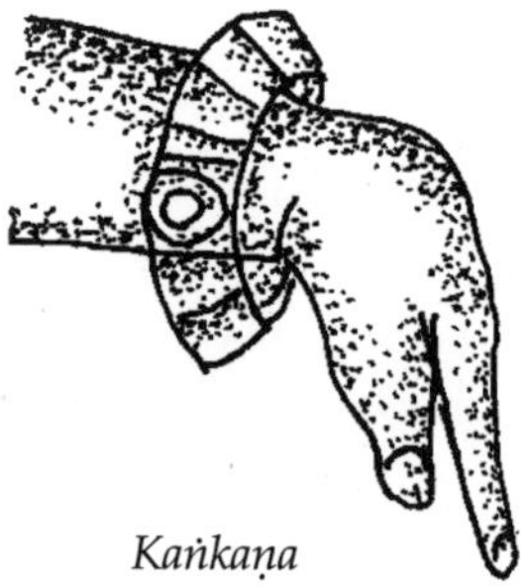

Kaṅkaṇa

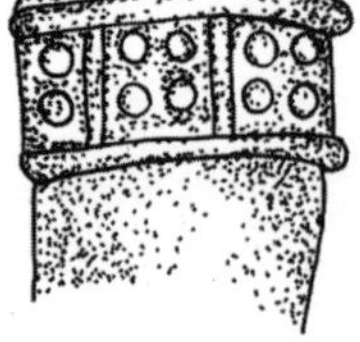

Valaya

PĀDA-ĀBHŪṢAṆA (पाद-आभूषण) OR FEET ORNAMENTS

***Mañjarī* (मञ्जरी)** : Strings embedded with small bells.

***Mundarī* (मुंदरी)** : Ring worn on toes.

BĀHU (बाहु) AND BHUJĀ ĀBHŪṢAṆA (भुजा-आभूषण) OR ARMLETS AND WRISTLETS

***Aṅgada* (अंगद)** : Wrist ornaments.

***Kaṅkaṇa* (कंकण)** : Wrist-band.

***Keyūra* (केयूर)** : Armlets of various shapes.

***Valaya* (वलय)** : Armlet.

NĀSA-ĀBHŪṢAṆA (नास-आभूषण) OR NOSE ORNAMENTS

The most popular nose ornament, called *vesara* (वेसर), was worn by Rādhā and Kṛṣṇa.

Paridhāna (परिधान) or Dress

Gods are also known by their special dresses. These are of two kinds — *bandha* (बन्ध) and *vastra* (वस्त्र).

BANDHA (बन्ध) OR BELT

***Kaṭibandha* (कटिबन्ध)** : Belt of cloth or metal tied at the hips.

***Udarabandha* (उदरबन्ध)** : The part of loincloth or a separate piece of cloth used as a belt round the belly. Used mainly by *yakṣas*. It is also called *ūrdhabandha* (ऊर्धबन्ध) particularly when it is just above the belly.

VASTRA (वस्त्र) OR CLOTH

***Dhotī* (धोती)** : One piece of long cloth which covers the lower body fully and upper body partially.

***Laṅgoṭī* (लंगोटी)** : A small piece of cloth worn by ascetics just to cover the private parts.

***Uttarīya* (उत्तरीय)** : A piece of cloth that is separately used to cover the upper part of the body.

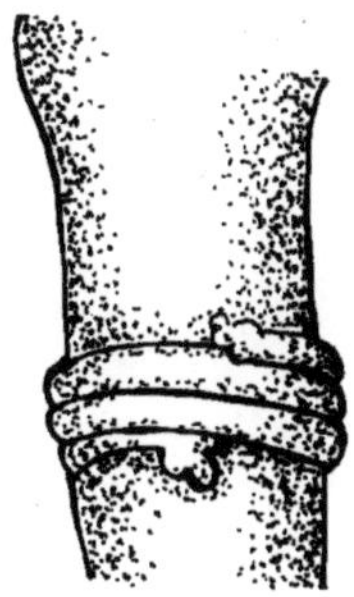

Keyūra

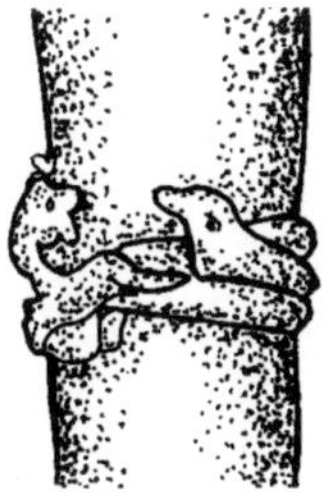

Keyūra

SPECIAL DRESS OF THE BUDDHA (बुद्ध के वस्त्र)

***Antaravāsaka* (अन्तर्वासक)** : Innermost garment.

***Uttarsaṅga* (उत्तरसंग)** : Garment covering the *antaravāsaka*.

***Saṁghāti* (संघाति)** : Cloak. Also called *cīvara* (चीवर).

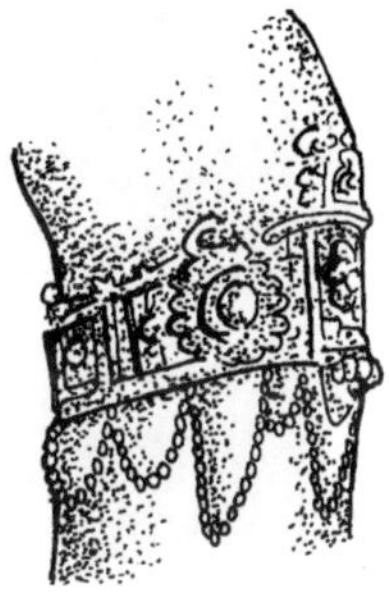

Keyūra

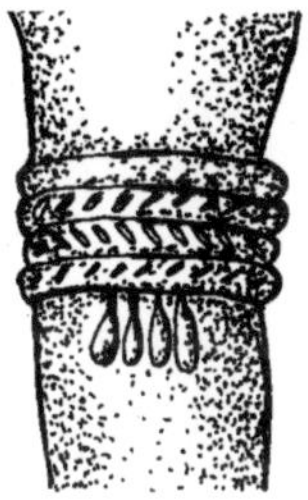

Valaya

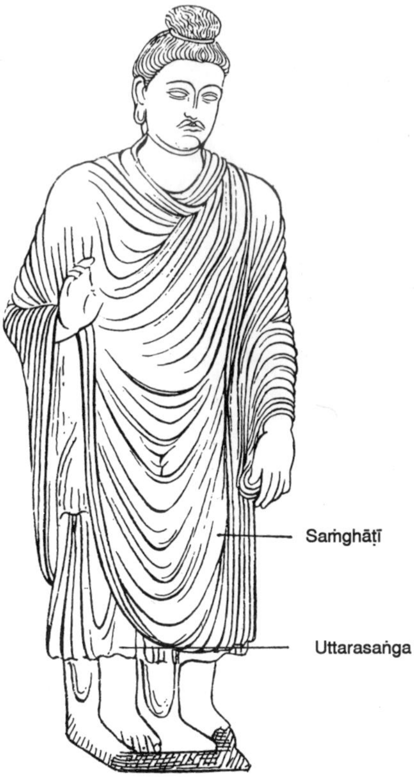

Dress of Buddha, Gāndhāra, 1st century CE

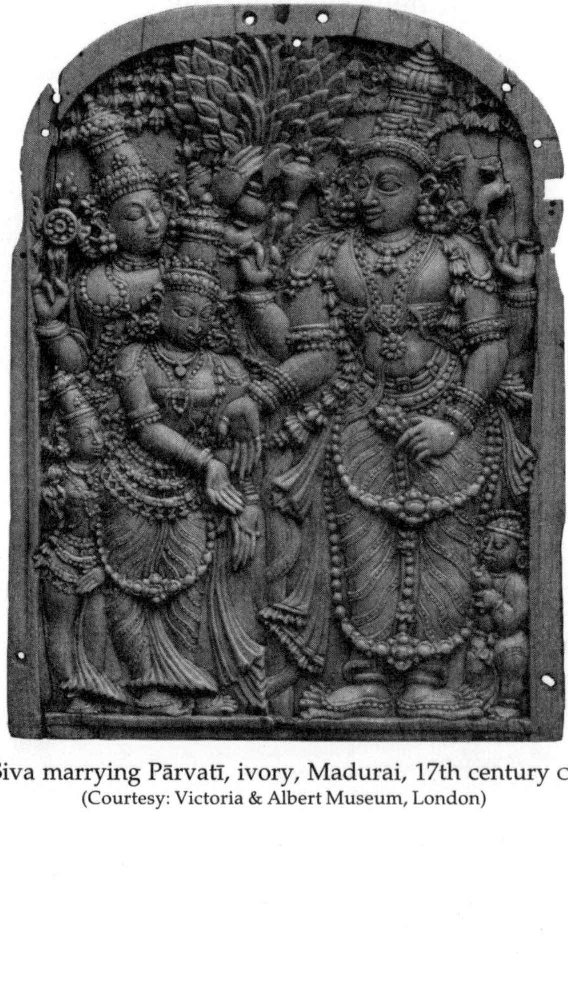

Śiva marrying Pārvatī, ivory, Madurai, 17th century CE
(Courtesy: Victoria & Albert Museum, London)

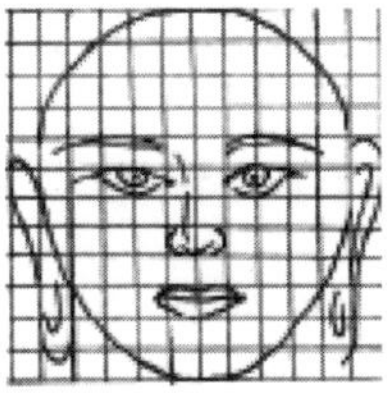

6

Principles of Iconometry

THE Hindu Iconometry or Tālamāna (तालमान) has the grammar of proportionate measurements of different parts of the body of human beings as well as of gods (देवता) and devils (दानव); of birds and animals too. At one stage it became necessary since iconometric forms also laid down the rules of *āyudhas*, *ābhūṣaṇas*, *mukuṭas*, etc. and for a balanced composition of Paurāṇic and Āgamic scenes, this important aspect could not be left to the whims of every individual artist. True, it created unsurmountable constraints for the real artists since he could not now take initiative to do otherwise and use his talents freely, but at the same time the common sculptors now also produced objects which was in conformity with those made by the masters. In any case, in the mediaeval times, it became essential for the sculptors to know the proportions of different parts of the body in relation to each other, whether it was the body of a human being, or of a god, or of an animal, or of a bird, or of a devil or *rākṣasa* or a *daitya* or a *dānava* as laid down by the masters and codified in texts.

However, in order to allow some variety, texts have suggested variations also, and of different kinds. In one kind of variation, the canon writers made five kinds of human beings, each with one set of measurements. In another kind of variation, the height differed — eight units or nine units or ten units.

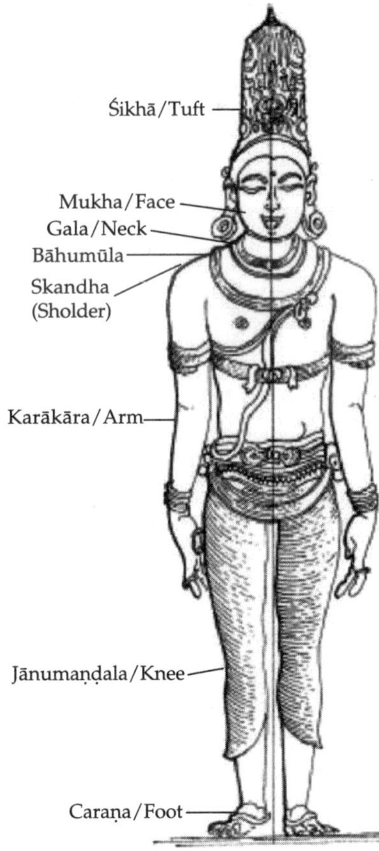

Parts of Human Body

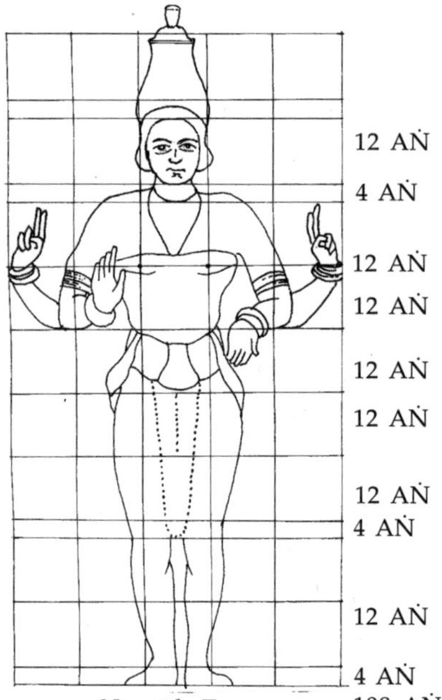

Navatāla Type

Tāla (ताल) as Main Unit of Measurement

In Hindu iconometry, one unit is called *tāla* (ताल). One *tāla* is one palm-length, i.e. when the palm is spread, the longest length is measured from the tip of the thumb to the tip of the middle finger. *Tāla* is also called *vitasti* (वितस्ति), *mukha* (मुख), *yama* (यम), *arka* (अर्क), *rāśi* (राशि), and *jagati* (जगति).

Aṅgula (अंगुल) as the First Unit of Measurement

This *tāla* unit is, however, further divided into *aṅgula*s, one *aṅgula* (अंगुल) is the thickness of the middle finger. One *tāla* has twelve *aṅgula*s.

Height and Girth Measurements

All measurements given in the texts are according to this *tāla* system. As noted earlier, Varāhamihira says that there are five kinds of men — each has a measurement for the height and girth as follows:

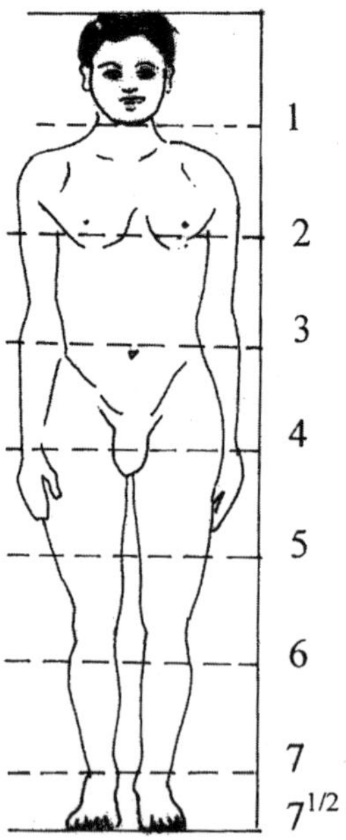

Proportions of the Male Body

Tālamāna

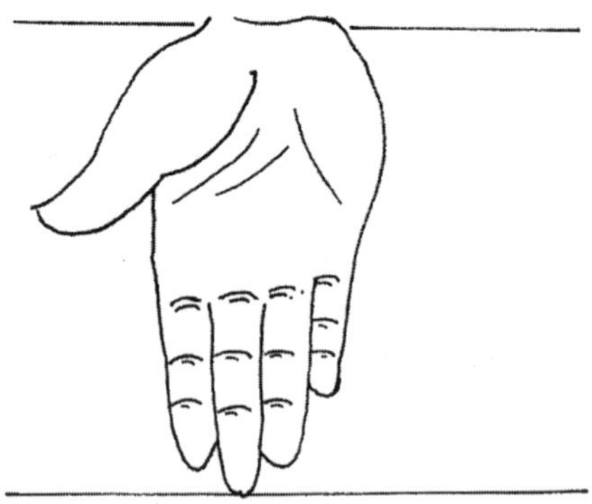

Length of the Hand
= 1 *tāla* (12 *aṅgula*)
Middle Digit of the Medius
= 1 *aṅgula*

(i) ***Haṁsa* (हंस)** : 96 *aṅgula*s, height as well as girth.

(ii) ***Śaśa* (शश)** : 99 *aṅgula*s, height as well as girth.

(iii) ***Rūcaka* (रूचक)** : 102 *aṅgula*s, height as well as girth.

(iv) ***Bhadra* (भद्र)** : 105 *aṅgula*s, height as well as girth.

(v) ***Mālavya* (मालव्य)** : 108 *aṅgula*s, height as well as girth.

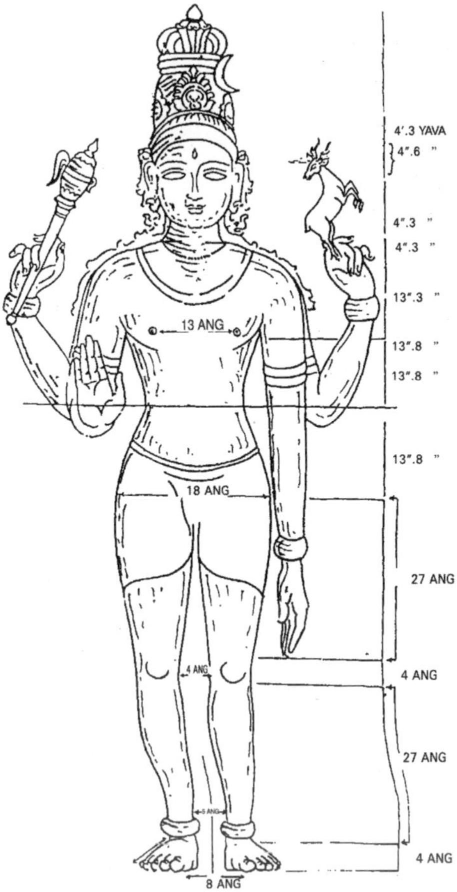

In this, the first, i.e. the *haṁsa* type is *daśatāla* type, while the last, the *mālavya* type is *navatāla* type, *daśa* is ten while *nava* is nine. The measurement is taken from the top of the head, up to hair-line or *keśa-rekhā,* to the bottom of the feet.

Measurements of Different Parts of the Body

The *Vaikhānasāgama* (वैखानसागम) of south India mentions six ways of the measurements of different parts of human body:

(i) ***Māna* (मान)** : Measurement of the length (height) of the body.

(ii) ***Pramāṇa* (प्रमाण)** : Breadth of the body.

(iii) ***Unmāna* (उन्मान)** : Thickness of the body.

(iv) ***Parimāṇa* (परिमाण)** : Girth or periphery of the body.

(v) ***Upamāna* (उपमान)** : Interspaces between different parts of the body, i.e. between one limb and the other.

(vi) ***Lambamāna* (लम्बमान)** : Total height, taken along the plumb lines.

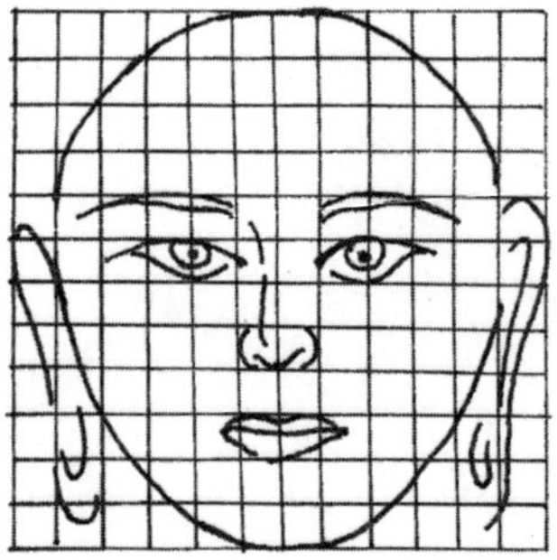

Length and Breadth of the face = 1 *tāla* (12 *aṅgula*)

The *Bṛhat-Saṁhitā* has given the measurements of face, neck, etc. so that all remain proportionate and balanced.

It is interesting to note that the northern texts, except for the *Matsya Purāṇa*, do not use the term *tāla*, they use *aṅgula*. The southern ones use *tāla* frequently. *Matsya* mentions that while Rāma, Narasiṁha, and other great men and gods were of *daśatāla* measurement, *Vāmana Purāṇa* recommends *saptatāla* measurement.

Uttama, Madhyama and Adhama Measurements

The texts like *Vaikhānasāgama* also mention *uttama* (उत्तम), *madhyama* (मध्यम) and *adhama* (अधम) *daśatāla* measurements — the first is 124 *aṅgulas*, the second is 120 *aṅgulas*, and the third is 116 *aṅgulas*.

The *Vaikhānasāgama* lays down the following rules:

(i) Brahmā, Viṣṇu and Śiva: *Uttama daśatāla* (उत्तम दशताल) (124 *aṅgulas*).

(ii) Śrī, Bhūdevī, Umā and Sarasvatī : *Madhyama daśatāla* (मध्यम दशताल) (120 *aṅgulas*).

(iii) Indra, Lokapālas, Sūrya, Candra, 12 Ādityas, 11 Rudras, 8 Vasus, the Aśvins, Bhṛgu, Mārkaṇḍeya, Garuḍa, Śeṣa, Durgā, Guha (Kārttikeya) and seven ṛṣis : *Adhama daśatāla* (अधम दशताल) (116 *aṅgulas*).

(iv) Yakṣas (including Kubera), Navagrahas, other deities : *Navārdhatāla* (नवार्द्धताल) (114 *aṅgulas*).

(v) Rākṣasas, Asuras, Indras : *Navatāla* (नवताल) (108 *aṅgulas*).

(vi) Men : *Aṣṭatāla* (अष्टताल) (96 *aṅgulas*).

(vii) Vaitāla : *Saptatāla* (सप्तताल) (84 *aṅgulas*).

(viii) Pretas : *Ṣaṭtāla* (षट्ताल) (72 *aṅgulas*).

(ix) Hunchbacks : *Pañcatāla* (पञ्चताल) (60 *aṅgulas*).

(x) Dwarfs : *Catuśtāla* (चतुश्ताल) (48 *aṅgulas*).

(xi) Bhūtas, Kinnaras : *Tritāla* (त्रिताल) (36 *aṅgulas*).

(xii) Kuṣmāṇḍas (Kumbhāṇḍas) : *Dvitāla* (द्विताल) (24 *aṅgulas*).

(xiii) Kabaṅdhas : *Ekatāla* (एकताल) (12 *aṅgulas*).

This text also suggests that each of these *tāla* measurements has three varieties, viz. *uttama*, *madhyama*, and *adhama*. Recently, P.O. Sompura has illustrated a set of other measurements for different categories of images which have come into use in modern times following some old traditions. Obviously, although the southern text *Vaikhānasāgama* (वैखानसागम), used by T.A. Gopinath Rao and others, as given above, has been the basis of iconometric studies, there have been many other traditions, one of which has been given by Sompura and which is being practised by his family of traditional architects, the *sthapatis* (स्थपति).

Some Textual Differences

It is interesting to note that the term *tāla* is comparatively of late usage; also, used more in southern system than in northern. As we know, neither the earlier portion of chapter 57 of *Bṛhat-Saṁhitā*, nor Utpala's commentary on it explicitly refers to the word *tāla* or its equivalent(s). Kaśyapa is also silent about it. The *Pratimālakṣaṇam*, as edited by J.N. Banerjea, is based on early texts, but it is also silent about it. According to W.S. Hadaway, terms like *daśatāla*, *navatāla*, etc. refer to the divisions of the "whole used length of an image," e.g. in *daśatāla* an image, say meant to be 5 m high, is divided into ten equal parts for the measurement of other parts of the body. But Banerjea has rightly observed that this is based on the present-day practice of the south Indian architects — *sthapatis* (स्थपति) and not on the authority of the old texts.

It is also interesting to note that many early texts tell us that the face should be of one *tāla* length and the same one *tāla* breadth, which, in effect, makes it round. But possibly from very early times, maybe early Gupta, if not pre-Gupta, the south Indian or Dravidian system had long faces — 14 or 13½ *aṅgula*s in length and 12 *aṅgula*s in width. This conclusion is based on the fact that one canon-writer, Nagnajit, from whom Varāhamihira quotes some passages, was of early or pre-Gupta period, as has been shown by Dr Priyabala Shah, who has edited the *Viṣṇudharmottara* in the Gaikwad Series, Baroda. According to the verse of Nagnajit, the length of the face of the image, with the hair on the head, should be 16 *aṅgula*s.

अस्यं सकेशनिचयम् षोडश
दैर्ध्येण नग्नजित् प्रोक्तम् ।।
asyaṁ sakeśanicayam ṣoḍaśa
dairdhyeṇa nagnajit proktam ।।
— 57.V.15

Significantly, some of the important south Indian Āgamas, such as *Karṇāgama* and *Vaikhānasāgama*, mention that the length of the face should be 14 or 13½ *aṅgula*s.

All these details show that while the general practice in the north was of round faces of 12 *aṅgula*s length and 12 *aṅgula*s breadth, the practice in the south was of long faces of 13½ or 14 or 16 *aṅgula*s in length and 12 *aṅgula*s in width.

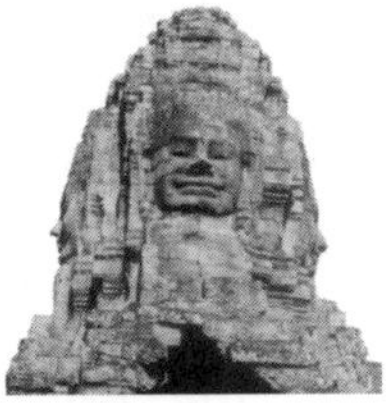

7

Indian Art Beyond the Indian Frontiers

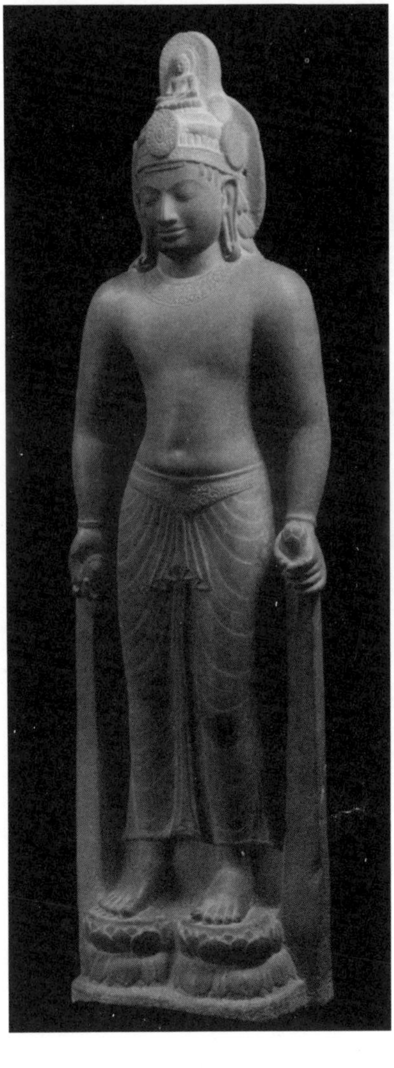

Tân Long, Vietnam: Avalokiteśvara

THE story of Indian Art and Architecture will hardly be complete unless something is told about its extension beyond the frontiers of India. In the south is Sri Lanka while in the east are the present-day countries of Myanmar (Brahmadeśa), Thailand (Siam), Cambodia (Kāmboja), Laos (Lava), Vietnam (Champa) and Malaysia (Malayadeśa) forming the mainland, and Indonesia (including Java or Yavadvīpa and Sumātrā or Suvarṇabhūmi). The history of these countries, particularly of the mainland South-East Asia and to some extent the islands, has been of long-drawn battles, often changing their capitals and frontiers. However, there was hardly any major break in the continuity of their culture which remained one and the same from about the first century CE to the fifteenth century CE. This culture is generally called "Hindu-Buddhist." The justification of this term lies in the fact that throughout this long period, these countries witnessed the simultaneous entry and growth of Hinduism and Buddhism. It became possible because there was constant movement of the *ācārya*s (आचार्य), i.e. masters, saints and apostles, between India's mainland and the countries of South and South-East Asia. The movement was primarily maritime, since trade amongst the Indian Ocean Rim countries from South China Sea through the Arabian Sea and the Red Sea was brisk. All this is

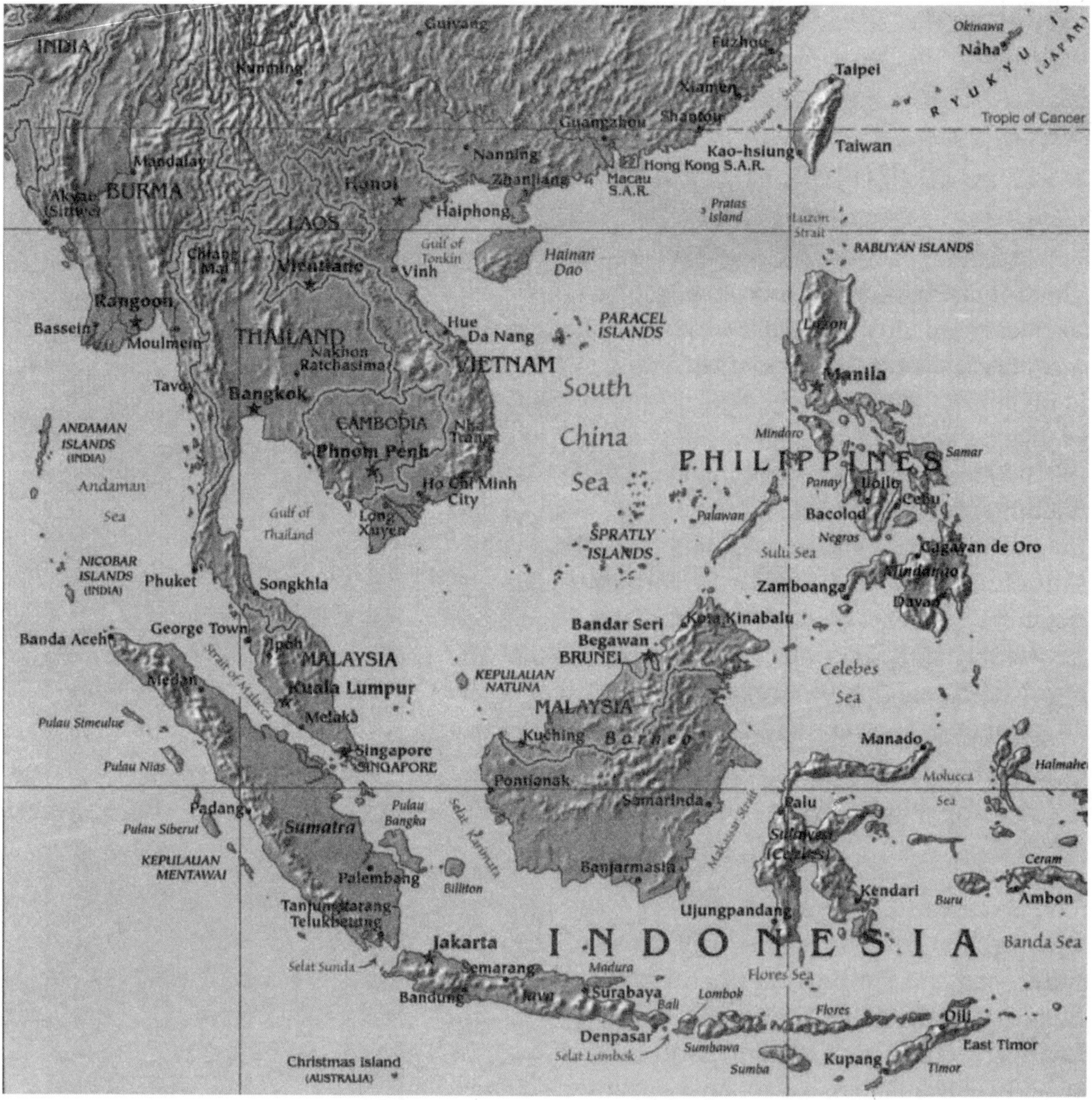

General Map of South-East Asia

borne out by the Chinese literary sources, South-East Asian epigraphical records and archaeological objects found in explorations and excavations conducted in these countries. However, it is not that Indian artists and craftsmen themselves executed the building projects in this region; in fact, there is ample evidence to show that in all these countries local talents developed in every field of cultural activity. Dance, drama and painting as well as decorative arts followed the same pattern — initial introduction by the Indian masters and occasional request for the new ones but establishment of local schools and workshops. That is why while Indian religions, mythologies and literature provided the contents to the art and architecture of South and South-East Asia, the actual forms of the figures, human and animal, remained fully rooted in the local soil. In temple and *stūpa* (स्तूप) architecture also, although their basic elements remained the same as in India, still several modifications and elaborations in them have been noted by all scholars. It is because of these factors, that the history of art and architecture of South and South-East Asian countries is so very exciting for all of us in India — it was Indian in one sense and non-Indian in another. It was in fact the stage of flowering of Indian art in different colours and in different gardens of the world.

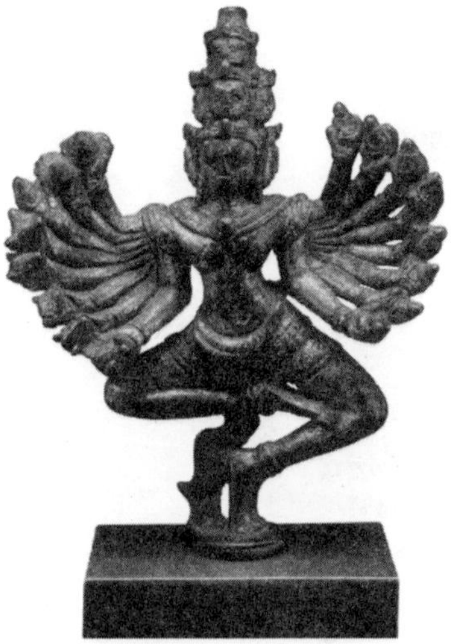

Cambodia: *Hevajra*, Bronze

Let us begin with Sri Lanka:

Sri Lanka

Tradition tells us that it was as far back in time as the fifth century BCE that a prince named Vijay, from somewhere in the mid-Gaṅgā plains, founded in Sri Lanka the first city called "Tamrapanni" (Skt. Tāmraparṇī) (ताम्रपर्णी). Around 400 BCE, a still larger city, called "Anurādhapura" was founded.

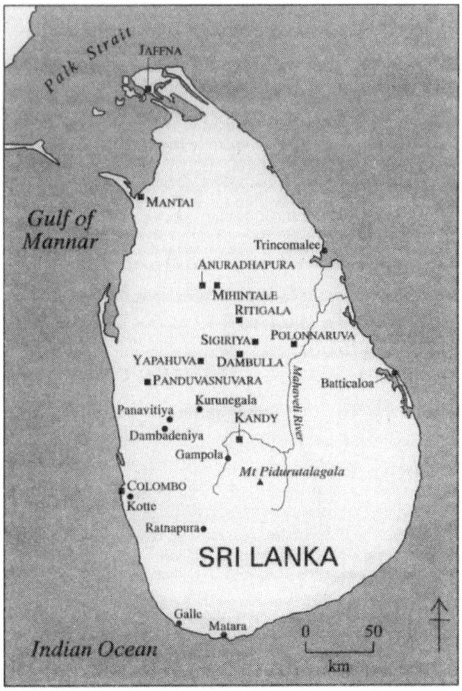

Historical map of Sri Lanka

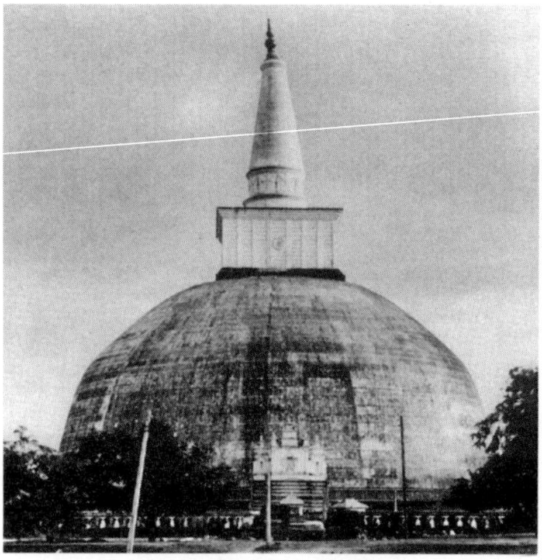

Anurādhapura: Ruwanweli Seya

However, the first historically attested reference to a king of Sri Lanka comes from literary and traditional sources — his name was Devānāmapiya Tissa (247-207 BCE). King Aśoka had sent his son Mahendra and daughter Saṅghamitrā to the court of this very king with a branch of the *bodhi* tree from Bodha-Gayā to be planted in honour of Buddha Śākyamuni at Anurādhapura with the message that he would see now onwards the spread of true Dharma. Although soon after, the Tamil people from south India established their rule at this place, another Sinhalese warrior king, by the name Dutthagāminī (101-77 BCE), re-established the rule of the local people. However, this incident unfortunately also led to Sinhalese-Tamilian feud for all time to come. It may be mentioned that in subsequent times while the Sinhalese favoured Buddhist religion, Buddhist art and Buddhist architecture, the Tamilians favoured Hinduism and built Hindu temples with Vaiṣṇava and Śaiva deities. In fact, during the Coḷa period, in tenth century CE, Sri Lanka was conquered and it became just a provincial seat under a Governor. Still, soon after, Poḷonnāruva, besides Anurādhapura, became another seat of governance by the Sinhalese who were more numerous and now more powerful in the southern part of the island. In the eighteenth-century Kandy became the third important city of the island. It, in course of time, also became an important centre of Sri Lankan art and culture.

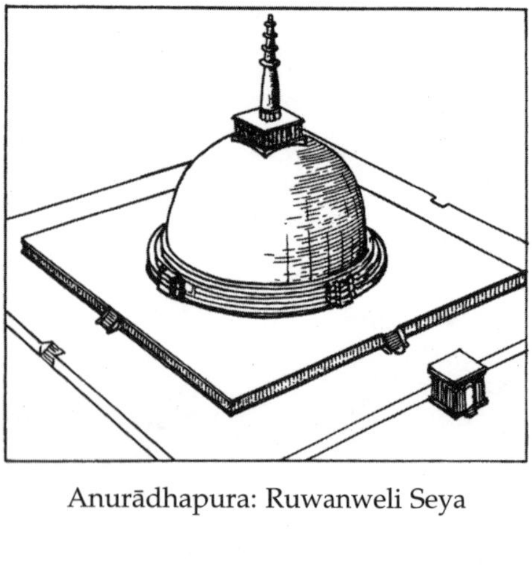

Anurādhapura: Ruwanweli Seya

The Sinhalese Buddhists constructed *stūpa*s, they called *dāgaba*s (दागब), with hemispherical dome or *aṇḍa* (अण्ड), following the model of the *mahāstūpa* (महास्तूप) at Sāñcī. However, unlike Sāñcī, it has three moulded rims or rings at the base. The entire structure though stands on a square platform was concealed below the ground since for them it was only a constructional device for providing strong

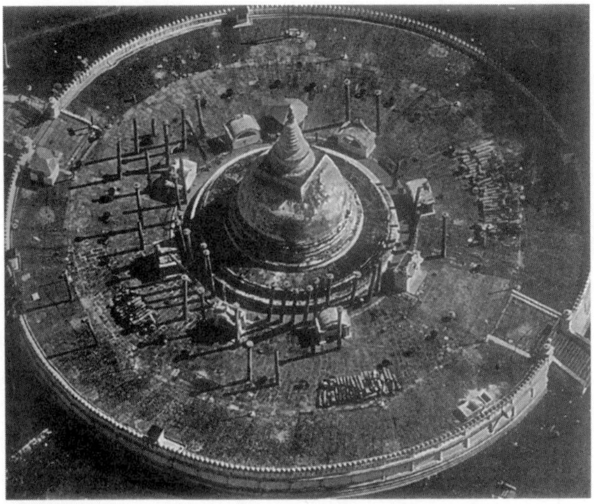

Anurādhapura: Thupārāma

foundation to the huge and heavy mass of the solid drum. The *stūpa* was, however, approached from all the four cardinal directions by flights of steps. The first of such *dāgabas*, surrounded by free-standing tall and slender pillars, arranged on a platform in as many as four rings, was built in 244 BCE at Thāpārāma. King Dutthagāminī built two of them at Anurādhapura. Of them, the most famous is of Ruwanweli, with the dome measuring 254 ft in diameter. It had paintings also on it. Here, there stood two colossal images, one of Buddha and the other of a *bodhisattva*, both conceived and carved in the Amarāvatī style. King Mahāsena (CE 277-304), on the other hand, built a monastic complex, called the "Jetavana Vihāra" with a large *stūpa* in the centre. He also built the largest *dāgaba* of Sri Lanka, called "Abhayagiri Dāgaba." During the fifth century, something more imposing was built. A king named Kassapa I (CE 479-97) occupied the natural hill-fortress of Sigriyā (Lion Rock) for his palace. This tall and beautiful hill witnessed the creation of caves which contain some of the most exquisite wall paintings with men and women drawn with lyrical flowing lines and soft but colourful light-and-shade leading to the creation of the illusion of the third dimension, i.e. thickness in the body in the Gupta-Ajantā style. The Jetavana Vihāra had, of course, a number of other buildings. Of these, the one called "Laṅkātilaka" has the largest Buddha image built in bricks and plastered as well as painted.

Sīgiriya: Fresco on rock face

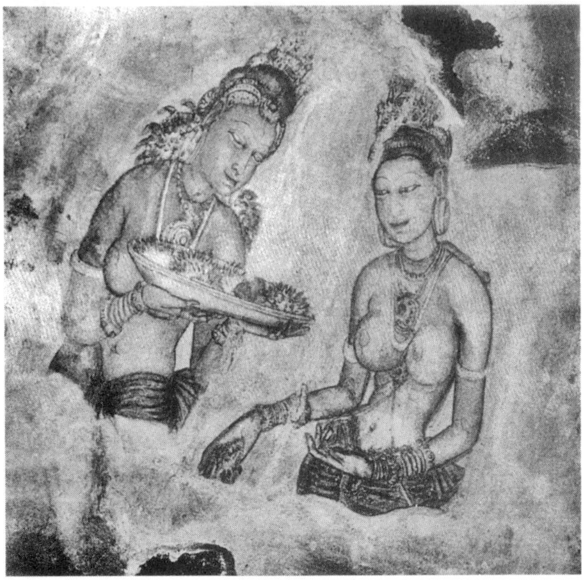

At Poḷonnāruva, on the other hand, the Coḷas had built several Hindu temples,

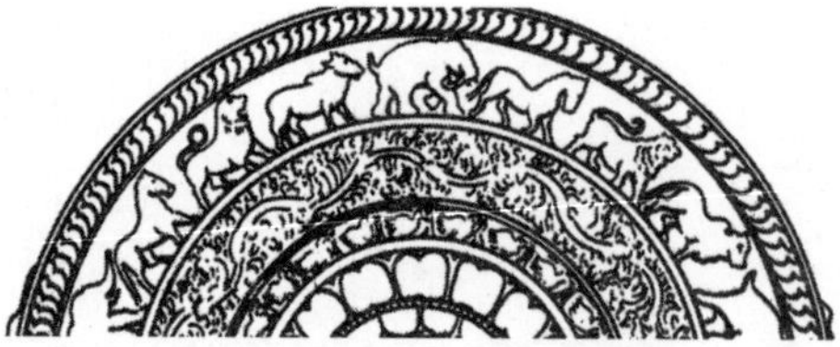

Anurādhapura: Candraśilā

of which a beautiful one, the most imposing one, is devoted to Śiva. The temple called *devāle* (देवाले), has the usual *garbha-gṛha* (गर्भ-गृह), *antarāla* (अन्तराल), *ardha-maṇḍapa* (अर्द्ध-मण्डप) and *maṇḍapa* (विमान), with a four-storied *vimāna* or spire, all conceived in the south Indian temple style. There are three Vaiṣṇava temples also, at Kataragama, Kandy and Ratanpura. All these temples are adorned with a multitude of images carved in stone. They also contained beautiful bronze images with graceful bodies and meaningful gestures, following the prescriptions of Hindu iconography.

Sri Lanka is indeed full of sculptures in stone and bronze of Buddhist and Hindu icons, exhibiting south Indian art traditions. The bronze images of Buddha and *bodhisattvas* as well as of Śiva, Kārttikeya, Gaṇeśa, etc. found in large numbers, however, show many local features which make them a lot different from the Indian ones. Hence these are Sinhalese in their own terms. The world-famous Sigriyā cave paintings are also imbued with features, not only facial but also representational, which make them exclusive as Sinhalese, although the models before the painter-artists were undoubtedly Ajantan and Bāgh, both in terms of contents and technical devices.

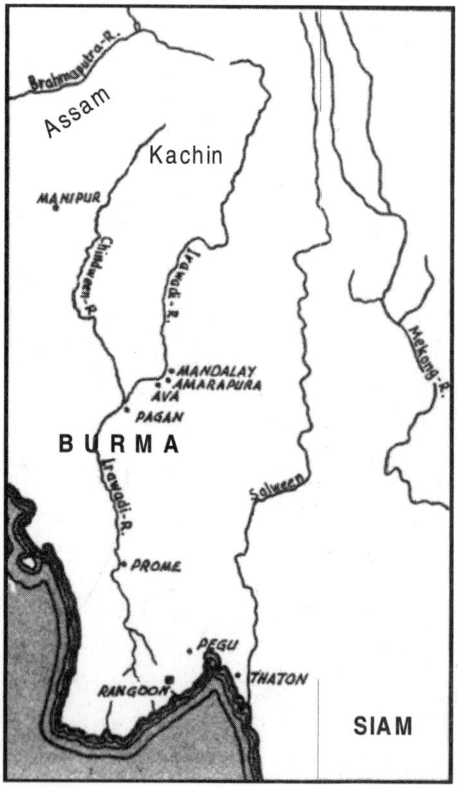

Myanmar

Like Sri Lanka, Myanmar was also the next-door neighbour of India which has yielded enough evidence of not only the original peoples, like the Pyus, but also the settlements of the Indians, particularly in the coastal regions. The evidence shows that from about 300-200 BCE, i.e. during the Mauryan rule, people of Indian origin came to Myanmar; in all likelihood, they were engaged in trading activities, even in luxury items like beads of the semi-precious stones like carnelian and agate. There is, however, much more evidence of the Indians settling in Myanmar between first century and fifth century CE at places like Tagaun, Prome and Thaton, respectively located in the north, centre and the south of the country. These places are known in later history for their eminence and prosperity as well as for the Hindu and Buddhist temples, existing side by side, from at least the Gupta times of the fifth and sixth centuries of the Common Era (CE).

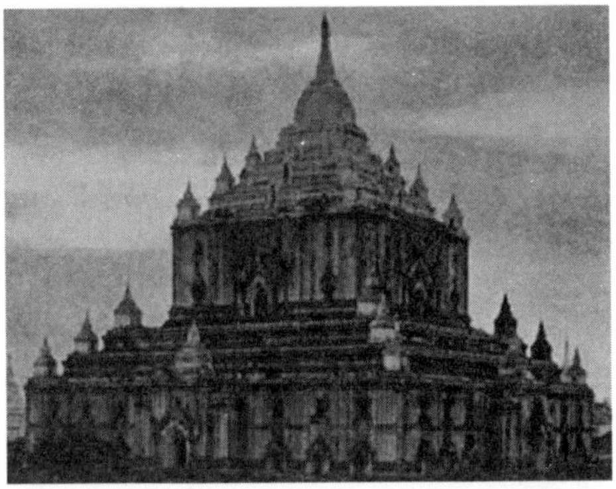

The Hindu temples were devoted to Viṣṇu as well as to Śiva which is reflected in numerous stone and terracotta sculptures found in their precincts. The Buddhist *stūpa*s, monasteries and temples, also adorned with religious sculptures and paintings, belong both to Hīnayāna (हीनयान) and Mahāyāna (महायान). The Hīnayāna temples and *stūpa*s (स्तूप) are there at Thaton, a place which was, it is said, visited by Buddhaghoṣa, a great teacher, around CE 450. He came loaded with Pāli canons which contributed greatly to the growth and spread of Hīnayāna

Bagan: Dhammayangyi Pahto

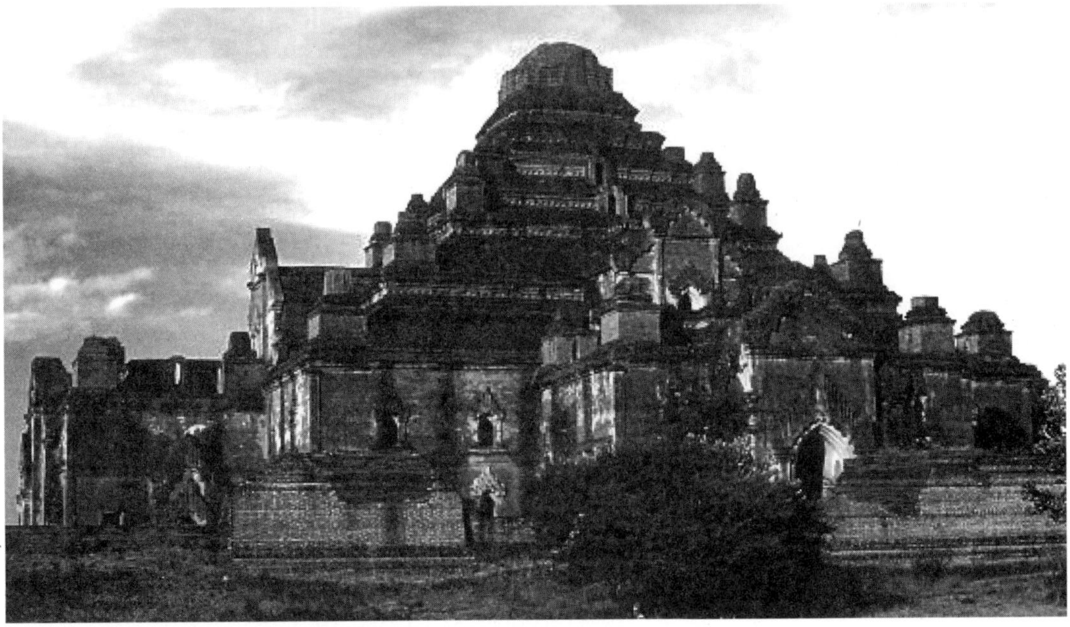

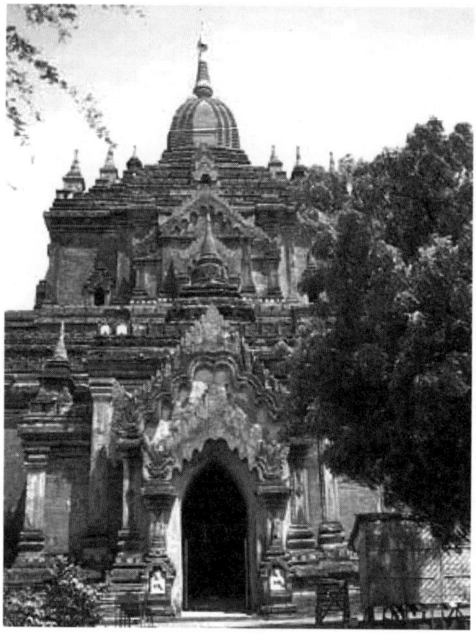

Bagan: Htilominlo temple, CE 1211

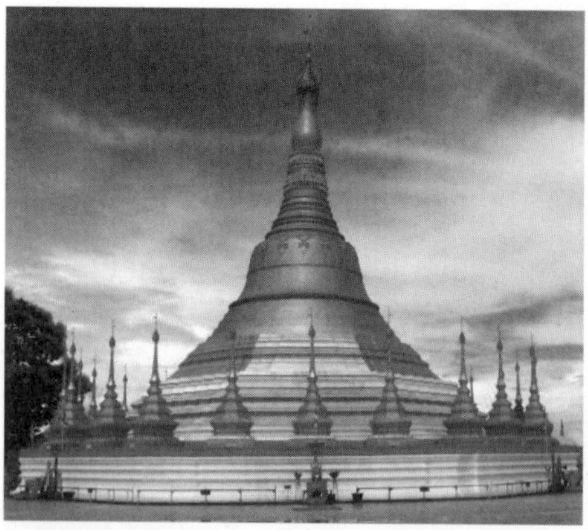

Tachileik: Golden *pagoḍā*

Buddhism. The Mahāyānist temples, on the other hand, are there at Prome. These were visited by several pontiffs in course of time. As a matter of fact, Tagaun and other places in the northern region of the country witnessed the growth of even Tantrism of the Nepalese origin. Myanmar, as a country, has, however, been predominantly Hīnayānist. By the ninth century, there were political changes brought about by the establishment of new capital towns, such as the one in Pagan, a fortified settlement with several Buddhist and Hindu establishments. In the tenth century, a Vaiṣṇava temple-complex came up prominently at Pagan. However, now only one such temple, named Nat Hlaung Gyaung, is surviving. The Buddhist complexes are many. There the *stūpa*s are cylindrical as well as bulbous like the one at Dhamekh at Sārnāth. These are located at Ngakywe Nadaung.

It was the eleventh century, which had really witnessed the real growth in Hīnayānist monastic establishments. At this point of time the distinguished warrior king of Pagan, named Anawrata, in Sanskrit Aniruddha, conquered most of the country and built virtually a multitude of *stūpa*s or *pagoḍā*s (पगोडा) in and around Pagan, a practice that continued for several centuries. In the eleventh century even cave-temples were carved out by the Buddhists, such as the one at Kyanzitha. Ānanda and Nanpaya were yet other great *pagoḍā*s of this century. Belonging to the twelfth century are some of the extremely important Buddhist *stūpa*-monastery complexes. They are found existing at Sapada and Thatabinnu. The thirteenth century also witnessed the founding of a large number of *pagoḍā*s, such as Mahābodhi, Tilominlo, etc. It may be noted that most of them were built of bricks and beautifully decorated with stucco, glazed tiles and mural paintings. Many of these paintings and stuccos contain scenes from Buddhist Jātaka stories, connected with the supposed-to-be previous births of the Buddha, as *bodhisattvas*, around 500 of them.

It may be noted that the Myanmar Pagoḍā or *stūpa* architecture, when analysed in detail, show influences in their forms coming not only from India but also Sri Lanka, Cambodia, Indonesia, and even China, since there was a great mobility of the people amongst all these Buddhist countries, and devotees of those countries also contributed to their establishments as they are doing presently at Bodh-Gayā and Sārnāth. However, there did develop a style and form in art and architecture which was earlier called "Burmese," because the country was thus called in the nineteenth and twentieth centuries, but now Myanmarese. The best examples of this style of monuments are Ānanda, Thatabinnu and Gawdapalin, although there are several others also of the same style. This style shows, besides other characteristics, like terraces, lying flat on square base but rising one above the other and giving the structure a tall vertical effect, the element of niche-shrines. These are carved within the mass of the *pagoḍā* structure, a feature which was only rarely seen in India.

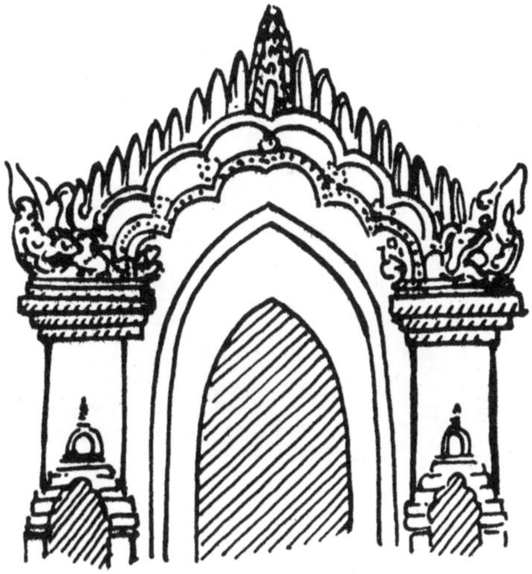

Pagan: Ānanda Temple

The art of Myanmar includes, besides murals, beautiful bronzes in late Gupta style, of the seventh ...d eighth centuries. It appears that at least a few ...m were brought by the monks or sculptors ...Buddhist centres of Bihar and Bengal. There ...ne images and relief sculptures also, both ... Hindu. The Ānanda Pagoḍā has as ...hes, each one of which contained ...in low relief and others in high ...utiful works of art which show ... the instruments generating ...duced lyrical human figures

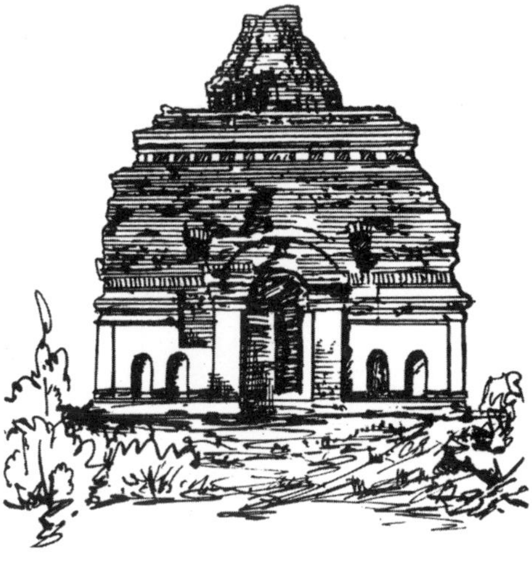

Nat Hlaung Gyaung: Ancient Brahmanical Temple

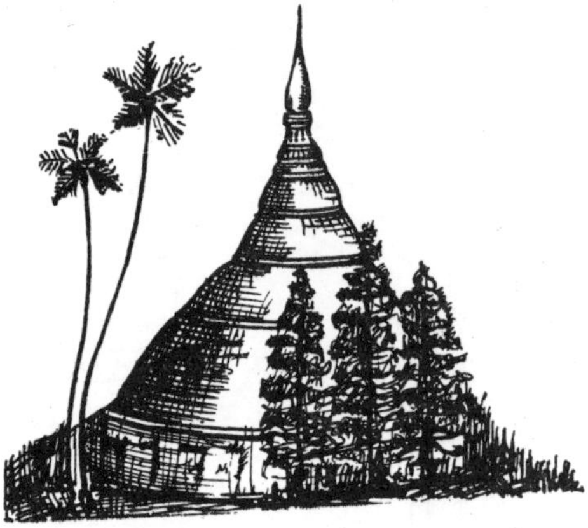

Rangoon: Shwe Dagon

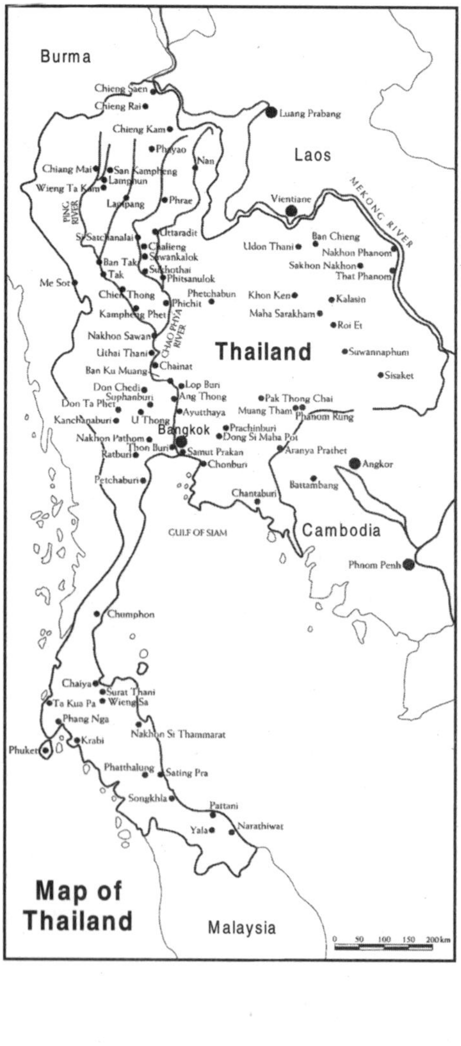

Map of Thailand

with floral decorations and flowing costumes. The humans are imbued with graceful poise and gait, making them superb in quality. Such examples can be seen in the Nanpaya Pagoḍā decorations also. Ānanda Pagoḍā also has several of such beautiful sculptures. So also is the case with Kyanzitha *pagoḍā*.

The Hindu sculptures of the Viṣṇu's Daśāvatāra figures at Nat Hlaung Gyaung are, it may be mentioned, equally beautiful with markedly Indian elements.

One thing may also be noted. Tāntric Buddhist art of Myanmar contains many iconographic novelties. Those found in the Payathonzu triple temple at Minnanthu, located near Pagan, for example, clearly exhibit a curious mixture of Hindu, Buddhist and local elements and features.

There are at least two establishments, that of Yathemya and Hmawza, in which sculptures of different periods, in the fifth and eleventh-century styles, are found in large numbers. At Peagu, there is a very large sculpture of Buddha lying in *mahāparinirvāṇa-mudrā* (महापरिनिर्वाण-मुद्रा). It is 181 ft in length. In late thirteenth century, unfortunately Kublai Khan attacked and destroyed the city of Pagan, ending a great tradition in art although the creation of works of art continued and occurs even to this day, but the perfection and glory of the past centuries are found replaced by mechanically drawn figures lacking th grace and spirituality of the past ages.

Thailand

Modern Thailand formed part of ancien which was larger in expanse. As a matte the southern part of the country was for part of the Khmer empire conce

Cambodia. It was, therefore, natural that Thailand inherited Hinduism as well as Buddhism from the Khmer culture. Still, Siam, located in northern Thailand, had its independent status for a very long time. In CE 575 its capital was Lamphun which has the remains of several temples. Slightly south of it there developed the kingdom of Sukhothai, which, in course of time, became the most important centre of Thai rule and Thai culture, from around the eleventh century to the fourteenth century. Still south was the kingdom of Lopburi, which was under the Khmers also for centuries together. Dvārāvatī was its great city.

Lopburi: Prasat Hin Phimai

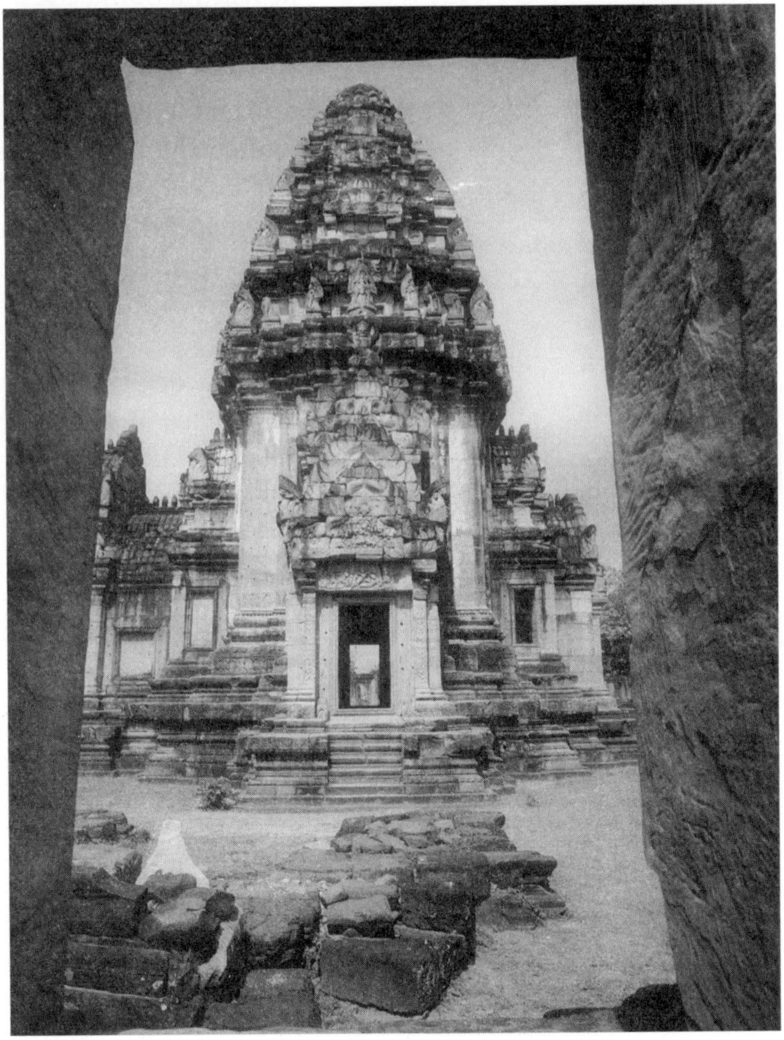

In Thailand, as in other parts of South-East Asia, Gupta and Pallava art and architecture exerted great influence as can be seen in the monuments at places like Rājburi, Chantaburi, Kedah, etc. In fact, only by CE 1400, Thai power is felt in the mainland. They even invaded and sacked Angkor Wat of the Khmers heralding the end of one of the greatest art traditions of South-East Asia and the birth of another one, this time in Thailand. In 1350, the Thais founded at the old capital township of Sano an entirely new capital city named Ayuthiā, named after the famous city of the

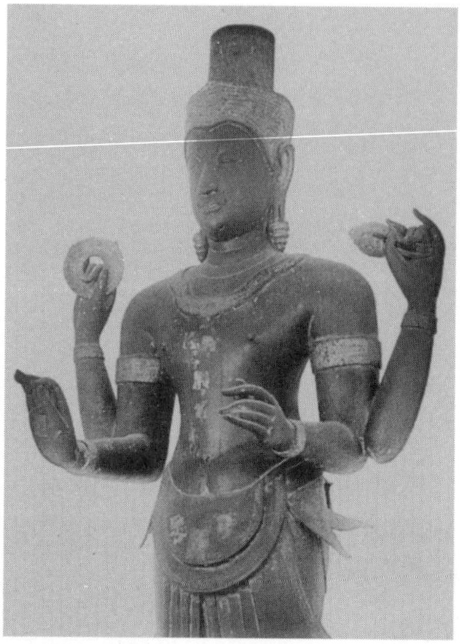

Sukhothai: Bronze Viṣṇu, *c.* 14th CE

Lopburi: Bronze Buddha, *c.* 13th CE

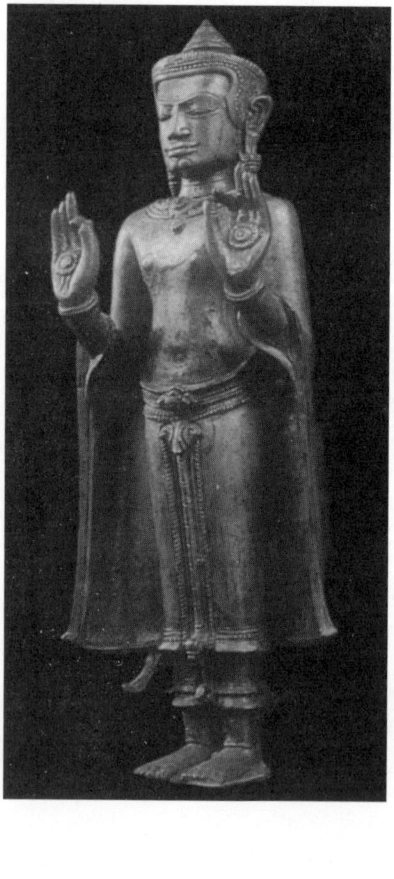

Rāmāyaṇa (रामायण), Ayodhyā. Here they ruled for around four centuries with great prosperity in material wealth and cultural output. But in 1757, Myanmar gave a crushing defeat to the Thais and sacked the township of Ayuthiā due to which the capital was shifted to the present site of Bangkok.

It was, however, the eleventh century which witnessed the typical Thai or Siamese art. The human faces in this art are found "characterized by the curved elevated eyebrows, doubly curved upward sloping eyelids, aquiline nose and sharply moulded lips." Buddha heads from Pitsanulok and Lopburi are clearly marked by these features. The fourteenth-century engravings of the Jātaka stories found at Wat Si Jun are also certainly high in quality but these are not sculptures in relief, only linear outlines. In fact, these figures have a Sri Lankan influence, maybe it came with the Buddhist Sri Lankan high priest Saṁgharāja who was invited by the king and given a mango-grove to conceive and supervise the building of some *stūpa* (स्तूप) complexes in the west of Sukhothai.

The art of Thailand has, of course, produced in the late fourteenth century some of the most serene-looking and majestically standing images of Buddha and Viṣṇu in stone as well as bronze, at Kampen Phet, for example. Each one of them is imposing and graceful, sporting very few ornaments but endowed with countenance of self-assured power, ready to bless the devotees in poise. The roots of this style, of course, go deep into the Gupta and Coḷa traditions.

The first Sukhothai style architecture is Wat Mahathat. "Wāṭa" or "Vāṭa" is a complex of structures like Nālandā and Odantapurī which were *mahāvihāras* (महाविहार) containing not only the *stūpas* and monastery but also library, teaching blocks, residential quarters, etc. In this the lotus bud, the most sacred symbol, was employed as the finial on the spire of the *stūpa* which was imposingly tall and slender in two distinct forms — one is like a tower and the other is like a dome releasing a long needle meant to pierce the sky. There are also bell-shaped domes of the *stūpa*s. These are called *cedi*: These are topped with spires. Prang is also a tall monument, often with 33 rings, arranged in tapering form, finally crowned by a piercing finial. These differences in the forms of the *stūpa* or *cedi* are stylistic and not fundamental.

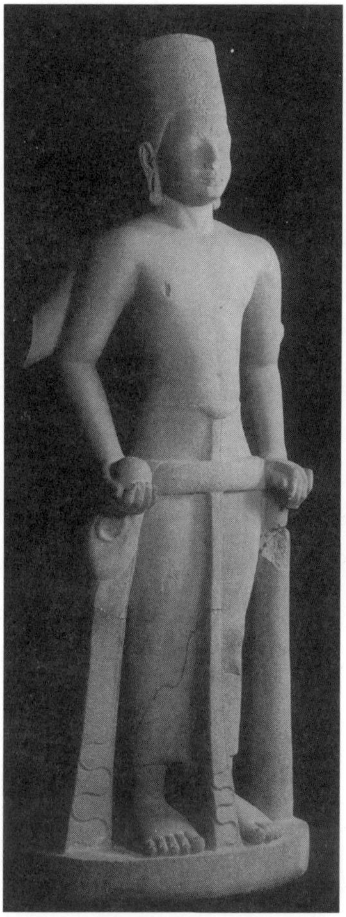

Dong Si Mahaphot: Stone Viṣṇu

Thai art is best represented in the Sukhothai bronzes, particularly in the images of the Buddha, fashioned after the Sārnāth style with plain body-clinging drapery or else Mathurā style, with drapery showing pleats. The Sārnāth types are extremely lyrical marked by flowing lines which create not only the transparent garments but also the body parts peeping through it. The *mudrā*s (मुद्रा) or hand-gestures are depicted so softly that the *karuṇā* (करुणा) or compassion of Buddha becomes apparent. The Gupta-style eyes set in yogic manner, the upper eyelid covering the eye three-fourth, leaving only the lower portion open to concentrate on the tip of the nose. The "Walking Buddha" bronze in *vitarka-mudrā* (वितर्क-मुद्रा), with flame on the *uṣṇīṣa* (उष्णीष), like the Indian Nāgapaṭṭinam bronzes, is the finest example of the fourteenth-century Sukhothai style of art. Although called "walking," it is as if floating in the air with one hand dangling at ease along the side, and the other hand raised in *abhaya-mudrā* (अभय-मुद्रा). At a later period, these Buddha bronzes are shown wearing a crown, somewhat in the Pāla style. On the walls of the buildings of the Wat we get even beautiful stucco images of the Buddha, standing and sitting both. Their facial features, like

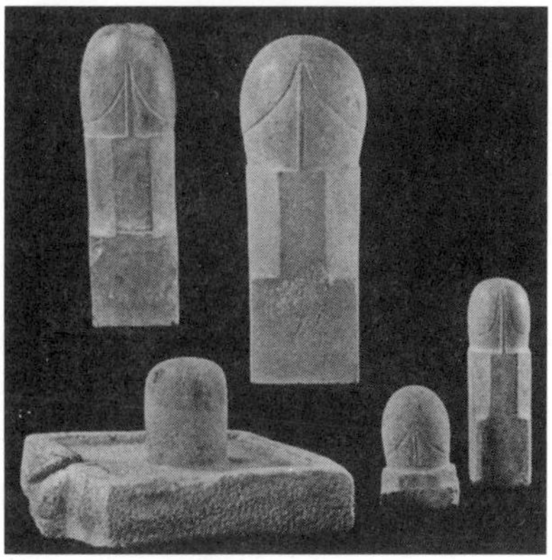

Stone *liṅga*s from various sites from the region of Nakhon Si Thammarat

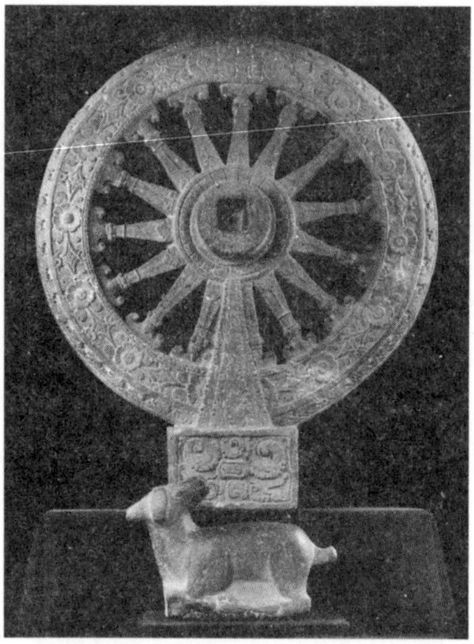

Nakhon Pathom: Stone *Dhammacakra*
c. 7th - 8th CE

those of the bronzes, are so soft and gracile that they border on being effeminate.

In some examples, the lines of the eyes, eyebrows, eyelids, nose and lips are flowing but sharp, as if betraying some formula, since contrasting to this are the full rounded faces, almost bulging and somewhat awkward.

Thai art and architecture is a highly vibrant living tradition although emphasis is shifting more and more towards ornate roofings.

Cambodia

Cambodia is the modern name of ancient Kāmboj, also called "Kampuchea." Its people are known as Khmers, even Mon-Khmers; Mons, the first part, being the name of the supposed-to-be original inhabitants of the northern parts of the country. Our knowledge about Kāmboj, which was immensely larger than the present-day Cambodia, embodying parts of south and south-eastern parts of Thailand, Laos and Vietnam, collectively, called in Chinese as "Funan," comes from hundred of inscriptions found in temple and monastic complexes as well as Chinese literary sources.

Map of Cambodia

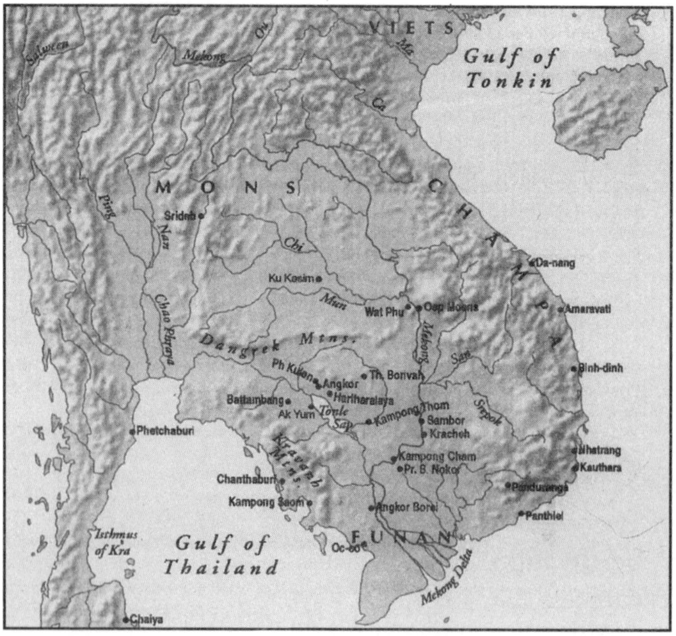

Funan proper, the land along the delta of the Mekong River or "Mai-Gaṅgā," we are told in the traditional accounts, including inscriptional, became Hinduized, as early as the first century CE. The credit for this goes to one named Kauṇḍinya, a young handsome brāhmaṇa boy from India, who

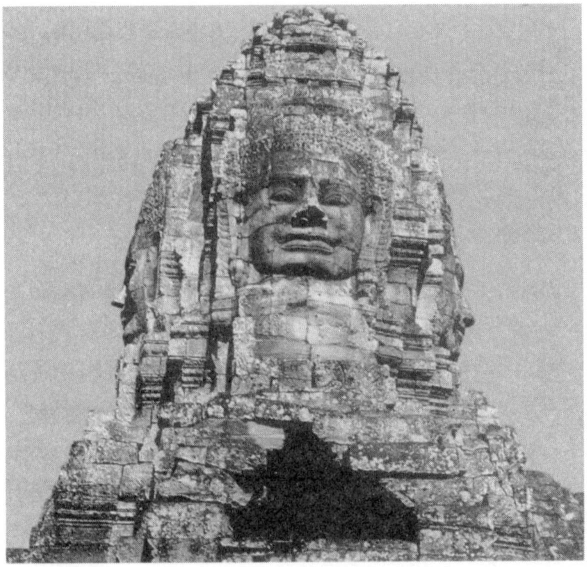

Angkor Thom: Colossal face of Lokeśvara

landed here from a merchant boat. Legend tells us that for him the local princess, named "Somā," also Nāginī, developed a liking and married. Now onwards started a Hindu dynasty of rulers. Not much is, however, known about the history of Cambodia-Funan till we reach the Gupta period, in CE 400, when we hear of one Śrutavarman, probably of the Indian descent of the Pallavas of Andhra Pradesh, ruling over this land and patronizing Hinduism. For about four hundred years, i.e. till the end of the seventh century, even eighth, we hear of, in inscription after inscription composed in Sanskrit language and written in Pallava script, the knowledge contained in the Vedas, the *Rāmāyaṇa* (रामायण), the *Mahābhārata* (महाभारत) and the Purāṇas. However, along with Hinduism, Buddhism also grew in the fifth century and developed slowly and gradually through the following centuries. At Vyādhapur, the old capital of Funan, there are the remains of a sixth-seventh-century fortified complex of several temples of bricks and of stones, including laterite. At Hanchai, near Sambour, there is a single-cella sandstone slab temple with the lintel of the

Angkor Wat

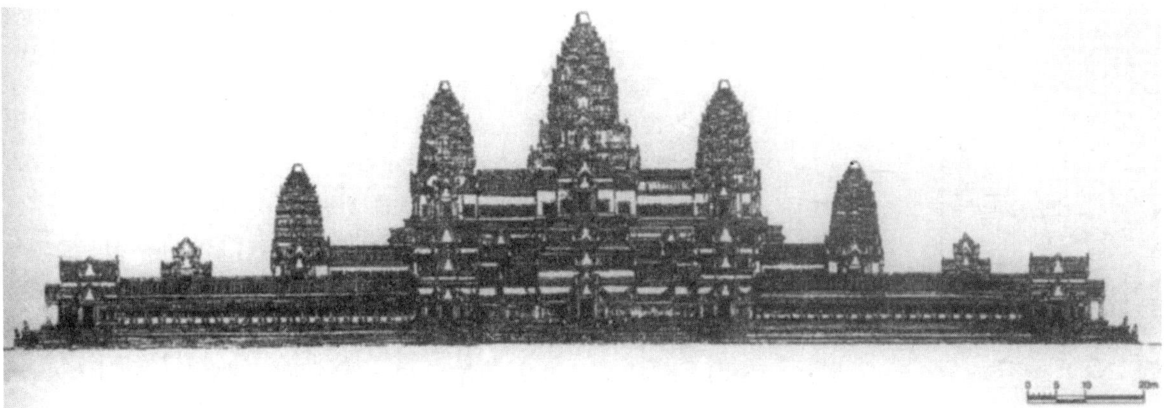

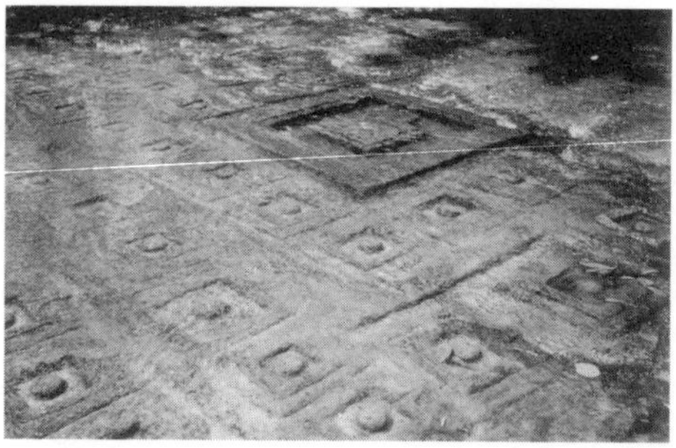

Under water 'Thousand *Liṅgas*' in the sacred Ruisey Stream

porch bearing a very beautiful sculpture of Viṣṇu lying on Śeṣanāga. In the same complex are two other shrines, of the seventh century, with pyramidal tower-like *śikhara*s (शिखर) built of bricks and containing the sculptures of *makara*s and *haṁsa*s (हंस) in the *caitya* (चैत्य)-windows. Similar, perhaps much more elegant, are the brick-tower sandstone shrines, more than fifty of them, decorated with niches adorned by images, as the earlier ones, at the site of Prei Kuk, Kompon Thom. They also betray Gupta traditions in art. Of the same Gupta style is the temple of Āśram Mahā Rosei in granite rock, probably dedicated to Harihara. One similar brick temple of this date, along with an *in situ* carved monolithic elephant, is located on Mt. Kulen. To the fifth-sixth centuries belong some of the Sārnāth-style Buddha images with transparent upper garment, and also Buddha heads, such as those at Romlok and Ta Keo. In fact, it is from the sixth century that we start getting local inscriptions. To the early seventh century belong Hindu images, like that of Harihara from Prasāt Andet, Kompon Thom. There are several other examples of Buddha heads, Hindu deities and male and female figures in some foreign museums, like Mussè Guimet, Paris, and private collections in Europe and America, which show that during this period of Cambodian Art (CE 100-700) Indian style of Sārnāth Buddha and Pallava style of Kailāsanātha temple of Kāñcīpuram played the major role. It appears that there was not only the exchange of scholars, stone-cutters and actual works of art between the two regions but also the opening of regular workshops of masons, artists and sculptors in the deltaic region of the mighty River Mekong in Funan.

Bantây Srei: Phimean-âkas or "Aerial Palace"

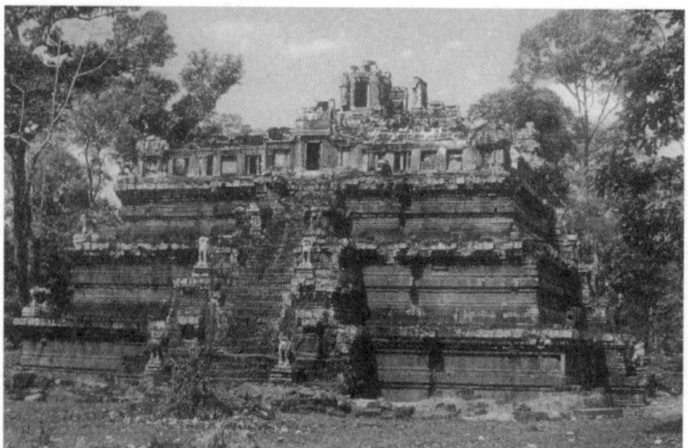

The period of late seventh and the whole eighth century was less productive, maybe due to the severe political unrest in the country witnessing uprisings of local rulers against kings like Bhavavarman, Mahendravarman and Īśānavarman I, who is also known to have initiated the early Angkorean style of architecture, of the ninth century, by getting erected a temple at Sambor Prei Kuk with distinctive features. Chinese then gave a new name to Funan — "Chenla."

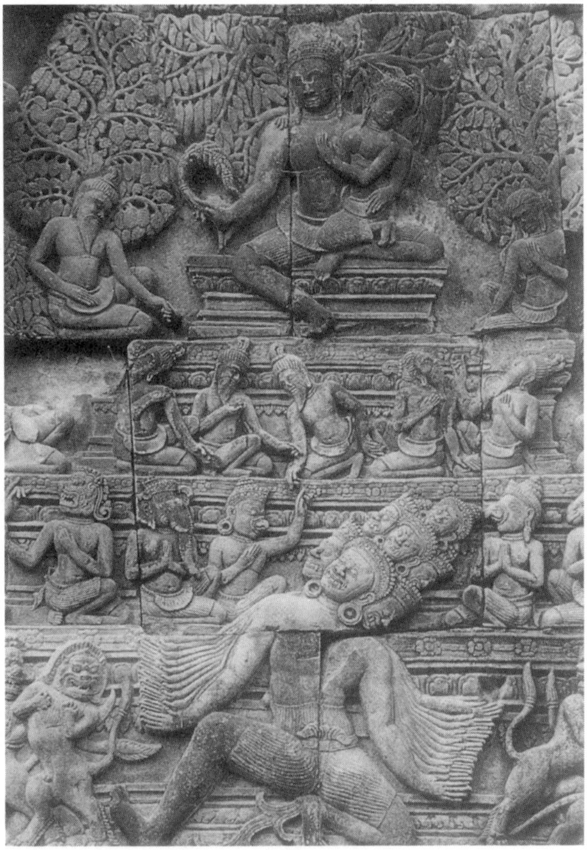

Bantây Srei: A *toraṇa* depicting Śiva-Pārvatī on mount Kailāsa and Rāvaṇa below

The next phase of Cambodian art and architecture is called "Khmer," even Angkorean because Angkor Wat became the main centre of art activities under a long succession of powerful rulers, starting from Jayavarman II who ascended the throne in CE 790. His dynasty, in one form or the other, continued to rule up to the end of CE 1300. The period from the ninth through the thirteenth century, is considered to be the "Golden Period" as well as "Classical Period," because neither before nor after this period Cambodia witnessed better structural and artistic activities.

Preah Pithu, Angkor: Aparṇā (Pārvatī)

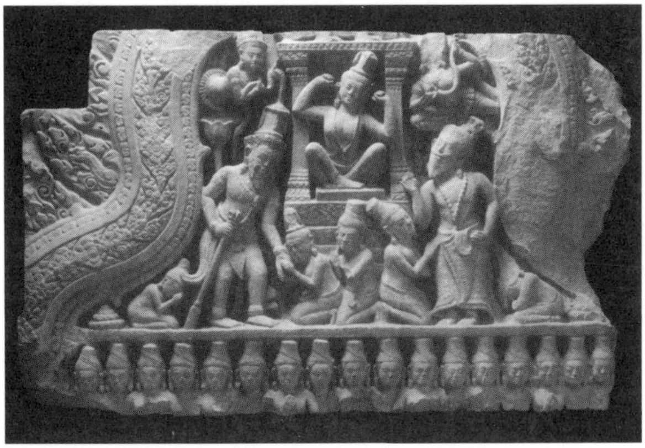

The Khmer style of art and architecture did not favour the Pre-Khmer "Pallava motifs of the *makara toraṇa* (मकर तोरण) lintel, the *caitya*-window, the use of *haṁsa*s with extended wings as abacus supports, its round and square columns are un-Indian, and new and quite un-Indian elements such as the towers with human faces, Garuḍa caryatides and Nāga balustrades are introduced," rightly observes Coomaraswamy. He also observes that, "In sculpture, too, a national formula is evolved, this type is characterized by the

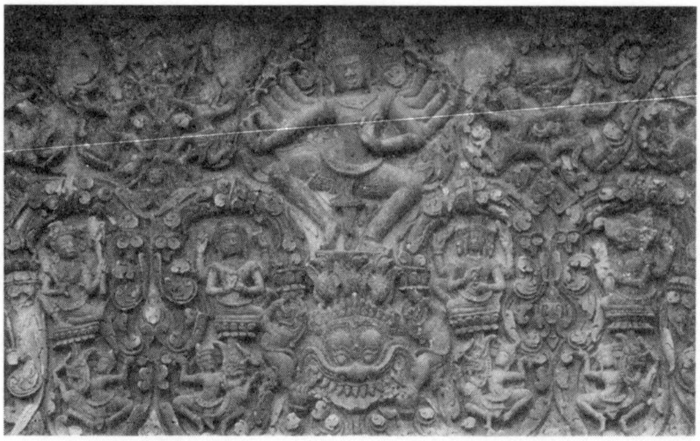

Sikhoraphum: Ten-armed dancing Śiva

straight line of the hair, the level brows, the scarcely sloping eyes, full and wide lips and impassable serenity, often, especially in the case of the beautiful faces of the *apsaras*, by an exotic smile and peculiar sweetness."

While all this is true, as far as the art style of the Khmer period is concerned, it must be noted that the contents of the art, the themes, their religious background, their belief systems, their underlying mythology, etc. were provided by Hinduism and Buddhism (generally, Mahāyānist) except for the cult of deified kingship, which was of local development in conceptualization of ancestors in the form of their chosen gods, and the cult of "Devarāja," or king-god, always represented by a *liṅgam* (लिंगम्), the centre of divine powers founded by Jayavarman II at Mahendra Parvata and served by the brāhmaṇa priest Śivakaivalya, the king's chaplain, and his descendants for several generations. The Angkor Wat temples of the typical Khmer style were built in stone and surrounded by long fortification walls, generally made of blocks of laterite stone. To begin with, their constructional peculiarities show that some features were the copies of the wooden architecture, for example, the vaulted and half-vaulted roofs, stone tiles used in sloping roofs, long galleries having walls decorated with low-relief sculptural panels and friezes depicting scenes from Hindu epics. Because of the use of huge moats and lakes round the temples and causeways erected on them for people to cross over, the causeways had to have long railings on both the sides, the coping of which was given the form of serpents or *nāgas*, with open hoods, of course in highly stylized forms. As in the *samudra-manthana* (समुद्र-मन्थन) scenes, these are

Ayuthiyā: A 14th-century temple

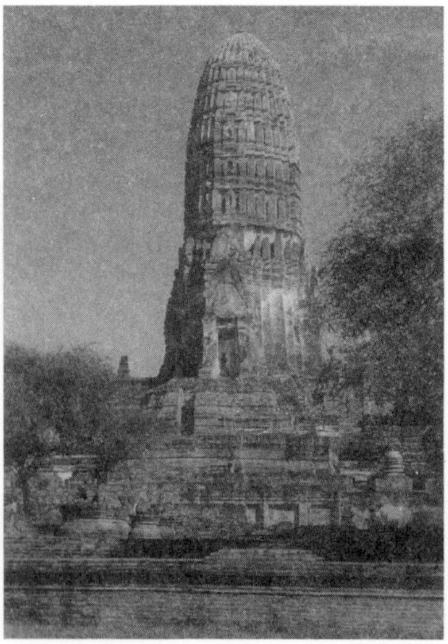

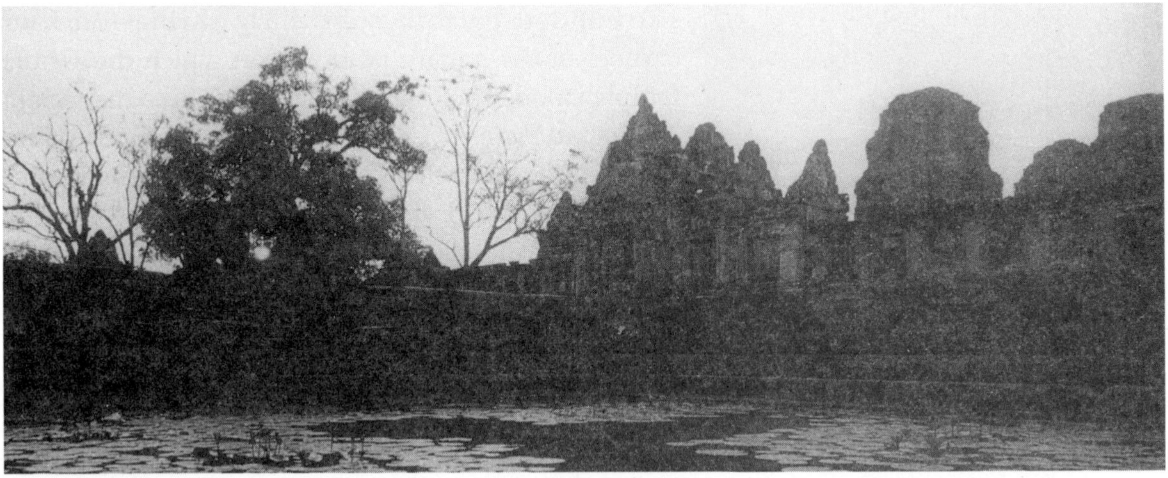

Muang Tam: A general view of temple complex and moat

often shown supported by *devas* (देव) and *asuras* (असुर). There are also staircases from the four cardinal directions, and *bhāravāhakas* (भारवाहक) or caryatides, in the form of Garuḍa or eagle, the vehicle of Viṣṇu. The gates were crowned by towers carrying human masks, possibly representing Lokeśvara.

Bantây Samre: A carving depicting Skanda on his peacock

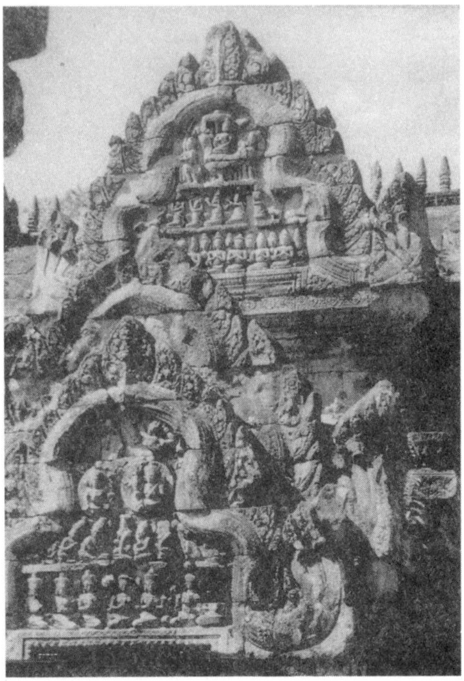

Cambodia is known world over for the most magnificent city with a temple, called Angkor Wat. It was built by emperor Sūryavarman II between CE 1113 and 1150, i.e. in the first half of the twelfth century. The building-complex covers around 200 ha of area. It is surrounded by a huge fortified moat, generally found filled with water even now. It has four gateways, called *gopuras* (गोपुर), following the terminology of south Indian temples of late Coḷa and Nāyaka periods (eleventh-sixteenth centuries). Within this unusually large campus stands in the centre the temple built over a huge solid terrace measuring 332 × 258 m, i.e. covering 9 ha of land. By its side once stood the palace of the king, possibly made of wooden architecture. The temple, built in stone, is in typical Khmer style of pyramids or towers and galleries. These were pre-planned on the *pañcāyatana* (पञ्चायतन) principle: one central shrine,

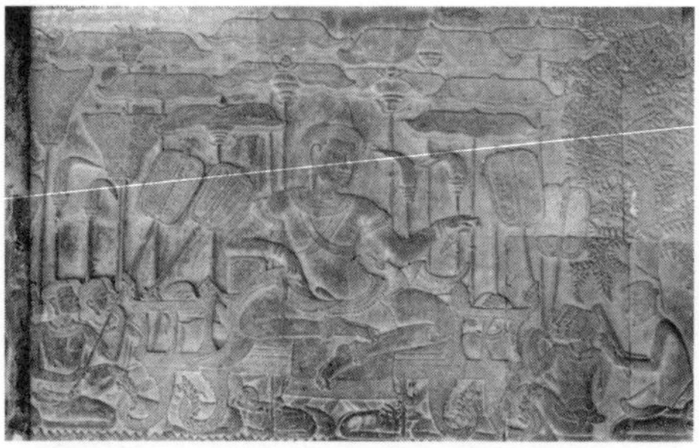

Angkor Vat: Scene from a carved stone panel

surrounded by four subsidiary shrines on four corners of the square platform on which the whole temple stood. The tower in the centre, like the *śikhara* on the *garbha-gṛha*, was constructed at three rising levels, each one enclosed by a gallery. The four corner towers surround the central shrine. The temple symbolizes the cosmos — moat with water stands for ocean surrounding the earth. The galleries represent mountain ranges surrounding Mount Meru, the home of the gods, located at the navel or centre of the earth; Meru is the central tower.

Angkor Wat is known for the low relief sculptures running in unending long friezes in the galleries depicting scenes from the *Mahābhārata*, for example, the war of Kurukṣetra. Some episodes from the *Rāmāyaṇa* have also been included, such as the death of monkey king Vāli. The emperor Sūryavarman sitting on his throne is also represented.

The Angkor Wat complex of temples includes many huge structures, such as Angkor Thom, Bayon, Ta Keo, Ta Prohm. One of the most beautifully carved temples of smaller size is Banteay Srei. While Bayon temple is famous for the huge mask-images of Lokeśvara, located on the tops of the towers, the Banteay Srei is known for its minute carvings depicting scenes from the life of Kṛṣṇa. All the Khmer temples are, however, decorated with the beautiful images of the *apsaras* or celestial nymphs.

Bayon: A general view

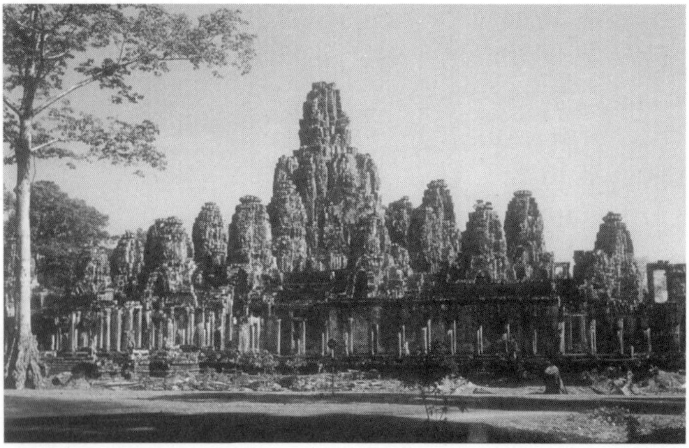

Cambodia has many more temples built in stone as well as in bricks but nothing like those at Angkor Wat.

Indonesia

Indonesia has several large and small islands some of which witnessed the world's greatest monuments, Hindu as well as Buddhist. Its history begins from the western island of Sumātrā which records the rule of the kingdom of Śrīvijaya with the capital city located at Palembang, the most important trading port of South-East Asia in use till CE 700. Archaeological evidence shows that there were coastal sites where Indians may have come and settled much earlier, from the third–second century BCE to the early centuries of the Common Era. Since it was an extremely rich country, even in natural wealth, it was called Suvarṇabhūmi or the "land of gold" as well as "Yavadvīpa" in the Jātakas as well as the *Rāmāyaṇa*. One Guṇavarman from Kashmir is credited with introducing Mahāyāna Buddhism in this land during the fifth century. It kept on flourishing till the end of the eighth century.

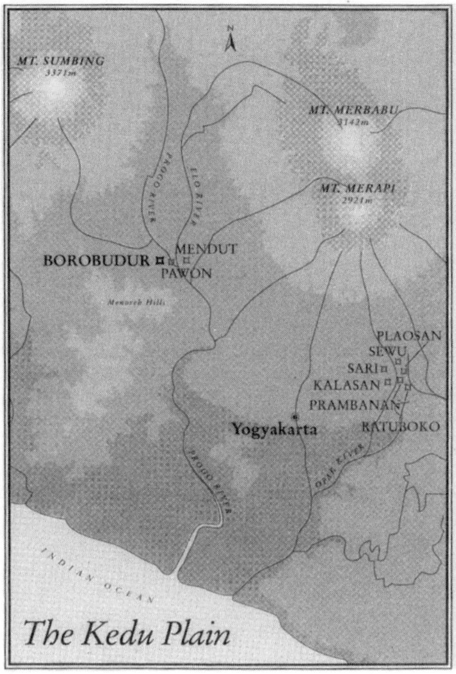

Map of The Kedu Plain in Jāvā

Borobudur Temple

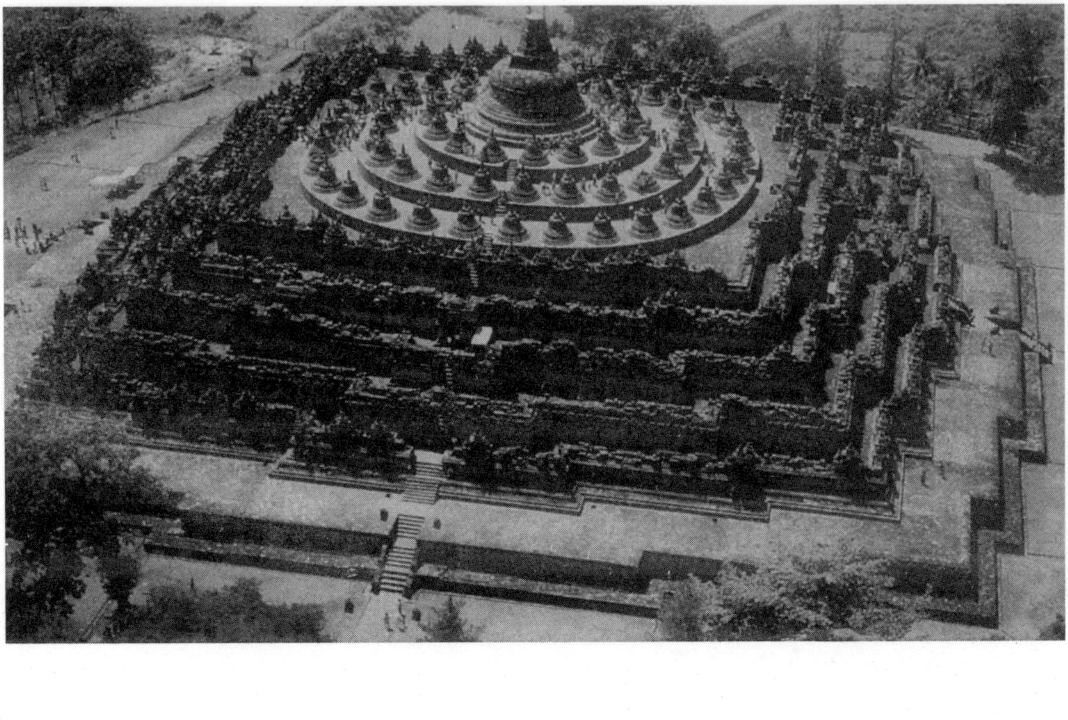

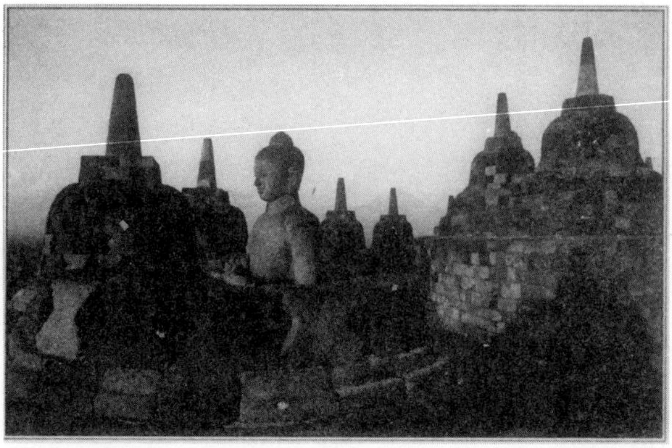

Borobudur: Buddha in *dharmacakra-pravartana-mudrā*

Java, in fact, western Java, remained Hindu till about the sixth century. Central Java, on the other hand, kept the Hindu character up to the sixth century; there is no evidence of Hīnayāna Buddhism in Java till that date. However, soon Tāntric Mahāyānism enters into this region. What is of greatest significance is something else. Here "Buddhism and Śaiva Hinduism are inseparably combined" as may be seen in terms like Śivabuddha.

The Dieng plateau of central Java island has, on the other hand, the remains of a temple-city with Hindu shrines of simple square *garbha-gṛha* or cella, approached from a porch built in front of it; the three outer walls of the cella are divided by pilasters or half-pillars into three parts decorated with projecting niches or else with panels containing sculptures of religious themes; the roof was *śikhara* type, i.e. pyramidal. The entrance as well as top of the niches bore *kīrttimukha* (कीर्त्तिमुख), while floriated *makara* decorations are seen elsewhere on the front tops. Brahmā, Viṣṇu and Śiva images, slender and light in visual weight, are found sculptured in these temples, called "Caṇḍī" locally. In this style were built and decorated four temples of the so-called "Arjuna Group."

Middle Java witnessed the rule of the Śailendra dynasty (CE 732–860), with the succession of some of the great rulers. It is in the year CE 778 that we get for the first time a Buddhist shrine called "Caṇḍī Kalasan," located west of the famous site of the Prambanan, which was dedicated to the Mahāyānist goddess Tārā; till then it was all Hindu. The art and architecture of this temple is in the Dieng style but conceived in larger dimensions, including the figures of *kīrttimukhas* and *makaras* of

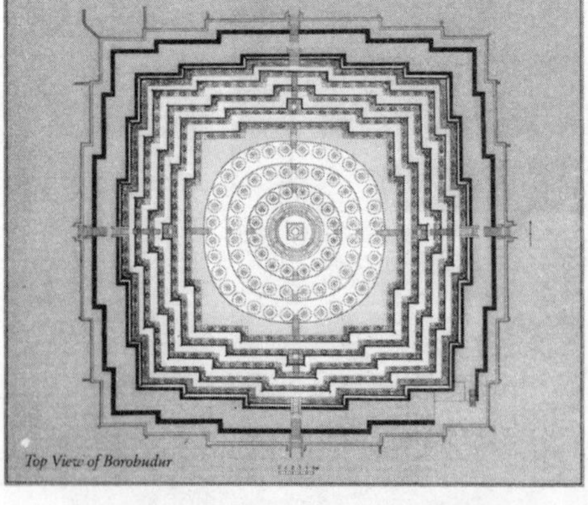

Borobudur Temple Plan

the *toraṇas* (तोरण), i.e. gateways. Towards further east of this place is located the Caṇḍī Sewu complex of temples of the ninth century marked by developed Kalasan design "with side chapels open to the exterior and lavishly decorated with arches and niches, originally containing images of Buddhist deities."

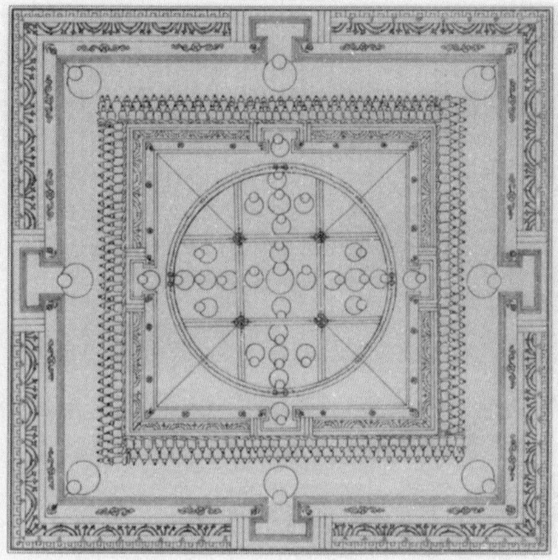

A Vajradhātu Maṇḍala, on which the Borobadur Temple plan was based

As Cambodia is known in the history of world art for the Angkor Wat temples and their art and architecture, Indonesia is known in the same way for Borobudur *stūpa*-complex, or Caṇḍī, belonging to late eighth and early ninth century (CE 760-847). In art history, Borobudur is studied along with two other contemporary and related Buddhist monuments of great significance in art and architecture, those of Caṇḍī Mendut and Caṇḍī Pawon located in the same Kedu region. The former, with a central temple, has open vestibule or *antarāla* exhibiting beautiful large relief-sculptures of Buddhist goddesses like Hārīti and Pañcikā. Three other side-walls of the *garbha-gṛha* contain equally beautiful images of *bodhisattvas* as well as Tārā carved in relief. However, the most elegant are the two images of the *bodhisattvas* and one large image of Buddha with a halo at the back, sitting on a throne with legs down, like the famous one at Sārnāth.

Line Drawing of Frontal view of Borobudur Temple

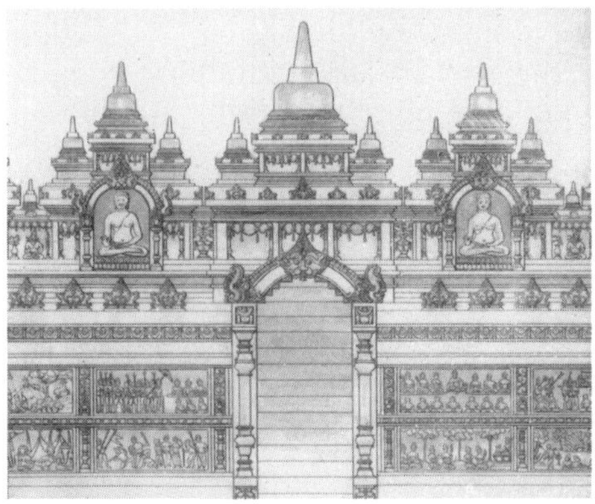

Located in the background of a living volcano, of course at a far distant place, but visible from here, the huge and imposing Borobudur *stūpa*-complex of the Kedu plains is partly rock-cut and largely built. This, unlike any other monument of its period, was created by cutting and terracing step by step a round hill. It is like a truncated pyramid rising high amidst the green paddy fields. It has a *stūpa*, not too large, at the top, which is surrounded by 72 smaller but perforated *stūpas* with finials arranged in three concentric circles at different heights of the rock-cut terraces. These are reached by staircases

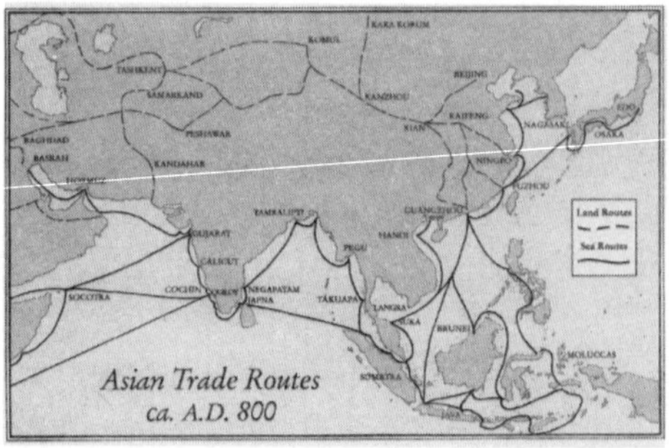

Asian Trade Routes around CE 800

created in the middle of each side of the pyramidal structure. The ground plan of the Borobudur is also unique — the six lower terraces are square while the three upper ones are round. From the art historian's point of view the most important part of the monument are the galleries of the lower terraces since it is in them that we get long series of sculptures in relief, covering almost 5 km in length, illustrating the life of the Buddha as described in the *Lalitavistara* (ललितविस्तर) as well as the narratives contained in *Divyāvadāna* (दिव्यावदान), in *Jātakamālā* (जातकमाला) of Ura, in *Gaṇḍavyūha* (गण्डव्यूह) and other literary and traditional accounts. It can only be compared with the *Mahābhārata* friezes of Angkor Wat, although the latter, because of the war scenes, are extremely animated exhibiting great force and tension in body parts of men and animals which is generally absent in the Buddhist themes of Borobudur. Borobudur certainly reflects the cultural ethos of the eighth-century rulers of the Śailendra dynasty whose empire covered not only Java but also Sumātrā, although the roots of the pyramidal plan of temples may go back to some earlier and some contemporary sacred structures in India, for example, at Pratihāspur in Kashmir which has an eighth-century shrine of the pyramidal type. There are also two Gupta brick temples of somewhat this type at Ahicchatra. As far as the metal images from the central Java monuments are concerned, there are many of them, some in copper and gold also. However, they appear to have on them the stamp of Bihar bronzes in characteristic features.

Stone relief depicting *Sibi Jātaka*

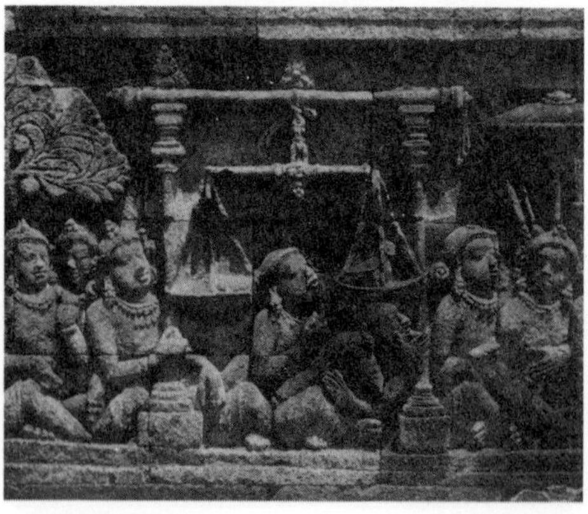

The period that follows the Śailendras in Java is called the "Period of Restoration" (CE 860–915). During this period, Hinduism again received the royal patronage. Comparable to Buddhist Borobudur, we have now the huge temples of Loro Jongrang, in Prambanan. This complex consists of eight temples built on a "walled terrace surrounded by smaller chapels and two outer walls." The three largest of these temples are devoted to Brahmā, Viṣṇu and Śiva, the last one being the central one and also the largest one. The Śiva temple was conceived in the form of Borobudur, which is a truncated pyramid, square in plan with stairways located in the middle of each of the three sides. The upper terrace contains a large image of standing Śiva. However, the art contained in the terrace below is known the world over for its "continuous series of reliefs illustrating the earlier part of the *Rāmāyaṇa* story." The figures are fully animated, capturing the dramatic moments of the stories they narrate. These are usually considered superior in quality to the Borobudur reliefs. The Viṣṇu temple has, as expected, the stories connected with the life of Kṛṣṇa. It is surmised that the Brahmā temple, now in ruins, may have carried the *Rāmāyaṇa*-related themes in sculpture, extending the works of art seen in the Śiva temple. The Prambanan temples, some of which got destroyed in the recent tsunami disaster, were soon deserted, maybe due to natural causes, but the style of its monuments and art continued to be in use in the tenth and eleventh centuries, not in mid-Java but in eastern Java where there are the remains of the Caṇḍīs of Sumber Nanas and Sangariti as well as Belahan gateways. King Erlaṅga (CE 1010-42) was responsible for some sculptural creations of great significance such as the one of Viṣṇu riding Garuḍa; Viṣṇu was here no other than the king himself. However, not many examples of his works of art have survived. There is then a gap. But the period from twelfth to fifteenth century saw in eastern Java some of the most beautiful examples of Javanese art and architecture. In Siṅgasārī there is an impressive Śiva temple, called Caṇḍī Kidal built with heavy pyramidal roof. Then there is also a Buddhist temple,

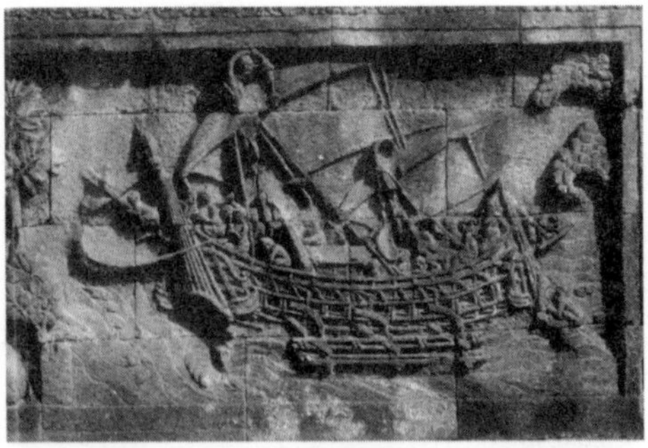

Borobudur: A stone relief depicting a ship

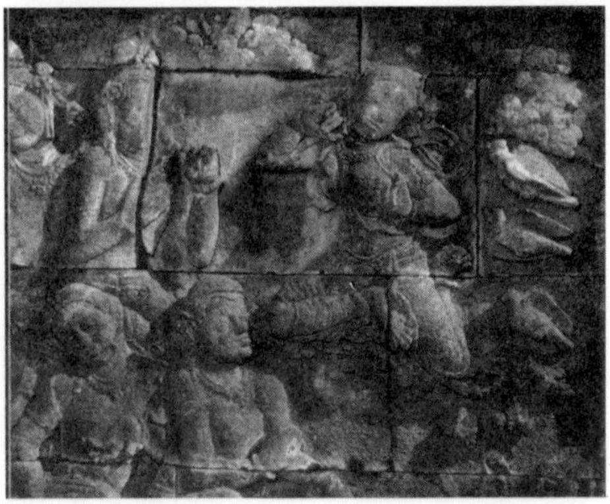

A stone relief depicting a *Jātaka* story

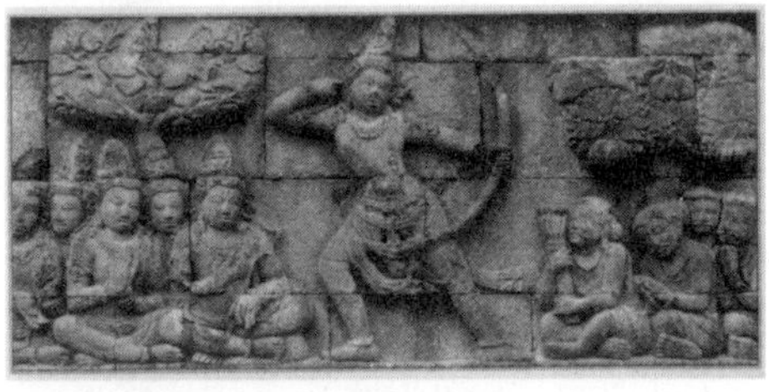

Borobudur: A stone relief depicting noblemen and an archer

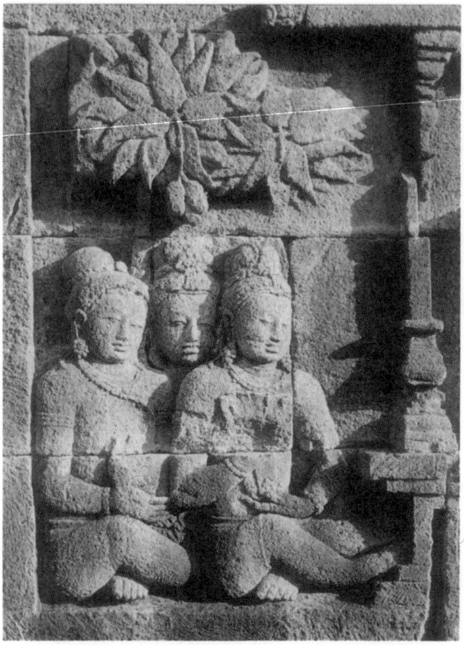

A Stone relief

called Caṇḍī Jāgo, decorated with *wayang*-like shadow images in relief narrating, strangely as if, the stories from the life of Kṛṣṇa. In Caṇḍī Jawi, on the other hand, we see in the art representations Śaiva-Buddhist syncretism where in the *garbha-gṛha* there is the Śiva image with the image of Buddha above it. The circular temple of Caṇḍī Jabung with rich works of art, is, however, considered the best of its times in eastern Java, although Majapahit also had many temples and Panataran has given us many sculptural scenes from the *Rāmāyaṇa*.

Bali, an Indonesian island, still preserves the Vedic–Hindu system of worship, rituals and festivals in temples and shrines containing images of Hindu gods and goddesses. However, here also we have many examples of Hindu-Buddhist mixed traditions as seen in many parts of South-East Asia. Amongst the very few early temples in Bali is the royal burial-complex temple of eleventh-twelfth centuries at Tampak Siring. The fourteenth-century Pura ye Gaṅgā temple art and architecture is like that of Panataran of Java. So is true of the temples of the same date found at Pejeng. There are several individual later-day temples, generally small in size, as at Bargli and Batur, important mainly for carrying on old traditions more for the devotees than for the connoisseurs of art.

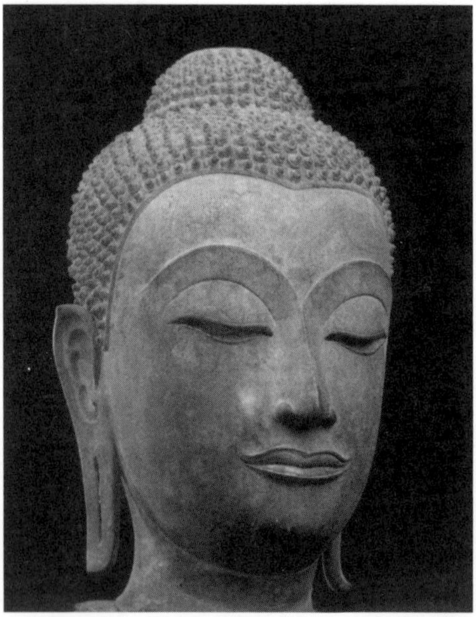

Apart from the art traditions of the SE Asian countries discussed above, some other countries in this region — like Laos or Lava, Vietnam or Champa, Malayasia or Malaya and Borneo — also show the influence of Indian art and architecture in their cultural heritage. This was due to the shared history of SE Asian countries in particular and maritime contacts among the Indian Ocean Rim countries in general.

Select Bibliography

EPICS AND PURĀṆAS (महाकाव्य एवं पुराण)

1. *Mahābhārata* (महाभारत, महाकाव्य)
2. *Rāmāyaṇa* (रामायण, महाकाव्य)
3. *Viṣṇudharmottara Purāṇa* (विष्णुधर्मोत्तर पुराण)
4. Important Purāṇas such as the *Matsya* and *Śiva* (मत्स्य पुराण, शिव पुराण, आदि)

ŚILPAŚĀSTRAS AND OTHER SIMILAR TEXTS (शिल्प शास्त्र, आदि)

1. *Aparājitapṛcchā* (अपराजितपृच्छा)
2. *Citralakṣaṇam* (चित्रलक्षणम्)
3. *Mānasāra* (मानसार)
4. *Mānasollāsa* (मानसोल्लास)
5. *Nāṭyaśāstra* (नाट्यशास्त्र)
6. *Pratimālakṣaṇam* (प्रतिमालक्षणम्)
7. *Rūpamaṇḍana* (रूपमण्डन)
8. *Sādhanamālā* (साधनमाला)
9. *Samarāṅgaṇa Sūtradhāra* (समरांगण सूत्रधार)
10. *Śilparatna* (शिल्परत्न)
11. *Viśvakarmāvatāraśāstra* (विश्वकर्मावतारशास्त्र)

ASTRONOMICAL, GRAMMATICAL, ETC. WORKS

1. *Bṛhat-saṁhitā* (बृहत्संहिता)
2. *Aṣṭādhyāyī* (अष्टाध्यायी)
3. *Śukranītisāra* (शुक्रनीतिसार)
4. *Raghuvaṁśaṁ* (रघुवंशम्)
5. *Kumārasambhavam* (कुमारसम्भवम्)

MODERN WRITINGS

Agrawal, V.S., 1965, *Indian Art*, Varanasi.

Asthana, Shashi Prabha, 2000, *Mathurā Kalā*, New Delhi.

Bachhofer, Ludwig, 1929, *Early Indian Sculpture*, Paris.

Banerjea, J.N., 1941, *Development of Hindu Iconography*, Calcutta.

Beek, S.V. and L.I. Tettoni, 1999, *The Arts of Thailand*, Hongkong: Periplus Press.

Briggs, L.P., 1999, *The Ancient Khmer Empire*, Bangkok: White Lotus Press.

Brown, Percy, 1942, *Indian Architecture*, Bombay.

Chakravarty, K.K. and R.G. Bednarik, 2004, *Indian Rock Art and its Global Context*, Delhi: Motilal Banarsidass.

Chandra, Lokesh, S.P. Gupta, et al. (eds.), *India's Contribution to World Thought and Culture*, Kanyakumari: Vivekanand Rock Memorial.

Chandra, Pramod (ed.), 1975, *Studies in Indian Temple Architecture*, New Delhi. *On the Study of Indian Art*, 1983, New York, Asia Society.

Coomaraswamy, A.K., 1965, *History of Indian and Indonesian Art*, New York: Dover Publications.

Craven, Ray C., 1976, *A Concise History of Indian Art*, New York.

Ferguson, Geroge, 1961, *Signs and Symbols in Christian Art*, New York.

Ghosh, A. (ed.), 1974, *Jaina Art and Architecture*, New Delhi.

Gupta, S.P. (ed.), 2003, *Masterpieces of the National Museum Collection*, New Delhi: National Museum.

Gupta, S.P., 1996, *The Indus-Saraswati Civilization*, New Delhi: Pratibha Prakashan.

Gupta, S.P., 1982, *The Roots of Indian Art*, New Delhi. Also *The Kuṣāṇa Art of Sanghol* (ed.) 1985, New Delhi. *The Catalogue of the National Museum Collection* (ed.), New Delhi.

Havell, E.B., 1928, *Indian Sculpture and Painting* (2nd edn.), London.

Jarriage, C., J.F. Jarrige, R.H. Meadow, and G. Quivron, 1995, *Mehrgarh: Field Reports 1974-1985*, Karachi: Department of Culture & Tourism, Pakistan.

Kramrisch, Stella, 1946, *The Hindu Temple*, Calcutta.

Krishna Deva, 1996, *Temples of North India*, New Delhi: NBT.

Kvorn, N.J., 1927, *Barabudur : Archaeological Description*, The Hague: Martinus Nijhoff.

Lal, B.B., 2002, *The Saraswati Flows On*, New Delhi: Aryan Books International.

Miksic, John, 1990, *Borobudur — Golden Tales of the Buddhas*, London: Bamboo Publishers Ltd.

Mitra, Debala 1980, *Buddhist Monuments, Calcutta. Bhubaneswar*, 1966, New Delhi: Archaeological Survey of India.

Mitter, Partha, 1977, *Much Maligned Monsters* (History of European Reactions to Indian Art), Oxford. *Indian Art*, Oxford, 2001.

Purākalā, Annual Journal of the Rock Art Society of India, Nos. 14-15. 2005.

Ray, Nihar Ranjan, 1975, *Maurya and Post Maurya Art*, New Delhi.

Rowland, Benjamin, 1970, *Art and Architecture of India*, Pelican Books.

Saraswati, S.K., 1970, *Survey of Indian Sculpture*, New Delhi.

Sharma, R.C., 1995, *Buddhist Art* (Mathura School), New Delhi.

Singh, Harihar, 1982, *Jaina Temples of Western India*, Varanasi.

Sivaramamurti, C., 1974, *The Art of India*, Paris. Also *Indian Painting*, 1970, New Delhi: NBT.

Snellgrove, David, 2004, *Angkor — Before and After: A Cultural History of Khmers*, Bangkok: Orchid Press.

Srinivasan, K.R., *Temples of South India*, New Delhi: NBT.

Turner, Jane, (ed.) 1996, *The Dictionary of Art*, vol. 29, London: Grove.

Wakankar, V.S., 2005, *Painted Rock-Shelters of India*, Bhopal: Directorate of Archaeology and Museums, Madhya Pradesh Government.

Wakankar, V.S. and R.R.R. Brooks, 1976, *Stone Age Painting in India*, Mumbai: D.B. Taraporwala, Sons & Co.

Williams, Joanna G., 1982, *The Art of Gupta India*, New Jersey.

[There are many small and nominally priced guide-books but written by great authorities and published by the Archaeological Survey of India, New Delhi, which give detailed accounts of many important monuments and sites in India. National Book Trust, New Delhi has also produced many reasonably priced books on art, architecture, numismatics, etc.]

BOOKS IN HINDI

कृष्ण दत्त बाजपेयी, 1991, *भारतीय कला*, भोपाल, मध्य प्रदेशः हिन्दी ग्रंथ अकादमी।

कृष्ण देव, 1969, *उत्तर भारत के मंदिर*, दिल्ली: नेशनल बुक ट्रस्ट, वाराणसीः पृथ्वी प्रकाशन।

वासुदेव शरण अग्रवाल, 1966, *भारतीय कला*, वाराणसीः पृथ्वी प्रकाशन।

श्री नारायण चतुर्वेदी, *नागर शैली के नए हिन्दू मन्दिर*, दिल्ली: प्रभात प्रकाशन।

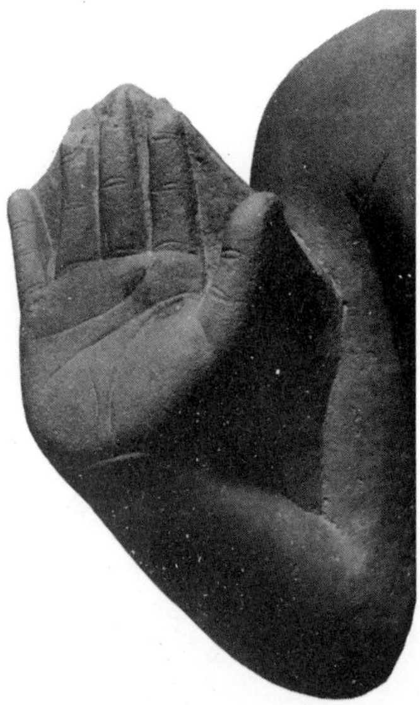

Abhaya of Buddha, Maṅkuwar, U.P., Gupta, 5th century AD

Index

Abhayagiri Dāgaba, 161
Ābhijñānaśākuntalam, 57
Abhilāṣitārthacintāmaṇi, 37
Abhinaya Darpaṇa, 108
Ādamgaṛh, 2
adhiṣṭhāna, 16-17, 19-20
Ādināth, 6
Āgamas, 1, 20, 37-38, 76, 85, 89, 100, 103
Āgamic, 94, 105
agate, 12, 162
Agathocles, 69
Agni, 29, 108
Ahicchatra, 77, 86, 180
Ai-Khanum, 69, 81
Aihoḷe, 90
Ajantā, 4, 6-7, 55-56
Ajantan, 162
ākāśa, 11
Akoṭā, 89
alabaster, 12
Alexander, 9
Altamira caves, 2
āmalak-sārikā, 18
*āmalaka*s, 17-18, 27
Amarāvatī, 9, 72-73, 79, 161
AMS method, 6
Ānanda, 164-66
Anawrata, 164
aṇḍa, 8-9, 160
Andhakāsura, 41
Angkor Thom, 176
Angkor Wat, 167, 173-76, 179-80
Annapūrṇā, 42
antarāla, 16, 162, 179
antarpatra, 19
Anurādhapura, 159, 160
anuratha-paga, 27
Aparājitapṛcchā, 37
apasmāra, 33
Apollo, 82
apsaras, 19
Apsidal Fire temple, 19
ardha-maṇḍapa, 16, 162
Ardhanārīśvara, 36
Arjuna Group, 178
arsenic, 12
Aśoka, 160
Āśram Mahā Rosei, 172
*aṣṭa-māṅgalika cihna*s, 50
Asuramardinī, 37
Atharvaveda, 44
Aurignacian Culture, 3
*avadāna*s, 49
avatāra, 4
*āyāgapaṭṭa*s, 78
āyaka, 9
*āyudha*s, 26, 33, 70
Ayuthiā, 167
Azilises, 70

Bachhofer, Ludwick, 2, 57
Bactria, 71, 74, 81, 82
Bāḍā, 25
Bādāmī, 90
Bāgh, 55, 162
Balarāma, 5, 69, 71
Bali, 182
Baṇāwalī, 11, 19
Banda, 2
Bandhana, 26
Banerjea, J.N., 104, 135-36
Bangkok, 168
Banteay, 176
Barābar, 67
Baraṇḍā, 26
Bargli, 182

Batur, 182
Bauddha, 2-3, 29, 44, 47, 105
Bayon, 176
beads, 16
Bekī, 26
Belahan, 181
Beḷur, 97
bhadras, 18, 23
Bhagavad Gītā, 57
Bhaja, 73
Bharhut, 72-73
Bhavavarman, 173
Bhīmbeṭkā, 2-3, 8, 53
Bhirrānā, 11
bhitti, 20, 23
bhoga deul, 24
Bhṛgu, 106
Bhūmi, 26, 42
bhūmi-āmalakas, 17-18, 26
bhūta, 22, 24
Bhūteśvara, 77-78
Biṣama, 26
bījapūraka, 18
bilingual inscriptions, 9
Billasurgam caves, 8
bimba, 61-62, 70-71
Bisht, R.S., 11
Bodha-Gayā, 5, 69, 72, 96, 165
bodhi-ghara, 9
bodhisattvas, 9, 48, 78, 81, 87, 165, 179
Borneo, 182
Borobudur, 179-81
Brahmā, 3, 28, 36, 42, 46, 90, 178, 181
brahmāṇḍa, 11
Brāhmī, 35
Bṛhat-Saṁhitā, 134-35
bronze, 12
bronze Age in India, 9
Buddha, 5-6, 28, 48-49, 51, 81-82, 87, 106, 165, 168, 179-80, 182
Buddhaghoṣa, 163
Buddha-*pāda*, 73
Buddha Śākyamuni, 160
Buddhism, 32, 55, 65-66, 75-76, 167, 171, 174, 178
Buddhist, 1, 45, 56-57, 72-73, 77, 96, 104
Buddhist religion, 160
Bulandībāgh, 68
Butkarā, 65
Buxar, 68

caitya, 9, 11
caityagṛha, 9, 10
cakras, 28, 32, 34, 43, 70
Cambodia, 165, 167, 170, 173, 175-76, 179
Caṇḍa, 41
Caṇḍī, 178-79, 81
  Jabung, 182
  Jāgo, 181
  Jawi, 182
  Kalasan, 178
  Kidal, 181
  Mendut, 179
  Pawon, 179
  Sewu, 179
candrikā, 18
Canhu-dāṛo, 13-14
Carlleyle, A., 2
carnelian, 12, 162
Caturvargacintāmaṇi, 37
Cave, 67
cedi, 169
Chadanta Jātaka, 55
chādya, 17-18
Chalcolithic, 5
Champa, 182
Chantaburi, 167
Charles Masson, 9
chatra, 9, 32
Chenla, 173
Chilas, 69
China, 31, 44, 79
Chinese Turkestan, 110
Chittor, 99
Christ, 29, 31
Christian, 10, 12, 58
Christianity, 4, 31
Chunār, 66
cihna, 28
cire-perdue, 16, 94
Citralakṣaṇa, 54
citrasūtra, 53
Clarke, J.D., 8
Cockburn, John, 2
Coḷa, 168, 175, 160-61
Coomaraswamy, A.K., 57-58, 82

corbelled arches, 20
costumes, 6
Crucifixion, 31
Cunningham, 11
cup-marks, 2, 6
cupule, 2

Ḍābar Koṭ, 14
dāgabas, 160
Dāmb Sadāt, 14
darśana, 15
Daśāvatāra, 166
Datiā, 39
Deogaṛh, 15, 86-87, 107
devakanyās, 19, 98
devakoṣṭhas, 24
Devānāmapiya Tissa, 160
Devarāja, 174
Devatāmūrtiprakaraṇa, 37
Devī Bhāgavata Purāṇa, 40
Devī Māhātmya, 41
dhamma, 49
Dhamekh, 164
dhāriṇīs, 45
dharma, 64
dharma-stambhas, 63
dharmacakra, 48, 63, 66, 73
dharmacakra-pravartana, 5
Dhauli, 67
Dholāvīrā, 11, 17-19
dhyāna-mudrā, 32
Dīdārgañj, 64, 67
Digambara, 49
discstones, 66, 68
Divyāvadāna, 180
Dockyard, 18
drains, 20
Draviḍa, 13-14, 90
Durgā, 28, 32, 37-38, 42-43
Dutthagāminī, 160-61
dvāra-śākhās, 19
dvārapālas, 19
Dvārāvatī, 167

Egyptian, 9, 17
Elephaṇṭā, 90
Ellorā, 56, 90
English Bond, 17
Erlaṅga (King), 181
etched carnelian beads, 17

faience, 16
Fatehpur Sīkrī, 99
faunal elements of art, 12
figurines,
  bronze, 16
  bull, 14
  female, 14
  male, 15
  mythical, 14
fire altars, 19
floral elements of art, 12
fortifications, 19
Funan, 170, 173

Gaja-Lakṣmī, 37, 70
Gajendramokṣa, 86
Gaṇḍavyūha, 180
Gaṇḍī, 25
Gaṇeśa, 34, 46, 71, 108, 162
Gaṅgā, 19
Gaṅgaikoṇḍacoḷapuram, 52, 93
garbha-gṛha, 14-16, 19-21, 24-26, 30, 97, 105, 162, 179
garuḍa, 22
gavākṣa, 10, 16, 27
Gawdapalin, 165
geometric designs, 16
geometric motifs, 12, 17
Ghosh, Manoranjan, 2
Ghosuṇḍī, 65
Gilgamesh, 15
Glacial Age, 3
Glazing, 16
Gopā, 89
Gopinatha Rao, T.A., 135
Gordon, D.H., 2
grāsapaṭṭī, 19
Granary, 18
Great Bath, 18
Greco-Roman, 75, 81
Greek, 47, 61, 69-71, 81, 88
Greeks, 71, 74-75, 82, 95
grīvā, 14, 18, 21
gūḍha-maṇḍapa, 16
Guḍimallam, 65, 72
Guṇavarman, 177
Gupta period, 168, 180
Gupta-style, 169

Gupta, Jagdish, 2
Guru Grantha Saheb, 29
Gwalior, 99

Hadaway, W.S., 135
haematite, 4
Halebiḍ, 96
haṁsa, 35
Hanchai, 171
hāra, 22, 23
haraṅtara, 23
harmikā, 9
harmya, 21
Haṛappā, 9, 11, 13, 17-20
Haṛappan,
  architecture, 17
  civilization, 9, 20
  Late Haṛappan, 11
  pre-Haṛappan, 11
Harappan Art, Early and Mature, 11
Harihara, 172
Hārīti, 179
Havell, 57
Hayagrīva, 46
Heliodoros, 65
Higher Tradition, 50
Hīnayāna, 163, 178
Hīnayānist, 164
Hindu, 12, 56
Hinduism, 160, 167, 171, 174, 180
Hmawza, 166
hybrid personages, 12

Icon, 61
Idol, 3, 61
īhāmṛga, 46-47
Image, 61
Indo-Greeks, 75
Indonesia, 165, 177, 179
Indra, 42
Indus Valley, 9
Indus-Sarasvatī civilization, 9, 11, 20
Īśānavarman I, 173
Islam, 4
intaglio, 15

jagamohana, 24, 27
jagati, 16, 19, 20
Jaina, 1-3, 47, 56, 73, 77, 98, 105
Jainas, 6, 28, 32
Jainism, 7, 32, 76
jāla, 11
jālī, 27
jaṅghā, 17
Jarrige, J.F., 11
jasper, 12
jaspery stone, 13
jaṭā-mukuṭa, 34
Jātakas, 49, 73, 76, 165, 177
Jātakamālā, 180
Java, 178, 180-82
Jayavarman II, 173-74
Jetavana Vihāra, 161
jewellery, 12, 16

jinas, 6, 49, 64
Joshi, J.P., 11
Jūnī Kurāṇ, 11

Kailāsanātha temple, 172
Kaimūr, 3
Kaiṭabha, 41
kālacakras, 46
kalaśa, 12, 18, 21, 25-27, 37
Kalasan, 179
Kālī, 28, 38, 42
Kālībaṅgā, 11, 13, 17, 19
Kālidāsa, 47, 84, 86
Kālīghāṭa, 40
Kalki, 5
Kāmagiri, 40
kamaṇḍalu, 35
Kāmboj, 170
Kampen Phet, 168
Kampuchea, 170
Kāñcīpuram, 90, 92-93, 172
Kandy, 160, 162
kaṇikā-paga, 27
Kaniṣka, 74
kaṅkars, 4
kaṇṭhī, 26
kaolin, 12
Kapilavastu, 5
kapota, 19, 21
karmayoga, 58
karṇa, 17, 23
Karṇāgama, 136
Kārttikeya, 34, 162

Kassapa I, 161
Kataragama, 162
Kauḍaṇī, 14
Kaula-Kāpālikas, 43, 98
Kauṇḍinya, 170
Kauṇḍinyapur, 6
Kauśāmbī, 66, 77, 79, 86, 115
Kedah, 167
Keśava, 35
Khajurāho, 98
khakharā-muṇḍī, 27
Kharpurī, 26
Khmer, 166-67, 170, 173-76
Khiciṅga, 96
Khotan, 79
khura, 19
kinnara, 46
kinnarī, 46
kirīṭa-mukuṭa, 34, 35, 50
kīrtimukha, 27, 178
Kompon, 172
Kompon Thom, 172
Koṇārka, 97
koṣṭhas, 23-24
Kramrisch Stella, 11, 57
Kṛṣṇa, 28, 176, 181-82
Kublai Khan, 166
Kumar, Giriraj, 2
Kumāra, 42
Kumbakoṇam, 93
Kumrahār, 68
Kurkihāra, 96
Kūrmāvatāra, 5
Kurukṣetra, 40, 79
Kuśīnagara, 6
kūṭa, 7, 8, 22-23
kuṭī, 7
Kyanzibha, 164
Kyanzitha, 166

Lahiri, A.N., 70
Lakṣmī, 42, 71, 86
Lal, B.B., 11, 20
lalāṭa-biṁba, 19
Lalitavistara, 180
Lamb, 31
Lamphun, 167
lāñchanas, 22
Laṅkātilaka, 161
Laos, 170
Lascaux, 2, 5
latā, 18
Laughing Buddha, 31
Lauria-Nandangarh, 66
Lekhaniā, 3
liṅgam, 28, 174
Lohānīpur, 64, 67
Lohuizen-de Leeuw, 65
Lokeśvara, 175-76
Lopburi, 167-68
Loro Jongrang, 180
lost-wax, 16
Lothal, 11, 17-18
Lower Tradition, 50
Lumbinī, 5
Madhu, 41
madhyama mārga, 5
Madhyama-carita, 41
Madurai, 99
magico-religious purpose, 5-6
Mahābalipuram, 91
Mahābhārata, 171, 176, 180
Mahābodhi, 164
mahāmaṇḍapa, 16
Mahāpīṭhanirūpaṇa, 40
mahāpuruṣa lakṣaṇas, 48
Mahāsāṁghika, 82
Mahāsena, 161
mahāstūpa, 160
Mahāvidyās, 37, 39, 46
mahāvihāras, 168
Mahāvīra, 4, 6
Mahāyāna, 163, 177
Mahāyānist, 174
Mahendra, 160
Mahendra Parvata, 174
Mahendravarman, 173
Maheśa, 90
Māheśvarī, 42
Mahiṣāsuramardinī, 32, 36, 41, 46, 77
maithuna, 33
Majapahit, 182
makara, 178
Malaya, 182
Malayasia, 182
Malhār, 64

Mānasāra, 37, 99
maṇḍalas, 29, 44-45
maṇḍapa, 15-16, 24-25, 162
mandira, 29
mantras, 29, 45
Māra, 111
Marco Polo, 57
Mārkaṇḍeya Purāṇa, 41
Marshall, John, 11, 20
Mastaka, 25
Mathurā, 36, 65, 67, 72, 73, 74, 77-79, 81-83, 87, 169
Mātṛkās, 37, 41-42
Matsyāvatāra, 5
Maues, 70
Mauryan rule, 162
Mauryan-Śuṅga Brāhmī, 5
Mayamata, 37
Mayūrbhañja, 96
Mehrgaṛh, 11
Mekong River, 170
Meru, 30
Mesolithic period, 3
Mesopotamia, 9, 13, 17
Minnanthu, 166
Miran, 79
mithuna, 32, 33
Mirzapur, 2
Mitra, 29
Moḍherā, 99
Moheñjo-dāṛo, 11, 13-14, 17-18
Mon-Khmers, 170
Mother Goddess, 14, 36
moulds, 14
Mt. Abu, 99
Mount Meru, 176
mudrās, 32, 76
Muṇḍa, 41
muṇḍī, 27
murals, 165
mūrti, 70
Muslim, 12
Myanmar, 162, 164-65
Mythology, 47

nāga-nāgī, 27
nāgadeva, 77
Nāgapaṭṭinam, 169
Nāgara, 13-14, 16, 19, 90, 97
Nāgārjunakoṇḍa, 9, 79
Nāgārjunī, 67
Nālandā, 95-96, 168
Nandī, 34
Nanpaya, 164, 166
Nara-Nārāyaṇa, 86
Narain, A.K., 70
Narasiṁha, 4, 46
Narmadā, 3
Nāsik, 40
Nat Hlaung Gyaung, 164, 166
Naṭarāja, 33
naturalistic, 15
nāṭya deul, 24
Nāṭyaśāstra, 84, 93, 108
Navarātra, 28
nave, 10
Nāyaka, 175
Neolithic, 7
Ngakywe Nadaung, 164
nīḍas, 23
nirvāṇa, 5-6, 28, 48, 58
Niśumbha, 38, 41
Niya, 79

ochres, 4
Odantapurī, 168
open-air shrines, 8

Pābhāga, 25
padas, 46
padma, 19, 34
pādukā, 31
Pagan, 164, 166
pagoḍā, 164-65
Pahalava, 75
Paintings, 52, 53, 56
Palace, 66
Pāla style, 169
Pāli, 99
Palembang, 177
Pallava, 171, 173
Panataran, 182
Pañcamaṛhī, 3
pañca-makāra, 44
pañcāyatana, 105, 175
Pañcikā, 179
Pandey, S.K., 2
pañjara, 11

pañjaras, 23
Paraśurāma, 5
Pārvatī, 28, 34, 40, 86
Paśupati, 15
pātāla, 11
Pāṭaliputra, 64
Paṭne, 7
Paṭṭaḍakal, 90
Payathonzu, 166
peacocks, 16
Peagu, 166
Pejeng, 182
Periāno Ghuṇḍaī, 14
Peshawar, 74
pīḍhā, 25, 27, 97
pīḍhā-muṇḍī, 27
Pillars, 66
pīpala leaf, 16, 30, 31
Pītalkhora, 55, 72, 73
pīṭha, 16, 19
Pīṭha-Devīs, 37
Pīṭhanirṇaya, 40
Pitsanulok, 168
Pleistocene Period, 3
Poḷonnaruva, 160-61
polychrome paintings, 5
pothī, 35
pradakṣiṇā, 8, 9
pradakṣiṇāpatha, 16, 20
Prambanan, 178, 180-81
Prang, 169
prāsāda, 7, 14, 17
Prasāt Andet, 172
prastara, 20, 21, 22
prati-bhadras, 18
pratīka, 31
pratimā, 61, 62
Pratimālakṣaṇam, 135
Pratihāspur, 180
Prayāga, 40
Prei Kuk, 172
Prome, 163
pṛthvī, 11
Purāṇas, 1, 12, 37, 47, 102-03, 134
Pura ye Gaṅgā, 182
pūrṇa-ghaṭas, 19, 31
Purushapur, 81
Pūrvacarita, 41
pyrites, 4
Pyus, 162

radiocarbon, 6
rāhapaga, 27
rahas, 27
Rāhul, 5
Rājburi, 167
Rājaghāṭa, 77
Rajashāhī, 96
Rākā, 36
Rākhīgaṛhī, 11, 19
Raktabīja, 41
Rāma, 28
Rāmāyaṇa, 171, 176-77, 181-82
Raṅganātha, 35
Rao, S.R., 11
Rasa, 55
Ratanpura, 162
ratha, 23, 91
rathika, 18
rekhā deul, 24, 25
Ṛgveda, 46, 62
Ṛgvedic, 2
ringstones, 66, 68
Rock Art, 1, 2
Rock-cut caves, 66
Romans, 82, 95
Romlok, 172
Ropar, 95
Ṛṣabhanātha, 6
Ruanweli, 161
Rudrayāmala Tantra, 36, 46
Rūpamaṇḍana, 37

sabhā, 23
ṣaḍāṅga, 53
Sadāśiva, 90
sādhanā, 29
Saidu Sharif, 65
Śailendra, 178, 180
śaitāna, 31, 58
Śaiva, 1-2, 43-44, 47, 69-72, 76, 81, 98, 103, 160
Śaiva Hinduism, 178
Śaivism, 7
Śaivite, 30, 32, 104
Śaka, 75
Śākta, 2, 28, 40, 45, 103

Śāktapīṭhas, 40
Śakti, 3, 28, 36-38, 40, 43, 45, 104
Śaktipīṭha, 46
Śaktis, 42, 105
Śāktism, 7, 32
śālā, 7, 8, 22-23
vimāna, 23
śāligrāma, 28
Samarāṅgaṇa Sūtradhāra, 37, 108, 113
Sambor Prei Kuk, 173
Sambour, 171
Saṁgharāja, 168
samudra-manthana, 174
Sāñcī, 15, 72, 73, 160
sandstone, 12
Saṅgariti, 181
Saṅghamitrā, 160
śaṅkha, 34
Sannati, 72
Sano, 167
Sapada, 164
Sārnāth, 5, 66, 79, 86, 87, 164-65, 169, 179
Sārnāth Buddha, 85
sealings, 9
seals, 9, 15
semi-precious stones, 12
Śeṣanāga, 35, 172
Shah, Priyabala, 136
Shāmalājī, 89
Sharma, D.V., 99
Sharma, G.R., 8
shell, 16
Shugh, 79
Siam, 166
Sign, 31
Sigriyā, 161-62
śikhara, 14-15, 17, 20-26, 52, 90, 97, 178
Silk Routes, 78
śilpa, 20-21
Śilparatna, 38
silver, 12, 16
Siṅgasārī, 181
Sinīvalī, 36
Sirpur, 92
śīrṣa, 18
Sītā, 86
Śiva, 3, 15, 28, 33-36, 41-42, 45-46, 65, 69, 71, 90, 105, 108, 114-15, 162 63, 178, 181-82
Śivabuddha, 178
Śivakaivalya, 174
*Śivaliṅga*s, 34, 65
skandha, 18
soap stone, 15
Somā, 171
Sompura, P.O., 135
Soṅkh, 36, 77
śramaṇa paramparā, 48-49
Śrāvastī, 42, 66, 108
Śrī, 42
Sri Lanka, 159, 165
śrīphala, 30
Śrīraṅgapaṭṭanam, 97, 99
Śrītattvanidhi, 39
śrīvatsa, 32
Śrīvijaya, 177
*śṛṅga śikhara*s, 17
Śrutavarman, 171
*stambha*s, 10, 20
steatite, 12-13, 15-16
Stencil Style, 51
stepped wells, 19
Stone Age, 1, 7
Stone Age Architecture, 8
stone pillars, 20
stūpa, 7-11, 21, 28, 73, 161, 163-65, 168, 179
*stūpī*s, 21-22, 25
*sūcī*s, 10
suka-nāsikā, 18
Sukhothai, 167-69
Śukranītisāra, 104
Sumātrā, 177, 180
Sumber Nanas, 181
Śumbha, 38, 41
Śuṅga–Indo–Bactrian, 80
Śuṅga–Sātavāhana, 6
Sūr–Jaṅgal, 14
Sūrkoṭaḍā, 11, 17, 19
Sūrya, 35, 69, 70, 108
Sūryavarman, 176
Sūryavarman II, 175
Suvarṇabhūmi, 177
svarga, 11
svastika, 28, 30-32
Śvetāmbara, 49

Syādvāda, 6
Symbol, 31

Ta Keo, 176
Ta Prohm, 176
Tagaun, 163, 164
Takeo, 172
tala, 21
Tala jaṅghā, 26
Tālamāna, 14, 131
Tampak Siring, 182
Tamrapanni, 159
Tantras, 29, 43, 44, 103
Tāntric, 166
tāntrikas, 29, 39, 43
Tāntrik Mahāyānism, 178
Tantrism, 164
Taoism, 44
Tārā, 178-79
Tarkhānewālā Ḍerā, 11
terracotta, 12, 14
Thailand, 166-68, 170
Thañjāvur, 52, 93
Thāpārāma, 161
Thatabinnu, 164-65
Thaton, 163
tilaka, 47
Tilominlo, 164
tīrthaṁkaras, 6, 29, 32, 49, 51, 114
Tiruvālangāḍu, 94
tools bronze, 12
toraṇa, 24, 179
trefoil design, 13
tripuṇḍra, 30, 34
triratna, 49, 73
triśūla, 31-32
Tulasī, 42
turquoise, 16

Udaigiri–Khaṇḍagiri, 72-73
Ujjayinī, 40
UNESCO, 2
Ūpara jaṅghā, 26
Upper Palaeolithic, 3, 7, 8
ūrdhva-retasa, 34
ūrṇā, 47
uru-śṛṅgas, 17
uṣṇīṣa, 10, 47

vāhanas, 22, 33
vaijayantī-mālā, 34
Vaikhānasāgama, 106, 133-34, 136
Vaiśālī, 6, 66, 115
Vaiṣṇava, 1-2, 30, 44, 47, 69-72, 76-77, 81, 98, 103, 160, 162, 164
Vaiṣṇavism, 7, 32, 76
vajra-muṇḍī, 27
Vāmana Purāṇa, 41
Vāmanāvatāra, 5
vanamālā, 34
Varāha, 5, 42
Varāha Purāṇa, 41-42
Varāhamihira, 132
Vārāhī, 46
Vārāṇasī, 5, 40, 66
varāṇḍikā, 17
Vardhamāna, 6
Varuṇa, 29
Vāstu Śāstras, 20
vāstupuruṣa, 16
Vāsudeva, 70-71
Vedas, 1, 4, 62
vedī-bandha, 16
Vedic, 3, 5, 29, 32, 63, 70
Vedic-Hindu, 182
vedikā, 8, 10, 19
Vesara, 13-14
Vidiśā, 65
Vietnam, 170, 182
Vighna-Vināyaka, 34
Vijay, 159
Vikramaśilā, 96
vimāna, 20-22
Viṣṇu, 3, 4, 28, 32, 35-36, 42, 46, 51, 64, 90, 105-108, 113, 115, 163, 166, 168, 172, 175, 178, 181
Viṣṇudharmottara Pusāṇa, 53, 85, 88, 104, 108, 114, 136
viṣṇupāda, 30
votive *stūpas*, 11
Vṛndāvana, 40
Vyādhapur, 171
vyāla, 24, 46-47
Wakankar, V.S., 2-3
Warehouse, 18
Wat, 169

Wat Mahathat, 168
Wat Si Jun, 168
Water Reservoirs, 18-19
weapons, 6
World Heritage Site, 2
Worship,
  bull, 21
  fire, 21
  mother-goddess, 21
  Paśupati Śiva, 21
  pīpala, 21
  serpent, 21
  Śivaliṅga, 21
  svastika, 21
  tree, 21
  water, 21

*yakṣa*s, 19, 49-51, 64, 73, 77, 82-83, 87, 134
*yakṣī*s, 19, 49-51, 64, 67, 69, 73, 78, 83
Yama, 42
Yamunā, 19
*yantra*s, 29, 44, 46
Yaśodharā, 5
yaṣṭi, 9
Yathemya, 166
yatu, 46
Yavadvīpa, 177
yoga, 43-44, 46
yogī, 32, 65
yogic postures, 14
*yoginī*s, 28, 37, 42-43
yoni, 43
yoni-pīṭha, 34

Zhob and Bolan valleys, 14